Catholic Controversies

Catholic Controversies

Understanding Church Teachings and Events in History

Stephen Gabriel, Editor

Moorings Press

Falls Church, Virginia

Nihil obstat: Reverend Thomas J. Lehning
                  Censor Librorum

Imprimatur: + Paul S. Loverde
                  Bishop of Arlington
                  September 9, 2010

The *Nihil Obstat* and *Imprimatur* are official declarations that a book or pamphlet is free of doctrinal or moral error. No implication is contained therein that those who have granted the *Nihil Obstat* and *Imprimatur* agree with the contents, opinions, or statements expressed.

Moorings Press
P.O. Box 6050
Falls Church, VA 22040
www.MooringsPress.com

Cover design: Kathryn Marcellino, www.marcellinodesign.com

ISBN: 978-0-9827-6620-0

Library of Congress Control Number: 2010912629

Printed in the United States of America

To my children and grandchildren,
my eternal legacy

and

To the memory of my father, Edmund Philip Gabriel,
a convert to the Catholic faith,
loving husband and father,
master mariner

Contents

Part III. Misunderstood Doctrines of the Church

Introduction

Preparing this book has been a labor of love for me—love for the Church and love for my family. As a father, my primary goal is that my wife and children go to Heaven. The best way for them to achieve this goal is to embrace the Catholic faith. I want my family to be Catholic, not so we will all be in the same club—the Catholic club. But because I believe the Catholic Church teaches the truth: about God, about our relations with God, and about our relations with each other. The Church is the surest path to happiness on earth and beatitude in Heaven. Love for my family demands this concern. In an absolute sense, it is all that matters.

The idea for this book was born of the many encounters my college-aged children had with their classmates and professors. My children's faith was challenged at every turn. Professors proclaimed with great authority that the Gospels are a myth or that science and religion are incompatible. The media made great sport of belittling the Church for its actions during the Inquisition or the Crusades. I could usually come up with a response, but it was frequently not quite adequate to satisfy the more sophisticated and inquisitive minds of university students. I found myself running to the Internet to find a good article addressing the issue at hand.

This book is intended for anyone who wishes to dispel the many myths and misperceptions about the Catholic Church and its teachings that are promoted by university professors, the media, and the uninformed. The book is divided into four parts covering 26 topics. These topics are "hot-button" issues that come up repeatedly.

The material is organized to maximize its usefulness. Each topic has a brief introduction, frequently with a reference to an authoritative source such as the *Catechism of the Catholic Church* or an official Church document. This introduction is followed by a short presentation of the highlights, in bulleted format, of one or more articles addressing the topic, and then the articles themselves, which are reprinted with permission. The book may be read cover to cover or from topic to topic, according to readers' interests and inclinations.

The articles were chosen for their reliability and clarity. Although some of the articles are more challenging, all should be accessible to readers with varying backgrounds and education. The bulleted highlights provide the key points and conclusions. However, the articles should be read in their entirety to get a solid understanding of how the authors derived their conclusions. If we are to understand and later explain these issues to others, we need to digest the ideas and arguments presented. This book is intended as an invitation to further exploration, and additional reading is highly recommended.

Part I.

The Credibility of God, the Church, and Scripture

The foundations of our faith are based on our belief in God and his revelation through the Scriptures and Sacred Tradition, as interpreted and safeguarded by the Church. Those who wish to undermine our faith tend to attack these foundational issues and to question their credibility. Part I presents a reasoned defense of our belief in God, the consistency of our religion and science, and the reliability of Sacred Scripture.

Chapter 1

Chapter 1

Can the Existence of God Be Proven?

The question of God's existence is not a new one. It has been the subject of man's inquiry throughout the ages. For many, the existence of God is something taken for granted, having been taught this truth since childhood. For others, God's existence has been a gnawing question for a long time. Some have believed and then ceased to believe; others have become ardent believers after a journey of disbelief, doubt, and maybe crisis.

The Catholic Church teaches that we can arrive at the knowledge of God's existence through the use of our reason.[1] If we have the capacity to "discover" God in our lives and we are not yet convinced, let us not put off the quest to find Him. It is of monumental importance to us, to our families, and to society. The discovery of God is the first step in finding true purpose and meaning in our lives.

The articles in this chapter present many of the "ways" we can come to see that God exists. Although these are not light reading, a careful reading will pay off handsomely.

In **"The Reasons to Believe,"** Peter Kreeft explores several arguments for belief in God.
- ➤ **Creation's Design:** Our universe and everything in it is characterized by such a high degree of order that it is unlikely it was caused by random events and is far more likely caused by an intelligent designer.
- ➤ **First Cause:** Observation of our everyday world reveals that everything has a cause. Nothing causes itself. Accordingly, there must be an ultimate first cause. That cause is God.

---

[1] *Catechism of the Catholic Church.* 1997. 2nd ed., nos. 31 and 35. Vatican City: Libreria Editrice Vaticana.

➤ **Conscience:** The universal acceptance of the absolute moral authority of conscience and the fact that the only absolute authority is a Perfect Will points to the existence of a divine Being.

➤ **History:** History provides at least eight arguments for the existence of God. First, human history shows a storyline and must be told by an intelligent storyteller. Second, history has a moral design. When moral law is followed, people thrive; when it is not followed, they do not thrive. Third, Providential "coincidences" such as the parting of the Red Sea suggest God's hand. Fourth, the fact that documented miracles happen points to the existence of God. Fifth, Christ claimed to be God and the evidence suggests that his claims are true. Sixth, the life and witness of many of the saints strongly indicate that God exists. Seventh, the unlikely conversion of much of the world to Christianity suggests God's role. Eighth, the life experiences of the Christian attest to the existence of God.

➤ **Pascal's Wager:** French philosopher Blaise Pascal suggested that a person should "wager" as though God exists, because in doing so he has everything to gain and nothing to lose.

In **"Anthropic Coincidences,"** physicist Stephen Barr sheds light on the question: Is the human race an accident, or were we meant to be here? Barr introduces the concept of anthropic coincidences and what they tell us about where humanity fits into the universe.

➤ Many features of the laws of nature seem arranged, even "fine-tuned," to make possible the existence of life, including intelligent life. These "anthropic coincidences" support the argument that life has an intelligent origin.

➤ Examples of anthropic coincidences include: Had the strong nuclear force been a bit weaker or a bit stronger, the prospects of life on earth would have been quite dim. Also, Helium nuclei must fuse to allow the formation of larger elements. Yet, this process is very precise and perplexed nuclear theorists and astrophysicists until discovered. If this process did not happen, the result would likely be a universe without life.

➤ Life depends on a delicate balance among many fundamental forces of nature, particularly on the relative weakness of electromagnetic effects.

- ➢ Some scientists remain skeptical about the significance of anthropic coincidences and believe they can be explained by natural causation. Though Barr agrees these skeptics should be taken seriously, he states that "even if all apparently anthropic coincidences could be explained in this way, it would still be remarkable that the relationships dictated by physical theory happened also to be those propitious for life."
- ➢ Anthropic coincidences point out that the "laws of physics have to be very special to allow life to exist."
- ➢ This physicist concludes that the facts of science point to a cosmic Designer.

Further Reading

Jimmy Akin. 2003. "Eternal Gamble: Is Pascal's Wager a Good Bet?" *This Rock* 14 (3) (March).

Mark Shea. 2003. "Mere Theism: The Case for God." *Crisis* 21 (11): 12-17.

The Reasons to Believe

By Peter Kreeft

Why do you believe all the things you believe as a Catholic? Because of the reliability of the Church which teaches them, of course.

You didn't figure out the Trinity and Transubstantiation and the Immaculate Conception all by yourself. But why believe in the authority of the Church? Because it was founded and guaranteed by Christ, and Christ is not a fallible man but the infallible God-become-man.

The teachings are the Church's, the Church is Christ's, and Christ is God. But why do you believe in God? Sooner or later that primary question comes up.

There are many arguments for God's existence. They're like roads, starting from different points but all aiming at the same goal. In this article, we'll explore the arguments from cause and effect, from conscience, from history and from "Pascal's Wager." But first of all, let's concentrate on the "argument from design."

Does God Really Exist? The Argument from Design

The argument starts with the "major premise" that where there's design, there must be a designer. The "minor premise" is the existence of design throughout the universe. The "conclusion" is that there must be a universal designer.

Why believe that all design implies a designer? Because everyone admits this in practice. For example, suppose you came upon a deserted island and found "S.O.S." written in the sand. You wouldn't think the waves had written it by mere chance, but that someone had been there, someone intelligent enough to write the message. If you found a stone hut on the island with windows, doors and a fireplace, you wouldn't think a hurricane had piled up the stones by chance. We immediately infer a designer when we see design.

When the first moon rocket took off from Cape Canaveral, two U.S. scientists stood watching it, side by side. One was a believer, the other an unbeliever. The believer said, "Isn't it wonderful that our rocket is going to hit the moon by chance?" The unbeliever objected, "What do you mean, chance? We put millions of man-hours of design into that rocket." "Oh," said the believer, "You don't think chance is a good explanation for the rocket? Then why do you think it's a good explanation for the universe? There's much more design in a universe than in a rocket. We can design a rocket, but we couldn't design a whole universe. I wonder who can?"

Later that day the two were strolling down a street and passed an antique store. The atheist admired a picture in the window and asked, "I wonder who painted that picture?" "No one," joked the believer, "it just happened by chance."

Is it possible that design happens by chance without a designer? There is perhaps one chance in a trillion that "S.O.S." could be written in the sand by the wind. But who would use a one-in-a-trillion explanation? Someone once said that if you sat a million monkeys at a million typewriters for a million years, one of them would type out all of "Hamlet" eventually, by chance.

But when we read a text of *Hamlet*, we don't wonder whether it came from chance and monkeys. Why then does the atheist use that incredibly improbable explanation for the universe? Clearly, because it's his only chance of remaining an atheist. At this point we need a psychological explanation of the atheist rather than a logical explanation of the universe. We have a logical explanation of the universe, but the atheist doesn't like it. It's called God.

There is one especially strong version of the argument from design that hits close to home because it's about the design of the very thing we use to think about design: our brains. The human brain is the most complex piece of design in the known universe. In many ways, it's just like a computer. Now just suppose there were a computer that was programmed only by chance. For instance, suppose you were in a plane and the public address system announced that there was no pilot, but the plane was being flown by a computer that had been programmed by a random fall of hailstones on its typewriter keyboard, or by a baseball player in spiked shoes dancing on computer cards. How much confidence would you have in that plane? But if our brain computer has no cosmic intelligence behind the heredity and environment that program it, why should we trust it when it tells us about anything— even about the brain?

Another uniquely strong aspect of the design argument is the so-called "anthropic principle." The universe seems to be specially designed from the beginning for human life to evolve. If the temperature of the primal fireball that resulted from the "Big Bang" some 15-20 billion years ago which was the beginning of our universe had been a trillionth of a degree colder or hotter, the carbon molecule that's the foundation of all organic life could never have evolved. The number of possible universes is trillions and trillions. Only one of them could support human life: this one. Sounds suspiciously like a plot.

But doesn't evolution explain everything without a divine Designer? Just the opposite: Evolution is a beautiful example of design, a great clue to God. There's very good scientific evidence for the evolving, ordered appearance of species, from simple to complex. But there is no scientific proof of "natural selection" as the mechanism of evolution. Natural selection "explains" the emergence of higher forms without intelligent design by the "survival of the fittest" principle. But this is sheer theory. There is no evidence that abstract, theoretical thinking or altruistic love make it easier for man to survive. How did they evolve, then?

Furthermore, how could the design that obviously exists now in man and in the human brain come from something with less or no design? It violates the principle of causality, which states that you can't get more in the effect than you had in the cause. If there is intelligence in the effect (man), there must be intelligence in the cause. But a universe ruled by blind chance has no intelligence. Therefore there must be a cause for human intelligence that transcends the universe: a Mind behind the physical universe. (Most great scientists have believed in such a Mind, by the way, even those who did not believe any revealed religion.)

How much does this argument prove? Not all that the Christian means by "God," of course—no argument can do that—but it proves a pretty thick slice of God: some designing intelligence great enough to account for all the design in the universe and the human mind.

If that's not God, what is it? Steven Spielberg?

If the cosmic rays had bombarded the primordial slime at a slightly different angle or time or intensity, the hemoglobin molecule necessary for all warm-blooded animals could never have evolved. The chance of this happening is something like one in a trillion trillion. Add together each of the "chances" and you have something far more unbelievable than a million monkeys writing "Hamlet."

There are relatively few atheists among neurologists and brain surgeons or among astrophysicists, but many among psychologists, sociologists and historians. The reason seems obvious: the first study divine design, the second study human undesign.

Does God Really Exist? The Argument from Conscience "First Cause"

The most famous arguments for God's existence are the "five ways" of Thomas Aquinas. One of them is the argument from design, which we looked at last week. The other four are versions of the "first cause" argument, which we explore here.

The argument is really very simple: Everything needs an explanation. Nothing just is. Everything has some "sufficient reason" why it is.

Example: My parents caused me, my grandparents caused them, etc. But it's not that simple. I wouldn't be here without billions of causes, from the Big Bang through the cooling of the galaxies and the evolution of the protein molecule to the marriages of my ancestors. So the universe is a vast and complex chain of causes.

But does the universe as a whole have a cause? Is there a First Cause, an uncaused Cause, of the whole process?

If not, then there's an "infinite regress" of causes, with no first link in the great cosmic chain. If so, then there is a First Cause, an eternal, independent, self-explanatory Being with nothing above it, before it or supporting it. It would have to explain itself as well as everything else— for if it needed something else as its explanation, then it wouldn't be the First Cause.

Such a Being would have to be God. If we can prove there is such a First Cause, we'll have proved there is a God.

If there is no First Cause, then the universe is like a railroad train moving without an engine. Each car's motion is explained, proximately, by the motion of the car in front of it: The caboose moves because the boxcar pulls it: the boxcar moves because the cattle car pulls it: etc. But there's no engine to pull the first car, and thus the whole train. That would be impossible, of course. But that's what the universe is like if there is no First Cause.

There's one more analogy: Suppose I tell you there's a book that explains everything you want explained. You want that book very much. You ask me whether I have it. I say no, I have to get it from my wife. Does she have it? No, she has to get it from a neighbor. Does he

have it? No, he has to get it from his teacher, who has to get it ...
etcetera, adinfinitum. No one actually has the book. In that case, you
will never get it. However long or short the chain of book-borrowers
may be, you will get the book only if someone actually has it and
doesn't have to borrow it.

Well, existence is like that book. Existence is handed down the
chain of causes, from cause to effect. If there's no First Cause, no Being
who is eternal and self-sufficient, who has existence by His own nature
and does not have to borrow it from someone else—if there's no such
Being, then the gift of existence can never be passed down the chain to
the others, and no one will ever get it.

But we did get it! We exist. We got the gift of existence from our
causes, down the chain, and so did every actual being in the universe
from atoms to archangels. Therefore, there must be a First Cause of
existence—a God.

Dependent beings cannot cause themselves. They are dependent
on their causes. If there's no Independent Being, then the whole chain
of dependent beings is dependent on nothing and could not exist. But
they do exist. Therefore there is an Independent Being.

Aquinas has four versions of this basic argument.

First, he argues that the chain of movers must have a First Mover
because nothing can move itself. If the whole chain of moving things
had no First Mover, it could not now be moving—but it is. If there were
an "infinite regress" of movers with no First Mover, no motion could
ever begin, and if it never began, it could not go on and exist now. But
it does go on: it does exist now. Therefore it began, and therefore there
is a First Mover. ("Motion" here refers to any kind of change, not just
change of place.)

Second, he expands the proof from proving a cause of motion to
proving a cause of existence. He argues that if there were no cause for
the universe coming into being, then there could be no second causes,
since second causes (i.e. caused causes) are dependent on a First Cause.
But there are "second causes" all around us. Therefore there must be a
First Cause.

Third, he argues that if there were no eternal, necessary and immortal being: if everything had a possibility of not being, of ceasing to
be, then eventually this possibility of ceasing to be would be realized

for everything. In other words, if everything could die, then given infinite time, everything would eventually die. But in that case nothing could start up again; we would have universal death, for a being that has ceased to exist cannot cause itself or anything else to begin to exist again. But if there is no God, then there must have been infinite time; the universe must have been here always, with no beginning and no First Cause. Yet this universal death has not happened and things do exist. Therefore there must be a necessary Being which cannot not-be and cannot possibly cease to be. That's a description of God.

Fourth, there must also be a First Cause of "perfection," or goodness, or value. We rank things as more or less perfect, good or valuable. Unless this ranking is false, unless souls don't really have any more perfection than slugs, there must be a real standard of perfection to make such a hierarchy possible. For a thing is ranked higher on the hierarchy of perfection only insofar as it is closer to the ideal. Unless there is a Most Perfect Being to be that real standard of perfection, all our value judgments are meaningless. Such a Most Perfect Being, or real-ideal standard of perfection, is another description of God.

There is a single, common, logical structure to all four proofs. Instead of proving God directly, they prove Him indirectly, by refuting atheism. Either there is a First Cause or not. The proofs look at "not" and refute it, leaving the only other possibility that He is.

Each of the four "ways" makes the same point for four different kinds of cause: first, cause of motion; second, cause of a beginning to existence; third, cause of present existence; and fourth, cause of goodness or value. The common point is that if there were no First Cause, there could be no second causes, and yet there are second causes (moved movers, caused causers, dependent and mortal beings, and less-than-wholly perfect beings). Therefore, there must be a First Cause of motion, beginning, existence and perfection.

How can anyone squirm out of this tight logic? Here are four ways in which different philosophers try:

First, many say the proofs just don't prove God, but only some vague "first cause" or other. "God of Abraham, Isaac and Jacob, not the God of philosophers and scholars," cries Pascal, who was a passionate Christian but did not believe you could logically prove God's existence.

It's quite true that the proofs do not prove everything the Christian means by "God." But they do prove a transcendent, eternal, un-caused, immortal, self-existing, independent, all-perfect Being. That certainly sounds more like God than like Superman. It's a pretty thick slice of God, at any rate—much too much for any atheist to digest.

Second, some philosophers, like David Hume, say that the concept of "cause" is ambiguous and not applicable beyond the physical universe to God. How dare we use the same term for what clouds do to rain, what parents do to children, what authors do to books, and what God does to the universe? The answer is that the concept of "cause" is analogical; that is, it differs somewhat but not completely from one example to another. Human fatherhood is like divine fatherhood, and physical causality is like divine causality. The way an author conceives a book in his mind is not exactly the same as the way a woman conceives a baby in her body either, but we call both "causes." (In fact, we also call both conceptions.") The objection is right to point out that we don't fully understand how God causes the universe, as we understand how parents cause children or clouds cause rain. But the term remains meaningful. A cause is the *sine qua non* for an effect: If no cause, no effect. If no creator, no creation; if no God, no universe.

Third, it's sometimes argued (e.g by Bertrand Russell) that there is a self-contradiction in the argument, for one of the premises is that everything needs a cause but the conclusion is that there is something (God) which does not need a cause. The child who asks, "Who made God?" is really thinking of this objection. The answer is very simple: The argument does not use the premise "Everything needs a cause." Everything in motion needs a cause, everything dependent needs a cause, everything imperfect needs a cause.

Fourth, it's often asked why there can't be infinite regress, with no First Being. Infinite regress is perfectly acceptable in mathematics. Negative numbers go on to infinity just as positive numbers do. So why can't time be like the number series, with no highest number either negatively (no First in the past) or positively (no Last in the future)?

The answer is that real beings are not like numbers. They need causes. For the chain of real beings moves in one direction only, from past to future, and the future is caused by the past. Positive numbers are not caused by negative numbers.

There is, in fact, a parallel in the number series for a First Cause: the number one. If there were no first positive integer, no unit one, there could be no subsequent addition of units. Two is two ones, there is three ones, and so on. If there were no First, there could be no second or third.

If this is getting too tricky, the thing to do is to return to what's sure and clear: the intuitive point we began with.

As C.S. Lewis put it, "I felt in my bones that this universe does not explain itself."

Does God Really Exist? The Argument from Conscience

Almost no one will say that we ought to sin against our conscience. Disobey the Church, the state, parents, "authority figures"—but do not disobey your conscience. Thus people usually admit—though not usually in these words—the absolute moral authority of conscience.

Such people are usually surprised to find out that Thomas Aquinas, of all people, agrees with them to such an extent that he says if a Catholic comes to believe the Church is in error in some essential, officially binding doctrine, it is a mortal sin against conscience, a sin of hypocrisy, for him to remain in the Church and call himself a Catholic, but only a venial sin against knowledge for him to leave the Church in honest but partly culpable error.

So one of the two premises of an argument for God's existence is already established: Conscience has an absolute authority over us. The second premise is that the only possible source of absolute authority is an absolutely Perfect Will, a divine Being. The conclusion follows that such a Being exists.

How would someone disagree with the second premise? By finding an alternative basis for conscience besides God. There are four such possibilities:

1. something abstract and impersonal, like an idea
2. something concrete but less than human, on the level of animal instinct
3. something on the human level but not the divine and
4. something higher than the human level but not yet divine.

The **first** possibility means that the basis of conscience is a law without a lawgiver. We are obligated absolutely to an abstract ideal, a pattern of behavior. The question then comes up: Where does this pattern exist? If it does not exist anywhere, how can a real person be under the authority of something unreal? How can More be subject to Less? If, on the other hand, this pattern or idea exists in the minds of people, then what authority do they have to impose this idea of theirs on me? If the idea is only an idea, it has no personal will behind it; if it is only someone's idea, it has only that someone behind it. In neither case do we have a sufficient basis for absolute, infallible, no-exceptions authority.

The **second** possibility means that we trace conscience to a biological instinct. "We must love one another or die," writes the poet W.H. Auden. We unconsciously know this, says the believer in the second possibility, just as animals unconsciously know that unless they behave in certain ways the species will not survive. That's why animal mothers sacrifice for their children, and that's a sufficient explanation for human altruism too. It's "the herd instinct."

The problem with this explanation is that it, like the first, does not account for the absoluteness of conscience's authority. We believe we ought to disobey an instinct—any instinct—on some occasions. But we do not believe we ought ever to disobey our conscience. You should usually obey instincts like mother-love, but not if it means keeping your son back from risking his life to save his country in a just and necessary defensive war, or if it means injustice and uncharity to other mothers' sons. There is no instinct which should always be obeyed. Instincts are like the notes on a piano (the illustration comes from C.S. Lewis); the moral law is like sheet music. Different notes are right at different times.

Furthermore, instinct fails to account not only for what we ought to do but also for what we do do. We don't always follow instinct. Sometimes we go to the aid of a victim even though we fear for our own safety.

A **third** possibility is that other human beings, or "society," are the source of the authority of conscience. That's the most popular belief. But it's also the weakest of all four possibilities. For "society" does not mean something over and above other human beings.

Society is simply other people like myself. What authority do they have over me? Are they always right? Must I never disobey them? What kind of blind status quo conservatism is that? Should a German have obeyed "society" in the Nazi era?

The **fourth** possibility remains: that the source of conscience's authority is something above me but not God. What could this be?

Society is not above me, nor is instinct. An ideal? But that's possibility number one, already dealt with. It looks like there are simply no candidates in this area. And that leaves us with God.

To sum up the argument most simply: Conscience has binding moral authority over us, demanding unqualified obedience. But only a perfectly good, righteous Divine Will has this authority and a right to absolute, exceptionless obedience. Therefore, conscience is the voice of the will of God.

This doesn't mean, of course, that we always hear that voice aright. Our consciences can err. That's why the first obligation we have, in conscience, is to form our conscience by seeking the truth—especially the truth about whether this God has revealed to us clear moral maps (Scripture and Church). If so, whenever our conscience seems to tell us to disobey those maps, it is not working properly, and we can know that by conscience itself, if only we remember that conscience is more than just immediate feeling.

Does God Really Exist? The Argument from History

There are at least eight different arguments for the existence of God from history, not just one.

First, history, both human and prehuman, shows a story line. It is not just random. If atheism is true, there are no adventures; life is "a tale told by an idiot, full of sound and fury, signifying nothing." But life isn't like that. Life is a story. And stories aren't told by idiots.

Rather, a story points to a Storyteller. Thus, the general argument from history is a version of the argument from design.

A second argument concentrates on history's moral design. The historical books of the Old Testament are an argument for the existence of God from the justice displayed in the history of the Jewish people: They're an invitation to see the hand of God in human affairs. Whenever God's laws are followed, the people prosper. When they're violated, the people perish.

History shows that moral laws are as inescapable as physical ones. Just as you can flout gravity only temporarily, then you fall, so you can flout the laws of God only temporarily, then you fall. Great tyrants like Hitler flourish for a day, then perish. Great saints suffer apparent failure, then emerge into triumph. The same is true of nations. History proves you can't cut the corners of the moral square.

Now, is this fact which the East calls karma mere chance, or the design of a wise lawgiver? But no human lawgiver invented history itself. So, the only adequate cause for such an effect is God.

A third argument flows from providential "coincidences," like the Red Sea parting (moved by an east wind, according to Exodus) just at the right time for the Jews to escape Pharaoh. Our own individual histories usually have similar bits of curious timing. Unprejudiced examination of these "coincidences" will bring at least a suspicion, if not the conviction, that an unseen divine hand is at work.

The writers of the Bible often shortcut the argument and simply ascribe such natural events to God. Indeed, another passage in Exodus says simply that God parted the sea. This is not a miracle: God worked here, and continues to work, through the second causes of natural agents. But it is God who works, and the hand of the Worker is visible through the work if we only look.

A fourth argument from history, the strongest of all, is miracles. Miracles directly show the presence of God, for a miracle, in the ordinary sense of the word, is a deed done by supernatural, not natural, power. If miracles happen, they demonstrate God's existence as clearly as rational speech shows the existence of thought.

If I were an atheist, I would study all published interviews of any of the 70,000 who saw the miracle of the sun at Fatima; I would ransack hospital records for documented, "impossible," miraculous cures.

Yet nearly all atheists argue against miracles philosophically rather than historically. They are convinced *a priori*, by argument, that miracles can't happen. So they don't waste their time on empirical investigation. Those who do, soon cease to be atheists—like the skeptical scientists who investigated the Shroud of Turin, or like Frank Morrison, who investigated the evidence for the "myth" of Christ's resurrection with the careful scientific eye of the historian—and became a believer. (His book, *Who Moved the Stone?*, is still a classic and still in print after 60 years.)

God provided just enough evidence of Himself for any honest seeker whose heart really cares about the truth of the matter. But not so much that hardened hearts will be convinced by force. Even Christ did not convince the world of His divinity by His miracles. He could have remained on earth, impervious to death, indefinitely. He could have come down from the cross, and then the doubters would have believed. But He didn't. Even His resurrection was kept semiprivate. The New Testament speaks of only 500 who saw Him. Why did He not reveal Himself to all?

He will—on the Last Day, when it's too late to change sides. His mercy gives us time and freedom to choose. Jesus is like a lover with a marriage proposal, not a cop with a warrant.

A fifth argument is Christ Himself. Here is a man who lived among us and claimed to be God. If Christ was God, then, of course, there is a God. But if Christ was not God, He was a madman or a devil—a madman if He really thought He was God but was not; a devil if He knew He was not God and yet tempted men to worship Him. Which is He—Lord, lunatic or liar?

Part of the data of history is the Gospel record of His life. Reading the Gospels is like reading Boswell's account of Dr. Johnson: an absolutely unforgettable character emerges. Christ's personality is compelling even to unbelievers, even to enemies like Nietzsche. And the character revealed there is utterly unlike that of a lunatic or a liar. So if it's impossible for a lunatic to be so wise or a liar so loving, then He must be the One He claims to be.

A sixth argument is the saints, especially their joy. Chesterton once said that the only unanswerable argument against Christianity was Christians. (He meant bad and sad Christians.) Similarly, the only unanswerable argument for Christianity is Christians—saintly Christians. You can argue against Mother Teresa's theology if you're skeptical of mind, but you can't argue against Mother Teresa herself, unless you're hopelessly hard of heart.

If there is no God, how can life's most fundamental illusion cause its greatest joy? If God didn't do it, who put smiles on the lips of martyrs? "By their fruits you shall know them." Illusions don't have the staying power that the faith has.

And that brings us to our seventh argument from history: the conversion of the world. How to explain the success of the faith in winning the hearts of men? Hard-hearted Romans give up worldly pleasures and ambitions and often life itself, and take a leap in the dark; worldly men pin their hopes on otherworldly goals and do it consistently, en masse, century after century, until the whole civilized Western world is converted—if Christianity is not true and there are no miracles, then this record is an even greater miracle.

Greek philosophy won converts through rational proofs, and Mohammed through force of arms in the jihad or holy war. But Christ won hearts by the miracle of "amazing grace, how sweet the sound, that saved a wretch like me."

(I almost believe it's our high and holy duty to loudly sing the original "wretch" line that our liturgical experts have bowdlerized out of that great old hymn whenever the congregation sings today's sanitized version instead. God in His wisdom saw that the American Church lacked persecutions—and so sent her liturgists.)

The eighth and last argument from history is from our own life experiences. The Christian faith is verifiable in a laboratory, but it's a subtle and complex laboratory: the laboratory of one's life. I always tell a skeptic to pray "The Prayer of the Skeptic" if he really wants to know whether God exists. It's the scientific thing to do: to test a hypothesis by performing the relevant experiment. If God exists, He wants to get in touch with us and reveal Himself to us, and He has promised that all who seek Him will find Him. Well then, all the agnostic has to do is to sincerely seek, honestly and with an open mind, and he will find, in God's way and in God's time. That's part of the hypothesis.

How to seek? Not just by arguing but by praying, not just by talking about God, as Job's three friends did, who did not find Him, but by talking to God, as Job did, who found Him. Go out into your back yard some night and say to the empty universe above you: "God, I don't know whether You exist or not. Maybe I'm praying to nobody, but maybe I'm praying to You. So if You're really there, please let me know somehow, because I do want to know. I want only the truth, whatever it is. If You are the truth, here I am, ready and willing to follow You wherever You lead."

If our faith is not a pack of lies, then whoever sincerely prays that prayer will find God in his or her own life, no matter how hard, long or complex the road, as Augustine's was in the "Confessions." "All roads lead to Rome"—if only we follow them.

Pascal's Wager: Betting on Eternity

Suppose someone precious to you lay dying, and the doctor offered to try a new "miracle drug" that he couldn't guarantee, but which seemed to have a 50-50 chance of saving your loved one's life.

Would it be reasonable to try it, even if it cost a little money? And suppose it were free—wouldn't it be utterly reasonable to try it and unreasonable not to?

Suppose you hear that your house is on fire and your children are inside. You don't know whether the report is true or false. What's the sensible thing to do—to ignore it or at least phone home in case the report is true?

No reasonable person can be in doubt in such cases. But deciding whether or not to believe in God is a case like these, argues Pascal. It's therefore the height of folly not to "bet" on God, even if we have no guarantee that our bet will win.

To understand Pascal's Wager we have to understand its background. Pascal lived in a time of huge skepticism. Medieval philosophy was dead, and theology was sneered at by the new intellectuals of the 17th century's scientific revolution. The classic arguments for the existence of God were no longer believed. What could the Christian apologist say to the skeptical mind of this era? Suppose such a mind lacked both the gift of faith and the confidence in reason to prove God's existence: Could there be a third ladder out of the pit of unbelief?

Pascal's Wager claims to be that third ladder. He knew well that if we believe in God only as a "bet" that is certainly not a mature or adequate faith. But it's a start. The Wager appeals not to a high instinct, like love or reason, but to a low one: self-preservation. But on that low, natural level, it has tremendous force. Thus he prefaces his argument with the words, "Let us now speak according to our natural lights."

Pascal says, "Either God is, or He is not. But to which view shall we be inclined? Reason cannot decide this question. (Pascal's Wager is an argument for skeptics.) Infinite chaos separates us. At the far end of this infinite distance (death), a coin is being spun which will come down heads (God) or tails (no God). How will you wager?"

The most powerful part of Pascal's argument comes next, and it's not his refutation of atheism as a foolish wager (that comes last) but his refutation of agnosticism as impossible. After all, agnosticism—not knowing, maintaining a skeptical, uncommitted attitude—seems to be the most reasonable option. The agnostic says, "The right thing is not to wager at all."

Pascal replies, "But you must wager. There is no choice. You are already committed (or 'embarked')." We are not observers of life, but participants. We're like ships which need to get home, sailing past a port that has signs on it proclaiming that it is our true home and happiness. The ships are our own lives and the signs on the port say "God."

The agnostic says he will neither put in at that port (believe) nor turn away from it (disbelieve), but stay anchored a reasonable distance until the weather clears and he can see better whether this is the true port or a fake (for there are lots of fakes around). Why is this attitude unreasonable—even impossible?

Because we're moving. The ship of life is moving along the waters of time and there comes a point when our fuel runs out. The Wager works because of the fact of death.

Suppose Romeo proposes to Juliet but Juliet says, "Give me some time to make up my mind." And suppose Romeo keeps corning back, day after day, but Juliet keeps saying the same thing: "Perhaps tomorrow." There comes a time when there are no more tomorrows. Then "maybe" becomes "no." Romeo will die. Corpses do not marry.

Christianity is God's marriage proposal to the soul. To keep saying "maybe" and "perhaps tomorrow" cannot continue indefinitely because life doesn't continue indefinitely. The weather will never be clear enough for the agnostic navigator to be sure whether the port with the signs on it is true or false just by looking at it through binoculars from a distance. He has to take a chance, or he'll never get home.

Once it is decided that we must wager; once it is decided that there are only two options, theism and atheism, not three, theism, atheism and agnosticism; then the argument is simple. Atheism is a bad bet. It gives us no chance of winning.

"You have two things to lose: the true and the good; and two things to stake: your reason and your will, your knowledge and your happiness; and your nature has two things to avoid: error and wretchedness. Since you must necessarily choose, your reason is no more affronted by choosing one rather than the other.

But your happiness? Let us weigh the gain and the loss in calling heads that God exists. Let us assess the two cases: If you win, you win everything; if you lose, you lose nothing. Do not hesitate then: Wager that He does exist."

If God does not exist, it doesn't matter how we wager, for there's nothing to win after death and nothing to lose after death. But if God does exist, our only chance of winning eternal happiness is to believe, and our only chance of losing it is to refuse to believe. As Pascal says, "I should be much more afraid of being mistaken and then finding out that Christianity is true than of being mistaken in believing it to be true." If we believe too much, we neither win nor lose eternal happiness. But if we believe too little, we risk losing everything.

But is it worth the price? What must be given up to wager that God exists? Whatever the correct answer it is only finite, and it's very reasonable indeed to wager a finite bet on the chance of winning an infinite prize. Perhaps we must give up autonomy, or illicit pleasures, but we'll gain infinite happiness in eternity, and "I tell you that you will gain even in this life"—purpose, peace, hope, joy, the things that put smiles on the lips of martyrs.

It's fitting that Pascal next imagines the listener offering the very practical objection that he just cannot bring himself to believe. Pascal answers this with stunningly practical psychology: with the suggestion that the prospective convert "act into" his belief if he cannot yet "act out" of it. It's the same advice Dostoyevsky's guru Father Zossima gives to the "woman of little faith" in "The Brothers Karamazov":

"If you are unable to believe, it is because of your passions, since reason impels you to believe and yet you cannot do so. Concentrate then not on convincing yourself by multiplying proofs of God's existence but by diminishing your passions. You want to find faith and you do not know the road. You want to be cured of unbelief and you ask for the remedy: Learn from those who were once bound like you and who now wager all they have . . . they behaved just as if they did believe."

The behavior Pascal mentions is "taking holy water, having Masses said, and so on." Father Zossima counsels to the same end an "active and indefatigable love of your neighbor . . . I am sorry I cannot say anything more comforting to you, for love in action is a harsh and dreadful thing compared with love in dreams." In both cases, living the faith can be a way of getting the faith. As Pascal says, "That will make you believe quite naturally and will make you more docile."

"But that is what I am afraid of."

"But why? What have you to lose?"

An atheist once visited the great rabbi-philosopher Martin Buber and demanded that Buber prove the existence of God to him. Buber refused, and the atheist got up to leave in anger. As he left, Buber called after him, "But can you be sure there is no God?"

That atheist wrote 40 years later, "I am still an atheist. But Buber's question has haunted me every day of my life."

The Wager has just that haunting power.

Source: Kreeft, Peter. 1988. "The Reasons to Believe." *National Catholic Register* (April 10). Reprinted with permission of *National Catholic Register*.

Peter Kreeft, Ph.D., is a professor of philosophy at Boston College and at the King's College (Empire State Building), New York City. He is a regular contributor to several Christian publications, is in wide demand as a speaker at conferences, and is the author of over 59 books, including *Handbook of Christian Apologetics*, *Christianity for Modern Pagans*, and *Fundamentals of the Faith*.

Anthropic Coincidences

by Stephen M. Barr

How important is the human race in the scheme of things? According to the *Epistle to Diognetus*, a Christian work of the early second century, "God loved the race of men. It was for their sakes that He made the world." The consensus of later Christian tradition does not go quite that far, holding that the purpose of Creation is to manifest God's glory, not simply to benefit mankind. And yet Scripture and tradition certainly concur in teaching that the human race has a central place in the divine plan. In the Book of Genesis, the six days of creation culminate in the creation of man, and man alone of all the creatures is said to be made "in the image of God." If we are not the sole or the chief end of Creation, it is nevertheless the Jewish and Christian view that in creating the world God had the human race in mind. Indeed, St. Paul tells the Ephesians that they were chosen by God and destined to be His sons "before the foundation of the world."

On the other hand, we have often been told, science regards man and his place in the world very differently. In the story of science as it is told by materialists the human race is not central to the purpose of the universe for the simple reason that the universe has no purpose. This is the view set forth in a well-known passage in Steven Weinberg's best-selling book *The First Three Minutes*:

> It is almost irresistible for humans to believe that we have some special relation to the universe, that human life is not just a farcical outcome of a chain of accidents . . . but that we were somehow built-in from the beginning. . . . It is very hard for us to realize that [the entire earth] is just a tiny part of an overwhelmingly hostile universe. . . . The more the universe seems comprehensible, the more it also seems pointless.

It is the view not only of Weinberg but of many scientists that the progress of science has more and more made the universe appear "pointless," and the human race an accidental by-product of blind material forces. Indeed, this is thought by many to be the key lesson that science has to teach us. A particularly forthright champion of this view is the zoologist Richard Dawkins, who writes that "the universe we observe has precisely the properties we should expect if there is at bottom no design, no purpose, no evil, no good, nothing but pointless indifference."

The pointlessness of the cosmos and its indifference to human beings is also a main theme in the writings of the zoologist Stephen Jay Gould, who claims that the human race is a freak accident of evolutionary history, merely "a tiny twig on an ancient tree of life." We are, said Bertrand Russell, but "a curious accident in a backwater" of the universe.

Certainly, much in the history of science encourages this "marginalization of man." If nothing else, the very size of the cosmos seems to tell of our insignificance. And yet, discussions about the size and age of the universe do not come to grips with the real question: Is the human race an accident, or were we meant to be here? To put it in Weinberg's terms, were we "somehow built-in from the beginning?"

As it happens, new light has been shed on this question by the discoveries of modern physics. It has been noticed, especially since the work of the astrophysicist Brandon Carter in the 1970s, that there are many features of the laws of nature that seem arranged, even "fine-tuned," to make possible the existence of life, including intelligent beings such as ourselves. At least on the face of it, these so-called "anthropic coincidences" would appear to support the idea that we *were* built-in from the beginning. Even some former atheists and agnostics have seen in them impressive evidence of a divine plan. And yet, many others maintain that a perfectly naturalistic explanation of these coincidences is possible. Rather than settling the age-old questions, then, the "anthropic" arguments seem only to have generated new controversy. Before getting into that controversy, it will be helpful to look at a few examples of anthropic coincidences. I will start with a detailed look at two of the most famous examples, both of which concern the origin of the chemical elements needed for life.

All life is based on chemistry-very complex chemistry, as even a cursory look at a biochemistry textbook makes clear. The human body, for instance, is made up of no fewer than twenty-five different chemical elements. Altogether, almost a hundred chemical elements occur naturally, the smallest being hydrogen, and the largest uranium. Where did all these elements come from? And why are the chemical possibilities of our universe so rich?

Hydrogen has been around since very soon after the Big Bang. But almost all of the other elements were forged later, either in the deep interiors of stars, or in the violent explosions called supernovas with which some stars end their lives. These supernova explosions are also important for life because they spew the elements made within stars out into space where they can form new stars, or planets, or people. Indeed, most of the elements in our bodies were made inside stars that exploded before the sun was born. We are quite literally made of stardust.

For our purposes, it is crucial to note that the elements are formed in a sequential manner by nuclear reactions in which the nuclei of smaller atoms fuse together to make the nuclei of larger atoms. These same "nuclear fusion" reactions also produce the energy radiated by stars (including, of course, the sun), energy that is essential to support life. The first step in the process of forging the elements is the fusing together of pairs of hydrogen nuclei to make something called "deuterium." Deuterium is the first and vital link in the whole chain. If deuterium had been prevented from forming, none of the later steps could have taken place, and the universe would have contained no elements other than hydrogen. This would have been a disaster, for it is scarcely conceivable that a living thing could be made of hydrogen alone. Moreover, had the deuterium link been cut, the nuclear processes by which stars burn would have been prevented.

Everything thus depends on hydrogen being able to fuse to make deuterium. Here is where the first remarkable anthropic coincidence comes in. The force of nature that cements nuclei together is called the "strong nuclear force." Had the strong nuclear force been weaker by even as little as 10 percent, it would not have been able to fuse two hydrogens together to make deuterium, and the prospects of life would have been dim indeed. But this is only the half of it. Had the strong nuclear force been only a few percent *stronger* than it is, an opposite disaster would have occurred. It would have been *too easy* for hydrogen nuclei to fuse together. The nuclear burning in stars would have gone much too fast. Stars would have burned themselves out in millions of years or less, rather than the several billion years that stars like the sun last. However, the history of life on earth suggests that billions of years are required for the evolution of complex life such as ourselves. The upshot of all these considerations is that the strong nuclear force has just the right strength: a little stronger or weaker and we would not have been here.

Once deuterium is made, deuterium nuclei can combine by fusion processes to make helium nuclei. These steps happen very readily. At this point, however, another critical juncture is reached: somehow, helium nuclei must fuse to make yet larger elements. But all the obvious ways this could happen are forbidden by the laws of physics. In particular, two helium nuclei cannot fuse together. This was quite a puzzle for nuclear theorists and astrophysicists. How did all the elements larger than helium come to be made?

The answer was found by Fred Hoyle, who suggested that nature in effect did a large double step to get past the missing rung in the ladder. When two helium nuclei collide in the interior of a star they cannot fuse permanently, but they do remain stuck together momentarily-for about a hundredth of a millionth of a billionth of a second. In that tiny sliver of time a third helium nucleus comes along and hits the other two in a three-way collision. *Three* heliums, as it happens, *do* have enough sticking power to fuse together permanently. When they do so they form a nucleus called "carbon-12." This highly unusual triple collision process is called the "three-alpha process," and it is the way that almost all of the carbon in the universe is made. Without it, the only elements around would be hydrogen and helium, leading to an almost certainly lifeless universe.

It was in looking closely at the three-alpha process that Hoyle discovered one of the most dramatic of the anthropic coincidences. Hoyle's preliminary calculations showed him that such a rare event as the three-alpha process would not make enough carbon unless something greatly enhanced its effectiveness. That something, he realized, must be what is called in physics a "resonance." There are many examples of resonance phenomena in everyday life. A big truck going by a house can rattle the window panes if the frequency of the sound waves matches up, or "resonates," with one of the "natural modes of vibration" of the window. Similarly, opera singers can shatter wine glasses by hitting just the right note. In other words, an effect that would ordinarily be very feeble can be greatly enhanced if it occurs resonantly.

Now, it happens that atomic nuclei too have characteristic "notes" or "modes of vibration," called "energy levels," and nuclear reactions can be enormously facilitated if they hit upon one of these energy levels. Hoyle pointed out that the three-alpha process could have produced enough carbon only if the carbon-12 nucleus has an energy level in just the right place. Indeed, experiments done shortly thereafter confirmed that it does. Had this energy level of carbon-12 been only a few percent higher or lower in frequency, the three-alpha process would have been out of tune, as it were. Without carbon, and the elements heavier than carbon, life as we know it would have been unable to exist.

One sees that the making of the chemical elements needed for life was, to borrow the Duke of Wellington's comment on his victory at Waterloo, "a damn close run thing."

One can see anthropic coincidences not only in the nuclear processes that formed the elements, but in many quite various aspects of the laws of physics. To give a better idea of this variety, I will describe a few more examples, though in less detail.

The "strong nuclear force" is one of four basic forces of nature that is presently known. The others are the so-called "weak interaction," gravity, and electromagnetism. In the phenomena of our everyday lives, electromagnetism plays a dominant, although perhaps not obvious, role. For example, matter is held together by the electrical attraction of atoms, and light consists of electromagnetic waves. In contrast, the strong nuclear force plays no direct role in effects that we can experience. That is because its influence extends only over subatomic distances. Nevertheless, the electromagnetic force is intrinsically much weaker than the strong nuclear force. In fact it is, in a certain well-defined sense, about one hundred times weaker. This is very fortunate. Had the electromagnetic force *not* been intrinsically much weaker than the strong nuclear force, the electrical energy packed inside a hydrogen nucleus would have been so great as to render it unstable. The "weak interaction" would then have made all the hydrogen in the world decay radioactively, with a very short half-life, into other particles. The world would have been left devoid of hydrogen, and therefore almost certainly of life. For water, which is indispensable for life, contains hydrogen, as do almost all organic molecules. We see, then, how life depends on a delicate balance among the various fundamental forces of nature, and in particular on the relative feebleness of electromagnetic effects.

Another fortunate fact has to do with the flatness of space. Einstein taught us that space-time is not flat, but curved. Because of this curvature, bodies seem to attract each other by the force we call gravity. However, it turns out that the space of our universe, if looked at on large enough scales of distance, is on average astonishingly flat. The "spatial curvature," as it is called, is very small. In fact, shortly after the Big Bang the spatial curvature of the universe was, to the accuracy of many decimal places, equal to zero. For a long time, this was referred to as the "flatness problem," since no one could think of a good explanation for it. However, while long a difficult thing for theorists to explain, this flatness of space is very fortunate. Had the flatness of space *not* been fantastically small to begin with, the universe would either have collapsed and ended a very short time-a tiny fraction of a second-after it began, or would have undergone such a tremendously rapid expansion that it would have torn matter and even atoms asunder.

So far I have described various quantities, like the strengths of the strong nuclear force and the flatness of space, that had to be "fine-tuned" to very special numerical values to make life as we know it possible. But there are also certain gross qualitative features of the laws of physics that are "anthropically" important. One example is the fact that space is three-dimensional. We take this fact for granted, but we shouldn't. That space has three dimensions is an empirical fact, not a metaphysical necessity. Theoretical physicists study hypothetical universes with other numbers of dimensions all the time. If the world had not had three space dimensions, but four or more of them, the gravitational force between two objects would have depended in a different way upon the distance between them. And that, in turn, would have made it impossible for planets to orbit stably around stars: they would either have plummeted into stars or flown off into space. (Interestingly, the first person to point out this consequence of a different law of gravity was the Anglican clergyman William Paley. Paley was one of the first people to think about anthropic coincidences in the laws of nature.) In the same way, the orbits of electrons in atoms would not have been stable, and life based on chemistry would have been impossible.

On the other hand, had there been *fewer* than three space dimensions, complex organisms would doubtless have been impossible for quite a different reason. Complex neural circuitry, as is needed in a brain, would not be possible in one or two dimensions. If one tries to draw a complicated circuit diagram on a two-dimensional surface, one finds that the wires have to intersect each other many times, leading to short-circuits.

As a final example, the fact that nature obeys the principles of quantum theory is highly important for the possibility of life. It turns out that matter would not be stable in a non-quantum world. People generally suppose that the Heisenberg Uncertainty Principle makes the world, at least at the atomic level, a fuzzier and more indefinite place. However, paradoxical as it may sound, that principle is ultimately responsible for the fact that subatomic particles form stable atoms with well-defined chemical properties. Were it not for the principles of quantum theory, matter would be amorphous and protean to such a degree that it is hard to imagine a living organism being possible.

What do physicists make of such anthropic coincidences? There is a wide spectrum of opinion. Some of the greatest scientists of our time, including Yacov Zel'dovich, Andrei Sakharov, Lev Okun, Martin Rees, and Steven Weinberg, to name but a few, have been interested in them and have devoted study to them. Nevertheless, the subject provokes discomfort and even hostility in much of the physics community, partly due to the specter of teleology. Physicists have a strong instinctive professional aversion to teleological thinking, because, at least in the physical sciences, the scientific revolution was to a large extent made possible by the rejection of teleology in favor of mechanism. I suspect, though, that there is more to this nervousness about anthropic coincidences-namely, the specter of religion.

Yet, scientific skepticism about these ideas is not based entirely on such prejudices. There are several arguments against the idea of anthropic coincidences that must be taken seriously.

First, it is argued that we cannot really know what is necessary for life to arise. Life might take forms that are utterly alien to our experience. While the life that we know about makes use of a certain kind of physics, who knows whether, with different physical laws, completely different possibilities for life might have existed?

This objection has some real force. In some cases, I think, all we can honestly assert is that it appears highly unlikely that life could have arisen had the laws of physics been different in this or that respect—unlikely, but perhaps not utterly impossible. In such questions absolute certainty may not be attainable due to our limited imaginations. However, absolute certainty may be beside the point. We might still be left with strong *indications* that the cosmos was made with us in mind, even if those indications do not add up to a proof. After all, the reasons that scientists like Weinberg, Dawkins, and Gould give for reaching the opposite conclusion are also not subject to proof.

The second objection is that conventional scientific explanations may exist for some if not all of the facts that now appear to be anthropic coincidences. In fact, among the examples I gave of anthropic coincidences I included two where we may already have at least a partial scientific explanation of the facts involved. The fact that the electromagnetic force is much weaker than the strong nuclear force, for instance, is probably partly explained by the idea of "grand unification." There are reasons to believe that the electromagnetic force, the weak interaction, and the strong nuclear force are really all aspects of one underlying "grand unified" force. If that is so, then the strengths of the different forces are not independent of each other, but are tied together in a definite way. In fact, in a typical grand unified model—and many such models have been proposed—the electromagnetic force does indeed come out to be much weaker than the strong nuclear force. Another of the anthropic coincidences concerns the flatness of space. This too is a fact for which we now have a probable explanation: it is thought to be a consequence of an effect called "cosmic inflation."

Thus, it is more than likely that at least some of the facts about the laws of physics that appear favorable to our existence do have conventional scientific explanations. Even if that proved to be true of all of them, however, it would not explain away the coincidental nature of these facts. The critical point was well expressed by the noted astrophysicists Bernard Carr and Martin Rees:

> One day we may have a more physical explanation for some of the relationships . . . that now seem genuine coincidences. For example, [some of them] may eventually be subsumed as a consequence of some presently unformulated unified theory. However, *even if all apparently anthropic coincidences could be explained in this way, it would still be remarkable that the relationships dictated by physical theory happened also to be those propitious for life.* [emphasis added]

In other words, suppose that there are twenty numerical relationships that have to hold in order for life to be possible, and suppose that in some physical theory every one of those twenty relationships happens to hold as a consequence of some underlying physical principle. That would *itself* amount to an astonishing coincidence.

This brings us to the third objection, which is closely related to the second. Einstein famously asked whether God had a choice in how He made the world. Many physicists nowadays suspect not. They suspect that all mathematical relationships in the laws of physics will turn out to be dictated by some deep underlying principles that leave no room for things to have been otherwise. One frequently hears the possibility discussed that the laws of physics are "unique." The idea is that everything about the physical world-the kinds of particles that exist, the kinds of forces and their relative strengths, the number of dimensions of space and its degree of flatness, the energy levels of the carbon-12 nucleus, and so on, down to the smallest detail-may have to be as they are on account of some fundamental physical principles. If so, God could not have the freedom to arrange the laws of nature to be "propitious for life" or otherwise, since His hands were completely tied.

However, this is plainly wrong. Physical principles could not have tied God's hands, for the simple reason that He could have chosen some *other* principles upon which to base the laws of physics. For example, while the relative feebleness of the electromagnetic force, which we saw to be anthropically fortunate, may be a necessary outcome of a "grand unified" framework, it was by no means necessary that the world be built according to such a "grand unified" framework. In fact, we still do not know whether it is. So, in this particular matter God clearly did have a choice—indeed, many choices, as there are many mathematically self-consistent frameworks that involve "grand unification" and many that do not.

As a matter of fact, there are an infinite number of mathematically self-consistent sets of laws of physics that could have been chosen as the basis for the structure of a universe. This is incontestable. When those (good) physicists talk about the laws of physics being possibly "unique," they are speaking very loosely. What they really have in mind is the idea that a unique set of laws may be necessary if it has to satisfy certain assumed preconditions. For example, many theorists believe that there is only one possible set of laws—"superstring theory" —that can incorporate simultaneously the principles of quantum theory and the principles of Einsteinian gravity. However, there is certainly no reason to suppose *a priori* that the universe had to incorporate either quantum theory or Einsteinian gravity. In short, the universe could have been made differently, and if it had been life might not have been able to arise. These assertions, it seems to me, can hardly be disputed.

Before one leaps to the conclusion that the anthropic coincidences inevitably point to God, one should be aware of the fact that many of the scientists who have written about anthropic coincidences are atheists. (Steven Weinberg is a notable example.) It is their view that the laws of physics being "propitious" for life, far from pointing to the importance of life or human beings in some cosmic "plan," has a purely naturalistic, scientific explanation. The explanation that they offer is based on an idea that is called the Anthropic Principle. There are various anthropic principles that are discussed, but the only one taken seriously by scientists as being plausible and having any explanatory power is called the Weak Anthropic Principle, or WAP for short. It should be noted that careless writers often talk about "the anthropic principle" when what they really mean is "anthropic coincidences." The two ideas should not be confused: the anthropic coincidences are facts, while the anthropic "principle" is a speculative hypothesis for explaining those facts.

The idea of the Weak Anthropic Principle is easiest to grasp using an analogy. There are many things about conditions on the planet Earth that are propitious for life. If the Earth were much smaller, then it would not be able to retain an atmosphere. If it were much bigger, it would retain a lot of hydrogen in its atmosphere, which might be bad for life. If it were much closer to the sun it would be too hot to have liquid water, if much farther away it would be too cold. Has someone "fine-tuned" conditions here to make life possible? Not necessarily. There are presumably a vast number of planets in the universe. (In the context of present-day theory, it is not unlikely that there are an infinite number.) Some planets are hot, some cold. some big, and some small. They undoubtedly span a vast range of physical and chemical conditions. It seems inevitable that some of them would happen to have the right conditions for life.

To put it another way, if one tried one key in an unknown lock, it would be an astonishing coincidence if it worked. But if one tried a million keys it would not be greatly surprising if one of them did.

The idea of the Weak Anthropic Principle is that the same kind of argument can be used not just about planets, but about universes. Suppose that there are a huge number of universes. Some may have three space dimensions, some two, some four, and so on. In some, the electromagnetic force may be weaker than the strong nuclear force, in others it may be stronger, and in others there may be no such thing as the electromagnetic force at all. That is, all sorts of possible physical laws might be tried out in different universes. If so, it might not be surprising, assuming that a great enough number and variety of universes existed, that some of them would have just the right laws of physics to permit life. And of course, to the inhabitants of such an exceptional universe, it might seem that someone had arranged things in their universe with them in mind. This is an old idea, going back at least to David Hume, who suggested that "many worlds might have been botched and bungled, throughout an eternity, ere this system was struck out."

Before examining this idea critically, one must distinguish two versions of it. In the version that physicists take seriously, the many "universes" are not really distinct and separate universes at all, but domains or regions of one all-encompassing Universe. The domains are far apart in space, or otherwise prevented from communicating with each other. Conditions are assumed to be so different from one domain to another that they appear superficially to have different physical laws. However, at a deeper level all the domains are really controlled by one and the same set of fundamental laws. These laws also control what types of domains the universe has, and how many of each type.

The other version of the idea posits the existence of a large number of universes that really are universes, distinct and unconnected in any way with each other. Each has its own set of physical laws. There is no overarching physical system of which each is a part. One can understand why this version is not discussed among scientists. At least in the many-domains version all the domains are part of the same universe as we, so that, even if we cannot in practice observe them directly, we might hope at least to infer their existence theoretically from a deep understanding of the laws of nature. In the many-universes version, this is not the case.

Let us first consider the many-domains version of the idea. It is not, as many suppose, a foolish or extravagant one. In fact, some of the kinds of theories that fundamental physicists think about nowadays actually imply that the universe must have domains. In such theories the different domains can differ radically from each other, with even different kinds of particles and different forces. Thus it is not unreasonable to suppose that a many-domains version of the Weak

Anthropic Principle might turn out to be the explanation for some of the anthropic coincidences. Nevertheless, I do not believe that this would subtract much from the force of the anthropic coincidences as evidence for purpose in the universe. The reason is simple. The whole point of the anthropic coincidences is that the laws of physics have to be very special to allow life to exist. But this requirement is not avoided by the many-domains idea, for the laws of physics also have to be very special to give rise to a universe with domains, especially domains of a sufficiently rich variety to do what the Weak Anthropic Principle demands of them.

One can illustrate the point by means of a rather whimsical analogy. Suppose you were looking for a specific obscure recipe for, say, goulash. If the first book you took at random from the cooking shelf of the library happened to have exactly that recipe, you would regard it as a great coincidence. If you then discovered that the book contained *every* recipe for goulash ever invented, you would cease to regard it as coincidental that it had the one of particular interest to you. But you would be surprised nonetheless, for one does not expect a cookbook to treat that particular category of food so comprehensively. The fact that it happened to be so comprehensive in its selection of goulash, when it was goulash that you needed, would itself count as a remarkable coincidence.

Likewise, it is not something to be taken for granted that the universe would have as many domains as needed for the anthropic coincidences to seem unsurprising. On the contrary, in the kinds of theories physicists have found reason to study, the universe is not nearly so inclusive. True, some of those theories suggest that the universe has domains, but they typically realize only a few possibilities, not the vast smorgasbord of possibilities needed to explain *all* of the many anthropic coincidences that have been identified.

The many-universes version of the anthropic principle is in a way simpler. In the many-domains idea, one has to account for the domains by a physical mechanism. Consequently the laws of physics have to be "engineered," as it were, to produce a universe with a sufficiently rich variety of domains. In the many-universes idea, on the other hand, it is simply posited that many types of universe exist. What types of universe exist and what types do not? That is not a question that the laws of physics can possibly answer, since each universe has *ex hypothesi* its *own* laws of physics. If some kinds of universe exist while others do not, it would seem to suggest that Someone has made choices. Far from destroying the case that a cosmic Designer exists, the many-universes idea only strengthens it.

A last-ditch way out for the opponents of cosmic design would be to say that *all* conceivable universes exist, i.e., any universe that is logically and mathematically self-consistent actually exists. This idea has a breathtaking simplicity. It would explain existence: to exist is to be self-consistent. It would remove the need for a Designer or a Creator. Whereas the "unique laws of physics" idea got rid of a Designer by saying that there are no choices for a Designer to make as there is only one real possibility, here the Designer is eliminated by saying that there are infinitely many possibilities, but that no one has selected among them.

There is, however, a fatal problem with this way of getting rid of the cosmic Designer. It cannot explain why we live in a universe that is so astonishingly lawful. Among all the logically possible universes, ones that have the perfection of order and lawfulness that ours displays are highly exceptional, just as among all possible rocks, a perfect gem that has absolutely no flaws in it is almost infinitely unlikely. Why doesn't our universe exhibit occasional departures from its regularities—the regularities we call the laws of physics—just as gemstones have occasional departures from their regularities? No answer to this is possible. If all possible universes exist, it becomes a tremendous miracle that we live in a universe of perfect, or nearly perfect, lawfulness. It is a miracle, in other words, that miracles do not occur around us all the time.

The Weak Anthropic Principle, whether in its many-universes or many-domains versions, cannot succeed in explaining the anthropic coincidences away or making them any less coincidental. In the final analysis one cannot escape from two very basic facts: the laws of nature did not have to be as they are; and the laws of nature had to be very special in form if life were to be possible. In my view these facts lend themselves most naturally to a religious interpretation. Certainly, they tend to undercut the claim so often confidently made by materialists that the discoveries of science point to a universe without meaning or purpose, in which man is an accidental by-product.

Having said all this, we remain with a question very troubling to many: Why is the universe so big? How can we claim to be important in a universe that dwarfs us in its scales of space and time? There is at least a paradox here. It is a paradox that was not lost upon the Psalmist, who exclaimed, "When I consider the heavens, the work of thy fingers, the moon and the stars, which thou hast ordained; What is man, that thou art mindful of him, and the son of man, that thou visitest him?"

One answer, of course, is the traditional one. The universe was not made only for our benefit. As the Psalmist also said, "the heavens proclaim the glory of God." If it is the glory of God that they proclaim, then there is no particular reason why they should have to be made to human scale. In fact, in the fifteenth century Nicolas of Cusa argued that only a universe of infinite extent would be worthy of the Creator and able to manifest His glory.

The traditional answer is a good one, but there may be another. It turns out that the very age and vastness of the universe may have an "anthropic" significance. Life emerged in our universe in a way that required great stretches of time. As we have seen, most of the elements needed for life were made deep in stars. Those stars had to explode to disperse those elements and make them available before life could even begin to evolve. That whole process alone required billions of years. The evolution of human life from those elements required billions of years more. Thus, the briefness of human life spans and even of human history compared with the age of the universe may simply be a matter of physical necessity, given the developmental way that God seems to prefer to work. It takes longer for a tree to grow to maturity than the fruit of the tree lasts. It took much longer for the universe to grow to maturity than we last.

Physics can also suggest why the universe has to be so large. The laws of gravity discovered by Einstein relate the size of the universe directly to its age. The fact that the universe is many billions of light-years across is related to the fact that it has lasted several billions of years. Perhaps we would be less daunted by a cozy little universe the size, say, of a continent. But such a universe would have lasted only a few milliseconds. Even a universe the size of the solar system would have lasted only a few hours. A universe constructed in such a way as to evolve life may well have had to extend widely in space as well as in time. It may well be that the frightening expanses that are so often said to be a sign of human insignificance may actually, like so many other features of our strange universe, point to man, as they also proclaim the glory of God.

Source: Stephen M. Barr. 2001. "Anthropic Coincidences." *First Things* (114): 17-23 (June/July). Reprinted with permission from *First Things*.

Stephen M. Barr is a professor of Theoretical Particle Physics at the Bartol Research Institute and Department of Physics and Astronomy of the University of Delaware. His areas of expertise include Grand Unified Theories of the fundamental forces of nature, theories of the origin of quark and lepton masses, violation of spacetime symmetries, and an early universe cosmology. He is the author of over 120 physics papers, including the article on Grand Unified Theories for the *Encyclopedia of Physics*.

Chapter 2

─── ❧ ───

Are Religion and Science at Odds?

Any discussion with an atheist or most members of the media on the topic of religion and science would surely surface the argument that religion and science pose contradictory forces in our society. This fallacy is largely due to misunderstanding and confusion sown by ignorance. And the ignorance is held by believers and nonbelievers alike.

The Catholic Church makes it very clear that religion and science must be in harmony because both faith and reason come from God.[1] Truths cannot be in true conflict. Understanding how religion and science intersect is vitally important; each plays a role in advancing human knowledge.

The articles in this chapter provide a helpful perspective on how we should think about the role of religion and science in society.

Father Tadeusz Pacholczyk is a Catholic priest and a scientist. His **"Are Science and religion Really Enemies?"** tackles the question head on.

- ➤ Science and religion do not make competing claims of the same questions.
- ➤ As far back as the late 1500s, Cardinal Baronius stated that religion teaches us "the way to go to heaven, not the way the heavens go."
- ➤ Religion and science have "distinct and unique domains" making them objectively compatible.
- ➤ Einstein is cited as having said, "Science without religion is lame; religion without science is blind."

───────────────

[1] *Catechism of the Catholic Church*. 1997. 2nd ed., no. 159. Vatican City: Libreria Editrice Vaticana.

> Pope John Paul II said, "Science can purify religion from error and superstition. Religion can purify science from idolatry and false absolutes."
> One conflict that can arise occurs when religion insists on ethics with respect to scientific activity.
> The concluding quote from astronomer and mathematician Johannes Kepler states, "The chief aim of all investigations of the external world should be to discover the rational order and harmony which has been imposed on it by God and which He revealed to us in the language of mathematics."

In **"The Pope and the Apes,"** George Sim Johnston addresses misconceptions related to Pope John Paul II's comments that the Church has no problem with the concept of evolution, provided the mechanism involves God.

> There are many theories of evolution; Darwin's is just one.
> The Holy Father said, "[T]heories of evolution which, because of the philosophies which inspire them, regard the spirit either as emerging from the forces of living matter, or as a simple epiphenomenon of that matter, are incompatible with the truth about man."
> The notion of human evolution from ape-like creatures can be accepted as long as the theory includes an "ontological leap," according to the pope, to the first human person. This necessary leap is supported by the paleontological evidence that shows man's sudden emergence. In other words, one must accept the direct role of God, who creates each rational soul from nothing.
> Scripture does not teach science. The author states that "Genesis tells us what happened in the archaic, pre-scientific idiom of the ancient Hebrews. It does not tell us "how" it happened." Science tells us how it happened.
> There can be no true conflict between religion and science.

"Retelling the Story of Science" by physicist Stephen Barr is a superb essay that refutes several notions by materialists about the relationship between science and religion. He demonstrates how science and religion have never really been at odds.

➢ The conflict is not between religion and science, but between religion and materialism, a philosophy holding that nothing exists except matter.

➢ According to scholars, Genesis was a "polemic against pagan superstition."

➢ Genesis taught that the sun, moon, and animals were mere creatures that should not be worshiped. This cleared the way for the emergence of modern science.

➢ The Bible taught that the universe was a creation of God, governed by the laws of the cosmos that He established.

➢ Most ancient Christian texts do not focus on miraculous evidence of the existence of God. Rather, they point to the natural order of things.

➢ Galileo and Newton disputed the naturalistic theories of Aristotle that the Church defended because it was (mistakenly) defending the veracity of the Bible.

➢ The limitations placed on scientists and theologians are analogous. The scientist is subject to the data of an experiment, while the theologian must submit to the "data" of revelation. They both accept givens, despite how those data might conflict with knowledge obtained through other means.

➢ The scientist considers that certain scientific insights are yet to be discovered and may never be discovered, yet he believes they exist. Barr suggests that "faith in God is an extension of this attitude."

➢ Religion has never been an obstacle to scientific progress.

➢ A strictly materialistic notion of humanity cannot account for the power of man's reason. Nor can it account for consciousness, free will, and the unitary self.

➢ The materialist's "Story of Science" consists, largely, of five major themes. The author identifies five "twentieth-century plot twists" that undermine or even invalidate each of those themes or assertions:

   • The notion that the universe and time had a beginning originated in the Bible. Yet, scientific ideas at the beginning of the twentieth century held that space, matter, and time were eternal. They always existed and always would. This notion has been turned on its head by the theory and subsequent observational evidence of the "Big Bang."

- The laws of physics began to be appreciated for their "great subtlety, harmony, and beauty." This has undermined a merely mechanistic view of the cosmos and suggests that, in fact, there is a cosmic designer.
- The discovery of "anthropic coincidences" or aspects of the laws of physics that appear to provide precisely what is required for life to exist point to the likelihood that the universe has a purpose and that purpose is to support life.
- The development of quantum theory called into question the assumptions of determinism that held that we live in a world defined strictly by cause and effect. Quantum theory opened the door to the possibility of personal freedom that determinism would deny.
- Two twentieth-century discoveries, Quantum Theory and Gödel's Theorem, refute the idea that the human mind is just a biochemical machine.

➢ Barr concludes, "[T]he search for truth always leads us, in the end, back to God."

Further Reading

Stephen M. Barr. 2003. *Modern Physics and Ancient Faith*. South Bend, Indiana: University of Notre Dame Press.

Stephen Barr. 2006. "The Miracle of Evolution." *First Things (160):* 30-33 (February).

Rev. Stanley Jaki. 1997. "The Biblical Basis of Western Science." *Crisis* 15 (9):17-20 (October).

Michael W. Tkacz. 2008. "Aquinas vs. Intelligent Design." *This Rock* (19): 9 (November).

Are Science and Religion Really Enemies?

By Tadeusz Pacholczyk

A surprising number of people believe these two powerful forces in our society are incompatible with each other. Some even claim there is an "inherent conflict" between them.

When people learn that I am a scientist and a Catholic priest, a common response is, "Wow, how do you do it?" Although it may appear to a casual observer that science and religion make competing claims over the same questions, in reality they do not.

Already back in the late 1500s a well-known churchman named Cardinal Baronius made the point that religion teaches us "the way to go to heaven, not the way the heavens go." Science, on the other hand, addresses the physical world and "how the heavens go." This simple but important distinction, which was later incorporated into the writings of Galileo, reminds us that science and religion are objectively compatible with each other since they have distinct and unique domains.

Yet even if they deal with different domains, science and religion can and must speak to each other. Albert Einstein already saw this when he made his now-famous remark: "Science without religion is lame; religion without science is blind." Science and religion need each other and must work together. Pope John Paul II asserted this same fundamental point when he said: "Science can purify religion from error and superstition. Religion can purify science from idolatry and false absolutes."

This task of collaboration and purification, however, is not an easy one in an environment of mutual doubt, suspicion and hostility. One reason for such hostility is that religion often purifies science by insisting on the primacy of ethics. Yet many scientists are clearly unwilling to acknowledge that the interests of humanity are authentically served only when scientific knowledge is joined to a truthful conscience, and the pursuit of science is attenuated through the filter of ethics.

In fact, the much-hyped conflict between religion and science turns out to be largely a conflict between men of science and men of religion, rather than between science itself and religion itself. Ultimately, some scientists may become uncomfortable when they perceive that science cannot adequately address value questions or provide answers to the ultimate questions that religion addresses. Some men of faith may similarly feel threatened when they finally have to acknowledge that the Bible is not, in fact, a scientific textbook.

A further explanation for the suspicion between scientists and men of faith can be the ill will generated by a vocal minority of scientists who suggest that religion has a "softening influence on the brain," or that men and women of faith are "spared the trouble of thinking" when they live by religious dogma and strong ethical principles. Quite the opposite is actually the case. True religion, like good science, promotes a more measured rationality, and a more ordered thoughtfulness as we consider the created world we are a part of. Absolute religious dogmas and invariable ethical principles do not stifle thinking any more than absolute definitions and unalterable geometric postulates stifle the thinking of the student of geometry. The rules of geometry do not "spare us the trouble of thinking" but, on the contrary, help us to think in a structured way, providing us with the very categories we need in order to be able to enter more deeply into this branch of mathematics. Similarly, religious dogma and sound ethical teaching afford us the essential categories we need to enter reasonably into a discussion of the ultimate questions that every person faces, questions of purpose, morality and human destiny. Religion, in the words of G. K. Chesterton, is never "an arrest of thought, but a fertile basis and constant provocation of thought."

Moving past the mutual suspicion that has arisen between scientists and men of faith is thus a critical first step in seeing how religion and science are not, in fact, enemies at all. The two are able not only to co-exist peaceably, but within the person of the scientist, religion and science can ultimately interconnect and strengthen one another. The pioneering astronomer and mathematician Johannes Kepler, who first calculated the elliptical orbits of the planets, perhaps put it best when he wrote: "The chief aim of all investigations of the external world should be to discover the rational order and harmony which has been imposed on it by God and which He revealed to us in the language of mathematics."

That source of rationality, which is God himself, should be a source of continual wonder for each of us, as it was for Einstein when he mused: "The most incomprehensible thing about the universe is that it is comprehensible."

Source: Rev. Tadeusz Pacholczyk. 2008. "Are Science and Religion Really Enemies?" *Making Sense Out of Bioethics* (October). Reprinted with permission from Rev. Tadeusz Pacholczyk.

Rev. Tadeusz Pacholczyk, Ph.D., earned his doctorate in neuroscience from Yale University and conducted post-doctoral work at Harvard University. He is a priest of the diocese of Fall River, Massachusetts, and serves as the Director of Education at The National Catholic Bioethics Center in Philadelphia.

The Pope and the Apes

By George Sim Johnston

In October [1996], Pope John Paul II delivered a message to the Pontifical Academy of Sciences regarding the theory of evolution. The document touched on a number of important issues— scriptural, epistemological, and scientific—which are of supreme importance to Catholics. Inevitably, it was the least newsworthy item in the pope's message—that the Church has no problem with evolution so long as divine causality is not excluded—that produced screaming headlines around the world. "Pope Vindicates Darwin!"

The pope, in fact, did no such thing. *The New York Times* and other conduits of misinformation about the Church made the usual mistake of equating "evolution" with Darwin's explanation of evolution. Darwin did not discover evolution; he simply proposed a mechanism—gradual change via natural selection—that made materialistic evolution seem plausible. The mechanism was, and is, highly problematic. Many paleontologists and biologists, while calling themselves evolutionists, assert that Darwinian selection cannot explain the big, complicated jumps between life forms, starting with the Cambrian explosion 550 million years ago. A recent example is *Reinventing Darwin* (read: Retiring Darwin) by Niles Eldredge, chief paleontologist at the American Museum of Natural History.

The pope is aware of this controversy among evolutionists, writing that "rather than speaking about the theory of evolution, it is more accurate to speak of the theories of evolution. The use of the plural is required here . . . because of the diversity of explanations regarding the mechanism of evolution." And he goes on to reject the essence of Darwinism: "[T]heories of evolution which, because of the philosophies which inspire them, regard the spirit either as emerging from the forces of living matter, or as a simple epiphenomenon of that matter, are incompatible with the truth about man."

So the pope objects to philosophical materialism masquerading as science, which is what we find in books by Darwinists. Pop scientists like Richard Dawkins and Carl Sagan start with a philosophical prem-ise: There is no God. This allows them to embrace a teleological taboo that makes Darwin a winner by default. But their explanation of how the bacteria that appeared billions of years ago produced the incredible diversity of life we see today relies more on hidden postulates than empirical evidence. Darwinism in their hands really amounts to a countermetaphysics planted like a foreign body in the heart of biology.

The pope would have clarified matters greatly if he had repeated the observation of Catholic thinkers like Etienne Gilson that the real debate is not over evolution per se, but teleology. Either life forms came about by blind chance or they did not. Darwin's theory is the only one available that purports to explain how Homo sapiens and other species are the result exclusively of natural forces. There are no other theories available that do not smack of vitalism, than which there is no dirtier word in the lexicon of Darwinists.

Evolution actually has an ancient Catholic pedigree. St. Augustine was an evolutionist, although hardly a Darwinist. In his second com-mentary on Genesis, he surmised that God had planted "rational seeds" in nature that had fructified in due course. This is evolution in the strict etymological sense of the word, an unfolding of what is already there, like an acorn turning into an oak. At the time of the Scopes trial, Chesterton remarked that Catholics were not at all involved in a battle that set biblical and scientific fundamentalists against one another. As usual, there was a reasonable Catholic center that allowed both science and theology their due competence.

It makes no difference whether man is descended biologically from some ape-like creature, so long as we understand that there had to be what the pope calls an "ontological leap" to the first human person. This would have involved the direct action of God, who creates each rational soul out of nothing. Even the scanty paleontological evidence supports the scenario of man's sudden emergence. Homo sapiens, fully equipped with art, language, and toolmaking capabilities, appears with dramatic rapidity in the fossil record. There is no evidence of an ape trying to draw reindeer in the caves of south France or fashion a flute in the manner of the Neanderthals, who certainly were part of the human family.

The confusion over evolution among Christians boils down to the question of how to read the creation account in Genesis. Here the pope simply reiterates what the Magisterium has argued tirelessly since Leo

XIII's *Providentissimus Deus*. Scripture does not teach science, period. Genesis tells us what happened in the archaic, prescientific idiom of the ancient Hebrews. It does not tell us how it happened. We can learn what we can of that "how" from science, always keeping in mind that there can be no real conflict between two very different orders of knowledge: science and theology.

Source: Johnston, George Sim. 1997. "The Pope and the Apes." *Crisis* (16) 6: 33 (January). Reprinted with permission from InsideCatholic (www.insidecatholic.com).

George Sim Johnston is a writer living in New York City. His most recent book, *Did Darwin Get it Right?: Catholics and the Theory of Evolution* (1998*)*, is published by *Our Sunday Visitor*, Huntington, Indiana.

Retelling the Story of Science

By Stephen M. Barr

We often hear of a conflict between religion and science. Is there one? Certainly, some religious beliefs are scientifically untenable: for example, that the world is six thousand years old. However, for Jews and Christians not committed to a narrowly literalistic interpretation of Scripture, that kind of direct and clear-cut contradiction between scientific facts and religious doctrines does not exist.

What many take to be a conflict between religion and science is really something else. It is a conflict between religion and materialism. Materialism regards itself as scientific, and indeed is often called "scientific materialism," even by its opponents, but it has no legitimate claim to be part of science. It is, rather, a school of philosophy, one defined by the belief that nothing exists except matter, or, as Democritus put it, "atoms and the void."

However, there is more to materialism than this cold ontological negation. For many, scientific materialism is not a bloodless philosophy but a passionately held ideology. Indeed, it is the ideology of a great part of the scientific world. Its adherents see science as having a mission that goes beyond the mere investigation of nature or the discovery of physical laws. That mission is to free mankind from superstition in all its forms, and especially in the form of religious belief.

There are two grounds for the materialist's indictment of religion as superstition. First, religion is supernaturalist. It teaches that there is a spiritual realm, and supposedly embraces mythological explanations and magical practices. Second, religion is (in the materialist's eyes) irrationalist, because it is based on dogma, faith, and mystery. Science, being based on the natural and the rational, is therefore held to be fundamentally opposed to religion.

In other words, the scientific materialist maintains that there *is* a conflict between science and religion, and that it is intrinsic and a priori, in the sense that it would exist even if science had not yet made any definite discoveries about the world. This supposed opposition flows from what science and religion are in themselves, from their basic views of reality. However, the materialist claims more than this. He also says that many of the particular discoveries of science have demolished the credibility of religion. He claims, in other words, that there is also an a posteriori conflict between science and religion. This claim is based on a tendentious reading of scientific history, what I shall call the materialist's "Story of Science." According to this story, the great discoveries since the time of Copernicus and Galileo have disclosed a world that looks ever less like the picture religion painted of it, and have forced religious believers to fight a centuries-long rearguard action against the truth. Science has been the great debunker.

The claims of scientific materialism are hardly new. Indeed, they have not changed substantially in over a hundred years. And yet much else has changed in that time. We know much more than we did about the origins of science; we know vastly more about nature. It is a good time, therefore, to take a fresh look at the materialist ideology of science and its story of science to see how well they have held up in the light of new knowledge.

We begin with the issue of supernaturalism in religion and its supposedly superstitious character. I think we would all agree that most forms of belief in the supernatural are superstitious. However, we must remind ourselves of a vital historical fact, which is that many of these forms of supernaturalism were attacked, and at least partially overthrown, by biblical religion long before the advent of modern science. The Book of Genesis was itself in large part intended, scholars tell us, as a polemic against pagan superstition. For example, whereas the sun and moon were the objects of worship in pagan religion, the Book of Genesis taught that they were nothing but lamps set in the heavens to give light to day and night: not gods, but mere things, creatures of the one true God. Nor were animals and the forces of nature to be bowed down to by man as in pagan religion; rather man, as a rational being made in the image of God, was to exercise dominion over them.

It is true that the Bible is overwhelmingly supernatural in its outlook and literary atmosphere. However, what is critically important is that the Bible's supernaturalism is concentrated in a God who is outside of Nature, and radically distinguished from the world He has made. Therefore the world of nature is no longer seen as populated by capricious supernatural beings, by fates and furies, dryads and naiads, gods of war or goddesses of sex and fertility. The natural world has been "disenchanted." But whereas many give credit to science for this, the distinction belongs in the first instance to the monotheism of the

Bible, which by depersonalizing and desacralizing the natural world helped clear the ground for the eventual emergence of modern science.

The Bible taught, then, that whatever reverence it is proper to have for the sun, or the forces of nature, or living things is due not to any divinity or spirituality that they possess, but to the fact that they are the masterworks of God. The universe thus came to be seen as a great work of engineering. We observe this in the Book of Proverbs, where the divine Wisdom is portrayed as a master craftsman directing the work of creation. And according to the rabbis of old the divine craftsman worked from a plan that was none other than the Torah itself. As they put it, "the Holy One, blessed be He, consulted the Torah when He created the world." The Torah, then, was not merely a Law written in a perishable book, or part of a covenant with the people of Israel. It was an eternal Law in the mind of God which He imposed on the cosmos itself. The Lord says through the prophet Jeremiah: "When I have no covenant with day and night, and have given no laws to heaven and earth, then too will I reject the descendants of Jacob and of my servant David." Psalm 148 tells of the sun, the moon, the stars, and the heavens obeying a divinely given "law, that will not pass away." This emphasis on the lawfulness of the cosmos is found also in the earliest Christian writings. Minucius Felix in the second century wrote:

> If upon entering some home you saw that everything there was well-tended, neat, and decorative, you would believe that some master was in charge of it, and that he was himself much superior to those good things. So too in the home of this world, when you see providence, order, and law in the heavens and on earth, believe that there is a Lord and Author of the universe, more beautiful than the stars themselves and the various parts of the whole world.

Note that these ancient texts do not point to supernatural phenomena or to the miraculous as evidence of God's existence. Neither did St. Paul in the first chapter of Romans, where he discusses the grounds of belief in God. Nor did St. Thomas Aquinas in his famous five-fold proof. Belief in God is not founded upon supernatural manifestations but on the natural order, on the orderliness of things. The role of the miraculous in Judaism and Christianity is quite limited; it is to show God's favor to His people and testify to the authenticity of the oracles of divine revelation, not to ground belief in the Creator.

There is something else that can be observed in these ancient texts, I think, that has some relevance to the long-debated question of Darwin and design. Many seem to have gotten the impression that the old Argument from Design for the existence of God is primarily an argument from biology. Richard Dawkins says, for instance, that it was the discovery by Darwin that biological structure could arise without design that "made it possible to be an intellectually fulfilled atheist." However, most of the ancient Jewish and Christian texts seem to emphasize the structure of the cosmos as a whole more than the structure of living things. Jeremiah speaks of the covenant with day and night, and the laws given to heaven and earth; the Psalmist of the law obeyed by the sun, moon, stars, and heavens; and Minucius Felix of the providence, order, and law in the heavens and on earth.

It was in the heavens that the orderliness of nature was most evident to ancient man. It was this celestial order, perhaps, that first inspired in him feelings of religious awe. And it was the study of this order that gave birth to modern science in the seventeenth century. It is not altogether accidental, then, that it was an argument over the motions of the heavenly bodies that occasioned the fateful collision between science and religious authority that will forever be evoked by the name of Galileo. The case of Galileo raises another important historical point about supernaturalism and biblical religion.

Perhaps I can best introduce it with a personal story. I was asked a few years ago to give the response at a conference of scholars to a talk on the teaching of evolution in high schools. In my presentation I quoted the following piece of antireligious propaganda from a currently used high school biology textbook: "Every so often scientists stir up controversy when they explain part of the world that was considered beyond natural explanation—that is, belonging to the 'supernatural.'" I disputed the idea that such controversies arise "every so often," as the textbook asserted. I said that except for the battle over evolution I could think of no significant controversy that fit this description. At that point, as I had expected might happen, several members of the audience shouted out "Galileo!" But they had no reason to, for (as I went on to observe) the Galileo affair was most certainly not a debate about the supernatural. The geocentric theory that the Church in effect endorsed was no more supernatural than the heliocentric theory that it condemned. This was a clash between two perfectly naturalistic theories of astronomy. It was the veracity of Scripture that the Church authorities (mistakenly) saw themselves as upholding, not supernatural explanations of planetary motion over natural ones. (It is true that the inspiration of Scripture is supernatural, and that Galileo's opponents thus thought they had supernatural warrant for believing what they did. But one may believe a natural fact on supernatural authority. I may believe that figs grow on trees or that Pontius Pilate was procurator in Judea because the Bible says so, without thinking that those facts are in any way supernatural in themselves.)

It was the same in physics: what Galileo and Newton overthrew were the erroneous, but perfectly naturalistic, theories of Aristotle. The Scientific Revolution of the seventeenth century had to overcome the naturalism of Aristotle, not the supernaturalism of Christianity. Christianity had already embraced naturalism in science five hundred years earlier, when Western Christians first encountered Greek science (or as it was called, natural philosophy) through translations from Greek and Arabic texts. Under the aegis of the Church, natural philosophy became a staple of medieval university education and was even a prerequisite for the study of theology. So comfortable were Christians with a naturalistic conception of the cosmos that it was a cliché already in the twelfth century for theologians and other writers to refer to the cosmos as a "machine."

Now, while biblical religion has something to say about the existence of a natural order (which is simply a corollary of its teaching on God and creation), it has for the most part not regarded itself as having much to say about the detailed workings of that natural order. The materialist's notion that religion is about providing mythological explanations of nature in the absence of real scientific understanding—the "God of the gaps" idea—is, as applied to biblical religion at any rate, itself a piece of mythology. It is instructive to look, for instance, at the Roman Catechism, or Catechism of the Council of Trent, published in 1566, exactly fifty years before Galileo's first run-in with the Roman authorities. It contains not a word about botany, zoology, geology, or astronomy. Those were simply not considered part of Christian doctrine. That was the general attitude of the Catholic Church both before and after the Galileo affair, which can now be recognized as an adventitious and unique event in the history of the Church's relationship with science. It was a bump—admittedly, a very bad bump—in what has otherwise been a smooth road.

It is notable, in this regard, that the Catholic Church never condemned, or even criticized or warned against, the theory of evolution. Its first statement on that subject did not come until 1950, when Pius XII isolated two points concerning evolution as being of doctrinal significance. Both concerned only human evolution. First, he said, the original unity of the human race has to be upheld. And second, whereas the human body might have evolved, the human spiritual soul, not being reducible to matter, cannot be held to have evolved. It was specially created by God in the first human beings as in all subsequent human beings. Here, in this one case, we do see the Church upholding a form of supernaturalism. It is the one great exception to the depersonalizing of nature by Judaism and Christianity. Man himself must not be depersonalized or reduced to the merely natural in the sense of the merely physical. I shall return to this all-important point.

I would like to interject here a comment about what I regard as backsliding from the fundamental Jewish and Christian perspective on nature by some recent theologies. On the one hand, we have some process theologians blurring the distinction between God and the universe, and treating the Godhead itself as part of the cosmic evolutionary process. On the other hand, we have some critics of Darwinism not merely arguing the inadequacy of that theory, but attacking the very idea of naturalism in biology, even when it comes to plants and animals, as inherently unbiblical or irreligious. Although these schools of thought are in some ways opposite, they are equally guilty, it seems to me, of smuggling supernaturalism back where it does not belong, and where neither science nor theology has ever needed it. Some anti-Darwinists need to be reminded that there is a natural order that comes from God, and the process theologians need to understand that God is the author of it, not a part of it.

We turn now to the second reason that the materialist indicts religion as superstitious, namely, its supposed irrationalism. The materialist sees faith and dogma as simply a matter of believing without reason. Religious mystery he imagines to be something dark and off-limits, something we are not meant to understand, and indeed beyond all understanding. All of this adds up, in his eyes, to an obscurantism that sets itself against intellectual freedom and the search for truth.

In responding to these misconceptions, I would like to begin with the notion of intellectual freedom. The great physicist Richard Feynman once observed that the freedom of the scientist is quite different from that of the artist or writer. The artist is free to imagine anything he pleases. The imagination of the scientist, however, is chained to experimental facts. The theories he dreams up must conform to what is already known from observation, and must be abandoned, no matter how rationally coherent, beautiful, or compelling they seem, if they are contradicted by new experimental facts. To put it in religious language, the scientist is answerable to a very stern and peremptory magisterium, the magisterium of Nature herself.

There is a clear analogy between the limitations on the scientist and those on the theologian. The scientist must submit his mind to the data of experiment, the theologian must submit his to the data of revelation. The word "data" means "the things that are given." Both the religious person and the scientist accept givens. The givens may perplex. They may seem difficult to bring into harmony with each other or with what is known on other grounds. They may throw all our theories into confusion. But accepting the data must come before progress in understanding. That is why the words of St. Augustine apply, in a way, to the scientist as much as to the theologian: *credo ut intelligam*, "I believe in order that I may understand."

So we see in science something akin to religious faith. The scientist has confidence in the intelligibility of the world. He has questions about nature. And he expects—no, more than expects, he is absolutely convinced—that these questions have intelligible answers. The fact that he must seek those answers proves that they are not in sight. The fact that he continues to seek them in spite of all difficulties testifies to his unconquerable conviction that those answers, although not presently in sight, do in fact exist. Truly, the scientist too walks by faith and not by sight.

The scientist is convinced that there are certain acts of insight, which he has not yet achieved, and which indeed no human being may ever achieve, that would satisfy a rational mind on the questions he has raised about nature. Faith in God is an extension of this attitude. The believer in God is convinced that reality is intelligible, not merely on this or that point, but through and through. There is some all-embracing act of insight that would satisfy all questioning and leave no further questions to be asked. Such an infinite and perfect act of insight is the state of being of God, indeed for the Christian and Jew it *is* God. In the words of the Jesuit philosopher Bernard Lonergan, God is the "unrestricted act of understanding" that grasps all of reality, all of being.

The materialist imagines that a religious mystery is something too dark to be seen. But, as G. K. Chesterton noted, it is really something too bright to be seen, like the sun. As Scripture tells us, God "dwells in unapproachable light." The mystery is not impenetrable to intellect or unintelligible *in itself*; rather, it is not fully intelligible *to us*. And reason itself tells us that there must be such mysteries. For the nature of God is infinite, and therefore not proportionate to our finite minds. The mysteries of the faith primarily concern the nature of God, or they concern man in his relationship to God and as the image of God. They concern, that is, what is infinite or touches upon the infinite. Consequently, religious mystery hardly concerns, if it concerns at all, the matters studied by the physicist, chemist, or botanist. The things they study are quite finite in their natures and therefore quite proportionate to the human intellect. That is why there is nothing in Jewish or Christian belief that implies or suggests any limit to what human beings can understand about the structure of the physical world. Although the writings of scientific materialists are filled with hostility toward religious mystery, in fact religious mystery has never acted as a brake upon scientific progress.

This brings us back to the question of supernaturalism and its proper place. Supernaturalism is out of place in physics, astronomy, chemistry, or botany. However, it is necessary in anything that touches upon the nature of man, for man is made in the image of God. I have noted that biblical religion opposed the supernaturalism of the ancient pagan. In doing so, it clearly served the cause of reason. In our time, biblical religion serves the cause of reason just as much by opposing the absolute naturalism of the modern materialist. Where the ancient pagan went wrong is in seeing the supernatural everywhere in the world around him. Where the modern materialist goes wrong is in failing to see that which goes beyond physical nature in himself. By extending naturalism even to his own mind and soul, the materialist ends up sliding into his own morass of irrationalism and superstition. How so?

In the first place, a purely materialistic conception of man cannot account for the human power of reason itself. If we are just "a pack of neurons," in the words of Sir Francis Crick, if our mental life is nothing but electrical impulses in our nervous system, then one cannot explain the realm of abstract concepts, including those of theoretical science. Nor can one explain the human mind's openness to truth, which is the foundation of all science. As Chesterton observed, the materialist cannot explain "why anything should go right, even observation and deduction. Why good logic should not be as misleading as bad logic, if they are both movements in the brain of a bewildered ape." Scientific materialism exalts human reason, but cannot account for human reason.

Nor can materialism account for many other aspects of the human mind, such as consciousness, free will, and the very existence of a unitary self. In a purely material world such things cannot exist. Matter cannot be free. Matter cannot have a self. The materialist is thus driven to deny empirical facts-not the facts in front of his eyes, but, as it were, the facts behind his eyes: facts about his own mental life. He calls them illusions, or redefines them to be what they are not. In lowering himself to the level of the animal or the machine, the materialist ultimately denies his own status as a rational being, by reducing all his mental operations to instinct and programming.

Thus, like the pagan of old, the materialist ends up subjecting man to the subhuman. The pagan supernaturalist did so by raising the merely material to the level of spirit or the divine. The materialist does so by lowering what is truly spiritual or in the divine image to the level of matter. The results are much the same. The pagan said that his actions were controlled by the orbits of the planets and stars, the materialist says they are controlled by the orbits of the electrons in his brain. The pagan bowed down to animals or the likenesses of animals in worship, the materialist avers that he himself is no more than an animal. The pagan spoke of fate, the materialist speaks of physical determinism.

Pope John Paul II has said that divine revelation reveals not only God to man but man to himself. It reveals to man that he is made in the image of God and therefore endowed with the spiritual powers of rational intellect and free will. Thus the supernaturalism of religion with regard to man is not an attack upon human reason, but ultimately the only basis upon which human reason can be adequately defended.

Up to this point I have been discussing the materialist's claim that religion and science are intrinsically opposed because religion is incompatible with scientific naturalism and rationality. I now turn to the materialist's other claim, that the actual discoveries of science since

Copernicus have rendered the religious conception of the world incredible.

This is what I call the materialist's Story of Science. It pervades the atmosphere of the scientific world and of popular writing on science. Let me now briefly outline that story. It has five major themes.

The first theme is the overturning of the religious cosmology-the Copernican theme. We now know that we do not live at the center of a cozy little cosmos, but in what Bertrand Russell called a "backwater" of a vast universe. The earth is a tiny planet, orbiting an insignificant star, near the edge of an ordinary galaxy that contains a hundred billion other stars, in a universe with more than a hundred billion other galaxies.

The second theme is the triumph of mechanism over teleology. The biblical religions did have the concept of a natural order, but they saw that order as embodying purpose. The arrangement of the world and the processes of nature they saw as being directed toward beneficent ends. That is why Christianity had little difficulty in accepting the naturalistic science of Aristotle, which was based on final causes. However, the Scientific Revolution occurred when it was realized that final causes could be dispensed with altogether in physics and that phenomena could be adequately explained in a completely mechanistic way in terms of preceding physical events. Even in biology, apparent purpose is now thought to arise from the undirected mechanism of natural selection acting on random genetic mutations. The materialist argues that the disappearance of purpose from nature undercuts the idea that nature is designed.

These first two themes blend together to give the third theme of the story, what the late Stephen Jay Gould called the "dethronement of man." With the earth but an infinitesimal speck of flotsam in the limitless ocean of space, and the human race but a chemical accident, we can no longer believe ourselves to be the uniquely important beings for whom the universe was created.

The fourth theme, which goes back to Newton, is the discovery of physical determinism. The laws of nature were discovered to form a closed and complete system of cause and effect. Every event could be understood as arising inevitably from the past state of the universe in a way that is precisely determined by the mathematical laws of physics. As Laplace said in the eighteenth century, if the state of the world were completely known at one time, its whole future development could in principle be calculated down to the minutest detail. If this is true, it spells the death of the Jewish and Christian doctrine of free will. For even if we had wills that were free, they could have no effect upon the world of matter, including our bodily organs. They could not affect, in particular, what we say or do.

This leads to the fifth and final theme of the materialist's story, the emergence of a completely mechanistic view of man himself. Already in the seventeenth century the possibility was widely discussed that animals could be understood as machines or automata. The more radical thinkers of the Enlightenment, like La Mettrie and Baron d'Holbach, extended this view to man. Now, with the processes of life understood in terms of chemistry, and the brain understood to be a complex biochemical computer, the triumph of this mechanistic view of man seems virtually complete.

The story that I have just outlined should not be lightly dismissed. There are many people, not all of them hostile to religion, who find this interpretation of scientific history not only plausible but compelling. And it must be admitted that, in part, this is because much in scientific history up through the nineteenth century lent itself to this interpretation, or seemed to. And the startling developments in physics in the twentieth century only reinforced this view of things. People saw dramatic discoveries, like Einstein's theory of relativity and quantum theory, as demonstrating once again that all traditional or familiar or intuitively obvious notions are naive and fated to be cast aside. Science as debunker, it seemed, was continuing on its relentless course.

However, this view of twentieth-century science is misleading. It is true that science debunked many ideas in the twentieth century, but what it chiefly debunked, I will now argue, was the materialist's old Story of Science. This was not fully appreciated, because people saw what they expected to see. They extrapolated from the past story line. But the discoveries of the twentieth century threw some twists into the plot. Those twists have, in my view, invalidated, or at least called into serious question, every lesson that the materialist wished us to draw from scientific history.

What are those twentieth-century plot twists? There are, it so happens, five of them, which correspond rather closely to the five themes of the materialist's story of science.

We recall that the first theme of that story was the Copernican one, the overthrow of the religious cosmology, and in particular of the supposedly religious idea that man is at the center of the universe. I say supposedly religious idea, because in historical fact the notion that the universe has a center entered Western thought not from the Bible, which knows no such idea, but from Ptolemy and Aristotle. However, there was a question about the structure of the cosmos that historically really did divide Jews and Christians from materialists and pagans. That question was not about space and whether it has a center, it was about time and whether it had a beginning.

The idea that the universe and time itself had a beginning really did enter Western thought from the Bible, and indeed from the opening words of the Bible. Virtually all the pagan philosophers of antiquity, including Aristotle, and, according to most scholars, Plato, held that time had no beginning. Modern materialists and atheists, for obvious reasons, have generally followed the ancient pagan view.

For a very long time, all the indications from science seemed to tell against the idea of a beginning. In Newtonian physics it was natural to assume that both time and space were boundless and infinite in extent. The simplest assumption was that time coordinates, like space coordinates, extended from minus infinity to plus infinity. The discovery of the law of conservation of energy gave further support to the idea of the eternity of the world, for it said that energy could be neither created nor destroyed. And chemists discovered that the quantity of matter, as measured by its mass, is also unchanged in physical processes. Thus almost every scientific indication at the beginning of the twentieth century was that space, time, matter, and energy had always existed and always would. One more nail in the coffin of religion, it would seem. But then came the first plot twist.

The first intimation that time could have had a beginning came from Einstein's General Theory of Relativity—that is, his theory of gravity. In the 1920s, the Russian mathematician Alexander Friedmann and the Belgian physicist Georges Lemaître (who was also a Catholic priest) independently proposed mathematical models of the universe, based on Einstein's theory, in which the universe is expanding from some initial explosion, which Lemaître called the "primeval atom," and which is now called the "Big Bang." Observational evidence for this cosmic expansion was announced a few years later, in 1929, by the American astronomers Edwin Hubble and Milton Humason.

The initial reaction of some scientists to the idea of a beginning was extremely negative. The eminent German physicist Walter Nernst declared, "To deny the infinite duration of time would be to betray the very foundations of science." As late as 1959, thirty years after the discovery of the expansion of the universe, a survey of leading American astronomers and physicists showed that most still believed that the universe had no beginning. Not all, but certainly some, of the resistance to the idea of a beginning can be attributed to materialist prejudice.

None of this is to say that the Big Bang proves the biblical doctrine of creation, or even that it proves conclusively that time had a beginning. It is possible that something existed before the Big Bang, even though in the simplest and currently standard model of cosmology nothing did. Nevertheless, it remains true that on the one question of cosmology where Jewish and Christian doctrine really did have something to say that conflicted with the expectations of materialists and atheists—the question of a beginning—the evidence as it now stands seems strongly to favor the religious conception.

The second theme of the materialist's story was the triumph of mechanism over teleology. Instead of seeing purpose in nature, and thus a Person behind the purpose, science came to see only the operation of impersonal laws. There was no need for a cosmic designer, for it was the laws of physics that shaped and sculpted the world in which we live. When Laplace was asked by Napoleon why God was never mentioned in his great treatise on celestial mechanics, Laplace famously answered, "I had no need of that hypothesis." This revealed a shift in perspective. Whereas once the laws of nature had been seen as pointing to a lawgiver, they were now seen by some as constituting in themselves, and by themselves, a sufficient explanation of reality. This brings us to the second plot twist in the story of science. In the twentieth century another shift in perspective took place. One might call it the aesthetic turn. This requires some explanation.

Physics begins with phenomena that can be observed with the senses, perhaps aided by simple instruments, like telescopes. It finds regularities in those phenomena and seeks mathematical rules that accurately describe them. Physicists call such rules empirical formulas or phenomenological laws. At a later stage, these rules are found to follow from some deeper and more general laws, which usually require more abstract and abstruse mathematics to express them. Underlying these, in turn, are found yet more fundamental laws. As this deepening has occurred, two things have happened. First, there has been an increasing unification of physics. Whereas, in the early days of science, nature seemed to be a potpourri of many kinds of phenomena with little apparent relation, such as heat, sound, magnetism, and gravity, it later became clear that there were deep connections. This trend toward unification greatly accelerated throughout the twentieth century, until we now have begun to discern that the laws of physics make up a single harmonious mathematical system.

Second, physicists began to look not only at the surface physical effects, but increasingly at the form of the deep laws that underlie them. They began to notice that those laws exhibit a great richness and profundity of mathematical structure, and that they are, indeed, remarkably beautiful and elegant from the mathematical point of view. As time went on, the search for new theories became guided not only by detailed fitting of experimental data, but by aesthetic criteria. A classic example of this was the discovery of the Dirac Equation in 1928. Paul Dirac was looking for an equation to describe electrons that was consistent with both relativity and quantum theory. He hit upon a piece of mathematics that struck him as "pretty." "[It] was a pretty mathematical result," he said. "I was quite excited over it. It seemed that it must be of some importance." This led him to the discovery that has been justly described as among the highest achievements of twentieth-century science.

The same quest for mathematical beauty dominates the search for fundamental theories today. One of the leading theoretical particle physicists in the world today, Edward Witten, trying to explain to a skeptical science reporter why he believed in superstring theory in spite of the dearth of experimental evidence for it, said, "I don't think I've succeeded in conveying to you its wonder, incredible consistency, remarkable elegance, and beauty."

All of this has changed the context in which we think about design in nature. When the questions physicists asked were simply about particular sensible phenomena, like stars, rainbows, or crystals, it may have seemed out of place to talk about them, however beautiful they were, as being fashioned by the hand of God. They could be accounted for satisfactorily by the laws of physics. But now, when it is the laws of physics themselves that are the object of curiosity and aesthetic appreciation, and when it has been found that they form a single magnificent edifice of great subtlety, harmony, and beauty, the question of a cosmic designer seems no longer irrelevant, but inescapable.

In 1931, Hermann Weyl, one of the great mathematicians and physicists of the twentieth century, gave a lecture at Yale University in which he said the following:

> Many people think that modern science is far removed from God. I find, on the contrary, that it is much more difficult today for the knowing person to approach God from history, from the spiritual side of the world, and from morals; for there we encounter the suffering and evil in the world, which it is difficult to bring into harmony with an all-merciful and almighty God. In this domain we have evidently not yet succeeded in raising the veil with which our human nature covers the essence of things. But in our knowledge of physical nature we have penetrated so far that we can obtain a vision of the flawless harmony which is in conformity with sublime reason.

The third theme of the materialist's story was the "dethronement of man." A classic statement of this view was given by Steven Weinberg in his book *The First Three Minutes*. He wrote:

> It is almost irresistible for humans to believe that we have some special relation to the universe, that human life is not just a farcical outcome of a chain of accidents, . . . but that we were somehow built in from the beginning. . . . It is very hard for us to realize that [the entire earth] is just a tiny part of an overwhelmingly hostile universe. . . . The more the universe seems comprehensible, the more it also seems pointless.

Certainly, given the immensity of the universe and the impact of Darwinian ideas, it is easy to understand why this sentiment is widespread. However, in the last few decades there has been a development that suggests a very different estimate of man's place in the universe. This plot twist was not a single discovery, but the noticing of many facts about the laws of nature that all seem to point in the same direction. These facts are sometimes called "anthropic coincidences."

The term "anthropic coincidence" refers to some feature of the laws of physics that seems to be just what is needed for life to be able to evolve. In other words, it is a feature whose lack or minute alteration would have rendered the universe sterile. Some of these features have been known for a long time. For example, William Paley, already in 1802, in his treatise *Natural Theology*, pointed out that if the law of gravity had not been a so-called "inverse square law" then the earth and the other planets would not be able to remain in stable orbits around the sun. Perhaps the most famous anthropic coincidence was discovered in the 1930s, when it was found that except for a certain very precise relationship satisfied by the energy levels of the Carbon-12 nucleus, most of the chemical elements in nature would have occurred in only very minute quantities, greatly dimming the prospects of life.

Interest in and attention to anthropic coincidences has greatly intensified since the work of the astrophysicist Brandon Carter in the 1970s. Many such coincidences have now been identified. The most natural interpretation of them is that we were indeed "built in from the beginning," in Steven Weinberg's phrase, and that the universe, far from being "overwhelmingly hostile" to us, as he asserted, is actually amazingly, gratuitously hospitable.

Most scientists take a very jaundiced view of the whole subject of anthropic coincidences. They have some respectable reasons, but the major reason, in my experience, is a knee-jerk reaction against anything that smells like religion or teleology. Moreover, those well-known scientists who have shown interest in anthropic coincidences generally see them as having an explanation that does not invoke purpose in nature. They appeal to what is sometimes called the Weak Anthropic Principle. This is the idea that a variety of different laws of physics apply in different regions of the universe, or even in different universes, and that so many possible laws of physics are sampled in this way that there is really no coincidence in the fact that in some places the laws are "just right" for life. This is a very speculative idea, and as an explanation of all the anthropic coincidences it faces formidable difficulties. However, it cautions us that the anthropic coincidences may not point unambiguously to cosmic purpose. Yet these coincidences do completely vitiate the claim that science has shown life and man to be mere accidents. If anything, the prima facie evidence is in favor of the biblical idea that the universe was made with life and man in mind.

The fourth theme of the materialist's story was the determinism of physical law. Everything in the history of physics up until the last century seemed to support this idea. All the laws discovered—those of mechanics, gravity, and electromagnetism—were deterministic in character. If anything seemed securely established it was physical determinism. However, in the 1920s the ground rumbled under the feet of physicists. Determinism was swept away in the quantum revolution.

According to the principles of quantum theory, even complete information about the state of a physical system at one time does not determine its future behavior, except in a probabilistic sense.

This was terribly shocking to physicists. Indeed, one of the hallmarks of an exact science is its ability to predict outcomes. So shocking was this twist in the plot that several of the makers of the quantum revolution, including de Broglie and Schrödinger, were reluctant to accept this aspect of it. Einstein was never reconciled to the loss of determinism. "God," he famously said, "does not play dice." There have been many attempts to restore determinism to physics by modifying, reformulating, or reinterpreting quantum theory in some way. So far, however, it seems unlikely that the old classical determinism will be restored.

There are many who argue, nonetheless, that the indeterminacy of quantum theory does not create an opening or a space for free will to operate. They argue that the basic building blocks of the human brain, such as neurons, are too large for quantum indeterminacy to play a significant role. At this point, who can say? So little is known about the brain. What we can say is that there was for a long time a strong argument from the fundamental character of physical law against the possibility of free will, and this argument can no longer be so simply made. To quote Hermann Weyl again, from the same 1931 lecture:

> We may say that there exists a world, causally closed and determined by precise laws, but ... the new insight which modern [quantum] physics affords ... opens several ways of reconciling personal freedom with natural law. It would be premature, however, to propose a definite and complete solution of the problem.... We must await the further development of science, perhaps for centuries, perhaps for thousands of years, before we can design a true and detailed picture of the interwoven texture of Matter, Life, and Soul. But the old classical determinism of Hobbes and Laplace need not oppress us longer.

We return, now, to the final theme of the materialist's story, the mechanistic view of man himself. It is the final theme in more ways than one. Here the scientist debunks himself. Here all the grand intellectual adventure of science ends with the statement that there is no intellectual adventure. For the mind of man has looked into itself and seen nothing there except complex chemistry, nerve impulses, and synapses firing. That, at least, is what the materialist tells us that science has seen. However, the story is really not so simple. Here again the plot has twisted. Two of the greatest discoveries of the twentieth century cast considerable doubt upon, and some would say refute, the contention that the mind of man can be explained as a mere biochemical machine.

The first of these discoveries is quantum theory. In the traditional interpretation of quantum theory-sometimes also called the "Copenhagen," "standard," or "orthodox" interpretation-one must, to avoid paradoxes or absurdities, posit the existence of so-called "observers" who lie, at least in part, outside of the description of the world provided by physics. That is, the mathematical formalism which quantum theory uses to make predictions about the physical world cannot be stretched to cover completely the person who is observing that world. What is it about the "observer" that lies beyond physical description? Careful analysis suggests that it is some aspect of his rational mind.

This has led some eminent physicists to say that quantum theory is inconsistent with a materialistic view of the human mind. Eugene Wigner, a Nobel laureate in physics, stated flatly that materialism is not "logically consistent with present quantum mechanics." Sir Rudolf Peierls, another leading twentieth-century physicist, said, on the basis of quantum theory, "The premise that you can describe in terms of physics the whole function of a human being . . . including its knowledge, and its consciousness, is untenable. There is still something missing."

Admittedly, this is a highly controversial view. That is only to be expected, especially given the materialist prejudice that affects a large part of the scientific community. Moreover, the traditional interpretation of quantum theory has aspects that many find disturbing or implausible. Some even think (wrongly, in my opinion) that the role it assigns to observers leads to subjectivism or philosophical idealism. Dissatisfaction with the traditional interpretation has led to various rival interpretations and to attempts to modify quantum theory. However, these other ideas are equally controversial. The controversy over quantum theory will not be resolved any time soon, or perhaps ever. But, even if it is not, the fact will remain that there is an argument against materialism that comes from physics itself, an argument that has been advanced and defended by some leading physicists and never refuted.

The second discovery that arguably points to something nonmaterial in man is a revolutionary theorem in mathematical logic proved in 1931 by the Austrian Kurt Gödel, one of the greatest mathematicians of modern times. Gödel's Theorem concerns the inherent limitations of what are called "formal systems." Formal systems are essentially systems of symbolic manipulation. Since computers are basically just machines for doing such symbolic manipulations, Gödel's Theorem has great relevance to what computers and computer programs can do. It was recognized fairly quickly that Gödel's Theorem might have something to say about whether the human mind is just a computer-Gödel himself was firmly convinced that it is not. Indeed, he called materialism "a prejudice of our time." However, he never developed, at least in print, the argument against materialism based on his own theorem. That was first done by the Oxford philosopher John R. Lucas. In 1961, Lucas wrote,

> Gödel's theorem seems to me to prove that Mechanism is false, that is, that minds cannot be explained as machines. So has it seemed to many other people: almost every mathematical logician I have put the matter to has confessed similar thoughts, but has felt reluctant to commit himself definitely until he could see the whole argument set out, with all objections fully stated and properly met. This I attempt to do.

Both Gödel's Theorem and Lucas' argument are extremely subtle, but we can state the gist of them as follows. Gödel's Theorem implies that a computer program can be outwitted by someone who understands how it is put together. Lucas observed that if a man were *himself* a computer program, then by knowing how his own program was put together he could outwit himself, which is a contradiction. One may explain the Lucas argument in another way. Gödel's Theorem also showed that it is beyond the power of any computer program that operates by logically consistent rules to tell that it is doing so. However, a human being, Lucas noted, *can* recognize his own consistency-at least at times-and so must be more than a mere computer.

In recent years, the eminent mathematician and mathematical physicist Sir Roger Penrose has taken up the Lucas argument, further refined it, and answered criticisms that had been leveled at it by mathematicians and philosophers. This has not quieted the criticism.

However, the Gödelian argument of Lucas and Penrose, though often attacked, has never been refuted.

Where does this all leave us? After all the twists and turns of scientific history we look around and find ourselves in very familiar surroundings. We find ourselves in a universe that seems to have had a beginning. We find it governed by laws that have a grandeur and sublimity that bespeak design. We find many indications in those laws that we were built in from the beginning. We find that physical determinism is wrong. And we find that the deepest discoveries of modern physics and mathematics give hints, if not proof, that the mind of man has something about it that lies beyond the power of either physics or mathematics to describe.

Chesterton told the story of "an English yachtsman who slightly miscalculated his course and discovered England under the impression that it was an island in the South Seas." The explorer, he said, "landed (armed to the teeth and speaking by signs) to plant the British flag on that barbaric temple which turned out to be the pavilion at Brighton." Having braced himself to discover New South Wales, he realized, "with a gush of happy tears, that it was really old South Wales."

Science has taken us on just such an adventure. Armed not with weapons but with telescopes and particle accelerators, and speaking by the signs and symbols of recondite mathematics, it has brought us to many strange shores and shown us alien and fantastic landscapes. But as we scan the horizon, near the end of the voyage, we have begun to recognize first one and then another of the old familiar landmarks and outlines of our ancestral home. The search for truth always leads us, in the end, back to God.

Source: Stephen M. Barr. 2003. "Retelling the Story of Science." *First Things* *(131) 16-25* (March). This essay was originally presented in New York City on November 15, 2002, as the sixteenth annual Erasmus Lecture of the Institute on Religion and Public Life. Reprinted with permission from *First Things*.

Stephen M. Barr is a professor of Theoretical Particle Physics at the Bartol Research Institute and Department of Physics and Astronomy of the University of Delaware. His areas of expertise include Grand Unified Theories of the fundamental forces of nature, theories of the origin of quark and lepton masses, violation of space-time symmetries, and an early universe cosmology. He is the author of over 120 physics papers, including the article on Grand Unified Theories for the *Encyclopedia of Physics*.

Chapter 3

Are the Gospels Myths?

The possibility that the Gospels are merely myths has probably oc-curred to most Christians at some point in their faith journey. The Gospels, after all, are ancient texts relating various supernatural or miraculous events. Even though we may have embraced the Gospels as true based on the testimony of the Church, we may be at a loss to find a reasoned response to those who confidently assert that the Gospels are, in fact, a myth, much like the many ancient myths that preceded it. Fortunately, there are very good reasons to believe that the Gospels are not myths, but based on demonstrable facts, such as archeological and historical evidence. Nevertheless, as Avery Dulles, cautions, our faith is not based merely on historical research.

> For Catholics and, I suspect, most other Christians, faith does not rest on historical research but on the word of God authoritatively proclaimed by Scripture and tradition. As Newman said, no doctrine of the Church can be rigorously proved by history. In some cases the historical evidence may seem to point away from the Catholic doc-trines. "In all cases," Newman concluded, "there is a margin left for faith in the word of the Church. He who believes the dogmas of the Church only because he has reasoned them out of History, is scarce-ly a Catholic."[1]

Still, Christians can turn to history to confirm their faith in Christ, whom we believe to have lived in history as true God and true man. Again, faith and reason cannot be at odds and the historical facts available to us 2,000 years later point to the truth of the Gospels.

---

[1] Avery Dulles. 1992. "Historians and the Reality of Christ." *First Things* (28) 20-25 (December).

Carl Olson, in his "**Are the Gospels Myths?**," presents a convincing case for the historicity of the Gospels.

> ➤ Although less historical evidence exists for Caesar's crossing of the Rubicon than for the events presented in the Gospels, few, if any, historians doubt the Rubicon story.

> ➤ It is vitally important that the Gospels are based on actual people and events.

> ➤ Some of today's doubts about the veracity of the Gospels were sown in the Enlightenment when supernatural or miraculous events were rejected as not based on empirical evidence.

> ➤ It is clear from their writings that the Apostles and early Christians understood the difference between myth and fact.

> ➤ The historical value of the New Testament is found in the sheer volume of ancient copies available today compared to the writings of classical authors.

> ➤ Most Biblical scholars believe the Gospels were written prior to the end of the first century. Some believe they were written within 30 to 60 years after the Crucifixion. The New Testament makes reference to many historical figures, including Caesar Augustus, Pontius Pilate, Herod, and Caiaphas. Olson argues that these names are unlikely to be used inaccurately or in a "myth."

> ➤ Modern archeological finds validate specific details found in the Gospels.

> ➤ The writings of non-Christian Romans, such as Pliny the Younger (112 A.D.) and historian Tacitus (56 to 117 A.D.), referred to the Christian worship of Christ, the founder of their religion.

> ➤ Christians should be comfortable with honest historical examination of the Gospels.

In "**Myth Become Fact**," Mark Lowery takes the conversion story of C.S. Lewis as a point of departure in considering the truths contained in all ancient myths. The Christian Faith embodies those universal truths, suggesting that the myth actually became fact in the life, death, and resurrection of Jesus Christ.

> ➤ C.S. Lewis states that all the myths of the primitive religions were expressions of a deep yearning for redemption. He further argues Christianity is a myth that is also a fact that occurred in history at a particular place and a particular time.

➢ Lewis, as a young man, regarded the Gospels as just another myth in the mold of Adonis and Osiris. But a comment by an atheist friend wondering whether it might be that the Gospel is, in fact, a myth that actually occurred in history put Lewis on the path to conversion.

➢ Christoph Cardinal Schoenborn said, "Myth in general is . . . at its best, a real though unfocused gleam of divine truth falling on human imagination."

➢ Myth and Christianity are not opposed to each other. In fact, various myths have either anticipated or echoed Christianity.

Notre Dame Law professor Charles Rice, in **"The Resurrection,"** argues as if to convince a jury that Christ actually rose from the dead. He employs logic and reason to conclude that, based on the evidence, Jesus Christ did indeed rise from the dead as reported in the Gospel.

To come to this conclusion, he poses the following questions and proposes the reasonable answers.

➢ Did Christ die?

➢ Was he buried?

➢ Was the tomb empty on Easter?

➢ Where did the body go? There are only two alternatives: Either somebody took it, or Christ rose from the dead. If we exclude all the possibilities of the body having been taken, we have to conclude that he rose.

➢ Who could have taken the body?

➢ But was not the Resurrection a figment of the disciples' imagination, and were not the appearances of Christ after his Resurrection mere hallucinations?[2]

➢ The "legal evidence" presented by Rice is corroborated by the evidence of the Shroud of Turin.

---

[2] Another possible explanation is that the Resurrection account (and other miracles) was added to the Gospels after the Apostles died, and a myth came into being that ultimately came to be regarded as truth. Peter Kreeft and Ronald Tacelli point out, however, that the Gospels were written while eyewitnesses were still alive and available to refute this account. Yet, no such refutation exists. See Peter Kreeft and Ronald K. Tacelli, 1994. *Handbook of Christian Apologetics,* 190–91. Downers Grove, Illinois: InterVarity Press.

➤ The conclusion is that any other historical event presenting a similar degree of evidence would lead to no serious doubts as to its occurrence.

Further Reading

Paul Barnett. 2004. *Is the New Testament Reliable?* Downers Grove, Illinois: InterVarsity Press.

Craig L. Blomberg. 2004. *Making Sense of the New Testament: Three Crucial Questions.* Grand Rapids, Michigan: Baker Academic.

Marie-Christine Ceruti-Cendrier. 2005. "The Gospels—Direct Testimonies or Late Writings?" *Homiletic & Pastoral Review*: 46–52 (January).

Paul Rhodes Eddy and Gregory A. Boyd. 2007. *The Jesus Legend: A Case for the Historical Reliability of the Synoptic Jesus Tradition.* Grand Rapids, Michigan: Baker Academic.

Craig A. Evans. 2006. *Fabricating Jesus: How Modern Scholars Distort the Gospels.* Downers Grove, Illinois: InterVarsity Press.

J. Ed Komoszewski, M. James Sawyer, and Daniel B. Wallace. 2006. *Reinventing Jesus: How Contemporary Skeptics Miss the Real Jesus and Mislead Popular Culture.* Grand Rapids, Michigan: Kregel Publications.

Xavier Léon-Dufour, S.J. 1968. *The Gospels and the Jesus of History.* London: Collins.

Mark P. Shea. 2003. "If Christ Has Not Been Raised: The Evidence for the Resurrection." *Crisis Magazine* (February).

Are the Gospels Myths?

By Carl E. Olson

January 11, 49 B.C. is one of the most famous dates in the history of ancient Rome, even of the ancient world. On that date Julius Caesar crossed the Rubicon River, committing himself and his followers to civil war. Few, if any, historians doubt that the event happened. On the other hand, numerous skeptics claim that the Gospels of Matthew, Mark, Luke, and John are myth and have no basis in historical fact. Yet, as historian Paul Merkley pointed out two decades ago in his article, "The Gospels as Historical Testimony," far less historical evidence exists for the crossing of the Rubicon than does for the events depicted in the Gospels:

> There are no firsthand testimonies to Caesar's having crossed the Rubicon (wherever it was). Caesar himself makes no mention in his memoirs of crossing any river. Four historians belonging to the next two or three generations do mention a Rubicon River, and claim that Caesar crossed it. They are: Velleius Paterculus (c.19 B.C.–c.A.D. 30); Plutarch (c.A.D. 46–120); Suetonius (75–160); and Appian (second century). All of these evidently depended on the one published eyewitness account, that of Asinius Pollio (76 B.C.–c. A.D. 4)—which account has disappeared without a trace. No manuscript copies for any of these secondary sources is to be found earlier than several hundred years after their composition (*The Evangelical Quarterly* 58, 319-36).

Merkley observed that those skeptics who either scoff at the historical reliability of the Gospels or reject them outright as "myth" do so without much, if any, regard for the nature of history in general and the contents of Matthew, Mark, Luke, and John in particular.

The Distinctive Sign

So, are the four Gospels "myth"? Can they be trusted as historical records? If Christianity is about "having faith," do such questions really matter? The latter question is, I hope, easy to answer: Yes, it obviously matters very much if the narratives and discourses recorded by the four evangelists are about real people and historical events. Pope Benedict XVI, in his book *Jesus of Nazareth*, offers this succinct explanation:

> For it is of the very essence of biblical faith to be about real historical events. It does not tell stories symbolizing suprahistorical truths, but is based on history, history that took place here on this earth. The *factum historum* (historical fact) is not an interchangeable symbolic cipher for biblical faith, but the foundation on which it stands: *Et incarnates est*—when we say these words, we acknowledge God's actual entry into real history. (*Jesus of Nazareth*, xv)

Christianity, more than any other religion, is rooted in history and makes strong—even shocking—claims about historical events, most notably that God became man and dwelt among us. Of course, some Christians of a less-than-orthodox persuasion are content to discard large chunks of the Gospels as unnecessary (or even "offensive") or to interpret as "mythological" or "metaphorical" nearly each and every event and belief described therein. But such is not the belief of the Catholic Church (or of the Eastern Orthodox churches and most conservative Protestants). As the *Catechism of the Catholic Church* flatly states: "Belief in the true Incarnation of the Son of God is the distinctive sign of Christian faith" (CCC 463).

It is, ultimately, this distinctive sign—the conviction that Jesus of Nazareth was and is truly God and man—that is the focal point of attacks on the historical credibility of the Gospels and the New Testament. Over the past few centuries many historians and theologians have sought to uncover the "historical Jesus" and to peel away the many layers of what they believed were legend and theological accretion. Many abandoned hope that any historical (never mind theological) fact could be extracted from the Gospels.

A Work of Fiction

There were many complex reasons for this state of affairs, one of them being the Enlightenment-era doctrine that purely scientific, objective history could not only be found, but was necessary. Empirical data became for many scholars—men such as Isaac Newton, Francis Bacon, and René Descartes—the key to all scholarship, including the study of history. It became the accepted wisdom that supernatural or miraculous elements could not be considered scientific and truly historical and that they had to be rejected. Anything outside the realm of empirical data was liable to be labeled "myth" and "legend."

Fast-forward to our day. The results of this approach are all around us, both in the scholarly and popular realm. Not long ago, a young filmmaker named Brian Flemming produced a documentary titled *The God Who Wasn't There*. Its purpose, he explained in an interview, is to demonstrate that the "biblical Jesus" is a myth. Asked to summarize the evidence for this stance, Flemming explained:

> It's more a matter of demonstrating a positive than a negative, and the positive is that early Christians appeared not to have believed in a historical Jesus. If the very first Christians appear to believe in a mythical Christ, and only later did "historical" details get added bit by bit, that is not consistent with the real man actually existing. . . . I would say that he is a myth in the same way that many other characters people believed actually existed. Like William Tell is most likely a myth, according to many folklorists and many historians. Of course, [Jesus] is a very important myth. I think that he was invented a long time ago, and those stories have been passed on as if they are true. (David Ian Miller, "Finding My Religion," www.sfgate.com)

Here "myth" is synonymous with "fiction" or even "falsehood," reflecting the Enlightenment-era bias against anything bearing even trace amounts of the supernatural. "All I'm saying," remarked Flemming, "is that [Jesus] doesn't exist, and it would be a healthy thing for Christians to look at the Bible as a work of fiction from which they can take inspiration rather than, you know, the authoritative word of God."

"Serious Unicorns"

Thus the Gospels, according to skeptics such as Flemming, are compilations of "nice stories" or "silly tales," just like stories about unicorns and the Easter Bunny. Some skeptics mock Christians for holding fearfully onto childish tales while the truly mature people (self-described by some as "brights") go about the business of making the world a better place. "Meanwhile, we should devote as much time to studying serious theology," stated well-known atheist Richard Dawkins in column in *The Independent* (Dec. 23, 1998), "as we devote to studying serious fairies and serious unicorns." Fellow God-basher Daniel Dennett, in his book *Darwin's Dangerous Idea*, wrote,

> The kindly God who lovingly fashioned each and every one of us and sprinkled the sky with shining stars for our delight—that God is, like Santa Claus, a myth of childhood, not anything [that] a sane, undeluded adult could literally believe in. That God must either be turned into a symbol for something less concrete or abandoned altogether. (18)

Smarter than Thou

Such rhetoric rests both on the assumption that the Gospels are fanciful myth and that the authors of the New Testament (and their readers) were clueless about the difference between historical events and fictional stories. There is an overbearing sense of chronological snobbery at work: We are smarter than people who lived 2,000 years ago. Yet the Second Epistle of Peter demonstrates a clear understanding of the difference between myth and verified historical events: "For we did not follow cleverly devised myths when we made known to you the power and coming of our Lord Jesus Christ, but we were eyewitnesses of his majesty" (2 Pet. 1:16). The opening verses of Luke's Gospel indicate that the author undertook the task of writing about real people and events:

> Inasmuch as many have undertaken to compile a narrative of the things which have been accomplished among us, just as they were delivered to us by those who from the beginning were eyewitnesses and ministers of the word, it seemed good to me also, having followed all things closely for some time past, to write an orderly account for you, most excellent Theophilus, that you may know the truth concerning the things of which you have been informed. (Luke 1:1-4)

And the fourth Gospel concludes with similar remarks:

> This is the disciple who is bearing witness to these things, and who has written these things; and we know that his testimony is true. But there are also many other things which Jesus did; were every one of

them to be written, I suppose that the world itself could not contain
the books that would be written. (John 21:24-25)

These quotations do not, of course, prove the historicity of the
New Testament. Rather, they suggest that the authors, far from being
knuckle-dragging simpletons, set about to write works depicting real
people and events—especially since they believed the narratives they
recounted had meaning only if they really did occur. As such, their
historical content should be judged not against tales of unicorns and
Easter bunnies, but against other first-century works of history and
historical narrative.

What Is a Gospel?

The word *gospel* comes from the Greek word *euangelion*, meaning
"good news" and refers to the message of Christian belief in the person
of Jesus Christ. There has been much scholarly debate about the genre
of "gospel" and how it might relate to other forms of writings found in
first-century Palestine and the larger ancient world. Obviously, they do
contain biographical details, and some scholars have argued in recent
years that the gospels are as biographical in nature as anything in the
ancient Greco-Roman world.

"The majority of recent specialized studies," writes Evangelical biblical scholar Craig L. Blomberg in *Making Sense of the New Testament*,
"has recognized that the closest parallels are found among the com-
paratively trustworthy histories and biographies of writers like the
Jewish historian Josephus, and the Greek historians Herodotus and
Thucydides" (28). In his commentary on the Gospel of Matthew,
Catholic theologian and biblical scholar Erasmo Leiva-Merikakis writes:

> We must conclude, then, that the genre of the Gospel is not that of
> pure "history"; but neither is it that of myth, fairy tale, or legend. In
> fact, evangelion constitutes a genre all its own, a surprising novelty
> in the literature of the ancient world. Matthew does not seek to be
> "objective" in a scientific or legal sense. He is writing as one whose
> life has been drastically changed by the encounter with Jesus of Naz-
> areth. Hence, he is proposing to his listeners an objective reality of
> history, but offered as *kerygma*, that is, as a proclamation that bears
> personal witness to the radical difference that reality has already

made in his life. (*Fire of Mercy, Heart of the Word, Vol. II: Medita-tions on the Gospel According to St. Matthew*, 44)

Many early Christian authors, such as Justin Martyr, referred to the Gospels as memoirs of the apostles. Blomberg has used the descriptive "theological biographies," which captures well the supernatural and human elements found within them.

The Historical Evidence

Those supernatural elements—especially the miracles of Jesus and his claims to divinity—are, as we've noted, why skeptics call the Gospels "myth" while remaining unruffled about anything written about Julius Caesar and the Rubicon by Velleius Paterculus, Plutarch, Suetonius, and Appian. Yes, Suetonius did write in his account (Lives of the Twelve Caesars) about "an apparition of superhuman size and beauty . . . sitting on the river bank, playing a reed pipe" who persuaded Caesar to cross the river, but it has not seemed to undermine the belief that Caesar did indeed cross the Rubicon on January 11, 49 B.C. But, for the sake of argument, let's set aside the theological claims found in the New Testament and take a brief look at the sort of data a historian might examine in gauging the reliability and accuracy of an ancient manuscript.

First, there is the sheer number of ancient copies of the New Testament. There are close to 5,700 full or partial Greek New Testament manuscripts in existence. Most of these date from between the second to 16th century, with the oldest, known as Papyrus 52 (which contains John 18), dating from around A.D. 100-150. By comparison, the average work by a classical author—such as Tacitus (c. A.D. 56-c. 120), Pliny the Younger (A.D. 61-113), Livy (59 B.C.-A.D. 17), and Thucydides (460-395 B.C.)—has about 20 extant manuscripts, the earliest copy usually several centuries newer than the original. For example, the earliest copy of works by the prominent Roman historian Suetonius (A.D. 75-130) date to A.D. 950—over 800 years after the original manuscripts had been written.

In addition to the thousands of Greek manuscripts, there are an additional 10,000 Latin manuscripts, and thousands of additional manuscripts in Syriac, Aramaic, and Coptic, for a total of about 24,000 full or partial manuscripts of the New Testament. And then there are the estimated one million quotes from the New Testament in the writings of the Church Fathers (A.D. 150–1300). Obviously, the more manuscripts that are available, the better scholars are able to assess accurately what the original manuscripts contained and to correct errors that may exist in various copies.

When Were They Written?

Closely related is the matter of dating. While debate continues as to the exact dating of the Gospels, few biblical scholars believe that any of the four works were written after the end of the first century. "Liberal New Testament scholars today," writes Blomberg, "tend to put Mark a few years one side or the other of A.D. 70, Matthew and Luke–Acts sometime in the 80s, and John in the 90s" (*Making Sense of the New Testament*, 25). Meanwhile, many conservative scholars date the synoptic Gospels (and Acts) in the 60s and John in the 90s. That means, simply, that there exist four accounts of key events in Jesus' life written within 30 to 60 years after his Crucifixion—and this within a culture that placed a strong emphasis on the role and place of an accurate oral tradition. Anyone who denies that Jesus existed or who claims that the Gospels are filled with historical errors or fabrications will, in good conscience, have to explain why they don't make the same assessment about the historical works of Pliny the Younger, Suetonius, Julius Caesar, Livy, Josephus, Tacitus, and other classical authors.

Secondly, historical details are found in the Gospels and the other books of the New Testament. These include numerous mentions of secular rulers and leaders (Caesar Augustus, Pontius Pilate, Herod, Felix, Archelaus, Agrippa, Gallio), as well as Jewish leaders (Caiaphas, Ananias)—the sort of names unlikely to be used inaccurately or even to show up in a "myth." Anglican scholar Paul Barnett, in *Is The New Testament Reliable?* , provides several pages' worth of intersections between biblical and non-biblical sources regarding historical events and persons. "Christian sources contribute, on an equal footing with non-Christian sources," he observes, "pieces of information that form part of the fabric of known history. In matters of historical detail, the Christian writers are as valuable to the historian as the non-Christian" (167).

Then there are the specifically Jewish details, including references to and descriptions of festivals, religious traditions, farming and fishing

equipment, buildings, trades, social structures, and religious hierar-
chies. As numerous books and articles have shown in recent decades,
the beliefs and ideas found in the Gospels accurately reflect a first-
century Jewish context. All of this is important in responding to the
claim that the Gospels were written by authors who used Greek and
Egyptian myths to create a supernatural man-god out of the faint
outline of a lowly Jewish carpenter.

Pay Dirt

Various modern archeological discoveries have validated specific
details found in the Gospels:

- In 1961 a mosaic from the third century was found in Caesarea
  Maritima that had the name "Nazareth" in it. This is the first
  known ancient non-biblical reference to Nazareth.
- Coins with the names of the Herod family have been discovered,
  including the names of Herod the king, Herod the tetrarch of Galilee (who killed John the Baptist), Herod Agrippa I (who killed
  James Zebedee), and Herod Agrippa II (before whom Paul testified).
- In 1990 an ossuary was found inscribed with the Aramaic words,
  "Joseph son of Caiaphas," believed to be a reference to the high
  priest Caiaphas.
- In 1968 an ossuary was discovered near Jerusalem bearing the
  bones of a man who had been executed by crucifixion in the first
  century. These are the only known remains of a man crucified in
  Roman Palestine, and verify the descriptions given in the Gospels
  of Jesus' Crucifixion.
- In June 1961 Italian archaeologists excavating an ancient Roman
  amphitheatre near Caesarea-on-the-Sea (Maritima) uncovered a
  limestone block. On its face is an inscription (part of a larger dedi-
  cation to Tiberius Caesar) that reads: "Pontius Pilate, Prefect of
  Judaea."

Numerous other finds continue to demolish the notion that the
Gospels are mythologies filled with fictional names and events.

The External Evidence

Third, there are extra-biblical, ancient references to Jesus and early Christianity. Although the number of non-Christian Roman writings from the first half of the first century is quite small (just a few volumes), there are a couple of significant references.

Writing to the Emperor Trajan around A.D. 112, Pliny the Younger reported on the trials of certain Christians arrested by the Romans. He noted that those who are "really Christians" would never curse Christ:

> They asserted, however, that the sum and substance of their fault or error had been that they were accustomed to meet on a fixed day before dawn and sing responsively a hymn to Christ as to a god, and to bind themselves by oath, not to some crime, but not to commit fraud, theft, or adultery, not falsify their trust, nor to refuse to return a trust when called upon to do so. (*Letters*, Book 10, Letter 96)

The historian Tacitus, in his *Annals*—considered by historians to be one the finest works of ancient Roman history—mentioned how the Emperor Nero, following the fire in Rome in A.D. 64, persecuted Christians in order to draw attention away from himself. The passage is noteworthy as an unfriendly source because although Tacitus thought Nero was appalling, he also despised the foreign and, to him, superstitious religion of Christianity:

> Hence to suppress the rumor, he falsely charged with the guilt, and punished Christians, who were hated for their enormities. Christus, the founder of the name, was put to death by Pontius Pilate, procurator of Judea in the reign of Tiberius: but the pernicious superstition, repressed for a time broke out again, not only through Judea, where the mischief originated, but through the city of Rome also, where all things hideous and shameful from every part of the world find their center and become popular (*Annals*, 15:44).

Robert E. Van Voorst, author of *Jesus Outside the New Testament*, offers a detailed analysis of scholarly controversies about this passage, and then states, "Of all the Roman authors, Tacitus gives us the most precise information about Christ" (45). This includes Tacitus's understanding that "Christus"—not Paul or someone else—was the founder of the Christian movement. He notes that Christ was executed under Pilate during the reign of Tiberius, and that Judea was the source of the Christian movement. All of which further confirms the historical reliability of the Gospels.

Conclusion

As Pope Benedict XVI noted in his book on Jesus, there is much that is good about historical-critical and other scientific methods of studying Scripture. But these approaches have limits. "Neither the individual books of Holy Scripture nor the Scripture as a whole are simply a piece of literature" (*Jesus of Nazareth*, xx).

The Christian apologist should not be embarrassed to admit that he has a certain bias when it comes to reading and understanding the Gospels. He should point out that everyone has biases, and that the skeptic's bias against the supernatural and the miraculous shapes how he reads and understands history, especially the historical data found in Matthew, Mark, Luke, and John. The Christian, in other words, should have no problem with an honest historical examination of the Gospels. But why do so many skeptics shy away from a candid examination of their philosophical biases? That is the question apologists should pose and demand (politely, of course) to be answered.

Source: Carl E. Olson. 2008. "Are the Gospels Myth?" *This Rock* (19): 3 (March). Reprinted with permission from Carl E. Olson.

Carl E. Olson is the editor of IgnatiusInsight.com; the coauthor, with Sandra Miesel, of *The Da Vinci Hoax* (Ignatius, 2004); and the author of *Will Catholics Be "Left Behind"?* (Ignatius, 2003). He has written for numerous Catholic periodicals. He and his wife, Heather, have two children. Their conversion story appears in *Surprised by Truth 3: 10 More Converts Explain the Biblical and Historical Reason for Becoming Catholic*, volume 3, by Patrick Madrid (Sophia Institute Press, 2002).

Myth Become Fact

By Mark Lowery

I distinctly remember a time as a young man when it occurred to me that Christianity, with its teachings about God becoming man, the Virginal Conception, and the Resurrection, might in fact be one more myth in a long line of ancient religious myths; that Jesus may have been quite an admirable and charismatic person (if a bit mixed up as such people often are) and that his followers gradually mythologized their dead hero. I asked myself, a bit proud of my intellect, whether a rational person could be expected to believe that a God came down from heaven, became incarnate, was born of a Virgin, rose from the dead and then ascended right back up into heaven again. Isn't this the very essence of myth? Who can be expected to take such mythological data as true?

To make matters worse, these thoughts occurred to me on the feast of Christmas, at Midnight Mass. I didn't quite know what to make of it, but it certainly was discomfiting. I imagined how easily the whole edifice of Catholicism would come crashing down. For if the Church had taught for centuries that these "myths" were historical facts, and if the Church were wrong, then the Church was wrong about lots of other things too, from her teachings on the afterlife to her teachings on morality, and right on down the line.

Lots and lots of people have had a similar experience. Reading and listening to thinkers such as Joseph Campbell—vis-à-vis Bill Moyers—has only reinforced for them the possibility that Christianity is just another version of the ancient Roman, Greek, Persian, Egyptian, and Babylonian myths, a set of awesome stories that tell us a lot about the human condition, but still mythical for all that. And it hasn't helped young people much to have George Lucas come on the scene with his admittedly brilliant Stars Wars series, claiming that he thinks all religions are true, and that he is providing a new myth that will be of help in a modern technological age. Lucas is a great filmmaker but a bad philosopher.

Nor has the Jesus Seminar helped much. That's the group of "scholars" that gets a lot of publicity, usually around Christmas and Easter, for their "scientific" findings about the Gospels, namely, that only a tiny portion of the material therein is historically accurate. You guessed it—the Virginal Conception, the Resurrection, and of course Jesus' divinity are all mythological add-ons to the historical Jesus. While the Jesus Seminar claims objectivity, their conclusions represent instead very particular biases of the members, biases against the very possibility that God could have become man, died for our sins, and risen from the dead.

In the midst of such challenges, I myself was very lucky, or rather, very blessed. Fortunately, and providentially, a ready answer soon appeared, an answer that literally (no pun intended) turned upside down this argument about Christianity as a myth. The argument came from C.S. Lewis, in a brilliant little essay called "Myth Become Fact." Lewis opened up an entirely different possibility for me, based on two insights:

1. All the myths of mankind's primitive religions were expressions of a deep yearning—the deepest yearning—in mankind's consciousness, namely that the mysterious transcendent God would come into intimate contact with mankind, and do so in such a way that He would repair the damages made by mankind's sinfulness, and would grant to mankind a safety that would last forever.
2. Christianity, rather than being one myth alongside many others, is thus the fulfillment of all previous mythological religions. It is a myth, like the others, but this time a myth that is also a fact.

Here it is straight from the horse's mouth:

> The heart of Christianity is a myth which is also a fact. The old myth of the Dying God, without ceasing to be myth, comes down from the heaven of legend and imagination to the earth of history. It happens— at a particular date, in a particular place, followed by definable historical consequences. We pass from a Balder or an Osiris, dying nobody knows when or where, to a historical Person crucified (it is all in order) under Pontius Pilate. By becoming fact it does not cease to be myth: that is the miracle.[1]

---

[1] C.S Lewis. 1970. *God in the Dock. Essays on Theology and Ethics*, 66-67. Grand Rapids, Michigan: Eerdmans.

As Christoph Cardinal Schoenborn (yes, the mastermind behind the new *Catechism*) has pointed out, Lewis himself as a young man had fallen into the trap of thinking Christianity just another myth. He had read J. G. Frazer's celebrated twelve-volume work on myth, The Golden Bough (1890-1915), and was intrigued by the many parallels in the history of religions to the idea of the "dying god."

In this view, the myths of Adonis and Osiris, for example, are only myths of natural growth. These figures, who died and rose again to renew the world and their followers, are symbols of the grain that dies, is buried, and rises up in a new harvest. The myths symbolically apply this natural process to human life: Man, too, must endure death in order to live again.

As a young man, Lewis concluded that the Gospel stories were simply another myth of natural growth. Jesus says the wheat must die to bear fruit; He breaks the bread (grain) and calls it His body; He dies and rises again. Thus He seems to be just another harvest-god symbolically offering his life for the world.

Yet a moment came in Lewis' life that "turned the tables" as it were on such reductionism. As he notes in his autobiography, Surprised by Joy, one evening Lewis heard "the hardest boiled of all the atheists" he'd ever known make the startling observation that the evidence for the historicity of the Gospels was quite surprisingly good. The friend concluded: "All that stuff of Frazer's about the Dying God. Rum thing. It almost looks as if it had really happened once." The atheist was thus musing on the possibility that in the Gospel we could find, yes, all the old myths, but myths that really happened in history. This comment from such an unlikely source paved the way for Lewis' conversion![2]

Lewis had always been fascinated by myths, and in fact wrote some pretty good ones himself. Schoenborn describes what it was about myth that fascinated Lewis: [T]hey awaken in the reader a longing for something that is beyond his grasp. Myths have this fascination because they effect a catharsis, that is, they move us and purify us; thus they expand our consciousness, allowing us through them to transcend ourselves. So myths are not "poets' deceptions" (as Plato said in his Republic) nor demonic delusions (as many of the Church Fathers thought), nor clerical lies (as many Enlightenment figures asserted),

---

[2] C.S. Lewis. 1955. *Surprised by Joy*, 178-89. London: Collins.

but "Myth in general is . . . at its best, a real though unfocused gleam of divine truth falling on human imagination."[3]

In sum, all of mankind's religious and philosophical yearnings partake in, have an inchoate share in, the truth of the Incarnation. The particularity of Christianity—namely, that it is the true religion—is no longer scandalous, but a beautiful mystery that extends universally, seeing reality whole. As someone once said to me, even if this viewpoint is not true, it certainly is beautiful. I think it beautiful and true.

This also accounts for all the vestiges of Christianity found in ancient philosophy. For example, the teachings of the neo-Platonists, as the young St. Augustine discovered on his path to conversion, had lots of hints of Christianity in them, especially the notion of the Logos (the Word). They had remarkable similarity to the writings of St. John, who would not have known those works. But as St. Augustine notes, they lacked the historical flavor of Christianity, particularly the fact of the Word becoming flesh.

Myth and Christianity are not, therefore, antagonistic to each other. Various myths exist either as anticipations of Christianity or as echoes of Christianity. It then makes perfect sense that Christianity took various pagan holidays and feast days and "borrowed" them, or rather purified them and infused them with deeper meaning, instead of rejecting them. Too often we try to "hide" the fact that Christmas is really a pagan holiday that Christians borrowed. This is something rather to be proud of.

Many Christians recently went to Rome for a Holy Year pilgrimage. One of the big sights is the Pantheon, one of the best-preserved buildings from Roman times. (If you don't remember, it's the ancient-looking place that has a big opening at the top of the dome.) It was built by Marcus Agrippa in 27 B.C. as a shrine dedicated to the planetary gods and as an imperial monument.

In A.D. 609 the Byzantine emperor Phocas gave the building to Pope Boniface IV, who converted it into a Christian church. A famous legend tells us that Boniface had 28 cartloads of martyrs' bones brought to the Pantheon from Rome's various cemeteries—hence the Christian name of the Church, Santa Maria ad Martyres.

---

[3] Christoph Cardinal Schoenborn. 1983. *The Myth of the Incarnation*, 17. San Francisco: Ignatius Press.

When you visit the Pantheon, the true relationship between myth and Christianity can really come alive. What is the relationship between all the gods and goddesses of antiquity, shrouded in myth, and Christianity? Christianity is myth become fact. The Pantheon-become-Church is a reminder of this fulfillment, and a reminder that all of mankind's religious and philosophical yearnings have an inchoate share in the truth of the Incarnation.

The book I've been quoting from, *The Mystery of the Incarnation* by Christoph Cardinal Schoenborn (Ignatius Press, 1983), is now out of print. I used to have my students at the University of Dallas read this little book before they went on their sojourn in Rome and Greece—after all, when students see all the pagan shrines, it can easily occur to them that maybe Christianity is just another myth like all these other ancient ones. And if they've read or seen Joseph Campbell, who has popularized the idea of myth, then they can easily have their Christianity pulled out from under them.

That disaster is made all the more easy by the fact that it is convenient to put Christianity on the back burner for a while, to keep Christianity as a nice "mythical" religion on their shelf, practiced a bit on Christmas and Easter and maybe Ash Wednesday. It is particularly convenient to take Christianity's moral code and put it on the shelf for a while. If the Church is wrong when it teaches that God became man, died for our salvation, and rose from the dead, then the Church is probably equally wrong in its moral code that instructs us about euthanasia, just wages, homosexuality, just war, abortion, slavery, sterilization, and genocide.

Then, as one runs about flouting a new "enlightened" idea that Christianity is really just a myth, one neatly rationalizes any variety of immoral acts. The enlightened person's life soon becomes sheer misery, an enslavement to sin. In a word, this "enlightened" viewpoint isn't really very enlightened.

This Christmas, think about it the other way around. Christianity, without ceasing to be mythical, is solidly rooted in fact. Your faith is rooted in real events that happened in history. Did you ever notice how the first chapter of St. John's Gospel, accused of being the epitome of myth with its claims about the Word becoming flesh, sparkles with historical detail? ("A man named John..."). Have you ever noticed how St. Luke goes out of his way to state that his account is based on real facts (see Luke 1:1-4)? And St. Paul comes right out with it: "And if Christ has not been raised, then empty is our teaching" (1 Cor. 15:14).

One need not accept the historicity of the Gospels on blind faith. It is eminently reasonable to believe that in Jesus Christ, born in Bethlehem, the deepest yearnings of mankind, expressed in so many various mythological modes, have been fulfilled.

Source: Mark Lowery. 2001. "Myth Become Fact." *Envoy* (January/February). Reprinted with permission from Mark Lowery.

Mark Lowery, Ph. D., is Professor of Theology at the University of Dallas, departmental chair, and the editor-in-chief of the *Catholic Social Science Review*. He has published articles both in theological journals such as *Communio, The Jurist, Faith and Reason*, the *Catholic Social Science Review,* and the *Irish Theological Quarterly,* and in such popular periodicals as the *This Rock, New Oxford Review, The Catholic Faith, Homiletic and Pastoral Review*, and the *Social Justice Review.* His introductory book on moral theology, *Living the Good Life,* is published by St. Anthony Messenger Press. He and his wife Madeleine have nine children and live in Irving, Texas.

The Resurrection

By Charles E. Rice

Through our faith we know with absolute certainty that Christ rose from the dead. But we can give support to that faith by analyzing the resurrection as history.

If you were to try to convince a jury that Christ really rose, you would have to answer several questions:

1. Did Christ die?
2. Was he buried?
3. Was the tomb empty on Easter?
4. Where did the body go? There are only two alternatives: Somebody took it. Or Christ rose from the dead. If we exclude all the possibilities of the body having been taken we have to conclude that he rose.
5. Who could have taken the body? The realistic possibilities are:
   A. The Jews
   B. The Romans
   C. The Disciples of Christ

   When we exclude these three possibilities and realize that there are no other realistically possible explanations, we have to conclude that Christ rose from the dead.

6. But was not the Resurrection a figment of the disciples' imagination and were not the appearances of Christ after his Resurrection mere hallucinations?

The answers to the above questions can be summarized as follows:

1. Did Christ Die?

There is no doubt that Jesus Christ was crucified. This is confirmed by non-Christian sources such as Tacitus, Pliny the Younger and Josephus. If Christ had not been crucified, the references in the Gospels and Epistles to his crucifixion would have been contradicted by his enemies. The crucifixion of Christ, in light of his miracles and his claim to be God, was a major public event of the time.

Proof that Christ died from his crucifixion is found in the nature of crucifixion itself. This was a common mode of Roman execution and the procedures governing it were well settled in Roman law and military practice. Dr. Pierre Barbet, in his book, *A Doctor at Calvary* examines the medical aspects of the agony in the garden, the scourging, the crowning of Christ with thorns, his carrying of his cross, the method of crucifixion and the methods used by the Roman soldiers to verify the deaths of those crucified. [Barbet, *A Doctor at Calvary* (Doubleday, Image Books Edition, 1963)] The soldiers were duty bound, under penalty of their own deaths, to make absolutely certain that each crucified person died. In light of Dr. Barbet's analysis and in light of everything we know about the ritual of crucifixion, it is utterly unreasonable to believe that a crucified person could survive. This certainty is confirmed in Christ's case by the fact that his was a most noteworthy execution and large crowds were watching to see if he would perform a miracle at the last moment to escape. And he was placed in the arms of his mother and buried by his mother and his friends in a cold, airless tomb. Would his mother and those others who loved him have entombed him if there had been the slightest sign that he was still alive? Finally, there were no claims made at the time by Christ's enemies that he did not die. It contradicts all the evidence to believe that Christ did not die.

2. Was He Buried?

This question can be answered briefly. The tomb was a very short distance from the place of execution. Joseph of Arimathea received permission to take the body after Christ's death had been verified, the body was entombed and the Romans set a guard over the tomb. Nobody at the time or since has seriously questioned the fact that Christ was buried in that tomb.

3. Was the Tomb Empty on Easter?

Of course it was. If the body was still there, the Jewish leaders would have produced the body to refute the preaching and claims of the Christians.

4. Where Did the Body Go?

If Christ did not rise from the dead, somebody must have taken his lifeless body from the tomb. If we exclude all realistic possibilities of someone having taken the body, we must conclude that Christ rose under his own power.

5A. Did the Jews Take the body?

Certainly not. It was completely against their interest to do so.

5B. Did the Romans Take the Body?

They had no more reason than the Jews to take the body. The claims of Christ were not only contrary to the beliefs and material interests of the Jews, they were regarded by the Romans as a threat to the Empire. Neither the Jews nor the Romans would have done anything that would support the claim that Christ had risen.

5C. Did the Apostles or other Disciples of Christ Take the Body?

To answer this we have to answer two further questions: How could they have taken it? And if they took the body, how can we explain the transformation of the Apostles and their willingness to die for their belief in the Resurrection?

How could the Apostles have taken the body? The tomb was guarded by Roman soldiers who could pay with their own lives for dereliction of duty. The only ways the Apostles could have gotten the body were by bribery or by force. With respect to bribery, where would these poor men get the money? And how much money could induce a Roman soldier to hand over the body and thereby subject himself to the risk of capital punishment? We are not certain how many there were, but all of the guards would have had to have been bribed. Nor is it possible that the Apostles could have overpowered the guards and taken the body by force. The tomb was less than a quarter of a mile from Herod's palace. Any attempt to overpower the guards would have been heard. And would you really believe that the untrained Apostles would have been able to overcome the heavily armed and trained soldiers on guard?

If the Apostles stole the body and therefore knew that the claimed Resurrection was a fraud, would they have given up their lives for that claim? We know that most of the Apostles died as martyrs and all of them were willing to suffer martyrs' deaths. We can be sure that they must have been offered large bribes to renounce and "expose" Christianity and they must have known that they faced virtually certain death if they refused to recant and if they continued to preach. Yet none of them recanted and all of them continued to preach the risen Christ even at the price of their lives. It is a psychological impossibility that they would have so acted if they had known the Resurrection was a fraud. The transformation of the Apostles into heroic champions and martyrs for the faith makes it wholly unreasonable to believe that they had taken the body of Christ. The later conduct of the Apostles and other Disciples of Christ is explainable only on the grounds that they believed that they had seen the risen Christ; that belief could not have existed if they had taken the body. They were convinced that they had seen the risen Christ. It remains to be asked whether they actually did see what they thought they saw.

6. Did the Apostles and Disciples Merely Imagine that They Had Seen Christ?

Were the appearances of Christ mere hallucinations? The fact that a witness dies for his professed belief makes it entirely credible that he believes what he says. So we are certain that the Apostles believed that they had seen the risen Christ. Next we should ask whether the experiences they believed they had were the sort on which they could have been mistaken. The answer is no. It is incredible that they could have been mistaken in thinking that Christ walked and talked with them, took food from them, ate part of it and gave the rest back to them, cooked fish for breakfast on the shore, a breakfast which the Apostles themselves consumed. And so on. It is wholly unreasonable to think that the Apostles were deceived as to what they were certain they saw.

Could Christ's appearances have been hallucinations? There are certain characteristics of hallucinatory experiences which are not found in this case. Hallucinations commonly occur to high-strung people; but there is no reason to believe that all the people who saw Christ were of this type. Hallucinations are individualistic phenomena and it is highly unlikely that two people will have identical hallucinations. But Christ is recorded as appearing to 500 people on one occasion and on other occasions to smaller groups of various sizes. Normally, hallucinations concern some expected event, but the evidence is convincing that the disciples were not expecting Christ to rise from the dead. Another factor is that the alleged hallucinations of Christ occurred at widely different times and circumstances. And Christ's conduct at the time of his appearances was tangible. For example, he asked for food, ate some and gave the rest back to the Apostles; you cannot hallucinate a bite out of a hamburger. And if the appearances were hallucinations, why did they suddenly stop after 40 days, at the time of the Ascension? And finally, if the appearances of Christ were hallucinations, how do you explain the empty tomb? If the appearances of Christ were not real, where was his body?

If Christ did not really rise from the dead, the transformation of the Apostles and the spread and endurance of the Church in spite of persecution would be a greater miracle than the Resurrection itself. A fair-minded jury examining the facts could only conclude that the Resurrection of Christ is as much a fact of history as is George Washington's crossing of the Delaware. This is confirmed, incidentally, by the evidence of the Shroud of Turin. Scientists have demonstrated, as conclusively as science can, that the Shroud can be nothing other than the burial sheet in which the body of Christ was wrapped in the tomb. [See, for example, Humber; *The Sacred Shroud* (1977); Barbet, *A Doctor at Calvary* (Doubleday, Image Edition, 1963.)]

If we were discussing any other historical event there would be no serious challenge to the reality of its occurrence. But because it concerns religion, the clear historical proof of the Resurrection is rejected by some in favor of an absolute refusal to believe that such a miracle could occur. The evidence, however, demonstrates that not only is such a miracle possible, it actually happened.

Source: Charles E. Rice. 1983. "The Resurrection." In *Truth in Christ: Notes on Teaching Some Elements of the Catholic Faith,* 55-61. Notre Dame, Indiana: Cashel Institute.This article is reprinted with permission from the Charles E. Rice.

Charles E. Rice is Professor Emeritus at the University of Notre Dame law School. His areas of specialization are constitutional law and jurisprudence. He teaches Law and Morality at Notre Dame. His continuing 13-part series, *The Good Code: The Natural Law,* is available from the External Word Television Network. Among his books are *Freedom of Association; The Supreme*

Court and Public Prayer, The Vanishing Right to Live; Authority and Rebellion; Beyond Abortion: The Theory and Practice of the Secular State; No Exception: A Pro-Life Imperative; 50 Questions on the Natural Law; and *The Winning Side: Questions on Living the Culture of Life.* His latest books are *Where Did I Come? Where Am I Going? How Do I Get There?,* (2nd ed.) co-authored with Dr. Theresa Farnan, and *What Happened to Notre Dame?,* both published by St. Augustine's Press, South Bend, Indiana (2009).

Chapter 4

Making Sense of the Bible

Sacred Scripture and Sacred Tradition form the foundation of the Christian Faith. They compose all of God's revelation to mankind. As such, they are the root of all that we believe about God, our relationship with Him, and our relationship with our fellow man. Indeed, all of the Church's doctrine flows from both sources of Divine Revelation.

So, for the serious Christian, a mature and vibrant life of faith must involve regular, prayerful, and reflective reading of the Bible. We should not only read the Bible; we should seek to understand it as the Church understands it. The Church exhorts us to see the Scriptures as the living Word of God.[1]

For many years, taking pot shots at the truth of the Bible has become popular sport among so-called scholars, as well as the media. These attacks can undermine the faith of uninformed Christians if they do not promptly seek an explanation from a reliable source. The articles in this chapter provide insights into how to read and understand the Scriptures and how to address attacks on their authenticity.

Tim Gray helps us to see the "big picture" of the Bible in "**Seeing the Big Picture in Scripture.**"
- The Bible contains a diverse collection of writings, spanning over 1,000 years, in different languages, and in different genres.
- To understand the Bible properly, one must recognize that there is a unity to the different books. It is a unity due to the unity of God's plan.
- The interpretation of Scripture requires that one to take into consideration this unity.

---

[1] *Catechism of the Catholic Church.* 1997. 2nd ed., nos. 104 and 108. Vatican City: Libreria Editrice Vaticana.

> As St. Paul points out, all of Scripture points to Christ, its unifying principle—the new Adam.
> The overall plot presented in Scripture is God's plan of salvation.
> The fall of Adam and Eve was due to a lack of trust in God. The remedy was provided by the death and Resurrection of Christ and his profound trust in God, the Father.

In a two part series entitled **"Combating Biblical Skepticism,"** Frederick Marks provides answers to four key allegations; first, the claim that the Scriptures contain contradictions; second, the claim that the Bible contains errors; third, the claim that the reliability of the traditionally accepted authors, dates, and order of the composition of the Gospels is questionable; and fourth, the notion that the evangelists may have put "words in the mouth of Jesus," words that he did not utter. Finally, Marks addresses how we should regard the work of the "scholars" who have been muddying the water on these matters.

> Allegations of contradictions in the Scriptures have existed since the early days of Christianity.
> All of the alleged contradictions have been explained satisfactorily.
> It is likely that Jesus gave the same "speech" hundreds of times, modifying it somewhat to suit the audience and the circumstances.
> The reliability of the Bible has been supported by historians and archaeologists.
> Some scholars have attempted to show that the Gospels did not appear until the second century A.D. This enables them to call into question various aspects of the Bible's reliability. However, recent scholarship has dated the writing of three of the four Gospels to the period between 40 A.D. and 70 A.D.
> As late as 155 A.D. to 160 A.D., there were still individuals alive who had studied under one of the Apostles.
> Very early, Church historians and other early writers, not far removed from the Apostles, vouched for the traditional authorship of the Gospels.
> Internal evidence exists in the Gospels themselves that points to the authorship of Matthew, Mark, Luke, and John as tradition has held from the beginning.
> It is inconceivable that the evangelists would have falsified the discourses of Jesus, given Christian standards of honesty at the

time. Also, eyewitnesses were still alive when the Gospels were written.

➤ Even the Jews could not produce evidence that the words of the Gospels were anything but true.

➤ One must ask why the early Christians would have given their lives for a lie.

➤ Many of the scholars suggesting various problems with the Scriptures carry the baggage of materialism and their own pre-conceptions.

In "**Sacred Scripture Depends on Sacred Tradition**," Stephen Filippo demonstrates that the New Testament comes from the oral tradition that preceded it. Indeed, Sacred Scripture is drawn from Sacred Tradition, both being part of Divine Revelation.

➤ The Jews had an accurate oral tradition for centuries prior to the actual writing of the Bible.

➤ The oral teaching of Jesus was passed on to the earliest Christians before the Gospels were put to writing.

➤ Our Lord commanded his followers to preach the Gospel. At that time, the Gospel was communicated orally only; nothing was written down at that time.

➤ Many converted to the Christian Faith without a written New Testament. They relied on Sacred Tradition.

➤ Christ promised to protect the Church from error.

➤ Sacred Scripture is a part of Sacred Tradition.

➤ St. John wrote at the end of his Gospel, "There are also many other things which Jesus did; were every one of them to be written, I suppose that the world itself could not contain the books that would be written" (John 21:25).

Further Reading

Kenneth Baker, S.J. 1998. *Inside the Bible*. San Francisco: Ignatius Press.

Antonio Fuentes. 1999. *A Guide to the Bible*. Dublin, Ireland: Four Courts Press.

Edward Sri. 2010. *The Bible Compass: A Catholic's Guide to Navigating the Scriptures*. West Chester, Pennsylvania: Ascension Press.

Seeing the Big Picture in Scripture

by Tim Gray

The Bible is more a library than a book. It contains a diverse collection of writings that span a wide spectrum of time (more than 1,000 years), dozens of different authors, and several languages (Hebrew, Aramaic, and Greek). The many books range in genre from historical (1 Chronicles) to legal (Deuteronomy) to cultic (Leviticus) to poetic (Psalms) to prophetic (Isaiah) to personal letters (1-2 Timothy) to apocalyptic (Revelation). No other book contains so many different stories, characters, and genres.

How, then, does one get a handle on such a complex and sophisticated library? Is there any unity to the diversity contained in the Bible? The *Catechism* answers such questions when it observes, "Different as the books which comprise it may be, Scripture is a unity by reason of the unity of God's plan, of which Christ Jesus is the center and heart, open since his Passover" (no. 112). Behind the host of people, places, things, and the tremendous span of time stands God's plan.

In other words, history viewed through Scripture is really God's story ("His story"). God is the ultimate author of creation and history, and He has so designed history that it is shaped by the Person of His Son, Jesus Christ. Just as a novelist has a plan for weaving together all the incidents and characters in a novel, so too does the divine Author have a plan for uniting all things in His providential plot, revealed in Jesus Christ. So the key to the many books is the one story. But what is this one story? What is the Father's plan for Scripture and history?

The one overarching story that the Bible reveals is the key to discerning the unity of Scripture. This story enables us to interpret Scripture in light of its whole *content and unity*. This is one of the Church's principles for interpreting Scripture, and it keeps us from losing the larger meaning of the various stories and details (cf. *Catechism*, no. 112).

By inviting us to read Scripture with its content and unity in mind, the Church is asking us to read Scripture as St. Paul and the apostles did. Once Paul became a Christian, he no longer could read the stories of the Old Testament apart from Jesus. Indeed, he believed that those who read the Old Testament without Jesus in mind had a veil cast over their eyes, "but when a man turns to the Lord the veil is removed" (2 Cor. 3:16). Thus Paul always read Scripture in light of its unifying principle, Jesus, which is exemplified in his seeing Jesus as the new Adam who overcomes the problem brought about by the first Adam (cf. Rom. 5:12-19).

Now that we have simplified the library of Scripture to the unity of a single story, how do we understand the story? The key to a story is its plot. The ancient philosopher Aristotle once observed that "the most essential thing to a story, its life and soul, is the plot." We can further narrow our focus and say that the key to a plot is its problem. At the heart of a plot is a problem that is introduced very early in a story, with the rest of the story working toward its resolution. One doesn't have to read far into Scripture to find the problem. It appears in the third chapter of Genesis: the Fall. The problem created by the Fall—and God's plan to resolve it—is what the plot of Scripture is all about. Let's examine the Fall and see how it sheds light on the rest of the story.

As everyone knows, the story of Scripture and the world began with a happy bride and groom on a honeymoon in the Garden of Eden. But paradise is quickly lost. The subtle serpent sows doubt about God in the heart of the woman through a series of carefully crafted questions. "Did God say, 'You shall not eat of any tree of the garden?'" (Gen. 3:1). The subtle suggestion here is that God is a capricious tyrant who would keep back all the good trees of the garden from the young couple. Eve responds that they are free to eat of all of the trees but one, which they are not to eat or touch lest they die (cf. Gen. 3:3). The serpent then questions the purpose behind the prohibition: "You will not die. For God knows that when you eat of it your eyes will be opened, and you will be like God, knowing good and evil" (Gen. 3:5). The serpent has sown doubt about the purpose of God's law—is it for our good or is it a limitation set up by a God jealous of His prerogatives? Is the law concerning the forbidden fruit designed to keep the man and woman under God's thumb? These questions spark doubt about God and His law that is fanned into flame when Eve observes just how good the fruit looks. Why does God keep such a good thing from us unless . . .

Adam and Eve's fall from grace is caused by a failure to trust God. As the Catechism succinctly states, "Man, tempted by the devil, let his trust in his Creator die in his heart and, abusing his freedom, disobeyed God's command. This is what man's first sin consisted of. All subsequent sin would be disobedience toward God and lack of trust in his goodness" (*Catechism,* no. 397). This failure of trust is a failure to perceive God's fatherly goodness, and instead mistake God for a tyrant who wants to subjugate them. Original sin is the mistaken conviction that God's authority is tyrannical, not fatherly.

Pope John Paul II believes that understanding how original sin is the failure to trust God as Father is the "key for interpreting reality." He says, "Original sin attempts, then, to abolish fatherhood, destroying its rays which permeate the created world, placing in doubt the truth about God who is love and leaving man only with a sense of the master-slave relationship. As a result, the Lord appears jealous of His power over the world and over man; and consequently, man feels goaded to do battle against God." Created in perfection, Adam and Eve were still created and under God, and by rebelling against Him they "grasped at equality with God." Humanity ever since then has wrestled with the question of whether God is a trustworthy Father, or a tyrant to be appeased and liberated from. Is God Abba or Allah? Father or master?

Trust in God's goodness is what faith is all about. Indeed, the Hebrew word for faith, *amin*, literally means trust. The ultimate question is not whether God exists, but rather, can He be trusted? More pointedly, can *I* trust that He seeks *my* good, with fatherly love and care? This latter question is the one both Adam and Eve and all of us must confront. This struggle for faith sets the stage for the covenant drama of God and His people throughout Scripture. From Abraham to Mary, the drama played out is the drama of faith.

The story of Adam and his exile from Eden soon becomes the story of Israel as well. Israel followed in the footsteps of Adam, and after rebelling against God also ended up in exile. Both Adam and Israel stood in need of salvation, and the darkness that reigned from Adam on is overcome only by the coming of the true light into the world, Jesus Christ (cf. Jn. 1:9-10).

The principle of *content and unity* calls us to read Scripture through the lens of Jesus Christ. We have already observed how Paul is a model for such a unified reading of Scripture in Christ. In one of the most profound and succinct summaries of Jesus' life and mission, Paul contrasts Jesus' obedience to the Father with Adam's disobedience, and exhorts Christians to have the mind of Christ "who, though he was in the form of God, did not count equality with God a thing to be grasped, but emptied himself, taking the form of a servant, being born in the likeness of men. And being found in human form he humbled himself and became obedient unto death, even death on a cross" (Phil. 2:6-8).

Adam and Eve sought equality with God by rebelliously seizing the forbidden fruit, whereas Jesus, trusting in the Father, was obedient even unto death.

The story of disobedience and sin is resolved in Jesus' story of obedience and grace. In sharp contrast to Adam and Eve, who doubted God's fatherly goodness in the Garden of Eden, Jesus, in the midst of His agony in the Garden of Gethsemane, calls out in trust to God as "Abba, Father" (cf. Lk. 22:42). In His last words from the Cross He gives himself completely to the Father, "Father, into thy hands I commit my spirit" (Lk. 23:46). The problem of sin and death—the problem of Adam, Israel, and all humanity—is solved by the death and Resurrection of the faithful Son of God, Jesus Christ (cf. *Catechism*, no. 2606). Here the story of Scripture reaches its climax and resolution.

Although we have only painted with some broad strokes the outline to this picture, the point is that when reading Scripture with the mind of the Church, our minds must grasp this larger picture. The principle of *content and unity* helps us to read the Scriptures with the unveiled eyes of faith. Reading with this principle in mind will open the Scriptures and make our reading deeply spiritual.

St. Paul knew the power of such a reading of Scripture when he wrote his Second Letter to the Corinthians. Such a reading will transform us as we dwell upon the glory of the Lord Jesus Christ throughout Scripture. This is a bold promise indeed, but one borne over the centuries in the lives of the saints.

Source: Tim Gray. 2001. "Seeing the Big Picture in Scripture." *Lay Witness* (March). Reprinted with permission of Tim Gray.

Tim Gray is President and Professor at the Augustine Institute in Denver, Colorado. Dr. Gray holds a Ph.D. in Biblical Studies from Catholic University of America, a Th.M. in Scripture from Duke University, and an M.A. in Theology from the Franciscan University of Steubenville.

Combating Biblical Skepticism: Part One

By Frederick W. Marks

The Bible is our lifeblood. Paul calls it "the sword of the spirit" (Eph. 6:17). For evangelists it is indispensable, and the Catechism of the Catholic Church cites it innumerable times. Its cadences ring out during the consecration then again at Communion. Twice during the Mass we are reminded that what we are hearing is "the word of the Lord."

In the midst of so much outward display, many contemporary Catholic scholars have subjected the Bible to a drumfire of criticism. Contradictions are alleged; errors are charged. No sooner is a reading announced from the pulpit as being "from the Gospel of Matthew" than one is likely to hear that Matthew may not have been the author. At a recent Good Friday service, the homilist speculated that Christ might not have known who he was until after the Resurrection. Imagine this Jesus of ours—who was God from the moment of conception, who spoke as God throughout his public ministry, and who allowed his followers to worship him—not knowing who he was! So pervasive is the current climate of doubt that we are fortunate if we do not hear a priest say that certain scenes in Christ's life, as recounted by the evangelists, may never have occurred.

In this discussion, I would like to address five questions:
1. What is the proper response to allegations of contradiction?
2. Or error?
3. Are traditional notions of authorship, dating, and order of composition reliable?
4. Is it likely that the Gospel writers put words in Jesus' mouth for promotional purposes or to compensate for a loss of memory?
5. How impressed should we be with what "scholars" have been saying?

Contradictions

Allegations of contradiction have been around for a long time. Tatian, a student of Justin Martyr, penned a defense of biblical inerrancy in A.D. 170. Augustine, over two centuries later, wrote hundreds of pages on the harmony of the Gospels in response to Porphyry.

But even if a charge is new, there is not a single one that cannot be dealt with handily. What we face most often is a situation in which two statements differ but are not mutually exclusive. Some have assumed, for instance, that the Sermon on the Mount (Matt. 5–7) and Luke's Sermon on the Plain (Luke 6) are the same discourse edited in different ways for different audiences, possibly too that they are edited collections of diverse sayings spanning Jesus' three-year ministry.

But why resort to speculation when Jesus must have given the same basic speech hundreds of times? Undoubtedly there was a long form and a short form as well as intermediate forms. Surely he suited his words to his audience and the circumstances. How much time did he have? Was it late in the day when he spoke? Was a thunderstorm brewing?

The same may be said of the Lord's Prayer, of which we have two different versions. Is this really a problem? Jesus must have taught many groups how to pray. Some may have been children, others adults. Whatever the case, is it fair to assume that the "official version" never varied—or even that there was an official version?

It often is assumed that biblical accounts of the length of King Saul's reign are inconsistent. Luke gives a figure of forty years (cf. Acts 13:21) in comparison with 1 Samuel 13:1, where the figure is two. But could it not be—indeed, is it not likely—that both authors are correct? Saul was not king *de jure* for more than a very short interval, though he reigned *de facto* for the duration. From a spiritual point of view, he ceased to be king the moment Samuel announced that his reign was at an end. He had been found wanting because he was a proud man unwilling to follow God's instructions. He clung to his throne long after Samuel's anointing of David. But from this point on, he was no more king in God's eyes than Adonijah was king after Nathan's anointing of Solomon.

In the rare instance of an alleged contradiction that appears hard to crack, there are affordable, up-to-date encyclopedias of Bible difficulties. Since they are compiled mainly by Protestants, they tend to reflect Protestant theology, but they are exceedingly useful. Book by book, verse by verse, they solve thousands of ostensible problems. One begins by learning why the account of Creation in Genesis 1 is compatible with that found in Genesis 2, and by the end of the volume, one has harmonized divergent accounts of the death of Judas. (See, for example, Gleason Archer, *New International Encyclopedia of Bible Difficulties* [1982]; Norman Geisler and Thomas Howe, *When Critics Ask* [1992]).

Errors

How do we deal with allegations of error apart from contradiction? Academic texts routinely impugn the integrity of the Bible. A text currently in use at Catholic schools (Discovering God's Word [1995] by Marilyn Gustin) accuses Matthew of having erred in naming Herod as king of Judea in the year of Jesus' birth. Herod, we are told, died in 4 B.C. The same book—which, by the way, bears the imprimatur of a Catholic bishop—charges Luke with a similar mistake in naming Quirinius as governor of Syria. It also faults Mark for having described Jesus as traveling north from Galilee in order to go south to Jerusalem.

Such charges are dismissed easily. Jesus was most likely born in 6 B.C., a year that featured the confluence of Mars, Jupiter, and Saturn—something that occurs only every 800 years. So it was not Matthew who erred but rather a sixth-century scholar who fixed Jesus' birth approximately six years after the actual event. Although Roman records locate Quirinius's governorship in later years, Quirinius was a leading general active in the area north of Palestine, and there was a changing of governors in 6 B.C. Quirinius may have served as acting governor between terms, even if only for a few months. As for the possibility of Jesus going north in order to go south, he might have done so in order to transact business, visit friends, or take advantage of special modes of transportation to Jerusalem. Besides, Jewish authorities were plotting to take his life, and direct routes would not have been the safest to take.

The reliability of the Bible has been vindicated again and again by historians and archaeologists. Scholars questioned the probability of a number of strange-sounding patriarchal names in the Old Testament until a Sumerian tablet was found inscribed with the very names in question. In the same way, the Jews were judged wrong for having traced the Nile and Euphrates Rivers to the same source until an Arabian river was discovered with the same name as the one in Egypt.

The sudden annihilation of 185,000 Assyrians as recounted in the Bible was likewise doubted until confirmation surfaced in the works of ancient historians. Archaeologists have confirmed Lot's testimony on the fertility of the lower Jordan Valley, long questioned, just as they have validated the biblical account of a sudden crumbling of the walls of Jericho. Noah's flood, once the butt of scholarly ridicule, finds support in the oral and pictorial record of primitive peoples. By the same token, biblical reference to the destruction of Canaanite cities, once suspect in academia, has found acceptance.

There is more. Sodom and Gomorrah were once thought to be legendary cities, but no longer. Even the possibility of fire and brimstone raining down on Sodom is reinforced by modern geological analysis as well as by Greek and Roman writings. Old Testament details relating to the Jewish exile in Egypt have come to be regarded as accurate down to the price of an ordinary slave (twenty shekels). We have confirmation, moreover, of the existence of the Queen of Sheba along with Belshazzar's Feast and the Pool of Bethesda's five porticoes, all previously doubted.

Traditional attribution of certain psalms to King David, once rejected by scholars, is back in favor. At the same time, archaeological excavation points to a close association between Hebrews and Moabites as implied by the book of Ruth. Finally, Jesus and his followers invariably accepted Old Testament accounts of miracles at face value. Take, for example, Jesus' reference to fire and brimstone destroying Sodom "on the day when Lot went out" (Luke 17:29).

Because we do not have entire original manuscript copies of any of the books of Scripture, one may encounter an occasional copyist error (e.g., 22 for 222), not to mention, here and there, a slip in translation. But the vast majority of allegations are utterly groundless, and those that have not been disproven will falter given time. Once in a great while God's word fails to jibe with secular records. But secular record-keepers have been known to make mistakes. Why should the most thoroughly tested and rigorously authenticated book in the entire ancient world be called into question unless one can prove *beyond any reasonable doubt* that it is wrong?

Traditional notions of authenticity

Can we rely on traditional notions of Gospel authorship, dating, and order of composition? If one could establish that the Gospels were not written until the second century, as many modern scholars have attempted to do, then it would be easier to question their authorship and, by implication, their reliability. Late dating also lends itself to speculation that Jesus' stunning prediction regarding the fall of Jerusalem may have been an interpolation that was inserted at a later date for dramatic effect or to blame Jewish leaders for rejecting the Messiah.

Regarding order of composition, it should be noted that Matthew is our only source for some of Jesus' most important sayings and actions, including his presentation of the "keys" to Peter (signifying Petrine leadership). If one could establish that Mark preceded Matthew, as many have tried to do, Matthew would be more vulnerable to the charge that his Gospel is not original but is merely an embroidered version of Mark and hence less useful as a buttress for Catholic teaching.

Experts in manuscript dating (papyrology), using state-of-the-art, high-power microscopes, have estimated that fragments of Matthew currently at Oxford University were in circulation before A.D. 70 and most likely before 60. (Especially good on this point is Carsten Thiele and Matthew D'Ancona, *Eyewitness to Jesus: Amazing New Manuscript Evidence about the Origin of the Gospel* [1996]). In addition, we have the findings of language specialists. Just as Professor Henry Higgins in *My Fair Lady* could place strangers within a few blocks of their birthplace in London by the idioms in their accents, so too can philologists pinpoint the date of an ancient manuscript to within a decade or two of its composition on the basis of which expressions were popular with a given generation. Some of the latest philological research on the Gospels places all four somewhere between 40 and 50. (Here I would refer readers to Jean Carmignac's pioneer volume *The Birth of the Synoptics* [1987]. Carmignac, a translator of the Dead Sea Scrolls, is one of the foremost French biblical scholars of the twentieth century.)

As important as science is the historical foundation undergirding Sacred Tradition. Among those who confirm authorship, early dating, and order of composition during early Christian times are heretics, Jewish writers, and pagan commentators, not to mention Orthodox writers living near the Holy Land—hardly a friendly constituency.

Bearing in mind that, until around 155 to 160, there were still some alive who had studied under one of the twelve apostles, the list is impressive. Polycarp (c. 69–155) studied under John, and Irenaeus (c. 125–203)—who was Polycarp's student as well as the author of several scholarly volumes—vouches for Tradition on authorship, dating, and order of composition. Bishop Papias of Hierapolis, the first prominent post-apostolic Church historian, writing around A.D. 140, affirms that the first Gospel was by Matthew, just as he speaks of another Gospel by Mark. Papias is quoted by Eusebius. Almost thirty years before Papias, Hermas, in his work *Shepherd*, identified Luke and John as the authors of the third and fourth Gospels.

Tertullian, writing from Africa about A.D. 160, makes a telling distinction between Matthew and John, whom he calls "apostles," as compared with Mark and Luke, whom he describes as "apostolic men." The *Anti-Marcion Prologues to the Gospels* (c. 150–200) gives the order of composition as Matthew, Mark, and Luke. There are additional sources for one or more of the above points, including Clement of Rome (first century); Ignatius of Antioch (early second century); the *Didache* (90–100); the fragment of Muratori (second century); Clement of Alexandria (140–215); Theophilus, bishop of Antioch (c. 150); Justin (c. 160); and Origen (185–253).

In manuscripts of a still earlier date, such as a letter of Polycarp and the seven letters of Ignatius of Antioch (martyred about 107), we find quotations from and allusions to the Gospels. The *Epistle of Barnabas* (c. 120) quotes from Matthew. Even the first heretics— Cerinthus (first century), Valentinus (d. 160), Marcion (c. 110–165), Basilides (early second century), and Tatian (late second century)—all agree that the first three Gospels were written by Matthew, Mark, and Luke at approximately the dates agreed on by orthodox Christian authors.

Internal evidence of authorship may be adduced as well. John is reputed to have been from a priestly family, and the author of the fourth Gospel displays knowledge of Jerusalem, along with its Temple and liturgy, that is unmistakably clerical. John claims to have been an eyewitness, and this too is confirmed by displays of firsthand knowledge. For example, he tells us that at Cana the water jars were filled "to the brim" (John 2:7) and that when Lazarus' sister Mary used a perfumed balm to anoint Jesus' feet, the whole room was suffused with the sweetness of its scent (12:3). Finally, John's insistence on being a witness to the Crucifixion is borne out by Matthew, Mark, and Luke, who identify one and only one apostle, John, as having stood at the foot of the cross.

Luke is said to have been a doctor, and his Gospel contains a variety of specialized medical terms that clearly identify the author as a physician. Noted Bible translator William Barclay sees medical expertise in the way Luke describes the cure of a withered hand and also in his use of a verb that suggests clinical observation and a noun that implies symptoms of insanity (cf. *The Gospel of Luke* [1975] 52, 72, 86, 219, 294). When Luke refers to a needle, he alone uses a term signifying a surgical needle as opposed to the kind used for sewing. And Luke alone includes Jesus' words "Physician, heal yourself" (Luke 4:23).

For his part, Matthew is reputed to have been a tax collector (Levi), and his Gospel is uniquely concerned with matters of coinage and money. He alone refers to the precious gifts of the Magi; he alone relates the parable of the talents (as opposed to Luke's "gold pieces") and writes of the paying of the Temple tax with a coin drawn from the mouth of a fish (cf. Matt. 17:27). Typically, instead of relating that Judas received "money" for betraying Jesus (as do Mark and Luke), Matthew specifies kind and amount: "thirty pieces of silver."

Early dating for all four Gospels is indicated in the first instance by their lack of reference to the fall of Jerusalem in A.D. 70. Matthew especially stands out in this respect because of his emphasis on the fulfillment of biblical prophecy. Secondly, Luke speaks in his *Acts of the Apostles* (c. 63) of having written an earlier treatise (cf. Acts 1:1). Thirdly, all four Gospels contain hundreds of details relating to people, places, and events not likely to have been familiar to authors of a later period.

In part two of this article we will consider whether the evangelists put words in Jesus' mouth and how impressed we should be with what biblical "scholars" have been saying.

Source: Frederick Marks. 2004. "Combating Biblical Skepticism: Part One," *This Rock* (15): 5 (May/June). Reprinted with permission from Frederick Marks.

Frederick Marks holds a Ph.D. in history from the University of Michigan and is the author of six books, including *A Brief for Belief: The Case for Catholicism* (Queenship, 1999). He writes from Forest Hills, New York.

Combating Biblical Skepticism: Part Two

By Frederick W. Marks

In the last issue, we dealt with three interrelated questions concerning Scripture: (1) What is the proper response to allegations of contradiction? (2) How does one deal with charges of error (apart from contradiction)? (3) Can one rely on traditional notions of authorship, dating, and order of composition? In this article we will address two more questions of importance: (4) Did the Gospel writers put words in Jesus' mouth? (5) How impressed should one be with the findings of scholars?

Words in Jesus' mouth?

Is it likely that the Gospel writers put things in Jesus' mouth for promotional purposes or to compensate for faulty recollection? Certainly not. Apart from the retentiveness of students' memories in those days (phenomenal by our standards); apart from the fact that Matthew and John studied for several years—spring, summer, fall, and winter—at the feet of the greatest teacher the world has ever known; apart from the fact that Jesus must have used numerous techniques to stamp his teaching indelibly upon impressionable minds, there was the working of the Holy Spirit. Our Lord promised his apostles that "The Holy Spirit . . . will teach you *everything* and remind you of *all* that I told you" (John 14:26, emphasis added). According to the *Catechism of the Catholic Church*, we may take such words at face value because "the Church holds firmly that the four Gospels, 'whose historicity she unhesitatingly affirms, faithfully hand on what Jesus, the son of God, while he lived among men, really did and *taught*'" (*CCC* 126, emphasis added). It is worth noting that Jesus wanted his words reported with precision. "My words will never pass away," he prophesied, adding that "every word that comes forth from the mouth of God" is spiritually nourishing.

As for charges that the sacred writers invented sayings or entire discourses for the sake of evangelization, no student with any respect for his mentor would ever have dreamed of doing such a thing, let alone individuals who took their cue from the God-Man. In an age when one rarely took notes owing to the scarcity of paper, the rabbis used to say that a good pupil was like a cistern that never leaked. Faking a mentor's teachings would have reflected as much on the mentor as it did on the student. It would also have been exceedingly risky, for such fraud would almost surely have come to light in an age of eyewitnesses. No one during early apostolic times ever questioned the veracity of the Gospel records of Jesus' teachings. Later on, Christian apologists from Justin Martyr to Augustine challenged Jewish leaders to deny the reliability of the Gospels, and the answer was silence (Hilarin Felder, *Christ and the Critics*, vol. 2, 294–295).

Could there have been substantial tampering with the original copies? Again, highly unlikely. A skewed manuscript would have stood out in comparison with manuscripts located elsewhere, and, once detected, it could have been corrected by members of a faith community that imposed severe penalties for falsification. John, in his *Book of Revelation*, warns against the slightest addition or subtraction from his words (22:18–19). Tampering is doubly ruled out by virtue of the uniformity that characterizes extant copies.

Luke and John, who go out of their way to claim accuracy, are also remarkably fastidious. Scholars have studied Luke's books and concluded that he is right even in minor historical details. Why, moreover, would unscrupulous "spin" artists have included so many homely details? Why would they have recorded Jesus' claims to be God, along with his insistence on the Real Presence in the Eucharist (John 6)? Such teachings served merely to make Christianity a hard sell. Why would John, who stressed Jesus' divinity, have included so much material damaging to his case? John's Gospel has been called "the gospel of truth" because of its singular emphasis on integrity. Its author might likewise be called the "apostle of truth" since his letters highlight the same theme. One finds no less than four such references in one paragraph, six more in a brief chapter (1 John 1:5–10; 1 John 2).

Christianity in general represents a greatly stepped-up insistence on truth telling. Not that the Old Testament was lax in this regard. On the contrary, Proverbs and Deuteronomy warn against altering the inspired text, and lying is condemned by Leviticus (cf. 19:11) and Proverbs (cf. 6:17). Sirach describes lying as worse than stealing (cf. 20:24)—an interesting inversion of the Commandments—while, according to the book of Wisdom, falsehood destroys the soul (cf. 1:11). But Jesus went further, telling his followers that the truth would set them free and that he was *himself* "the Truth" in comparison with the devil, whom he dubbed "the father of lies." Before his passion and death, he clashed with Pilate on the issue of absolutes and, following the Resurrection, he rebuked Peter for lying to inquirers in the court-yard of the high priest despite extenuating circumstances.

Not long after Pentecost, two of Christ's disciples felt the fire of this insistence on truth when Peter took them to task for deception, and both were struck dead. Paul exhorted his fellow Christians to feed on "the unleavened bread of sincerity" (1 Cor. 5:8). Some he chastised for duplicity, others he warned lest, like Ananias and Sapphira, they incur the wrath of the Almighty. This is why it makes little sense to compare liberties such as Plato may have taken in his literary portrait of Socrates with the writings of Christian evangelists. Unlike them, Plato did not come from a rabbinical background; he did not worship his subject or regard him as God; he was not working under any special power of the Holy Spirit; nor did he give his life for what he had written, as did many of the early Christians. Socrates, moreover, unlike Jesus, could not make a divinely backed claim that his words would "never pass away."

In the thirteenth century, Thomas Aquinas was adamant about the need for absolute integrity of discourse (*Summa Theologica*, 2:2:109), and the tradition continues. The *Catechism* condemns mere adulation (in the sense of hollow flattery) as sinful, even if the goal is only to avoid evil (cf. *CCC* 2480).

Why, in the final analysis, would the first generation of Christians have given their lives for a lie? According to Tacitus, dean of Roman historians and no friend to Christians, an "enormous multitude" of Christ's disciples were martyred under Nero (cf. *Annals* 15:44). Their deaths occurred at a time when many eyewitnesses were living who would have known if any of the standard accounts had been false.

What About the Findings of Scholars?

How impressed should one be with the findings of scholars? We have traversed some of this ground already. But there is more to be said. A good portion of conventional wisdom is based on the irrational assumption that miracles either do not or cannot happen. Rudolf Bultmann (1884–1976), professor of biblical studies at the University of

Marburg, Germany, and the father of modern "demythologization," said it was "impossible to use electric light . . . and at the same time to believe in the New Testament world of spirits and miracles" (William Most, *Catholic Apologetics Today*, 7). Bultmann came to the United States in 1958 and delivered an influential series of lectures entitled, "Jesus Christ and Mythology." From then on, it has been open season on the Bible for many Catholic intellectuals, who appear only too willing, in many cases, to second Bultmann's preposterous claim that we can know practically nothing about Jesus' life and personality.

Academia is full of individuals who suffer from mysterophobia. They would not believe in a miracle even if 75,000 people, including agnostics and atheists, witnessed it and even if it was reported in the newspapers—such as happened at Fatima in 1917. If one were to levitate twenty feet off the ground in broad daylight before their very eyes, they would not believe. Yet these are the folks who would dictate what we are to think about the Bible.

Modern scholarship piles assumption on top of assumption and treats speculation as fact. At once unscholarly and unhistorical, it is not even scientific. As Karl Keating has pointed out, the "Q" source theory that many rely upon to justify the idea that Mark preceded Matthew is overwhelmed by countervailing data, but "Q" marches merrily on.

The phrase "most scholars" should leave us cold, for scholars in overwhelming numbers have been wrong. In the fourth century, most of the Church's intelligentsia questioned the divinity of Christ. Centuries later, a preponderance of "brains" held that a Church council could override the pope. Both of these theories, Arianism and Conciliarism, were badges of academic respectability at one time, and both are heresies. Neither is the prestige of individuals any guarantee of orthodoxy. Tertullian (c. 150–230), the author of thirty-three books, was second to none during his lifetime as a Christian scholar-theologian. Yet he wound up apostatizing because he could not abide Catholic absolution of persons guilty of grave sexual sin.

Scholars are also notorious for their mutability. Until recently, many Bible exegetes placed the writing of the Gospels after the year 100, thereby excluding the possibility of direct eyewitness testimony. Now, based on advanced archeological science, most experts put the date before 90, most of them before 70. Once upon a time, Homer, King Arthur, and the city of Troy were viewed as figments of the literary imagination. No longer.

We tend, as a breed, to place too much credence in what "scholars" have to say and not enough in what Holy Mother Church has been saying for two thousand years and continues to say. Many of today's theologians have set themselves at odds not only with Sacred Tradition, the Bible, and common sense, but also with the *Catechism*, the Doctors of the Church, a long line of pontiffs, and the infallible pronouncements of Church councils.

Vatican II's teaching on Scripture, as set forth in *Dei Verbum*, is worth noting for the number of times certain phrases occur. For example: Scripture as "truth" (seven times), as "the Word of God" (nine times), as written "under the inspiration of the Holy Spirit" (seven times). We are assured that the evangelists "consigned to writing what he [God] wanted and no more"; that they did it "truthfully and without error"; that after the Ascension, they "handed on to their hearers what he had *said* and done" (italics added); that they then handed on in writing "the same message they had preached." Matthew, Mark, Luke, and John are named as authors of Gospels that "have told us the honest truth about Jesus." Finally, the Bible is described as an "unalterable" book which "stands forever." It is hard to imagine a sixteen-page document going any further by way of reassurance.

In 1995, twenty-four years after Pope Paul VI reorganized the Pontifical Biblical Commission, placing it under the aegis of the Congregation for the Doctrine of the Faith, John Paul had stern words for its members: "Your ecclesiastical task," he told them, "should be to treat the Sacred Writings inspired by God with the utmost veneration and to distinguish accurately the text of Sacred Scripture from learned conjectures, both yours and others' . . . A certain confusion can be noted inasmuch as there are some who have more faith in views which are conjecture than in words which are divine" (George Weigel, *Witness to Hope*, 919).

Veneration of the type recommended by John Paul II is perhaps best exemplified by Augustine, who handed down a famous rule of interpretation: namely, "not to depart from the literal and obvious sense except . . . where reason makes it untenable or necessity requires" (*De Gen ad litt. lib.* 8 cap. 7, 13, quoted in Leo XIII's *Encyclical Letter on The Study of Holy Scripture*). A spirit of veneration requires, in addition, that one accept biblical teaching on faith and morals as universal and timeless unless the magisterium of the Church indicates otherwise. Cultural change is no reason, in and of itself, to discount Sacred

Scripture. Jesus himself said, "Scripture cannot be broken" (John 10:35), "Heaven and earth will pass away, but my words will not pass away" (Mark 13:31), and "not an iota, not a dot, will pass from the law until all is accomplished" (Matt. 5:18). Paul added, in similar vein, "Jesus Christ is the same yesterday and today and for ever" (Hebrews 13:8) and "All scripture is inspired by God and profitable for teaching, for reproof, for correction, and for training in righteousness" (2 Tim. 3:16). We also have Psalm 119:151–52: "But thou art near, O Lord, and all thy commandments are true. Long have I known from thy testimonies that thou hast founded them for ever."

If we continue to regard Scripture as unreliable and teach others to do the same, our prospect for converting non-Christians will approach the zero mark. We will also lose more of our brethren to evangelical Protestant groups, whose respect for the Bible is a given. It is time for Catholic homilists and apologists who have allowed themselves to be infected by the virus of biblical skepticism to turn over a new leaf and to cry out for all to hear that the emperor has no clothes. He is naked, and the game is up.

Source: Frederick Marks. 2004. "Combating Biblical Skepticism: Part One." *This Rock* (15): 6 (July-August). Reprinted with permission from Frederick Marks.

Frederick Marks holds a Ph.D. in history from the University of Michigan and is the author of six books, including *A Brief for Belief: The Case for Catholicism* (Queenship, 1999). He writes from Forest Hills, New York.

Sacred Scripture Depends
on Sacred Tradition

by Stephen N. Filippo

It is historical fact that man communicated orally before he wrote things down. Whether one puts the beginning of mankind at 5000 B.C. or 5,000,000 B.C., there is no archeological evidence of any written communication earlier than 4000 B.C.

The outside date any Scripture scholars are willing to give for the beginning of the writing down of the Torah, the first five books of the Bible, is approximately 1450 B.C. Yet the Torah conveys facts relating to God's creating the universe and events that happened as far back as circa 1850 B.C., when God brought Abram "from Ur of the Chaldeans to go into the land of Canaan" (Gen. 11:31). Obviously, unless we were to dismiss the validity of the entire Bible, we must admit the Jews had an accurate oral tradition (from the Latin traditio, meaning "handed or passed down") centuries prior to its being recorded in writing.

The life of a human being works similarly. Once born, it learns to speak long before it can write. It learns what is right and wrong from what its parents say and do. Only after years of upbringing does a child learn to read and write. And so the life of a human being parallels that of Sacred Scripture: Oral tradition necessarily precedes the act of writing.

The same is true for the New Testament. Jesus spoke to his disciples long before the things he taught were written down. While tradition means a "handing down," Sacred Tradition means the handing down of divine revelation from one generation of believers to the next, as preserved under the divine guidance of the Catholic Church established by Christ.

The Second Vatican Council, in its *Dogmatic Constitution on Divine Revelation (Dei Verbum)*, defines Sacred Tradition as what "the apostles who, by their oral preaching, by example, and by observances handed on what they had received from the lips of Christ, from living with him, and from what he did, or what they learned from the prompting of the Holy Spirit" (*DV* 7). Sacred Tradition, of which Sacred Scripture is a part, is a deeply penetrating, living reality. It is transmitted to us through the practices of the Church since apostolic times. These include official professions of faith, from the Apostles' Creed (circa A.D. 120) and Nicene Creed (325) to the Credo of the People of God by Pope Paul VI (1968); the official teachings of the 21 ecumenical councils of the Church, from Nicea I (325–381) to Vatican II (1962–65); the writings of Church Fathers and doctors; papal documents; sacred Scripture; sacred liturgy; and even Christian art that portrays what we believed and how we worshiped over the centuries.

Many non-Catholics today claim to base their faith on the Bible alone, a doctrine known as sola scriptura. This was a phrase coined by the Reformation Protestants who broke away from the Church in the 1500s. In addition to rejecting papal authority in all matters, daily governance, teaching authority, et cetera, the Protestants reject Sacred Tradition.

But where did the Bible come from? It came from the Church, not vice versa. In apostolic times most people were illiterate. So what Christ said and did was passed on orally. Christ instructed the apostles were to "go into all the world and preach the gospel to the whole creation" (Mark 16:15). How could Our Lord order them to "preach the gospel" at a time when the gospels themselves did not exist in written form? Unless one is to accuse our Lord of being unreasonable, the only answer is that the gospel ("good news") already existed in oral form as a part of the Sacred Tradition of the Church, "handed on . . . from the lips of Christ" (*DV* 8).

From the year of Christ's Resurrection until roughly 100, the New Testament itself was not completely written. And in the view of many nothing was written prior to the year 50. Yet this was a period of tremendous growth for the Church. How could it have grown intact, with the same teachings being passed on orally and consistently, unless the Holy Spirit was safeguarding the transmission of Sacred Tradition? How were so many converted without the aid of Sacred Scripture, if not with the aid of Sacred Tradition?

Many Protestant churches, in order to circumvent the Sacred Tradition issue, maintain that the Catholic Church fell into error at some point before the Reformation. And they are somehow in a position to judge where God and his Church have gone wrong.

But Sacred Scripture contains many of Christ's promises to protect and safeguard his Church until the end of time. He tells the apostles, "I am with you always, to the close of the age" (Matt. 28:20). Again he promises, "I will pray to the Father, and he will give you another Counselor, to be with you forever, even the Spirit of truth" (John 14:16–17). Jesus promises, "When the Spirit of truth comes, he will guide you into all the truth; for he will not speak on his own authority, but whatever he hears he will speak, and he will declare to you the things that are to come" (John 16:13). And Paul calls the Church "the pillar and bulwark of the truth" (1 Tim. 3:15). These verses are quite clear: The one, true Church Christ founded cannot err because God, who can neither deceive nor be deceived, protects it for all time.

Another place Sacred Scripture is quite clear is the divine origin of the papacy and therefore its divine authority. Our Lord says to Peter, "You are Peter and upon this rock I will build my church, and the gates of hell shall not prevail against it. I will give you the keys of the kingdom of heaven, and whatsoever you bind on earth shall be bound in heaven, and whatsoever you loose on earth shall be loosed in heaven (Matt. 16:18–19).

A common Protestant argument against the Catholic interpretation of this passage is that our Lord's words refer only to Peter and nobody after him. But would the Creator of the universe, who took the awesome trouble to become man in order to save us from our sins, leave us without a competent guide after Peter? Did God not have enough foresight? Do not human families, governments, and even corporations institute appropriate structures to insure smooth transitions of power? Could our Lord have somehow forgotten this or not be concerned enough with the man's welfare?

If, when left on his own, man had ruined and perverted life since the fall of Adam and Eve, made things worse at the tower of Babel, killed God's prophets, and ultimately crucified God himself, do you think he would leave us without a clear succession of vicars on earth? I doubt it. In denying the clear meaning of Matthew 16:18–19, Protestants actually reject some of what they propose to accept completely and entirely: namely, Sacred Scripture.

Sacred Scripture positions itself as a part—albeit a very important part—of a much bigger picture: Sacred Tradition. At the end of his Gospel, John tells us that not everything taught by Christ was written down: "There are also many other things which Jesus did; were every one of them to be written, I suppose that the world itself could not contain the books that would be written" (John 21:25).

The things Paul taught orally he considered Sacred Tradition: "Follow the pattern of the sound words that you have heard from me, in the faith and love which are in Christ Jesus; guard the truth that has been entrusted to you by the Holy Spirit who dwells within us" (2 Tim. 1:13–14). Then he elaborates further, "And what you have heard from me before many witnesses entrust to faithful men who will be able to teach others also" (2 Tim. 2:2). Paul describes—in Sacred Scripture—exactly how Sacred Tradition is passed on: by hearing—in another word, orally.

At another time, Paul writes that Sacred Tradition may be handed on orally or by writing. "To this he called you through our Gospel, so that you may obtain the glory of our Lord Jesus Christ. So then, brethren, stand firm and hold to the traditions which you were taught by us, either by word of mouth or by letter" (2 Thess. 2:14–15).

God, out of the sheer, gratuitous goodness of his heart, has guaranteed the full integrity of divine revelation being simultaneously preserved and transmitted from one generation of believers to the next. Its fullness is embodied in his Son, our Lord Jesus Christ, and in the teachings he passed on to his apostles by his words and deeds. The apostles in turn communicated this deposit of faith to others by their words and deeds. Only some of what our Lord said and did they wrote down. "The apostles entrusted the 'sacred deposit' of the faith (the depositum fidei), contained in Sacred Scripture and Tradition, to the whole of the Church" (*Catechism of the Catholic Church*, 84). To this day, divine revelation is transmitted by two sources: Sacred Tradition and Sacred Scripture. Therefore, "Sacred Tradition and Sacred Scripture form one sacred deposit of the word of God committed to the Church" (DV 10).

These two sources of divine revelation which make up this one "sacred deposit" are safeguarded and defended by the Sacred Magisterium (the teaching authority of the Church), whose job it is to guarantee the authenticity of the message while at the same time remaining its servant:

> The task of authentically interpreting the word of God, whether written or spoken, has been entrusted exclusively to the living teaching office of the Church, whose authority is exercised in the name of Jesus Christ. This teaching office is not above the word of God, but serves it, teaching only what has been handed on, listening to it devoutly, guarding it scrupulously, and explaining it faithfully. In

accord with a divine commission and with the help of the Holy Spirit, it draws from this one deposit of faith everything which it presents for belief as divinely revealed (*DV* 10).

The Sacred Magisterium is embodied in the living teaching office and authority of the papacy. Immediately after declaring Peter the first pope, our Lord gives him the "keys to the kingdom of heaven," so that whatever the papacy declares "bind[ing] on earth shall be bound in heaven," and whatsoever the Papacy declares "loose on earth shall be loosed in heaven." It is here that Sacred Scripture confirms the reality and power of the Sacred Magisterium.

The subject of purgatory provides a clear-cut example of how Sacred Tradition works. Protestants object that purgatory is unbiblical. The Catechism explains the doctrine of purgatory in this way: "All those who die in God's grace and friendship, but still imperfectly purified, are indeed assured of their eternal salvation; but after death they undergo purification, so as to achieve the holiness necessary to enter the joy of heaven" (1030). The Catechism cites Sacred Scripture (1 Cor. 3:15, 1 Peter 1:7, Matt. 12:31, and 2 Macc. 12:46); it cites Sacred Tradition (three ecumenical councils—Lyons, Florence, and Trent); it cites a papal encyclical (Benedictus Deus by Pope Benedict XII); and it cites two Church Fathers who are also doctors of the Church (Gregory the Great and John Chrysostom). Or we can quote just the Scripture passages: "If any man's work is burned up, he will suffer loss, though he himself will be saved, but only through fire" (1 Cor. 3:15). Or, "Therefore, he made atonement for the dead, that they might be delivered from their sin" (2 Macc. 12:46).

Or, quite firmly, with full certitude because of Sacred Tradition, we can say we believe the doctrine of purgatory simply because that is what the Catholic Church teaches.

Source: Stephen N. Filippo. 2000. "Sacred Scripture Depends on Sacred Tradition." *This Rock* (11): 3 (March). Reprinted with permission from Stephen Filippo.

Stephen N. Filippo writes from Southbury, Connecticut. He earned an M.A. in Dogmatic Theology at St. Joseph's Seminary in Yonkers, New York, and an S.Y.D. in Dogmatic Theology at Holy Apostle's Seminary in Cromwell, Connecticut. He has taught theology and philosophy at the high school and university level.

Part II.

꧁꧂

The Church in History

The Catholic Church is over 2,000 years old. It has endured persecutions and chaotic times, and it has wielded great civil power. The long and influential history of the Church provides fodder for criticism for those who are so inclined. Part II provides needed perspectives on the circumstances surrounding the most frequently criticized events in the history of the Church. Much of the so-called "history" cited to condemn the Church is, in fact, myth. Church officials have clearly made mistakes over the centuries, but an accurate account of the events—combined with a proper perspective—puts the Church in a much better light than many believe. We should be grateful for the Church's pivotal role in shaping Western civilization for the better.

Chapter 5

Contributions of the Church to Western Civilization

The Catholic Church is a favorite whipping boy of intellectuals and many members of the media. This prejudice against the Church flows from ignorance and preconceived ideas about the role of the Church in history that were sown in high school and college and reinforced by popular media. The truth about the Church is frequently not sought because it is far too much fun to ridicule the institution responsible for reminding society of the moral law. Modern scholarship shows that the Church—rather than the intolerant obstacle to progress critics allege—has actually made substantial contributions to Western civilization.

> That Western civilization stands indebted to the Church for the university system, charitable work, international law, the sciences, important legal principles, and much else besides has not exactly been impressed upon them with terrific zeal. Western civilization owes far more to the Catholic Church than most people—Catholics included—often realized. The Church, in fact, built Western civilization.[1]

If we are to really understand a people of antiquity and the Catholic Church, we must view them through the eyes of that epoch. Making judgments about the morality and motives of people living hundreds of years ago through the prism of twenty-first century knowledge and experience is not only unfair; it distorts our understanding of history. This is not to say that truth is subjective, but that circumstances do matter in understanding the events of the past.

---

[1] Thomas E. Woods, Jr. 2005. *How The Catholic Church Built Western Civilization*, 1. Washington, DC: Regnery Publishing.

Historian Thomas Woods, senior fellow at the Ludwig von Mises Institute, provides an overview of the contributions of the monks to Western civilization. He documents how we benefitted from their work and ingenuity in areas ranging from agriculture to education.

> The Benedictines worked hard to convert vast areas of unproductive land into fertile farmland. They drained swamps, cleared forests, and advanced the current knowledge of animal husbandry.

> In twelfth-century France, the Cistercians used waterpower for milling tanning and other uses. They were also skilled in metallurgy. Their know-how was shared throughout Europe.

> Evidence suggests that the Cistercians of sixteenth-century England developed advanced blast furnaces for making cast iron. However, When Henry VIII closed their monasteries, he disrupted the transfer of this technology throughout Europe.

> The monks were known for their acts of charity, providing safe haven to travelers.

> Monks are well-known for preserving many literary works of classical antiquity through their work to copy and preserve manuscripts in their libraries and scriptorium.

> The monks were active in education, teaching not only future monks, but lay people as well.

> The monks' commitment to reading, writing, and education most likely saved Europe from a long period of illiteracy due to the barbarian invasions and the ensuing chaos.

> The foundation for the universities of Europe has been attributed to the work of the monks.

In **"How Christianity Led to Freedom, Capitalism, and the Success of the West,"** Rodney Stark points to Christian belief in reason and progress as the impetus of much of the success experienced in the West.

> Fifteenth-century Europeans were greatly superior technologically to Indians of South and Central America during the "Conquest" of America. They were superior, also, to the civilizations of China, India, and the Islamic nations.

> This technological superiority is attributed to the ascendancy of capitalism in Europe, which has its roots in Christianity's faith in reason.

> Although other religions focused on mystery and intuition, Christianity relied on reason and logic as guides to religious truth.

> Aided by medieval universities, founded by the Church, faith and reason permeated Western culture and fostered the study of science and the development of democratic ideas.

> Scientific progress had clear religious foundations, and those who facilitated this were Christians.

> The rise of capitalism in Europe came centuries before the Reformation, contrary to popular belief. Capitalism first appeared in Christian monasteries.

> St. Augustine (c. 354-430) taught that we can reach a better understanding of God by the use of reason.

> The notion that the Dark Ages constituted centuries of ignorance, superstition, and misery is a myth. It was during the Dark Ages that Europe achieved its technological and scientific advantage over the rest of the world.

> Great theologians such as Augustine and Aquinas taught respect for private property.

> By the seventh century, Christianity was the only world religion to articulate a specific theological opposition to slavery. By the eleventh century, slavery had been ended in Europe.

> Despite slavery's reemergence in America, it was vigorously condemned by the popes. The abolition movements that led to its final demise in America had primarily religious roots.

Further Reading

Vincent Carroll and David Shiflett. 2000. "Christianity and the Foundation of the West." In *Christianity on Trial: Arguments Against Anti-Religious Bigotry*. San Francisco, California: Encounter Books, 1-23.

Thomas E. Woods, Jr., 2005. *How The Catholic Church Built Western Civilization*. Washington, DC: Regnery Publishing, Inc.

Thomas E. Woods, Jr. 2005. "None So Blind: How Secularists Ignore the Value of Religion." *Crisis Magazine* (November).

What We Owe the Monks

by Thomas E. Woods, Jr.

When Joseph Cardinal Ratzinger took the name Benedict XVI in late April, observers immediately speculated as to what it meant. Papal names often carry great significance. The name John Paul, for example, indicated a profound sympathy with the pontificates of John XXIII and Paul VI, the popes of Vatican II. Although Benedict XVI has pointed to his desire to carry on the legacy of Pope Benedict XV (1914–22) as a primary reason behind the name, his choice of Benedict naturally calls to mind St. Benedict of Nursia (c. 480–547), by far the most important figure in the history of Western monasticism. Some have said that just as St. Benedict and his monks rescued Europe during a time of general collapse, Pope Benedict hopes to rejuvenate a Europe adrift from its moorings, overcome by relativism, and unwilling even to reproduce itself.

Although many people know that St. Benedict's monks were responsible for preserving much of the literature of the ancient world, that is where their knowledge of the subject ends. But the more familiar we are with the monastic tradition and its essential if largely unknown contributions to the West, the easier it is to understand why St. Benedict has vied with Charlemagne for the title of Father of Europe.

Agriculture. Although it is in scholarly and cultural pursuits where most educated people look to the medieval monasteries for their contribution and influence, we can hardly overlook the monks' important cultivation of what might be called the practical arts. Manual labor played a central role in the monastic life. Although the Rule of St. Benedict (c. 529) was known for its moderation and its aversion to exaggerated penances, we often find the monks freely embracing work that was difficult and unattractive, since for them such tasks were channels of grace and opportunities for mortification of the flesh. This is certainly true when it comes to the clearing and reclaiming of land. A swamp was utterly without value, and was only a source of pestilence. But the monks thrived in such locations, and embraced the challenges that came with them. Before long, they managed to dike and drain the swamp. Soon, what had once been a source of disease and filth became fertile agricultural land.

This contribution has not gone entirely unnoticed. "We owe the agricultural restoration of a great part of Europe to the monks," observes one expert. "Wherever they came," adds another, "they converted the wilderness into a cultivated country; they pursued the breeding of cattle and agriculture, labored with their own hands, drained morasses, and cleared away forests. By them Germany was rendered a fruitful country." Still another records that "every Benedictine monastery was an agricultural college for the whole region in which it was located."

Montalembert, the great nineteenth-century historian of the monks, likewise paid tribute to their great agricultural work. "It is impossible to forget," he wrote, "the use they made of so many vast districts (holding as they did one-fifth of all the land in England), uncultivated and uninhabited, covered with forests or surrounded by marshes." Although they cleared forests that stood in the way of human habitation and use, the monks were also careful to plant trees and conserve forests when possible.

Wherever they went, the monks introduced crops, or industries, or production methods with which the people had not previously been familiar. Here they would introduce the rearing of cattle and horses, there the brewing of beer or the raising of bees or fruit. In Sweden the corn trade owed its existence to the monks; in Parma it was cheese making, in Ireland salmon fisheries—and, in a great many places, the finest vineyards. They stored up the waters from springs, that they might distribute them in times of drought. In Lombardy it was the monks from whom the peasants learned irrigation. The monks have also been credited with being the first to work toward improving the breeds of cattle, rather than leaving the process to chance.

The monks also pioneered in the production of wine, which they used both for the celebration of Mass as well as for ordinary consumption, which the Rule of St. Benedict permitted. In addition, the discovery of champagne can be traced to Dom Perignon of St. Peter's Abbey, Hautvilliers-on-the-Marne. He was appointed cellarer of the abbey in 1688, and developed champagne over the course of experimenting with blending wines. The fundamental principles that he established continue to govern the manufacture of champagne even today.

Technology. The Cistercians, a reform-minded Benedictine order established at Cîteaux in 1098, are especially well known for their technological sophistication. Thanks to the great network of communication that existed between the various monasteries, technological information was able to spread rapidly. The Cistercian monastery of Clairvaux in France leaves us a twelfth-century report about its use of waterpower that reveals the surprising extent to which machinery had become central to European life. The world of classical antiquity had not adopted mechanization for industrial use on any considerable scale, but the medieval world did so on an enormous scale, a fact symbolized and reflected in the Cistercians' use of waterpower. The Cistercian monastic community generally ran its own factory. The monks used waterpower for crushing wheat, sieving flour, fulling cloth, and tanning. And as Professor Jean Gimpel points out in *The Medieval Machine*, this twelfth-century report could have been written 742 times, since that was the number of Cistercian monasteries in Europe in the twelfth century and the same level of technological achievement could have been observed in practically all of them.

The Cistercians were also known for their skill in metallurgy. Although they needed iron for their own use, Cistercian monasteries would come in time to offer their surplus for sale; in fact, from the mid-thirteenth through the seventeenth century the Cistercians were the leading iron producers of the Champagne region of France. Ever eager to increase the efficiency of their monasteries, the Cistercians used the slag from their furnaces as fertilizer, thanks to its concentration of phosphates.

No wonder the monks have been called "the skillful and unpaid technical advisers of the third world of their times—that is to say, Europe after the invasion of the barbarians." A French scholar writes:

> In effect, whether it be the mining of salt, lead, iron, alum, or gypsum, or metallurgy, quarrying marble, running cutler's shops and glassworks, or forging metal plates, also known as firebacks, there was no activity at all in which the monks did not display creativity and a fertile spirit of research. Utilizing their labor force, they instructed and trained it to perfection. Monastic know-how [would] spread throughout Europe.

The extent of monastic skills and technological cleverness is still being discovered. In the late 1990s, University of Bradford archeometallurgist Gerry McDonnell found evidence near Rievaulx Abbey in North Yorkshire, England—one of the monasteries that King Henry VIII ordered closed in the 1530s as part of his confiscation of Church properties—of a degree of technological sophistication that pointed ahead to the great machines of the eighteenth-century Industrial Revolution. In exploring the debris of Rievaulx and Laskill (an outstation about four miles from the monastery), McDonnell expected to find, based on the documentary evidence he had consulted, that the monks had built a furnace to extract iron from ore. And he did.

The typical such furnace of the sixteenth century had advanced relatively little over its ancient counterpart, and was inefficient by modern standards. The slag, or byproduct, of these relatively primitive furnaces contained a substantial concentration of iron, since they could not reach high enough temperatures to extract all of the iron from the ore. The slag that McDonnell discovered at Laskill, however, was low in iron content, similar to slag produced by a modern blast furnace.

McDonnell believes that the monks were on the verge of building dedicated furnaces for the large-scale production of cast iron—perhaps the key ingredient that ushered in the industrial age—and that the furnace at Laskill had been a prototype of such a furnace. "One of the key things is that the Cistercians had a regular meeting of abbots every year and they had the means of sharing technological advances across Europe," he said. "The break-up of the monasteries broke up this network of technology transfer." The monks "had the potential to move to blast furnaces that produced nothing but cast iron. They were poised to do it on a large scale, but by breaking up the virtual monopoly, Henry VIII effectively broke up that potential."

Charitable work. Another of the glories of the monastic tradition was the monks' attention to charitable activities, a subject worthy of lengthy treatment in itself. Here we may note simply that Benedict's Rule called for the monastery to dispense alms and hospitality to the extent that its means permitted. "All guests who come shall be received as though they were Christ," it said. Monasteries served as gratuitous inns, providing a safe and peaceful resting place for foreign travelers, pilgrims, and the poor. An old historian of the Norman Abbey of Bec wrote: "Let them ask Spaniards or Burgundians, or any foreigners whatever, how they have been received at Bec. They will answer that the door of the monastery is always open to all, and that its bread is free to the whole world."

In some cases the monks were even known to make efforts to track down poor souls who, lost or alone after dark, found themselves in need of emergency shelter. At Aubrac, for example, where in the late sixteenth century a monastic hospital had been established amid the mountains of the Rouergue, there rang a special bell every night in order to call to any wandering traveler, or to anyone overtaken by the intimidating forest darkness. The people dubbed it "the bell of the wanderers."

In a similar vein, it was not unusual for monks living near the sea to establish contrivances for warning sailors of perilous obstacles or for nearby monasteries to make provision for shipwrecked men in need of lodging. It has been said that the city of Copenhagen owes its origin to a monastery established by its founder, Bishop Absalon, which catered to the needs of the shipwrecked. In Scotland, at Arbroath, the abbots fixed a floating bell on a notoriously treacherous rock on the Forfarshire coast. Depending on the tide the rock may be scarcely visible at all, and many a sailor had been frightened at the prospect of striking it. The waves caused the bell to sound, thereby warning sailors of danger ahead. To this day the rock is known as "Bell Rock." Such examples constituted only a small part of the concern that the monasteries showed for the people who lived in their environs; the monks also contributed to the building or repair of bridges, roads, and other such features of the medieval infrastructure.

Preserving and appreciating the classical tradition. The monastic contribution with which many people are familiar involves the copying of manuscripts, both sacred and profane. This task, and those who carried it out, were accorded special honor. A Carthusian prior wrote, "Diligently labor at this work, this ought to be the special work of enclosed Carthusians. . . . This work in a certain sense is an immortal work, if one may say it, not passing away, but ever remaining; a work, so to speak, that is not a work; a work which above all others is most proper for educated religious men."

The monks appreciated the classical inheritance far more than modern students realize. Describing the holdings at his library at York, the great Alcuin (c. 735–804)—the polyglot who worked closely with Charlemagne in restoring study and scholarship in west-central Europe—mentioned works by Aristotle, Cicero, Lucan, Pliny, Statius,

Trogus Pompeius, and Virgil. In his correspondence he quotes still other classical authors, including Ovid, Horace, and Terence. Alcuin was far from alone in his familiarity with and appreciation for the ancient writers. Lupus (c. 805–862), the abbot of Ferrieres, can be found quoting Cicero, Horace, Martial, Suetonius, and Virgil. Abbo of Fleury (c. 950–1004), who served as abbot of the monastery of Fleury, demonstrates particular familiarity with Horace, Sallust, Terence, and Virgil. Desiderius, described as the greatest of the abbots of Monte Cassino after Benedict himself, and who became Pope (Blessed) Victor III in 1086, specifically oversaw the transcription of Horace and Seneca, as well as Cicero's De *Natura Deorum* and Ovid's *Fasti*. His friend Archbishop Alfano, who had also been a monk of Monte Cassino, possessed a similar fluency in the works of the ancient writers, frequently quoting from Apuleius, Aristotle, Cicero, Plato, Varro, and Virgil, and imitating Ovid and Horace in his verse. St. Anselm, while abbot of Bec, commended Virgil and other classical writers to his students, though he wished them to put aside morally objectionable passages.

The great Gerbert of Aurillac, who later became Pope Sylvester II, did not confine himself to teaching logic; he also brought his students to an appreciation of Horace, Juvenal, Lucan, Persius, Terence, Statius, and Virgil. We hear of lectures being delivered on the classical authors at places like St. Alban's and Paderborne. A school exercise composed by St. Hildebert survives to us in which he had pieced together excerpts from Cicero, Horace, Juvenal, Persius, Seneca, Terence, and others; John Henry Cardinal Newman, the nineteenth century's great convert from Anglicanism and an accomplished historian in his own right, suggests that St. Hildebert knew Horace practically by heart.

It was the monastic library and the scriptorium, the room set aside for the copying of texts, to which much of ancient Latin literature owes its transmission to us today, though at times the libraries and schools associated with the great cathedrals would play an important role as well. In the eleventh century, just as a variety of forms of monastic life were poised to eclipse the traditional Benedictine, the mother monastery of the Benedictine tradition, Monte Cassino, enjoyed a sudden revival. It has been called "the most dramatic single event in the history of Latin scholarship in the eleventh century." In addition to an outpouring of artistic and intellectual endeavor, Monte Cassino also displayed something of a classical revival, as a new interest in ancient texts emerged:

> At one swoop a number of texts were recovered which might otherwise have been lost for ever; to this one monastery in this one period we owe the preservation of the later *Annals* and *Histories* of Tacitus (Plate XIV), the *Golden Ass* of Apuleius, the *Dialogues* of Seneca, Varro's *De lingua latina*, Frontinus' *De aquis*, and thirty-odd lines of Juvenal's sixth satire that are not to be found in any other manuscript. (L.D. Reynolds and N.G. Wilson, *Scribes and Scholars: A Guide to the Transmission of Greek and Latin Literature*)

Education. Although the extent of the practice varied over the centuries, there can be no question that instruction was imparted in the monasteries, and not simply to future monks. St. John Chrysostom tells us that already in his day it was customary for people in Antioch to send their sons to be educated by the monks. St. Benedict himself personally instructed the sons of Roman nobles. St. Boniface established a school in every monastery he founded in Germany, and in England St. Augustine (of Canterbury, not St. Augustine of Hippo) and his monks set up schools wherever they went. St. Patrick is given credit for encouraging Irish scholarship, and the Irish monasteries would develop into important centers of learning, dispensing instruction to monks and laymen alike.

Most education for those who would not profess monastic vows would take place in other settings, and eventually in the cathedral schools established under Charlemagne. But even if the monasteries' contribution to education had been merely to teach their own how to read and write, that would have been no small accomplishment. When the Mycenaean Greeks suffered a catastrophe (the nature of which is still disputed by scholars) in the twelfth century B.C., the result was three centuries of illiteracy that students of classical antiquity refer to as the Greek Dark Ages. Writing simply disappeared amid the chaos and disorder. The monks' commitment to reading, writing, and education ensured that in their own dark age, when barbarian invasions and the collapse of civilized order portended complete cultural collapse, the same terrible fate that had befallen the Mycenaean Greeks in a similar situation would not be visited upon Europeans.

But they did much more than simply preserve literacy. Even an unsympathetic scholar could write of the monks, "They not only established the schools, and were the schoolmasters in them, but also laid the foundations for the universities. They were the thinkers and philosophers of the day and shaped the political and religious thought. To them, both collectively and individually, was due the continuity of thought and civilization of the ancient world with the later Middle Ages and with the modern period."

Perhaps Benedict really was the Father of Europe after all.

Source: This essay is adapted from the author's book, *How the Catholic Church Built Western Civilization* (Regnery, 2005). Reprinted with permission from Thomas E. Woods, Jr., and Regnery Publishing, Inc.

Thomas E. Woods, Jr., is a senior fellow at the Ludwig von Mises Institute. He holds a bachelor's degree in history from Harvard and his M.Phil. and Ph.D. from Columbia University. He is the author of nine books, including two *New York Times* bestsellers: *Meltdown: A Free-Market Look at Why the Stock Market Collapsed, the Economy Tanked, and Government Bailouts Will Make Things Worse* and *The Politically Incorrect Guide to American History,* and *How the Catholic Church Built Western Civilization.*

How Christianity Led to Freedom, Capitalism, and the Success of the West

By Rodney Stark

When Europeans first began to explore the globe, their greatest surprise was not the existence of the Western Hemisphere, but the extent of their own technological superiority over the rest of the world. Not only were the proud Maya, Aztec, and Inca nations helpless in the face of European intruders, so were the fabled civilizations of the East: China, India, and Islamic nations were "backward" by comparison with 15th-century Europe. How had that happened? Why was it that, although many civilizations had pursued alchemy, the study led to chemistry only in Europe? Why was it that, for centuries, Europeans were the only ones possessed of eyeglasses, chimneys, reliable clocks, heavy cavalry, or a system of music notation? How had the nations that had arisen from the rubble of Rome so greatly surpassed the rest of the world?

Several recent authors have discovered the secret to Western success in geography. But that same geography long also sustained European cultures that were well behind those of Asia. Other commentators have traced the rise of the West to steel, or to guns and sailing ships, and still others have credited a more productive agriculture. The trouble is that those answers are part of what needs to be explained: *Why did Europeans excel at metallurgy, shipbuilding, or farming?*

The most convincing answer to those questions attributes Western dominance to the rise of capitalism, which took place only in Europe. Even the most militant enemies of capitalism credit it with creating previously undreamed of productivity and progress. In *The Communist Manifesto*, Karl Marx and Friedrich Engels proposed that before the rise of capitalism, humans engaged "in the most slothful indolence"; the capitalist system was "the first to show what man's activity can bring about." Capitalism achieved that miracle through regular reinvestment to increase productivity, either to create greater capacity or improve technology, and by motivating both management and labor through ever-rising payoffs.

Supposing that capitalism did produce Europe's own "great leap forward," it remains to be explained why capitalism developed only in Europe. Some writers have found the roots of capitalism in the Protestant Reformation; others have traced it back to various political circumstances. But, if one digs deeper, it becomes clear that the truly fundamental basis not only for capitalism, but for the rise of the West, was an extraordinary faith in *reason*.

A series of developments, in which reason won the day, gave unique shape to Western culture and institutions. And the most important of those victories occurred within Christianity. While the other world religions emphasized mystery and intuition, Christianity alone embraced reason and logic as the primary guides to religious truth. Christian faith in reason was influenced by Greek philosophy. But the more important fact is that Greek philosophy had little impact on Greek religions. Those remained typical mystery cults, in which ambiguity and logical contradictions were taken as hallmarks of sacred origins. Similar assumptions concerning the fundamental inexplicability of the gods and the intellectual superiority of introspection dominated all of the other major world religions.

But, from early days, the church fathers taught that reason was the supreme gift from God and the means to progressively increase understanding of Scripture and revelation. Consequently Christianity was oriented to the future, while the other major religions asserted the superiority of the past. At least in principle, if not always in fact, Christian doctrines could always be modified in the name of progress, as demonstrated by reason. Encouraged by the scholastics and embodied in the great medieval universities founded by the church, faith in the power of reason infused Western culture, stimulating the pursuit of science and the evolution of democratic theory and practice. The rise of capitalism also was a victory for church-inspired reason, since capitalism is, in essence, the systematic and sustained application of reason to commerce—something that first took place within the great monastic estates.

During the past century Western intellectuals have been more than willing to trace European imperialism to Christian origins, but they have been entirely unwilling to recognize that Christianity made any contribution (other than intolerance) to the Western capacity to dominate other societies. Rather, the West is said to have surged ahead precisely as it overcame religious barriers to progress, especially those impeding science. Nonsense. The success of the West, including the rise of science, rested entirely on religious foundations, and the people who brought it about were devout Christians. Unfortunately, even many of those historians willing to grant Christianity a role in shaping Western progress have tended to limit themselves to tracing beneficial religious effects of the Protestant Reformation. It is as if the previous 1,500 years of Christianity either were of little matter, or were harmful.

Such academic anti-Roman Catholicism inspired the most famous book ever written on the origins of capitalism. At the start of the 20th century, the German sociologist Max Weber published what soon became an immensely influential study: *The Protestant Ethic and the Spirit of Capitalism.* In it Weber proposed that capitalism originated only in Europe because, of all the world's religions, only Protestantism provided a moral vision that led people to restrain their material consumption while vigorously seeking wealth. Weber argued that, before the Reformation, restraint on consumption was invariably linked to asceticism and, hence, to condemnations of commerce. Conversely, the pursuit of wealth was linked to profligate consumption. Either cultural pattern was inimical to capitalism. According to Weber, the Protestant ethic shattered those traditional linkages, creating a culture of frugal entrepreneurs content to systematically reinvest profits in order to pursue ever greater wealth, and therein lies the key to capitalism and the ascendancy of the West.

Perhaps because it was such an elegant thesis, it was widely embraced, despite the fact that it was so obviously wrong. Even today *The Protestant Ethic* enjoys an almost sacred status among sociologists, although economic historians quickly dismissed Weber's surprisingly undocumented monograph on the irrefutable grounds that the rise of capitalism in Europe preceded the Reformation by centuries. Only a decade after Weber published, the celebrated Belgian scholar Henri Pirenne noted a large literature that "established the fact that all of the essential features of capitalism—individual enterprise, advances in credit, commercial profits, speculation, etc.—are to be found from the 12th century on, in the city republics of Italy—Venice, Genoa, or Florence." A generation later, the equally celebrated French historian Fernand Braudel complained, "All historians have opposed this tenuous theory, although they have not managed to be rid of it once and for all. Yet it is clearly false. The northern countries took over the place that earlier had so long and brilliantly been occupied by the old capitalist centers of the Mediterranean. They invented nothing, either in technology or business management." Braudel might have added that, during their critical period of economic development, those northern centers of capitalism were Catholic, not Protestant—the Reformation still lay well into the future. Further, as the Canadian historian John Gilchrist, an authority on the economic activity of the medieval church, pointed out, the first examples of capitalism appeared in the great Christian monasteries.

Though Weber was wrong, however, he was correct to suppose that religious ideas played a vital role in the rise of capitalism in Europe. The material conditions needed for capitalism existed in many civilizations in various eras, including China, the Islamic world, India, Byzantium, and probably ancient Rome and Greece as well. But none of those societies broke through and developed capitalism, as none evolved ethical visions compatible with that dynamic economic system. Instead, leading religions outside the West called for asceticism and denounced profits, while wealth was exacted from peasants and merchants by rapacious elites dedicated to display and consumption. Why did things turn out differently in Europe? Because of the Christian commitment to rational theology, something that may have played a major role in causing the Reformation, but that surely predated Protestantism by far more than a millennium.

Even so, capitalism developed in only some locales. Why not in all? Because in some European societies, as in most of the rest of the world, it was prevented from happening by greedy despots. Freedom also was essential for the development of capitalism. That raises another matter: Why has freedom so seldom existed in most of the world, and how was it nurtured in some medieval European states? That, too, was a victory of reason. Before any medieval European state actually attempted rule by an elected council, Christian theologians had long been theorizing about the nature of equality and individual rights—indeed, the later work of such secular 18th-century political theorists as John Locke explicitly rested on egalitarian axioms derived by church scholars.

All of this stemmed from the fact that from earliest days, the major theologians taught that faith in reason was intrinsic to faith in God. As Quintus Tertullian instructed in the second century, "Reason is a thing of God, inasmuch as there is nothing which God the Maker of all has not provided, disposed, ordained by reason—nothing which He has not willed should be handled and understood by reason." Consequently it was assumed that reason held the key to progress in understanding scripture, and that knowledge of God and the secrets of his creation would increase over time. St. Augustine (c. 354-430) flatly asserted that through the application of reason we will gain an increasingly more accurate understanding of God, remarking that although there are "certain matters pertaining to the doctrine of salvation that we cannot yet grasp . . . one day we shall be able to do so."

Nor was the Christian belief in progress limited to theology. Augustine went on at length about the "wonderful—one might say stupefying—advances human industry has made." All were attributed to the "unspeakable boon" that God has conferred upon his creation, a "rational nature." Those views were repeated again and again through the centuries. Especially typical were these words preached by Fra Giordano, in Florence in 1306: "Not all the arts have been found; we shall never see an end of finding them."

Christian faith in reason and in progress was the foundation on which Western success was achieved. As the distinguished philosopher Alfred North Whitehead put it during one of his Lowell Lectures at Harvard in 1925, science arose only in Europe because only there did people think that science could be done and should be done, a faith "derivative from medieval theology."

Moreover the medieval Christian faith in reason and progress was constantly reinforced by actual progress, by technical and organizational innovations, many of them fostered by Christianity. For the past several centuries, far too many of us have been misled by the incredible fiction that, from the fall of Rome until about the 15th century, Europe was submerged in the Dark Ages—centuries of ignorance, superstition, and misery—from which it was suddenly, almost miraculously, rescued; first by the Renaissance and then by the Enlightenment. But, as even dictionaries and encyclopedias recently have begun to acknowledge, it was all a lie!

It was during the so-called Dark Ages that European technology and science overtook and surpassed the rest of the world. Some of that involved original inventions and discoveries; some of it came from Asia. But what was so remarkable was the way that the full capacities of new technologies were recognized and widely adopted. By the 10th century Europe already was far ahead in terms of farming equipment and techniques, had unmatched capacities in the use of water and wind power, and possessed superior military equipment and tactics. Not to be overlooked in all that medieval progress was the invention of a whole new way to organize and operate commerce and industry: capitalism.

Capitalism was developed by the great monastic estates. Throughout the medieval era, the church was by far the largest landowner in Europe, and its liquid assets and annual income probably exceeded that of all of Europe's nobility added together. Much of that wealth poured into the coffers of the religious orders, not only because they were the largest landowners, but also in payment for liturgical services—Henry VII of England paid a huge sum to have 10,000 masses said for his soul. As rapid innovation in agricultural technology began to yield large surpluses to the religious orders, the church not only began to reinvest profits to increase production, but diversified. Having substantial amounts of cash on hand, the religious orders began to lend money at interest. They soon evolved the mortgage (literally, "dead pledge") to lend money with land for security, collecting all income from the land during the term of the loan, none of which was deducted from the amount owed. That practice often added to the monastery's lands because the monks were not hesitant to foreclose. In addition, many monasteries began to rely on a hired labor force and to display an uncanny ability to adopt the latest technological advances. Capitalism had arrived.

Still, like all of the world's other major religions, for centuries Christianity took a dim view of commerce. As the many great Christian monastic orders maximized profits and lent money at whatever rate of interest the market would bear, they were increasingly subject to condemnations from more traditional members of the clergy who accused them of avarice.

Given the fundamental commitment of Christian theologians to reason and progress, what they did was rethink the traditional teachings. What is a just price for one's goods, they asked? According to the immensely influential St. Albertus Magnus (1193-1280), the just price is simply what "goods are worth according to the estimate of the market at the time of sale." That is, a just price is not a function of the amount of profit, but is whatever uncoerced buyers are willing to pay. Adam Smith would have agreed—St. Thomas Aquinas (1225-74) did. As for usury, a host of leading theologians of the day remained opposed to it, but quickly defined it out of practical existence. For example, no usury was involved if the interest was paid to compensate the lender for the costs of not having the money available for other commercial opportunities, which was almost always easily demonstrated.

That was a remarkable shift. Most of these theologians were, after all, men who had separated themselves from the world, and most of them had taken vows of poverty. Had asceticism truly prevailed in the monasteries, it seems very unlikely that the traditional disdain for and opposition to commerce would have mellowed. That it did, and to such a revolutionary extent, was a result of direct experience with worldly imperatives. For all their genuine acts of charity, monastic administrators were not about to give all their wealth to the poor, sell their products at cost, or give kings interest-free loans. It was the active participation of the great orders in free markets that caused monastic theologians to reconsider the morality of commerce.

The religious orders could pursue their economic goals because they were sufficiently powerful to withstand any attempts at seizure by an avaricious nobility. But for fully developed secular capitalism to unfold, there needed to be broader freedom from regulation and expropriation. Hence secular capitalism appeared first in the relatively democratic city-states of northern Italy, whose political institutions rested squarely on church doctrines of free will and moral equality.

Augustine, Aquinas, and other major theologians taught that the state must respect private property and not intrude on the freedom of its citizens to pursue virtue. In addition, there was the central Christian doctrine that, regardless of worldly inequalities, inequality in the most important sense does not exist: in the eyes of God and in the world to come. As Paul explained: "There is neither Jew nor Greek, there is neither bond nor fee, there is neither male nor female, for ye are all one in Christ Jesus."

And church theologians and leaders meant it. Through all prior recorded history, slavery was universal—Christianity began in a world where as much as half the population was in bondage. But by the seventh century, Christianity had become the only major world religion to formulate specific theological opposition to slavery, and, by no later than the 11th century, the church had expelled the dreadful institution from Europe. That it later reappeared in the New World is another matter, although there, too, slavery was vigorously condemned by popes and all of the eventual abolition movements were of religious origins.

Free labor was an essential ingredient for the rise of capitalism, for free workers can maximize their rewards by working harder or more effectively than before. In contrast, coerced workers gain nothing from doing more. Put another way, tyranny makes a few people richer; capitalism can make everyone richer. Therefore, as the northern Italian city-states developed capitalist economies, visitors marveled at their standards of living; many were equally confounded by how hard everyone worked.

The common denominator in all these great historical developments was the Christian commitment to reason.

That was why the West won.

Source: Rodney Stark. 2005. "How Christianity Led to Freedom, Capitalism, and the Success of the West." *The Chronicle of Higher Education* (52): 15 (December 2), B11. Reprinted with permission from Rodney Stark.

The essay above was adapted from Rodney Stark's book, *The Victory of Reason: How Christianity Led to Freedom, Capitalism, and Western Success.* New York: Random House, 2005.

Rodney Stark received his Ph.D. from the University of California, Berkeley, and joined the faculty of Baylor University in 2004. He has published 30 books and more than 140 scholarly articles on subjects as diverse as prejudice, crime, suicide, and city life in ancient Rome. However, the greater part of his work has been on religion. He is past president of the Society for the Scientific Study of Religion and of the Association for the Sociology of Religion. He has won a number of national and international awards for distinguished scholarship.

Chapter 6

----- ∞ -----

The Galileo Affair

The Galileo affair is one of the primary historical events that opponents of the Church cite as evidence that the Church of that era was anti-science. Furthermore, it is offered as proof that the Church cannot be infallible. An examination of the historical evidence reveals that neither of these myths is true. Indeed, the record shows three things:

1. The Church did not persecute Galileo.

2. Many churchmen, including Pope Urban VIII, were not opposed to the Copernican heliocentric theory that Galileo espoused. They were opposed to the heavy-handed manner employed by Galileo to use the yet unproven theory to encroach on Scriptural interpretation.

3. The Church made no *official* condemnation of Galileo's heliocentric theory. Moreover, the Church claims infallibility only in matters of faith and morals, not science, and then only under certain circumstances.

Nevertheless, objective reading of history leads to the conclusion that the Church overstepped its bounds by opining on a matter about which it had no authority. In 1979, Pope John Paul II acknowledged this.[1]

In **"The Dispute between Galileo and the Catholic Church,"** Donald DeMarco provides a detailed account of the Galileo affair. His account is balanced and factual, providing an honest perspective on this much misunderstood historical event.

➢ Most of the Church intelligensia supported Galileo, while most of his opposition came from secular sectors of society.

---

[1] Pope John Paul II. 1979. "On the Centenary of the Birth of Albert Einstein." A Discourse of His Holiness Pope John Paul II on November 10 at the Plenary Academic Session to commemorate the centenary of the birth of Albert Einstein.

➤ The Church did not launch an aggressive attack on Galileo as much as it was backed into a corner by an unyielding and ambitious scientist, that is, by Galileo himself.

➤ Without the support of the Church and many churchmen, Copernicus' book advancing his heliocentric theory would never have been published. Indeed, Copernicus dedicated the book to Pope Paul III.

➤ When Galileo produced an improved telescope and reported on his observations in *The Starry Messenger*, he was applauded by all, including Pope Paul V and other churchmen. Nevertheless, this work did not confirm the Copernican system.

➤ Other theories of planetary movement were widely endorsed by astronomers of the day.

➤ Galileo's enemies cited various Bible passages that seemed to suggest that the sun revolved around the earth to undermine Galileo's theories. Although a Dominican priest was instrumental in leading this attack, scholars point out that most of the other churchmen involved did not take the Dominican's position.

➤ Galileo stated that the validity of the Copernican system had been proven beyond doubt and that the Church must therefore reinterpret the passages of Scripture that contradicted it.

➤ Robert Cardinal Bellarmine, a leading Jesuit theologian, stated that, indeed, should the validity of the Copernican system be truly proven, then "it would be necessary to use careful consideration in explaining the Scriptures that seemed contrary. . . ." The needed proof, however, was lacking. This reflected the thinking of the Church as well as many of the scientists of the day.

➤ After Galileo went to Rome to aggressively promote the Copernican system, ridiculing anyone disagreeing with him, the Holy Office issued a decree declaring this notion of the motion of the earth to be "false and altogether opposed to Holy Scripture." The decree did not name Galileo nor prohibit his works.

➤ Galileo's abrasiveness toward the Jesuits and his demeaning portrayal in his writings of Pope Urban VIII alienated these former supporters.

➤ Both Galileo and Pope Urban VIII have been characterized as men of great pride and vanity, facts that contributed to their final showdown.

> ➤ The Inquisition called Galileo to Rome in 1632. It was not until the following year that he actually arrived in Rome due to poor health.
> ➤ While in Rome, Galileo was treated very well, occupying a five-room apartment overlooking the Vatican Gardens. He was never tortured, nor did he fear being tortured.
> ➤ One author concluded, "The worst that happened [in that age] to men of science was that Galileo suffered an honorable detention and a mild reproof, before dying peacefully in his bed."

Further Reading

George Sim Johnston. 1994. *The Galileo Affair*. Princeton, New Jersey: Scepter Press.

The Dispute Between Galileo and the Catholic Church

By Donald DeMarco

The dispute between Galileo and the Catholic Church is both complex and controversial. It is complex because it involves a host of delicate issues and a multitude of volatile personalities. It is controversial because its interpreters invariably attach deeply felt positive or negative evaluations to these issues and personalities. There should be no mystery, consequently, why misrepresentations abound.

Bertold Brecht's play, *Galileo*,[1] whose cast calls for a "Fat Prelate," a "Furious Monk," and an "Old Cardinal"; paintings depicting the subjection of Galileo to various forms of humiliation that never took place;[2] and certain television dramatizations that pander to popular prejudice,[3] are typical one-sided misrepresentations that take the part of Galileo against a presumed authoritarian hierarchy. We find this same tendency to be commonplace even among certain books that pass for scholarly studies. In a book entitled *Man on Trial*, for example, the author views the trial of Galileo as "the climax of the onslaught of organized religion against scientific progress."[4] Another author erroneously contends that Galileo "rigorously demonstrated the Copernican system."[5]

In Carl Sagan's popular picture book on astronomy, *Cosmos*, the author tells us that Galileo was unable to convince the Catholic hierarchy that there are mountains on the Moon and that Jupiter has moons of its own.[6] The historical fact is the polar opposite of what Sagan contends. Jesuit astronomers of the Roman College confirmed Galileo's telescopic observations and subsequently honored Galileo with a full

---

[1] Jerome J. Langford, O.P. 1966. *Galileo, Science and the Church*. New York: Desclee, p. 151.

[2] Colin Ronan. 1974. *Galileo*. New York: G.P. Putnam's Sons, p. 217.

[3] Such as Steve Allen's shallow and one-sided portrayal of Galileo in his series, "The Meeting of Minds."

[4] Gerald Dickler. 1962. *Man on Trial*. Garden City: Doubleday, p. 61.

[5] A. Fouille. 1955. *Historia general de la filosofia*. Santiago de Chile, p. 274.

[6] Carl Sagan. 1980. *Cosmos*. New York: Random House, p. 141.

day of ceremonies. And while Galileo was in Rome for these plaudits, he was given a hero's welcome by cardinals, prelates, and other dignitaries of the Church including Pope Paul V.

It has been known for quite some time now that the majority of Church intellectuals supported Galileo, and that the clearest and strongest opposition to him came from secular agencies. This fact, however, is not sufficiently well known to the public at large.

This paper is an attempt to examine the pertinent ideas, issues, and personalities in the Galileo affair and by trying to understand these, shed some light on what was at the very heart of the dispute between Galileo and the Catholic Church.

Part I

No thinker is so bold and innovative that he thinks and works independently of his predecessors. Galileo, his creativity notwithstanding, stood on the shoulders of thinkers who came before him. His indebtedness to one particular school of thought—Pythagoreanism—is immense. "It was only just," as Giorgio de Santillana has remarked, "that Galileo's natural philosophy should have been denounced by his opponents as "the Pythagorean doctrine."[7] Galileo himself does not shy away from referring to his thought by its proper name, the "Pythagorean philosphy."

Indebted to Pythagoreans

By Pythagoreanism, what is meant here is the philosophy which accepts three fundamental assumptions about the world: 1) that the sun is at the center of a universe which is organized in the most simple and harmonious way possible; 2) that the planets move in circular paths, the circle being a form of perfection; 3) that the truth of things is to be found in number, and therefore the truth of nature is revealed through the science of mathematics.

---

[7] Giorgio de Santillana. 1961. *The Origins of Scientific Thought*. New York: New American Library, p. 65. The author is referring to the decree by the Holy Office issued against Galileo in 1616. See Santillana. 1962. *The Age of Adventure*. New York: New American Library, p. 228: "Galileo, the so-called empiricist, is in fact an unyielding scientific rationalist."

It was not before his sixtieth year that Galileo dared to make his Pythagorean convictions fully known. By that time, however, they were buttressed by thirty-five years of careful investigation. He was now convinced that the Pythagorean supposition was not merely an hypothesis but corresponded to a state of fact.[8] He had affirmed the Pythagorean astronomical model which demanded planets that made perfect circles around the sun. But now he was willing to go further and affirmed a Pythagorean philosophy of nature. His Pythagorean assumptions concerning nature and number are clearly represented in the following well known passage from his masterpiece, *Dialogues and Mathematical Demonstrations Concerning Two New Sciences:*

> Philosophy is written in that great book which ever lies before our eyes—I mean the universe—but we cannot understand it if we do not first learn the language and grasp the symbols, in which it is written. This book is written in the mathematical language, and the symbols are triangles, circles, and other geometric figures, without whose help it is impossible to comprehend a single word of it; without which one wanders in vain through a dark labyrinth.[9]

Put simply, Galileo's world was one of pure quantity. It was not the world of Aristotle; for Aristotle and his followers, quantity was only one of ten predicaments and not the most important. Nor was it congruent with the Christian doctrine of the Incarnation. It was a world of matter in motion, knowable to the mathematician and alien to the man of ordinary sense perception. Concerning this world the senses perceive, he writes:

> Hence I think that tastes, odors, colors, and so on are no more than mere names as far as the object in which we place them is concerned, and that they reside only in the consciousness. Hence if the-

---

[8] Giorgio de Santillana. 1955. *The Crime of Galileo.* Chicago: University of Chicago Press, p. 71.

[9] *Opere Complete di Galileo Galilei.* 1842. (Firenza, Vol. 1V, p. 171). See R.G. Collingwood, 1960. *The Idea of Nature.* New York: Oxford University Press, p. 94: "... Galileo, the true father of modern science, restated the Pythagorean-Platonic standpoint in his own words by proclaiming that the book of nature is a book written by God in the language of mathematics."

living creature were removed, all these qualities would be wiped away and annihilated.[10]

This perfect dichotomy of Galileo's between the world of mathematics and the world of sense qualities is tantamount to a divorce of science from philosophy and a radical depreciation of the latter. It is essentially Pythagorean as well as anti-Incarnational.

Galileo's conflict with the Church—which resulted in confrontations with the Vatican on two separate occasions—would never have taken place if it were not for his unyielding insistence on trying to prove that the helio-centric theory proposed by Copernicus was a true physical system. Underlying this conflict was a philosophical one between a Pythagorean view that finds truth in idealized mathematics, and a Christian-Incarnational view which affirms the unity of mind and matter, form and substance.

But the conflict was not between a progressive scientist and a backward clergy, or between a blameless individual and an authoritarian Church. In fact, as we shall argue, Galileo's attempt to validate an essentially Pythagorean description of the universe owes more of its driving force to his own vanity and personal ambitions, than to the impersonal forces that motivate a disinterested scientist. The Church, on the other hand, did not initiate an aggressive attack against Galileo as much as it was forced into a position of having to defend its own integrity.

Whereas Galileo's Pythagorean outlook put him at odds with Rome, it put him in harmony with Copernicus, for the latter also worked under the spell of Pythagoreanism.[11] In order to gain a better understanding of Galileo's fierce loyalty to Copernicus' system, it is helpful to know something about the common commitment both these great scientists had to the Pythagorean idealization of the world.

---

[10] Galileo, "The Assayer." 1957. trans. S. Drake in *Theories and Opinions of Galileo*. New York: Doubleday, p. 274.

[11] According to Rheticus, a pupil of Copernicus, it was by his master following "Plato and the Pythagoreans, the greatest mathematicians of that divine age that [he) thought that in order to determine the cause of the phenomena, circular motions have to be ascribed to the spherical earth." Quoted in Alexander Koyré, *From the Closed World to the Ignite Universe* (New York: Harper and Row, 1957), p. 28-29.

Copernicus's friend and teacher during the six years he stayed in Italy was a mathematician-astronomer by the name of Dominicus Maria da Novara. Novara was a free critic of the geo-centric system of Ptolemy principally because he was thoroughly caught up with the Platonic Pythagorean current of his time and felt that this cumbrous system, with its "deferent circles" and innumerable "epicycles," violated the postulate that the astronomical universe is an orderly mathematical harmony.[12] Through the influence of Novara, Copernicus developed his interest in the early Pythagoreans, who almost alone among the ancients had ventured to theorize about a non-geocentric astronomy.

One important aspect of Copernicus's own Pythagorean thinking was his assumption of simplicity. Applied to nature it meant that nature always operated in the most mathematically simple and elegant manner possible. This thinking was in accord with a number of accepted maxims which were prevalent at the time: *"Natura simplicitatem amat." "Amat illa unitatem." "Natura semper quod potest per faciliora, non agit per ambages* (windings) *difficiles."*

Drew from Predecessors

Copernicus held that a sphere moves in a circular pattern because the motion of a body naturally and spontaneously follows from its geometric form. "For the motion of a sphere," he writes, "is to turn in a circle; by this very act expressing its form."[13] "The mind shudders," at the alternative, he adds, "because it would be unworthy to suppose such a thing in a Creation constituted in the best possible way."

Scholars have accused Copernicus of having an obsession with circularity and sphericity, and of constructing a heliocentric system that is justified by aesthetic judgment alone.[14] Sir Francis Bacon firmly rejected Copernicanism when he said: "I shall not stand upon that piece of mathematical elegance." Even Galileo had to admit that Copernicus's naive preoccupation with simplicity was the insouciance of genius. It was no doubt Copernicus's absolute Pythagorean faith that led him to

---

[12] Dorothy Stimson. 1917. *The Gradual Acceptance of the Copernican Theory of the Universe.* New York, p. 25.

[13] Nicholas Copernicus, On the Revolution of the Heavenly Spheres, Book 1.

[14] Herbert Butterfield. 1957. *The Origins of Modern Science.* New York: The Free Press, p. 44.

believe that his theory was not merely an abstract model of mathematical simplicity and elegance, but a true physical system.

At any rate, Copernicus presented the world with a new picture of the universe in which he dared to attribute to the earth a diurnal motion on its axis and an annual revolution around the sun, because such a model was one of greater mathematical simplicity than the one provided by Ptolemy. He could accept the metaphysical implications of his system because of the widespread Platonic-Pythagorean conception of the universe suggested to his mind by the preceding developments in the science of mathematics.

Although Copernicus himself was hesitant to publish his work and waited until he was 70 and in the last year of his life before he consented to its publication, he had received strong support and encouragement from other officials in the Church. In 1533, Pope Clement VII had listened to a lecture on the Copernican theory and was greatly impressed. A few years later Cardinal Schönberg, a scholar who had distinguished himself in all branches of learning, wrote to Copernicus that he had learned with great admiration about the Polish mathematician's "having created a new theory of the universe according to which the Earth moves and the sun occupies the basic and central position. . . . Therefore, learned man, without wishing to be opportune, I beg you most emphatically to communicate your discovery to the learned world."[15] In the Preface of his book, Copernicus acknowledges his indebtedness to his many friends and colleagues who encouraged him to publish his revolutionary findings, including Tiedeman Giese, Bishop of Culm who "spurred me on by added reproaches into publishing this book and letting come to light a work which I had kept hidden among my things for not merely nine years, but for almost four times nine years." Copernicus dedicated his work to Pope Paul III, Clement VII's successor.

Galileo's World of Quantity

Contrary to the legend, the Church did not initially oppose the helio-centric theory. In fact, the opposite was true. Without the patronage and encouragement of the clergy—from the local bishop to

---

[15] Quoted by Arthur Koestler in "The Greatest Scandal in Christendom," *The Critic*, Oct.-Nov., 1964, p. 16.

clergymen who occupied influential positions with the Vatican—Copernicus's book would never have been published.

The simplicity, mathematical elegance, and Platonic-Pythagorean quality of Copernicus's work appealed very strongly to Galileo, and he adopted the heliocentric system in his twenties. Yet, just as his Polish mentor delayed publishing his work for fear of being "laughed at and hissed off the stage," so too, Galileo, for fear of being ridiculed, kept his convictions to himself until he was nearly fifty. During the interim, he defended the geocentric model of Ptolemy in his lectures, repudiating the earth's motion by means of the traditional arguments. For example, he taught that the earth did not move, for if it did, the clouds would be left behind.[16]

In general, Galileo's deceptiveness has created no end of difficulties for his interpreters. One scholar has made the comment that perhaps, "*All* the pronouncements of Galileo have to be taken *cum grano salis*."[17] Many of Galileo's dissimulations were no doubt rooted in prudence. Nevertheless, those whose ridicule he feared were not members of the clergy, but his own lay colleagues who occupied chairs of astronomy and philosophy at Bologna, Pisa, Padua, and elsewhere. The risk of ecclesiastical censure during the first fifty years of his life never occurred to him. On his own account, Galileo regarded the Jesuits of the Roman College, who were the leading astronomers of the day, as "modern-minded humanists, friends of science and discovery."[18]

In 1610, Galileo's life took a dramatic turn. The telescope was invented in Holland two years before by an optician named Hans Lippershey. Upon learning of this invention, Galileo built his own telescope with vastly improved magnifying power (though the most powerful telescope he built magnified objects only thirty-three times).

---

[16] The proof of this claim is found in a surviving manuscript copy of a lecture of Galileo, dated 1601, *Trattato della Sfera* (Opere, Ediz. Nationale: Florence, 1929-30, Vol. II, pp. 203-55.

[17] Koyré, p. 98.

[18] See William Wallace, *Galileo and His Sources* (Princeton, N.J.: Princeton University Press, 1984). The author studies two early manuscripts of Galileo which are the results of lectures by Jesuits at the Collegio Romano, and shows how the materials in these lectures contributed to the evolution of Galileo's thought.

He published a booklet, *Sidereus Nuncius* (The Starry Messenger)[19] in which he recorded his observations. He reported seeing a moon with a surface just like that of the earth, "with huge prominences, deep valleys, and chasms"; stars "so numerous as almost to surpass belief"; and most momentous of all, four moons orbiting the planet Jupiter.

Galileo named the circumjovial moons the "Medicean Stars" to honor Cosimo II de' Medici, Grand Duke of Tuscany to whom he dedicated the *Nuncius*. This gesture proved to be politically astute. Four months after the booklet's publication, Cosimo appointed Galileo as the chief mathematician and philosopher to the Grand Duke of Tuscany at the handsome salary of 1,000 florins a year. Galileo was now financially secure for life.

Politically Astute

The Church rallied to his support. The Jesuits of the Roman College held a day of ceremonies in his honor. Pope Paul V received him in a long audience and showed him benevolence. He was well received by other dignitaries of the Church. Cardinal Francesco Mari del Monte, one of Galileo's patrons, stated in a letter: "If we were still living under the ancient Republic of Rome, I verily believe that there would be a column on the Capital erected in Galileo's honor."[20] Galileo described his reception in a letter to his friend Salviati: "I have been received and feted by many illustrious cardinals, prelates, and princes of this city, who wanted to see the things I have observed and were much pleased."[21]

Galileo's telescopic observations offered an empirical refutation of the claim that all celestial bodies revolved around the earth. They did not, however, nor did anything else he observed through the telescope, confirm the Copernican system. Nonetheless, the publication of *Nuncius* gave Galileo the fame and prestige he needed to risk making

---

[19] Kepler understood the title as meaning: the "messenger of stars." This mistranslation was generally accepted until it was corrected in 1948 in a new edition of the *Nuncius* as *The Message of the Stars*. The traditional title, *The Starry Messenger*, is nonetheless appropriate even though technically incorrect: *Se non è vero, è ben trovato.*

[20] Quoted in Koestler, p. 16.

[21] *Letter to Filippo Salviati*, quoted in de Santillana, 1955, p. 23.

known his long held allegiance to the Copernican system. His heightened fame and new boldness, however, moved other colleagues of his, mostly non-clerics, to bitter jealousy. They were so dazzled by what the telescope revealed that some of them, like the illustrious philosopher Cremonini, refused on principle, to look through it. In a letter to his esteemed friend, Kepler, Galileo writes about this matter as follows:

> Oh, my dear Kepler, how I wish we could have one hearty laugh together! Here at Padua is the principal professor of philosophy whom I have repeatedly and urgently requested to look at the moon and planets through my glass which he pertinaciously refuses to do. Why are you not here? What shouts of laughter we should have at this glorious folly! And to hear the professor of philosophy at Pisa labouring before the Grand Duke with logical arguments, as if with magical incantations, to charm the new planets out of the sky.[22]

The elite of Jesuit astronomers in various parts of Europe not only confirmed Galileo's empirical discoveries, but they improved on them. In addition, the Dutch mathematician-astronomer Christian Huygens discovered a satellite of Saturn and clarified Galileo's earlier observation of the peculiar configuration of that planet by announcing the presence of its surrounding ring. Galileo was victorious. His discoveries and genius were hailed throughout Europe. He now felt bold enough to go beyond merely endorsing the Copernican system. He began denigrating anyone who opposed it, referring to them as "mental pygmies" (*homunciones*), "dumb mooncalves" (*hebetes et pene stolidos*), and "hardly deserving to be called human beings."[23]

Galileo's triumphant attachment to the helio-centric theory of Copernicus was not exactly reasonable. Although the Jupiter moons

---

[22] Letter to Kepler, 1610, quoted in Oliver Lodge, *Pioneers of Science* (London, 1913), Ch. 4. The second philosopher to whom Galileo refers in this passage is Giulio Libri, a philosopher who taught at Pisa and at Padua during Galileo's service at those universities. Another colleague who refused to look through the telescope is Sizzi who held that the discovery of an additional planet would destroy the seven-day week which is based on the existence of seven and only seven planets. See James Christian, *Philosophy* (San Francisco: Rinehart Press, 1973), p. 419, from Sizzi's *Dianola astronomica*.

[23] De Santillana. 1955, p. 247. These remarks were brought out in the trial of Galileo in 1633 by Melchior Inchofer, one of the experts for the prosecution.

proved Ptolemy wrong, they did not prove Copernicus right. There existed alternative explanations of planetary movements. The great Danish astronomer, Tycho de Brahe, introduced an intermediate theory which, from a mathematical standpoint, was just as satisfactory as the Copernican system. De Brahe proposed a model in which the planets revolved around the sun and, together with the sun, revolved around a stationary earth. The general tendency among astronomers from about 1630 to 1687 was to prefer this model of explanation. In 1672 a scientist has as many as seven models to choose from.[24] But Galileo refused to consider even for a moment the possible legitimacy of the Tychonic "third system." To him it was a gratuitous red herring brought in at the last moment.[25] Nor was Galileo willing to consider the possibility that planets moved in patterns other than circles, although this notion had been brought to his attention. In his *Nuncius* he rejects even an oval motion that is nearly straight since it "seems unthinkable and quite inconsistent with the appearances."[26] Galileo's theory demanded circles as a physical reality.

The Copernican paradigm presented a major problem to scientists in the 17th century. If the earth did travel around the sun, as Copernicus claimed, the fixed stars ought to reveal an annual parallax (stellar displacement) due to the 186,000,000 mile difference in the position of the earth every six months. This question was not settled until Bessel's discovery of such a parallax in 1838. In Galileo's time, the absence of any visible stellar parallax implied that the stars were at a distance from the earth so immense as to be dismissed by all but a few as too astonishing to believe.[27]

Science and Scripture Clash

Meanwhile, Galileo's enemies had decided upon a new strategy with which they would attempt to topple him from his pedestal. Led by

---

[24] Butterfield, p. 83.

[25] De Santillana. 1955, p. 37.

[26] Galileo, *The Starry Messenger*. 1957. trans. S. Drake, p. 58. Kepler had discovered the elliptical patterns of the planets in the previous year and published his findings in *Astronomia Nova*.

[27] E. A. Burst. 1954. *The Metaphysical Foundations of Modern Science.* New York: Doubleday, pp. 37-38.

Lodovico delle Colombe, the "Pigeon-League,"[28] as Galileo contemptuously called them, sought to engage Galileo in a conflict between science and scripture. They endeavored to create a scandal surrounding the person of Galileo and thus compel the Roman authorities, who were reluctant to act on the grounds of theory, to act in the interest of restoring the good of public order. Colombe, who knew he was no match for Galileo on an intellectual level and had already been embarrassed in a dual of wits with him, was intent on defaming Galileo any way he could.

Colombe had been the first to use the Bible as a weapon directly against Galileo.[29] He had circulated in manuscript form his treatise, *Against the Motion of the Earth*, in which he cited several texts from Scripture that apparently contradicted the Copernican system. One such text, Joshua 10:12-13, used time and again, became closely identified with the controversy. Thus, Joshua, after defeating the Philistines, commanded the sun to stand still, which implied that the sun usually moves. Colombe prevailed upon a Dominican priest, Tommaso Caccini to join the fray. Goaded on by Colombe's "Pigeon-League," Caccini delivered a sermon on December 20, 1614 in Santa Maria Novella in Florence in which he strongly denounced Galileo and his followers and condemned the idea of a moving earth. He cited the Joshua passage to illustrate the contradiction that he believed existed between Scripture and Copernicanism.

Caccini's behavior, as scholars have pointed out, "stands out in contrast to that of nearly all the other churchmen involved" in the Galileo controversy.[30] Moreover, it was excessive and irrational. He had called for banishing "mathematicians" (in a very loose usage of the term) from Christian states. Father Maraffi, a Preacher-General of the Dominicans—and a fervid promoter of the Copernican cause—wrote a letter of apology to Galileo. "Unfortunately," he wrote, "1 have to answer for all the idiocies [bestialità] that thirty or forty thousand

---

[28] De Santillana. 1955, p. 21. Since *colombi* (masculine) means "pigeons," Galileo and his followers called the Peripatetic coalition formed by Lodovico, the "Pigeon-League."

[29] See J. Brodrick. 1961. *Robert Bellarmine: Saint and Scholar.* Westminster: Newman, p. 346.

[30] Langford, p. 55, f.n.8.

brothers may and do actually commit."[31] He had also made it clear to his Dominican subjects that he would not tolerate this kind of barbarity: "We should not open the door for every impertinent individual to come out with what is dictated to him by the rage of others and by his own madness and ignorance."[32] But perhaps the severest rebuke came from Caccini's own brother, Matteo. In letters addressed to his brother, Matteo writes: "It was a silly thing [for Tommaso] to get himself embroiled in this business by these pigeons [*colombi*] . . . What idiocy is this of being set abellowing at the prompting of those nasty pigeons . . . This performance of yours makes no sense in heaven and earth. . . . I who am no theologian can tell you what I am telling you, that you have behaved like a dreadful fool."[33]

Caccini's sermon brought the controversy between Scripture, Copernicanism, and Galileo out into the open for the first time. Galileo responded by writing a letter in which he argued that nothing he held was in conflict with Scripture. Accordingly, he reasoned that Scripture deals with natural matters in such a cursory and allusive way that it appears as though it wants to remind us that its proper concern is not about them but about the soul of man. It is willing to adjust its language about Nature to the simple minds of ordinary people.[34] He argued that it is not the business of Scripture to validate science, and defended this point by quoting Cardinal Baronius who had remarked that, "The Holy Ghost intended to teach us how to go to heaven, not how the heavens go."[35]

But the trap set for Galileo proved effective. He insisted that the Copernican system had been proved beyond doubt and that the Church must reinterpret scriptural passages that contradicted it. This set the

---

[31] Di Santillana. 1955, p. 45.

[32] *Ibid.*, P. 283.

[33] See A. Ricci-Riccardi. 1902. *Galileo e Fra Tommaso Caccini: Una corresponza inedita.*

[34] *Letter to Castelli* (Dec. 13, 1613): "Holy Scripture and nature proceed equally from the divine Word, the former as it were dictated by the Holy Spirit, the latter as a very faithful executor of God's orders."

[35] *Letter to the Grand Duchess Christina* (*National Edition of the Works of Galileo*, Vol. V, p. 315): "Holy Scripture can never lie, provided its true meaning is understood, which—I do not think it can be denied—is often hidden and very different from what a simple interpretation of the words seems to indicate."

stage for a confrontation with Rome, although the Church did everything it could to prevent it.

Part II

The Dispute between Galileo and the Catholic Church

The official view of the Church was represented by its highest theological authority at that time: the famous Jesuit theologian, Robert Cardinal Bellarmine. In a famous letter, Bellarmine stated as follows:

> I say that if there were a true demonstration that the sun was in the center of the universe and the earth in the third sphere, and that the sun did not go around the earth but the earth went around the sun, then it would be necessary to use careful consideration in explaining the Scriptures that seemed contrary, and we should rather have to say that we do not understand them than to say that something is false which had been proven.[36]

Bellarmine's letter reflects an informed and open mind. If the Copernican system were to be proven, then, rather than contradict science, the Church should reinterpret Scripture. But the proof was still wanting. And until such a proof appeared, as Bellarmine went on to say, to speak of the Copernican system *as an established truth* "is a very dangerous attitude." This cautionary note not only represented the mind of the Church, but also that of the responsible body of empirical scientists of the day. In fact, as Alfred North Whitehead and others have pointed out,[37] it was never a case of Galileo being right and the Inquisition being wrong on a scientific point. Galileo's formulation of the universe was not more true than that of the Inquisition, nor was the geo-centric system espoused by the Inquisition more true than the heliocentric one.

To be fair, it should also be pointed out that Bellarmine erred when he required a proof of the Copernican system as a condition for interpreting certain Scriptural passages—such as the Joshua text—in an

---

[36] *Letter of Cardinal Bellarmine to Foscarini.*
[37] Alfred North Whitehead. 1963. *Science and the Modern World.* New York: New American Library, p. 163.

allusive or non-literal manner. It is a curious paradox, as a scholar on the life and work of Bellarmine has remarked, that, "As a piece of Scriptural exegesis Galileo's theological letters are much superior to Bellarmine's, while as an essay on scientific method Bellarmine's letter is far sounder and more modern in its views than Galileo's."[38]

But Galileo was unwilling to wait until a proof could be discovered. He hurried off to Rome in the hope of winning support from Church authorities. While there, he displayed his talent for polemics by audaciously ridiculing opponents of the Copernican theory time and again in lively debates. But the Jesuits of the Roman College remained unimpressed. There was still the third system of Tycho de Brahe that had not yet been scientifically supplanted. They understood well that unqualified support for the helio-centric theory was impossible until de Brahe's system had been disproven.

Dr. Brahe's System Not Disproved

Galileo's over-eagerness to vindicate the Copernican system was only too evident. The Tuscan Ambassador made the observation that Galileo "is passionately involved in this quarrel so that he will be ensnarled in it and get himself into danger . . . For he is vehement and all impassioned in his affair."[39]

As a result of Galileo's importunity, the Holy Office finally issued a decree in 1616 declaring "the Pythagorean doctrine of the motion of the earth" to be "false and altogether opposed to Holy Scripture." Galileo's name was not mentioned in the decree, nor were his works prohibited. The incident ended on a decorous note with Pope Paul V gracefully receiving Galileo in a long audience in which the Pope assured Galileo that any rumors and calumny directed against him would be ignored by the Vatican.

Protestantism had not been so gracious toward Kepler when this great astronomer professed his intellectual sympathies for the Copernican system. Having been persecuted by the Protestant Faculty at

---

[38] Brodrick. 1928. *The Life and Work of Blessed Robert Francis, Cardinal Bellarmine*, SJ., vol. 11, p. 360.

[39] Koestler, p. 20.

Tubingen, Kepler actually took refuge with the Jesuits in 1596.[40] Luther had summarily dismissed Copernicus as "that fool." And Melancthon had condemned Copernicanism as "dishonest" and "pernicious."[41]

But the conflict between Galileo and the Church of Rome had not been put to rest and would flare up seventeen years later. In the meantime, Galileo set to work in an obsessive attempt to find scientific confirmation of Copernicus' theory. There can be no doubt as to what Galileo's intent was. He confided to a friend in 1629: "I have taken up work again on the *Dialogue* of the Ebb and Flow of the Sea . . . I trust, a most ample confirmation of the Copernican system."[42] The result was the *Dialogue on the Two Great World Systems* in which he contrasted the Ptolemaic and Copernican systems, though he curiously omitted any discussion of the newer systems of Kepler and de Brahe. In this work, its author juxtaposes masterly expositions with hollow rhetoric and the deliberate falsification of facts.

Most importantly, however, Galileo thought he had discovered the important proof of the earth's motion he had been looking for. "Rejecting Kepler's correct notion that the moon causes the alternation of the tides, Galileo argued that the seas "swapped over" once a day as a direct consequence of the earth's motion."[43] Accordingly, the tides were caused, so to speak, by the shaking of the vessel that contained them." This monumental error, inconsistent even with his own principles of dynamics, is unworthy of his genius and can only be understood as the effect of will being momentarily stronger than intellect, of vanity being more evident than a humble openness to truth. Arthur Koestler is unsparing in his criticism of Galileo's theory of the tides as it is presented in the *Dialogue*:

---

[40] Butterfield, p. 69. The first opposition to the helio-centric theory came from Luther and Melancthon and other Protestant theologians. They produced scathing condemnations of Copernicus' work. Luther called Copernicus "an ass who wants to pervert the whole of astronomy and deny what is said in the book of Joshua, only to make a show of ingenuity and attract attention."

[41] P. Melancthon, "Initia doctrinae physicae," *Corpus Reformatorum*, ed. Bretschneider, XIII, p. 216.

[42] *Letter to Diodati* (October 29, 1629).

[43] Arthur Koestler. 1964. "The Greatest Scandal in Christendom." *The Critic* (October-November). p. 19.

There can be no doubt that Galileo's theory of the tides was based on unconscious deception; but . . . there can also be little doubt that the sunspot argument was a deliberate attempt to confuse and mislead . . . We have seen that scholars have always been prone to manias and obsessions, and inclined to cheat about details; but impostures like Galileo's are rare in the annals of science. [44]

But there were other indiscretions that Galileo committed. Perhaps the most significant and damaging involves a series of abrasive dealings he had with Jesuit astronomers. In *The Assayer*, Galileo writes:

Others, not wanting to agree with my ideas, advance ridiculous and impossible opinions against me; and some, overwhelmed and convinced by my arguments, attempted to rob me of that glory which was mine, pretending not to have seen my writings and trying to represent themselves as the original discoverers of these impressive marvels. [45]

The Jesuit astronomer Christopher Scheiner took this remark to be unjustly aimed at him. Scheiner had published his observations of sunspots under a pseudonym on October 21, 1611, but had stated that he first noticed some spots on the sun seven or eight months before he began to record them. The first mention of sunspots by Galileo appears in a letter dated October 1, 1611. In his Dialogue, Galileo claimed for himself the honor of being the first to discover sunspots:

Harken then to this great new wonder. The first discoverer of the solar spots . . . was our Lincean academician [Galileo] and he discovered them in the year 1610. [46]

Scheiner contended forcefully that the honor belonged to himself. A great bitterness arose between these two astronomers about who really discovered the sunspots first, with each accusing the other of dishonesty. The dispute was a pointless one, however, since the honor belongs to Johann Fabricius of Wittenberg, whose booklet printed in

---

[44] Arthur Koestler. 1959. *The Sleepwalkers*. New York: Macmillan, p. 478.

[45] Galileo, "The Assayer," p. 232.

[46] Galileo. 1953. *Dialogue on the Great World Systems*, trans. de Santillana. Chicago: Chicago University Press, p. 354.

the summer of 1611 seems to have escaped the attention of the disputants. Nonetheless, it did much to antagonize Scheiner and other Jesuits, which resulted in Galileo losing a great deal of Jesuit support. Another incident, which further alienated the Jesuits from Galileo, involved the Jesuit mathematician-astronomer Horatio Grassi in a dispute over comets. Galileo's polemical refutation of Grassi in *The Assayer* was devastating. In fact, the whole of *The Assayer* was nothing more or less than an unremitting, sarcastic lampoon against Fr. Grassi. It left Grassi pulverized in the public eye. His fellow Jesuits ordered him to lie low and not attempt to answer Galileo. The following passage offers a fair indication of how unmerciful Galileo was toward his astronomical colleague:

> Let Sarsi [the imperfect anagram for Grassi) see from this how super-ficial his philosophizing is except in appearance. But let him not think he can reply with additional limitations, distinctions, logical technicalities, philosophical jargon, and other idle words, for I assure him that in sustaining one error, he will commit a hundred others that are more serious, and produce always greater follies in his camp....[47]

The frequency and sharpness of such remarks played an important role in causing many Jesuits to withdraw their support of Galileo, which he later needed very badly. Fr. Grienberger, another Jesuit astronomer, was to say in 1634, the year of Galileo's second confrontation with the Holy Office, that, "Galileo should have known how to keep the affections of the fathers of the Roman College. If he had, he would still be living gloriously in the world, he would not have fallen into trouble, he would be able to write on any subject he wished, even the rotation of the earth."[48] This remark may be over-stated. Nonetheless, there is no over-stating the point in saying that Galileo's unnecessary alienation of the Jesuits proved to be costly to him.

Galileo was to alienate another person—more important than any of the others—that was to seal his doom. This was Pope Urban VIII. Before ascending to the papal throne, Maffeo Barberini had been Galileo's most ardent admirer. He had written an ode in honor of

---

[47] Galileo, "The Assayer," p. 269.
[48] *Opere*, XVI, 117.

Galileo and, as Pope, gave him a testimonial extolling the virtues "of this great man, whose fame shines in the heavens and goes on earth far and wide." The year after he became Pope, he showered Galileo with gifts and favors.

A Penchant for Alienation

Urban had suggested to Galileo a line of reasoning which would allow him to speak favorably of the Copernican system without at the same time claiming it to be true. The reasoning is logically impeccable and asserts, in effect, that if a given theory is consistent with certain facts, it is possible that a totally different theory, perhaps known only to God, could be consistent with the same facts.[49] In other words, one cannot affirm the antecedent of a hypothetical proposition by affirming the consequent. The fact that the ground is wet can be accounted for by rain or by someone watering the lawn. The same logic applies to contemporary physics for, on a macroscopic level, both Newtonian Physics and Einsteinian Relativity explain physical motion equally well. The Pope's position was eminently orthodox. Robert Grosseteste had provided its epistemological basis in the thirteenth century.

At the close of his *Dialogue*, Galileo had the temerity or the imprudence to put the Pope's words in the mouth of Simplicio, the dunce—modelled after Lodovico delle Colombe—who had been shown up again and again throughout the book as a simpleton whose brain is cobwebbed with Aristotelian cosmology. It was as if Galileo had stuck his tongue out at the Pope in public. The Jesuits whom Galileo had alienated made certain that the Pope was aware of this passage and what it implied.[50] They also advised him that the *Dialogue* was an endorsement of Copernicanism, which, in their opinion, was a doctrine far more dangerous than anything of Luther's or Calvin's.[51]

There were also certain irregularities and deceptions involved in securing the *Imprimatur* for the *Dialogue*. As a result, the Pope discharged one of the men involved, Monsignor Ciampoli, the papal secretary.

---

[49] Quoted in full in Santillana, 1955, pp. 165-66.
[50] Ronan, p. 195.
[51] *Ibid.*, pp. 196-8.

Urban was deeply hurt by Galileo's conduct and regarded it as a personal betrayal. He never forgave him. He opposed Galileo's leaving Arcetri in 1636 to receive treatment for his eye, and even after Galileo's death, Urban balked at allowing his old friend to have a monument erected in his honor.

Human Flaw Caused Bitterness

Urban VIII, like Galileo, was a Florentine. And also like his compatriot, he was outgoing, ambitious, fiery, and impatient of opposition. He had a great deal in common with Galileo even on an intellectual level. As Cardinal Barberini, he once wrote to Galileo, who was sick at the time, and expressed his genuine affection for both the person and the work of that great scientist: "I write because men like you are of great value, deserve to live a long time for the public benefit, and I am also motivated by the particular interest and affection which I have for you and by my constant approbation of you and your work."[52]

But, like Galileo, Urban was not without vanity. When he was informed that certain notables wished to erect a monument in his honor he replied, fully mindful of the fact that this special honor was usually done for Popes only after their deaths: "Let them. I am not an ordinary Pope either." Urban's vanity was a fact well known. One eminent scholar and expert on the Galileo dispute has written of the radical change in conduct that took place when Cardinal Barberini took the name Urban VIII:

> Once in power, his latent pride and vanity were to break forth without restraint, and with them his natural temper, quick to anger and suspicions.[53]

It may very well have been the presence of this human flaw in both Urban and Galileo that accounted for, more than anything else, the bitter disputes, the rancor, the suspicions, the vindictiveness, and the final humiliating showdown in the trial of 1633.

The Inquisition summoned Galileo to Rome in 1632, the same year the *Dialogue* was published. Galileo delayed the meeting because of ill

---

[52] *Opere*, XI, 216.
[53] De Santillana, 1955, p. 161.

health until the following year. He was well treated. He never spent a day of his life in a prison cell, nor was he tortured or ever in fear of being tortured. While the proceedings continued, he and his valet occupied a five room apartment in the Holy Office overlooking the Vatican Gardens, while the Tuscan Ambassador's major domo looked after his food and wine.

It was the intent of the Inquisition to make Galileo recant and to show that not even so illustrious a personage as Galileo could mock the Pope and his theologians with impunity. Galileo, oddly enough, pleaded that his *Dialogue* was actually an attempt to *refute* the Copernican theory, despite the fact that innumerable passages clearly indicated the contrary. Apparently, as some scholars have concluded, Galileo realized the game was up, and lost his nerve.[54]

Finally, he was asked to recite a prepared statement clearing himself from the suspicion of heresy and denouncing the doctrine of the earth's motion. He knelt before the ten Cardinals and recited a text that, presumably, no one believed.

There followed a peaceful period of nearly ten years during which time Galileo wrote his masterpiece, the *Dialogue Concerning Two New Sciences*. This work summed up his life's work on motion, acceleration, and gravity, and furnished the basis for the three laws of motion laid down by Sir Isaac Newton in 1687. Whitehead has made the comment that, "The worst that happened [in that age] to men of science was that Galileo suffered an honorable detention and a mild reproof, before dying peacefully in his bed."[55] Another commentator has made the remark that, "It is probably true that no one had ever been treated so gently."[56]

Intelligent opinion concerning the nature of the dispute between Galileo and the Church has ranged over a wide variety of plausible theories. And the disagreements among scholars who have studied the life and times of Galileo in depth are strong and sharp. Was it a conflict between authority and freedom, or between science and Scripture? Was it fundamentally a tension between the Church and the secularization of society? Was it a clash between science and society, between science and the Church, or between the Church and philosophy? No

---

[54] Koestler, 1964, p. 20.
[55] Whitehead, p. 10.
[56] Ronan, p. 223.

doubt each of these conflicts played its part. At the same time, however, none of them was sufficient in itself to bring the dispute to the unfortunate denouement that history records. Each conflict created its own problem while helping to fuel the mounting controversy. Yet reason could have prevented any one of them from contributing to the *cause célèbre* had vanity and personal ambition not interfered with the exercise of that higher faculty.

A Clash of Souls

Galileo's caustic tongue and acid pen made him many a life-long enemy and even converted supportive colleagues into vindictive foes. The devastating sarcasm with which he frequently ridiculed the arguments and the character of his opponents created more bitterness than they shed light. Concerning his arch-rival, Colombe, Galileo remarked that Aristotle made many blunders, "Though neither so many nor so silly as does this author every time he opens his mouth on the subject."[57] Referring to the "Pigeon-League," he once stated that he had "an idea for an emblem those pedants could put on their shingle: A fireplace with a stuffed flue, and the smoke curling back to fill the house in which are assembled people to whom dark comes before evening."[58] De Santillana avers that Galileo's marginal jottings on his copy of a work by Fr. Grassi were so violent that, "The expletives alone would make a vocabulary of good Tuscan abuse."[59]

The Galileo affair is essentially a human drama played out by a cast of flawed and finite characters. It has the plausible pretext of being a loftier dispute involving science, philosophy, theology, and society. But in the main, it is a clash of souls, some less noble than others. There is a subtle irony to the fact that Galileo and Shakespeare were born in the same year. The world's pre-eminent playwright would have found the Galileo dispute much to his liking, and had he given it a script would doubtlessly have assigned the impersonal ideals a place of secondary significance.

Toward the end of his life, at age seventy-three, Galileo wrote a letter to Elia Diodati, his publishing liaison in France, in which he stated:

---

[57] *Opere*, iii:l, 253-34.
[58] Galileo. 1957, p. 21.
[59] De Santillana. 1955, p. 152.

Alas, your friend and servant Galileo has been for the last month hopelessly blind; so that this heaven, this earth, this universe, which I, by marvelous discoveries and clear demonstrations, have enlarged a hundred thousand times beyond the belief of the wise men of by-gone ages, henceforward for me is shrunk into such small space as is filled by my own bodily sensations . . .[60]

These words are not the ramblings of senescence, they accurately represent the man Galileo. They summarize his long life compressed into a single, brief paragraph. Here is faithfully recorded the friendship, self-pity, pride, boastfulness, exaggeration, scientific genius, and literary elegance. All these things were entwined within the same man. Galileo could never have been simply one thing or another. However extraordinary and powerful his genius, he never allowed it to eclipse his humanness. He was never less than an intricate complexity of powerful and well-developed tendencies. And this explains why the Galileo dispute can never be properly understood in impersonal terms. "One may understand the cosmos, but never the ego; the self is more distant than any star."[61] To no other person in human history could these words of G.K. Chesterton better apply.

Sources: Donald DeMarco. 1986. "The Dispute between Galileo and the Catholic Church." *The Homiletic & Pastoral Review* (3) (May): 23-51. Reprinted with permission from Donald DeMarco.

Donald DeMarco. 1986. "The Dispute between Galileo and the Catholic Church." *The Homiletic & Pastoral Review* (3) (June): 53-59. Reprinted with permission from Donald DeMarco.

Donald DeMarco earned a Ph.D. and M.A. in Philosophy from St. John's University in New York. He is adjunct professor at Holy Apostles College and Seminary in Cromwell, Connecticut, and professor emeritus at St. Jerome's University in Waterloo, Ontario.

---

[60] *Letter to Diodati.* 1637.
[61] G.K. Chesterton. 1957. *Orthodoxy,* p.54. Garden City: Doubleday.

Chapter 7

The Crusades

Many myths, perpetuated by poor popular history, persist regarding the Crusades. The misunderstandings and disinformation die hard due to the anti-Catholicism that exists in many segments of society.

Historian James Hitchcock suggests that the divine and human aspects of the Church are contributing factors.

> The Crusades, perhaps more than any other event in history, manifest the ambiguities and contradictions inherent in religion itself, the fact that what is perfect and eternal must be incarnated among imperfect human beings, subjected to the limitations of a merely temporal perspective.[1]

The Crusades are frequently characterized in terms of Christian brutality, greedy knights, and colonial designs. To be sure, there were instances of outrageous brutality, ignoble crusaders, and shameful behavior. These, unfortunately, have been found in every war ever fought whether in ancient or modern times.

Thomas Madden, Director of Saint Louis University's Center for Medieval and Renaissance Studies, sets the record straight in **"The Real History of the Crusades."** His presentation of the facts and perspective helps us to understand what the Crusades were all about.[2]

---

[1] James Hitchcock. 2002. "The Crusades and Their Critics." *Catholic Dossier* (8): 1 (January-February).

[2] Madden's article deals primarily with the major Crusades against the Muslims powers. However, there were additional Crusades against schismatics and heretics and others in Northeastern Europe as well as against secular powers of the West. A justification of defense was made for all these Crusades. For more

> The Crusades were defensive wars with the goal of defending Christian lands from Muslim attacks or reclaiming lands already taken.
> The expansion of Islam relied primarily on the sword. Previously Christian lands, such as Palestine, Syria, and Egypt, were conquered by Muslims.
> The emperor in Constantinople sent a desperate plea for help to Christians of the West. The First Crusade, called by Pope Urban II in 1095, was in response to this call for help.
> Contrary to popular opinion, the Crusaders were not the dregs of Europe, seeking only to plunder and kill far from home. They were the first sons of Europe who sacrificed greatly to participate in a worthy cause.
> The Crusades were regarded an act of penance, more a pilgrimage than a military campaign. Indeed, the Crusade indulgence was related to the pilgrimage indulgence.
> The twin goals given by Pope Urban II to the Crusaders were to rescue the Christians of the East and liberate Jerusalem and the other holy places.
> The reconquest of Jerusalem was a restoration of lands to Christian hands rather than an exercise in colonialism.
> The Crusades had nothing to do with forced conversions of Muslims. In the thirteenth century, the Franciscans began peaceful and largely unsuccessful attempts to convert them.
> There was brutality as in all wars, but less so than in modern wars.
> Various bands of Crusaders attacked Jews, but the Church strongly condemned these attacks.
> Against all odds, the First Crusade was a success. Nicaea and Antioch were restored to Christian control by 1098. Jerusalem was captured in 1099.
> The First Crusade was the only success in 500 years of efforts to effectively stop the advancement of the Muslim armies.
> The Muslims eventually recaptured the Christian holdings as successive crusades all ended in failure.

---

information on these Crusades, see Jonathan Riley-Smith. 2002. *What Were the Crusades?*, 9-26. 3rd ed. San Francisco: Ignatius Press.

> The Fourth Crusade (1201–1204) led to the brutal sacking of Constantinople, and Pope Innocent III strongly denounced the Crusaders.
> The Muslim kingdoms of the fourteenth, fifteenth, and sixteenth centuries were becoming increasingly powerful, having captured Constantinople and advanced deeply into Europe.
> By the fifteenth century, the Crusades became desperate attempts to save Christendom from extinction.
> Sultan Mehmed II threatened to invade Italy in 1480, leading to the evacuation of Rome. However, when he died, his invasion plans died with him.
> Suleiman the Magnificent laid siege to Vienna in 1529. Unusually bad weather caused him to abandon his efforts.
> Ultimately, Europe's economic advancement "defeated" the Muslim onslaught. As Europe grew in wealth and power, the Turks seemed "backward and pathetic."
> Without the Crusades, Christianity would likely have been driven into extinction.

Further Reading

Thomas F. Madden. 2007. "Crusaders and Historians." *First Things* (154): 26-31 (January).

Jonathan Riley-Smith. 2002. *What Were the Crusades?* 3rd ed. San Francisco: Ignatius Press.

Jonathan Riley-Smith. 2008. *The Crusades, Christianity, and Islam*. New York: Columbia University Press.

The Real History of the Crusades

By Thomas F. Madden

Many historians had been trying for some time to set the record straight on the Crusades—misconceptions are all too common. These historians are not revisionists, but mainstream scholars offering the fruit of several decades of very careful, very serious scholarship. For them, current interest is a ""teaching moment,"" an opportunity to explain the Crusades while people are actually listening. It won't last long, so here goes. With the possible exception of Umberto Eco, medieval scholars are not used to getting much media attention. We tend to be a quiet lot (except during the annual bacchanalia we call the International Congress on Medieval Studies in Kalamazoo, Michigan, of all places), poring over musty chronicles and writing dull yet meticulous studies that few will read. Imagine, then, my surprise when within days of the September 11 attacks, the Middle Ages suddenly became relevant.

As a Crusade historian, I found the tranquil solitude of the ivory tower shattered by journalists, editors, and talk-show hosts on tight deadlines eager to get the real scoop. What were the Crusades?, they asked. When were they? Just how insensitive was President George W. Bush for using the word "crusade" in his remarks? With a few of my callers I had the distinct impression that they already knew the answers to their questions, or at least thought they did. What they really wanted was an expert to say it all back to them. For example, I was frequently asked to comment on the fact that the Islamic world has a just grievance against the West. Doesn't the present violence, they persisted, have its roots in the Crusades' brutal and unprovoked attacks against a sophisticated and tolerant Muslim world? In other words, aren't the Crusades really to blame?

Osama bin Laden certainly thinks so. In his various video performances, he never fails to describe the American war against terrorism as a new Crusade against Islam. Ex-president Bill Clinton has also fingered the Crusades as the root cause of the present conflict. In a speech at Georgetown University, he recounted (and embellished) a massacre of Jews after the Crusader conquest of Jerusalem in 1099 and informed his audience that the episode was still bitterly remembered in the Middle

East. (Why Islamist terrorists should be upset about the killing of Jews was not explained.) Clinton took a beating on the nation's editorial pages for wanting so much to blame the United States that he was willing to reach back to the Middle Ages. Yet no one disputed the ex-president's fundamental premise.

Well, almost no one. Many historians had been trying to set the record straight on the Crusades long before Clinton discovered them. They are not revisionists, like the American historians who manufactured the Enola Gay exhibit, but mainstream scholars offering the fruit of several decades of very careful, very serious scholarship. For them, this is a "teaching moment," an opportunity to explain the Crusades while people are actually listening. It won't last long, so here goes.

Misconceptions about the Crusades are all too common. The Crusades are generally portrayed as a series of holy wars against Islam led by power-mad popes and fought by religious fanatics. They are supposed to have been the epitome of self-righteousness and intolerance, a black stain on the history of the Catholic Church in particular and Western civilization in general. A breed of proto-imperialists, the Crusaders introduced Western aggression to the peaceful Middle East and then deformed the enlightened Muslim culture, leaving it in ruins. For variations on this theme, one need not look far. See, for example, Steven Runciman's famous three-volume epic, *History of the Crusades*, or the BBC/A&E documentary, *The Crusades*, hosted by Terry Jones. Both are terrible history yet wonderfully entertaining.

So what is the truth about the Crusades? Scholars are still working some of that out. But much can already be said with certainty. For starters, the Crusades to the East were in every way defensive wars. They were a direct response to Muslim aggression—an attempt to turn back or defend against Muslim conquests of Christian lands.

Christians in the eleventh century were not paranoid fanatics. Muslims really were gunning for them. While Muslims can be peaceful, Islam was born in war and grew the same way. From the time of Mohammed, the means of Muslim expansion was always the sword. Muslim thought divides the world into two spheres, the Abode of Islam and the Abode of War. Christianity—and for that matter any other non-Muslim religion—has no abode. Christians and Jews can be tolerated within a Muslim state under Muslim rule. But, in traditional Islam, Christian and Jewish states must be destroyed and their lands conquered. When Mohammed was waging war against Mecca in the seventh century, Christianity was the dominant religion of power and wealth. As the faith of the Roman Empire, it spanned the entire Mediterranean, including the Middle East, where it was born. The Christian world, therefore, was a prime target for the earliest caliphs, and it would remain so for Muslim leaders for the next thousand years.

With enormous energy, the warriors of Islam struck out against the Christians shortly after Mohammed's death. They were extremely successful. Palestine, Syria, and Egypt—once the most heavily Christian areas in the world—quickly succumbed. By the eighth century, Muslim armies had conquered all of Christian North Africa and Spain. In the eleventh century, the Seljuk Turks conquered Asia Minor (modern Turkey), which had been Christian since the time of St. Paul. The old Roman Empire, known to modern historians as the Byzantine Empire, was reduced to little more than Greece. In desperation, the emperor in Constantinople sent word to the Christians of western Europe asking them to aid their brothers and sisters in the East.

That is what gave birth to the Crusades. They were not the brainchild of an ambitious pope or rapacious knights but a response to more than four centuries of conquests in which Muslims had already captured two-thirds of the old Christian world. At some point, Christianity as a faith and a culture had to defend itself or be subsumed by Islam. The Crusades were that defense.

Pope Urban II called upon the knights of Christendom to push back the conquests of Islam at the Council of Clermont in 1095. The response was tremendous. Many thousands of warriors took the vow of the cross and prepared for war. Why did they do it? The answer to that question has been badly misunderstood. In the wake of the Enlightenment, it was usually asserted that Crusaders were merely lacklands and ne'er-do-wells who took advantage of an opportunity to rob and pillage in a faraway land. The Crusaders' expressed sentiments of piety, self-sacrifice, and love for God were obviously not to be taken seriously. They were only a front for darker designs.

During the past two decades, computer-assisted charter studies have demolished that contrivance. Scholars have discovered that crusading knights were generally wealthy men with plenty of their own land in Europe. Nevertheless, they willingly gave up everything to undertake the holy mission. Crusading was not cheap. Even wealthy lords could easily impoverish themselves and their families by joining a Crusade. They did so not because they expected material wealth (which many of them had already) but because they hoped to store up treasure where rust and moth could not corrupt. They were keenly aware of their sinfulness and eager to undertake the hardships of the Crusade as a penitential act of charity and love. Europe is littered with thousands of medieval charters attesting to these sentiments, charters in which these men still speak to us today if we will listen. Of course, they were not opposed to capturing booty if it could be had. But the truth is that the Crusades were notoriously bad for plunder. A few people got rich, but the vast majority returned with nothing.

Urban II gave the Crusaders two goals, both of which would remain central to the eastern Crusades for centuries. The first was to rescue the Christians of the East. As his successor, Pope Innocent III, later wrote:

> How does a man love according to divine precept his neighbor as himself when, knowing that his Christian brothers in faith and in name are held by the perfidious Muslims in strict confinement and weighed down by the yoke of heaviest servitude, he does not devote himself to the task of freeing them? . . . Is it by chance that you do not know that many thousands of Christians are bound in slavery and imprisoned by the Muslims, tortured with innumerable torments?

"Crusading," Professor Jonathan Riley-Smith has rightly argued, was understood as an "an act of love"—in this case, the love of one's neighbor. The Crusade was seen as an errand of mercy to right a terrible wrong. As Pope Innocent III wrote to the Knights Templar, "You carry out in deeds the words of the Gospel, 'Greater love than this hath no man, that he lay down his life for his friends.'"

The second goal was the liberation of Jerusalem and the other places made holy by the life of Christ. The word crusade is modern. Medieval Crusaders saw themselves as pilgrims, performing acts of righteousness on their way to the Holy Sepulcher. The Crusade indulgence they received was canonically related to the pilgrimage indulgence. This goal was frequently described in feudal terms. When calling the Fifth Crusade in 1215, Innocent III wrote:

> Consider most dear sons, consider carefully that if any temporal king was thrown out of his domain and perhaps captured, would he

not, when he was restored to his pristine liberty and the time had come for dispensing justice look on his vassals as unfaithful and traitors . . . unless they had committed not only their property but also their persons to the task of freeing him?. . . And similarly will not Jesus Christ, the king of kings and lord of lords, whose servant you cannot deny being, who joined your soul to your body, who redeemed you with the Precious Blood . . . condemn you for the vice of ingratitude and the crime of infidelity if you neglect to help Him?

The reconquest of Jerusalem, therefore, was not colonialism but an act of restoration and an open declaration of one's love of God. Medieval men knew, of course, that God had the power to restore Jerusalem Himself—indeed, He had the power to restore the whole world to His rule. Yet as St. Bernard of Clairvaux preached, His refusal to do so was a blessing to His people:

Again I say, consider the Almighty's goodness and pay heed to His plans of mercy. He puts Himself under obligation to you, or rather feigns to do so, that He can help you to satisfy your obligations toward Himself. . . . I call blessed the generation that can seize an opportunity of such rich indulgence as this.

It is often assumed that the central goal of the Crusades was forced conversion of the Muslim world. Nothing could be further from the truth. From the perspective of medieval Christians, Muslims were the enemies of Christ and His Church. It was the Crusaders' task to defeat and defend against them. That was all. Muslims who lived in Crusader-won territories were generally allowed to retain their property and livelihood, and always their religion. Indeed, throughout the history of the Crusader Kingdom of Jerusalem, Muslim inhabitants far outnumbered the Catholics. It was not until the 13th century that the Franciscans began conversion efforts among Muslims. But these were mostly unsuccessful and finally abandoned. In any case, such efforts were by peaceful persuasion, not the threat of violence.

The Crusades were wars, so it would be a mistake to characterize them as nothing but piety and good intentions. Like all warfare, the violence was brutal (although not as brutal as modern wars). There were mishaps, blunders, and crimes. These are usually well-remembered today. During the early days of the First Crusade in 1095, a ragtag band of Crusaders led by Count Emicho of Leiningen made its way down the Rhine, robbing and murdering all the Jews they could find. Without success, the local bishops attempted to stop the carnage. In the eyes of these warriors, the Jews, like the Muslims, were the enemies of Christ. Plundering and killing them, then, was no vice. Indeed, they believed it was a righteous deed, since the Jews' money could be used to fund the Crusade to Jerusalem. But they were wrong, and the Church strongly condemned the anti-Jewish attacks.

Fifty years later, when the Second Crusade was gearing up, St. Bernard frequently preached that the Jews were not to be persecuted:

> Ask anyone who knows the Sacred Scriptures what he finds foretold of the Jews in the Psalm. "Not for their destruction do I pray," it says. The Jews are for us the living words of Scripture, for they remind us always of what our Lord suffered. . . . Under Christian princes they endure a hard captivity, but "they only wait for the time of their deliverance."

Nevertheless, a fellow Cistercian monk named Radulf stirred up people against the Rhineland Jews, despite numerous letters from Bernard demanding that he stop. At last Bernard was forced to travel to Germany himself, where he caught up with Radulf, sent him back to his convent, and ended the massacres.

It is often said that the roots of the Holocaust can be seen in these medieval pogroms. That may be. But if so, those roots are far deeper and more widespread than the Crusades. Jews perished during the Crusades, but the purpose of the Crusades was not to kill Jews. Quite the contrary: Popes, bishops, and preachers made it clear that the Jews of Europe were to be left unmolested. In a modern war, we call tragic deaths like these "collateral damage." Even with smart technologies, the United States has killed far more innocents in our wars than the Crusaders ever could. But no one would seriously argue that the purpose of American wars is to kill women and children.

By any reckoning, the First Crusade was a long shot. There was no leader, no chain of command, no supply lines, no detailed strategy. It was simply thousands of warriors marching deep into enemy territory, committed to a common cause. Many of them died, either in battle or through disease or starvation. It was a rough campaign, one that seemed always on the brink of disaster. Yet it was miraculously successful. By 1098, the Crusaders had restored Nicaea and Antioch to Christian rule. In July 1099, they conquered Jerusalem and began to build a Christian state in Palestine. The joy in Europe was unbridled. It seemed that the tide of history, which had lifted the Muslims to such heights, was now turning.

But it was not. When we think about the Middle Ages, it is easy to view Europe in light of what it became rather than what it was. The colossus of the medieval world was Islam, not Christendom. The Crusades are interesting largely because they were an attempt to counter that trend. But in five centuries of crusading, it was only the First Crusade that significantly rolled back the military progress of Islam. It was downhill from there.

When the Crusader County of Edessa fell to the Turks and Kurds in 1144, there was an enormous groundswell of support for a new Crusade in Europe. It was led by two kings, Louis VII of France and Conrad III of Germany, and preached by St. Bernard himself. It failed miserably. Most of the Crusaders were killed along the way. Those who made it to Jerusalem only made things worse by attacking Muslim Damascus, which formerly had been a strong ally of the Christians. In the wake of such a disaster, Christians across Europe were forced to accept not only the continued growth of Muslim power but the certainty that God was punishing the West for its sins. Lay piety movements sprouted up throughout Europe, all rooted in the desire to purify Christian society so that it might be worthy of victory in the East.

Crusading in the late twelfth century, therefore, became a total war effort. Every person, no matter how weak or poor, was called to help. Warriors were asked to sacrifice their wealth and, if need be, their lives for the defense of the Christian East. On the home front, all Christians were called to support the Crusades through prayer, fasting, and alms. Yet still the Muslims grew in strength. Saladin, the great unifier, had forged the Muslim Near East into a single entity, all the while preaching jihad against the Christians. In 1187 at the Battle of Hattin, his forces wiped out the combined armies of the Christian Kingdom of Jerusalem and captured the precious relic of the True Cross. Defenseless, the Christian cities began surrendering one by one, culminating in the surrender of Jerusalem on October 2. Only a tiny handful of ports held out.

The response was the Third Crusade. It was led by Emperor Frederick I Barbarossa of the German Empire, King Philip II Augustus of

France, and King Richard I Lionheart of England. By any measure it was a grand affair, although not quite as grand as the Christians had hoped. The aged Frederick drowned while crossing a river on horseback, so his army returned home before reaching the Holy Land. Philip and Richard came by boat, but their incessant bickering only added to an already divisive situation on the ground in Palestine. After recapturing Acre, the king of France went home, where he busied himself carving up Richard's French holdings. The Crusade, therefore, fell into Richard's lap. A skilled warrior, gifted leader, and superb tactician, Richard led the Christian forces to victory after victory, eventually reconquering the entire coast. But Jerusalem was not on the coast, and after two abortive attempts to secure supply lines to the Holy City, Richard at last gave up. Promising to return one day, he struck a truce with Saladin that ensured peace in the region and free access to Jerusalem for unarmed pilgrims. But it was a bitter pill to swallow. The desire to restore Jerusalem to Christian rule and regain the True Cross remained intense throughout Europe.

The Crusades of the 13th century were larger, better funded, and better organized. But they too failed. The Fourth Crusade (1201-1204) ran aground when it was seduced into a web of Byzantine politics, which the Westerners never fully understood. They had made a detour to Constantinople to support an imperial claimant who promised great rewards and support for the Holy Land. Yet once he was on the throne of the Caesars, their benefactor found that he could not pay what he had promised. Thus betrayed by their Greek friends, in 1204 the Crusaders attacked, captured, and brutally sacked Constantinople, the greatest Christian city in the world. Pope Innocent III, who had previously excommunicated the entire Crusade, strongly denounced the Crusaders. But there was little else he could do. The tragic events of 1204 closed an iron door between Roman Catholic and Greek Orthodox, a door that even today Pope John Paul II has been unable to reopen. It is a terrible irony that the Crusades, which were a direct result of the Catholic desire to rescue the Orthodox people, drove the two further—and perhaps irrevocably apart.

The remainder of the 13th century's Crusades did little better. The Fifth Crusade (1217-1221) managed briefly to capture Damietta in Egypt, but the Muslims eventually defeated the army and reoccupied the city. St. Louis IX of France led two Crusades in his life. The first also captured Damietta, but Louis was quickly outwitted by the Egyptians and forced to abandon the city. Although Louis was in the Holy Land for several years, spending freely on defensive works, he never achieved his fondest wish: to free Jerusalem. He was a much older man in 1270 when he led another Crusade to Tunis, where he died of a disease that ravaged the camp. After St. Louis's death, the ruthless Muslim leaders, Baybars and Kalavun, waged a brutal jihad against the Christians in Palestine. By 1291, the Muslim forces had succeeded in killing or ejecting the last of the Crusaders, thus erasing the Crusader kingdom from the map. Despite numerous attempts and many more plans, Christian forces were never again able to gain a foothold in the region until the 19th century.

One might think that three centuries of Christian defeats would have soured Europeans on the idea of Crusade. Not at all. In one sense, they had little alternative. Muslim kingdoms were becoming more, not less, powerful in the 14th, 15th, and 16th centuries. The Ottoman Turks conquered not only their fellow Muslims, thus further unifying Islam, but also continued to press westward, capturing Constantinople and plunging deep into Europe itself. By the 15th century, the Crusades were no longer errands of mercy for a distant people but desperate attempts of one of the last remnants of Christendom to survive. Europeans began to ponder the real possibility that Islam would finally achieve its aim of conquering the entire Christian world. One of the great best-sellers of the time, Sebastian Brant's The Ship of Fools, gave voice to this sentiment in a chapter titled "Of the Decline of the Faith":

> *Our faith was strong in th' Orient,*
> *It ruled in all of Asia,*
> *In Moorish lands and Africa.*
> *But now for us these lands are gone*
> *'Twould even grieve the hardest stone . . . .*
> *Four sisters of our Church you find,*
> *They're of the patriarchic kind:*
> *Constantinople, Alexandria,*
> *Jerusalem, Antiochia.*
> *But they've been forfeited and sacked*
> *And soon the head will be attacked.*

Of course, that is not what happened. But it very nearly did. In 1480, Sultan Mehmed II captured Otranto as a beachhead for his invasion of Italy. Rome was evacuated. Yet the sultan died shortly thereafter, and his plan died with him. In 1529, Suleiman the Magnificent laid siege to Vienna. If not for a run of freak rainstorms that delayed his progress and forced him to leave behind much of his artillery, it is virtually certain that the Turks would have taken the city. Germany, then, would have been at their mercy.

Yet, even while these close shaves were taking place, something else was brewing in Europe—something unprecedented in human history. The Renaissance, born from a strange mixture of Roman values, medieval piety, and a unique respect for commerce and entrepreneurialism, had led to other movements like humanism, the Scientific Revolution, and the Age of Exploration. Even while fighting for its life, Europe was preparing to expand on a global scale. The Protestant Reformation, which rejected the papacy and the doctrine of indulgence, made Crusades unthinkable for many Europeans, thus leaving the fighting to the Catholics. In 1571, a Holy League, which was itself a Crusade, defeated the Ottoman fleet at Lepanto. Yet military victories like that remained rare. The Muslim threat was neutralized economically. As Europe grew in wealth and power, the once awesome and sophisticated Turks began to seem backward and pathetic -- no longer worth a Crusade. The "Sick Man of Europe" limped along until the 20th century, when he finally expired, leaving behind the present mess of the modern Middle East.

From the safe distance of many centuries, it is easy enough to scowl in disgust at the Crusades. Religion, after all, is nothing to fight wars over. But we should be mindful that our medieval ancestors would have been equally disgusted by our infinitely more destructive wars fought in the name of political ideologies. And yet, both the medieval and the modern soldier fight ultimately for their own world and all that makes it up. Both are willing to suffer enormous sacrifice, provided that it is in the service of something they hold dear, something greater than themselves. Whether we admire the Crusaders or not, it is a fact that the world we know today would not exist without their efforts. The ancient faith of Christianity, with its respect for women and antipathy toward slavery, not only survived but flourished. Without the Crusades, it might well have followed Zoroastrianism, another of Islam's rivals, into extinction.

Source: Thomas F. Madden. 2002. "The Real History of the Crusades." *Crisis Magazine* (20): 4 (April). Reprinted with permission from InsideCatholic (www.insidecatholic.com).

Thomas F. Madden is Professor of History and Director of the Center for Medieval and Renaissance Studies at Saint Louis University. Dr. Madden's recent books include the *New Concise History of the Crusades, Empires of Trust,* and the award-winning *Enrico Dandolo and the Rise of Venice.* He has also written and lectured extensively on the ancient and medieval Mediterranean and the history of Christianity and Islam. Awards for his scholarship include the 2005 Otto Grundler Prize, awarded by the Medieval Institute, and the 2007 Haskins Medal, awarded by the Medieval Academy of America.

Chapter 8

The Spanish Inquisition

Catholics have been beating their breasts over the role of the Church in the Spanish Inquisition for a very long time. It conjures up images of torture, injustice, and hypocrisy. We enlightened moderns love to superimpose our values, and our culture for that matter, on societies of antiquity. Unfortunately, this does not help us to truly understand these societies and why they did what they did.

The Spanish Inquisition occurred during a brutal period in history. As Thomas Madden states in "**The Truth about the Spanish Inquisition,**" "This was a time, after all, when damaging shrubs in a public garden in London carried the death penalty." It was also a time characterized by a certain intermingling of Church and civil authorities, making it difficult to sort out who was responsible for the actions of public figures. This was all complicated by the relatively slow pace of communications during that era.

Church officials clearly made mistakes in their attempts to protect society from the corrosive effects of heresy. However, a proper perspective on the role of the Church and the era in which these events took place allows a more balanced understanding.

> The Spanish Inquisition was surely on the mind of Pope John Paul II when he made the Millennium apology for the wrongs of the past. But the real history of the Spanish Inquisition is far from the caricature that most people carry as part of their anti-Catholic cultural baggage. What we allege to know of the Spanish Inquisition is often little more than post-Reformation propaganda.[1]

---

[1] Robert P. Lockwood. 2007. "Secrets of the Spanish Inquisition Revealed." *This Rock* (18) 9 (November).

Thomas Madden does a masterful job as he introduces us to the Inquisition, showing us that much of what is popularly perceived is myth and has little to do with what actually took place hundreds of years ago.

> ➢ The Spanish Inquisition, which began in the late fifteenth century, was preceded by the medieval Inquisition.

> ➢ Religion in medieval times was woven into the fabric of all aspects of society. Heresy, therefore, constituted a grave threat to the fabric of the community. This phenomenon was true for many cultures around the world. Indeed, the notion of religious tolerance is relatively new and uniquely Western.

> ➢ Roman law regarded heresy as treason, because it was a source of unrest and rebellion, a challenge to royal authority.

> ➢ Rather than a tool of oppression, the medieval Inquisition helped bring order, justice, and compassion to an otherwise undisciplined secular persecution of heretics. The secular tribunals were largely conducted by illiterate laymen with little capacity to judge the merits of a case brought against a heretic.

> ➢ Pope Lucius III launched the medieval Inquisition in 1184 with instructions to use knowledgeable churchmen and Roman laws of evidence to try those accused of heresy.

> ➢ Most people whom the medieval Inquisition accused of heresy were found not guilty or given a suspended sentence. However, unrepentant heretics were generally excommunicated and handed over to the secular authorities. The Church did not burn heretics. However, the secular establishment regarded heresy as a capital offense.

> ➢ The medieval Inquisition actually *saved* untold thousands of innocent people from the hands of secular rulers or even from death at the hands of local mobs.

> ➢ The Inquisition, by the fourteenth century, employed the best legal practices of the day and educated specialists in theology and law.

> ➢ By the late Middle Ages, the power of kings had increased considerably. These rulers supported the Inquisition because it helped maintain the stability of their kingdoms. Eventually, the secular rulers took over the oversight of the Inquisitions within their own jurisdictions.

> ➢ The wave of anti-Semitism that had prevailed in most of Europe finally reached Spain in the late fourteenth century, leading to the

forced "conversions" of many Jews. Despite the opposition of the king of Aragon and the well-establish Church teaching of the invalidity of forced conversions, many of the new converts or *conversos* decided to remain Catholic while maintaining their Jewish culture. No doubt, many simply believed that it would be expedient to do so.

➢ Over the years the *conversos* gained wealth and power in Spain, leading to a backlash among Old Christians and conspiracy theories that the *conversos* really intended to destroy the Church.

➢ Although the conspiracy theories had no basis in fact, King Ferdinand and Queen Isabella persuaded Pope Sixtus IV to allow them to set up an Inquisition to investigate the matter of secret Jews within the kingdom. The Spanish Inquisition was under the control of the crown.

➢ The Spanish Inquisition focused on the fidelity of *conversos*. Old Christians and Jews had nothing to fear; many used the tribunals against their enemies. Most accused *conversos* were acquitted—however, not all were, and well-publicized burnings were carried out.

➢ In response to the Inquisition's expansion and abuses, Pope Sixtus IV tried to stop it by putting control in the hands of the bishops. However, King Ferdinand refused to comply, leaving the Spanish Inquisition under the control of the monarchy.

➢ As the Spanish Inquisition grew, opposition within the Church's hierarchy increased. Pope Sixtus' successor, Innocent VIII, wrote to the king twice, pleading for greater leniency for the *conversos*.

➢ Finally, in March 1492, Ferdinand and Isabella expelled all Jews from Spain, fearing they were influencing the *conversos*. The result was a large number of conversions, and consequently many more *conversos* were subjected to the Spanish Inquisition.

➢ In the first fifteen years of the Spanish Inquisition, under the direction of Tomas de Torquemada, about 2,000 *conversos* were burned at the stake. However, his successor, a Franciscan cardinal, introduced important reforms.

➢ After the reforms, the Spanish Inquisition became an exemplary tribunal leading to far fewer executions than any other court in Europe. In its 350 years, the Spanish Inquisition executed about 4,000 people. This compares with the roughly 60,000 victims of the witch-hunts that occurred across the rest of Catholic and Protestant Europe. The Spanish Inquisition prevented the witch-hunts from entering Spain.

> ➤ The prisons of the Inquisition were considered the best in Europe. In keeping with the times, the Spanish Inquisition used torture, but far less often than other courts, and strict limits were enforced.
> ➤ The Spanish Inquisition turned its focus on the Protestant Reformation because the Spanish monarchy was determined to prevent Protestantism from taking hold in Spain.
> ➤ Protestant Europe launched a propaganda campaign against Spain and its Inquisition, perpetuating legends of cruelty in Spain that modern scholarship has dismissed. Ultimately, a fictional Spanish Inquisition was invented by enemies of Spain and the Catholic Church.

Further Reading

James Hitchcock. 1996. "Inquisition." *Catholic Dossier* (2): 6 (November-December), 44-46.

Marvin R. O'Connell. "The Spanish Inquisition: Fact Versus Fiction." Ignatiusinsight.com. www.ignatiusinsight.com/features2005/print2005/moconnell_spaninquis_deco5.html. This article originally appeared in the November/December 1996 issue of *Catholic Dossier*.

The Truth about the Spanish Inquisition

by Thomas F. Madden

Because it was both professional and efficient, the Spanish Inquisition kept very good records. These documents are a goldmine for modern historians who have plunged greedily into them. Thus far, the fruits of that research have made one thing abundantly clear—the myth of the Spanish Inquisition has nothing at all to do with the real thing.

The scene is a plain-looking room with a door to the left. A pleasant young man, pestered by tedious and irrelevant questions, exclaims in a frustrated tone, "I didn't expect a kind of Spanish Inquisition." Suddenly the door bursts open to reveal Cardinal Ximinez flanked by Cardinal Fang and Cardinal Biggles. "Nobody expects the Spanish Inquisition!" Ximinez shouts. "Our chief weapon is surprise . . . surprise and fear . . . fear and surprise. . . . Our two weapons are fear and surprise . . . and ruthless efficiency. . . . Our three weapons are fear, surprise, and ruthless efficiency . . . and an almost fanatical devotion to the pope. . . . Our four . . . no. . . . Amongst our weapons . . . amongst our weaponry . . . are such elements as fear, surprise. . . . I'll come in again."

Anyone not living under a rock for the past 30 years will likely recognize this famous scene from *Monty Python's Flying Circus*. In these sketches three scarlet-clad, inept inquisitors torture their victims with such instruments as pillows and comfy chairs. The whole thing is funny because the audience knows full well that the Spanish Inquisition was neither inept nor comfortable, but ruthless, intolerant, and deadly. One need not have read Edgar Allan Poe's *The Pit and the Pendulum* to have heard of the dark dungeons, sadistic churchmen, and excruciating tortures of the Spanish Inquisition. The rack, the iron maiden, the bonfires on which the Catholic Church dumped its enemies by the millions: These are all familiar icons of the Spanish Inquisition set firmly into our culture.

This image of the Spanish Inquisition is a useful one for those who have little love for the Catholic Church. Anyone wishing to beat the Church about the head and shoulders will not tarry long before grabbing two favorite clubs: the Crusades and the Spanish Inquisition. I have dealt with the Crusades in a previous issue of *Crisis* (see "The Real History of the Crusades," April 2002). Now on to the other club.

In order to understand the Spanish Inquisition, which began in the late 15th century, we must look briefly at its predecessor, the medieval Inquisition. Before we do, though, it's worth pointing out that the medieval world was not the modern world. For medieval people, religion was not something one just did at church. It was their science, their philosophy, their politics, their identity, and their hope for salvation. It was not a personal preference but an abiding and universal truth. Heresy, then, struck at the heart of that truth. It doomed the heretic, endangered those near him, and tore apart the fabric of community. Medieval Europeans were not alone in this view. It was shared by numerous cultures around the world. The modern practice of universal religious toleration is itself quite new and uniquely Western.

Secular and ecclesiastical leaders in medieval Europe approached heresy in different ways. Roman law equated heresy with treason. Why? Because kingship was God-given, thus making heresy an inherent challenge to royal authority. Heretics divided people, causing unrest and rebellion. No Christian doubted that God would punish a community that allowed heresy to take root and spread. Kings and commoners, therefore, had good reason to find and destroy heretics wherever they found them—and they did so with gusto.

One of the most enduring myths of the Inquisition is that it was a tool of oppression imposed on unwilling Europeans by a power-hungry Church. Nothing could be more wrong. In truth, the Inquisition brought order, justice, and compassion to combat rampant secular and popular persecutions of heretics. When the people of a village rounded up a suspected heretic and brought him before the local lord, how was he to be judged? How could an illiterate layman determine if the accused's beliefs were heretical or not? And how were witnesses to be heard and examined?

The medieval Inquisition began in 1184 when Pope Lucius III sent a list of heresies to Europe's bishops and commanded them to take an active role in determining whether those accused of heresy were, in fact, guilty. Rather than relying on secular courts, local lords, or just mobs, bishops were to see to it that accused heretics in their dioceses were examined by knowledgeable churchmen using Roman laws of evidence. In other words, they were to "inquire"—thus, the term "inquisition."

From the perspective of secular authorities, heretics were traitors to God and king and therefore deserved death. From the perspective of the Church, however, heretics were lost sheep that had strayed from the flock. As shepherds, the pope and bishops had a duty to bring those sheep back into the fold, just as the Good Shepherd had commanded them. So, while medieval secular leaders were trying to safeguard their kingdoms, the Church was trying to save souls. The Inquisition provided a means for heretics to escape death and return to the community.

Most people accused of heresy by the medieval Inquisition were either acquitted or their sentence suspended. Those found guilty of grave error were allowed to confess their sin, do penance, and be restored to the Body of Christ. The underlying assumption of the Inquisition was that, like lost sheep, heretics had simply strayed. If, however, an inquisitor determined that a particular sheep had purposely departed out of hostility to the flock, there was nothing more that could be done. Unrepentant or obstinate heretics were excommunicated and given over to the secular authorities. Despite popular myth, the Church did not burn heretics. It was the secular authorities that held heresy to be a capital offense. The simple fact is that the medieval Inquisition *saved* uncounted thousands of innocent (and even not-so-innocent) people who would otherwise have been roasted by secular lords or mob rule.

As the power of medieval popes grew, so too did the extent and sophistication of the Inquisition. The introduction of the Franciscans and Dominicans in the early 13th century provided the papacy with a corps of dedicated religious willing to devote their lives to the salvation of the world. Because their order had been created to debate with heretics and preach the Catholic faith, the Dominicans became especially active in the Inquisition. Following the most progressive law codes of the day, the Church in the 13th century formed inquisitorial tribunals answerable to Rome rather than local bishops. To ensure fairness and uniformity, manuals were written for inquisitorial officials. Bernard Gui, best known today as the fanatical and evil inquisitor in *The Name of the Rose*, wrote a particularly influential manual. There is no reason to believe that Gui was anything like his fictional portrayal.

By the 14th century, the Inquisition represented the best legal practices available. Inquisition officials were university-trained specialists in law and theology. The procedures were similar to those used in secular inquisitions (we call them "inquests" today, but it's the same word).

The power of kings rose dramatically in the late Middle Ages. Secular rulers strongly supported the Inquisition because they saw it as an efficient way to ensure the religious health of their kingdoms. If anything, kings faulted the Inquisition for being too lenient on heretics. As in other areas of ecclesiastical control, secular authorities in the late Middle Ages began to take over the Inquisition, removing it from papal oversight. In France, for example, royal officials assisted by legal scholars at the University of Paris assumed control of the French Inquisition. Kings justified this on the belief that they knew better than the faraway pope how best to deal with heresy in their own kingdoms.

These dynamics would help to form the Spanish Inquisition—but there were others as well. Spain was in many ways quite different from the rest of Europe. Conquered by Muslim jihad in the eighth century, the Iberian peninsula had been a place of near constant warfare. Because borders between Muslim and Christian kingdoms shifted rapidly over the centuries, it was in most rulers' interest to practice a fair degree of tolerance for other religions. The ability of Muslims, Christians, and Jews to live together, called *convivencia* by the Spanish, was a rarity in the Middle Ages. Indeed, Spain was the most diverse and tolerant place in medieval Europe. England expelled all of its Jews in 1290. France did the same in 1306. Yet in Spain Jews thrived at every level of society.

But it was perhaps inevitable that the waves of anti-Semitism that swept across medieval Europe would eventually find their way into Spain. Envy, greed, and gullibility led to rising tensions between Christians and Jews in the 14th century. During the summer of 1391, urban mobs in Barcelona and other towns poured into Jewish quarters, rounded up Jews, and gave them a choice of baptism or death. Most took baptism. The king of Aragon, who had done his best to stop the attacks, later reminded his subjects of well-established Church doctrine on the matter of forced baptisms—they don't count. He decreed that any Jews who accepted baptism to avoid death could return to their religion.

But most of these new converts, or *conversos*, decided to remain Catholic. There were many reasons for this. Some believed that apostasy made them unfit to be Jewish. Others worried that returning to Judaism would leave them vulnerable to future attacks. Still others saw their baptism as a way to avoid the increasing number of restrictions and taxes imposed on Jews. As time passed, the *conversos* settled into their new religion, becoming just as pious as other Catholics. Their children were baptized at birth and raised as Catholics. But they remained in a cultural netherworld. Although Christian, most conversos still spoke, dressed, and ate like Jews. Many continued to live in Jewish quarters so as to be near family members. The presence of *conversos* had the effect of Christianizing Spanish Judaism. This in turn led to a steady stream of voluntary conversions to Catholicism.

In 1414 a debate was held in Tortosa between Christian and Jewish leaders. Pope Benedict XIII himself attended. On the Christian side was the papal physician, Jerónimo de Santa Fe, who had recently converted from Judaism. The debate brought about a wave of new voluntary conversions. In Aragon alone, 3,000 Jews received baptism. All of this caused a good deal of tension between those who remained Jewish and those who became Catholic. Spanish rabbis after 1391 had considered *conversos* to be Jews, since they had been forced into baptism. Yet by 1414, rabbis repeatedly stressed that *conversos* were indeed true Christians since they had voluntarily left Judaism.

By the mid-15th century, a whole new *converso* culture was flowering in Spain—Jewish in ethnicity and culture, but Catholic in religion. *Conversos*, whether new converts themselves or the descendants of converts, took enormous pride in that culture. Some even asserted that they were better than the "Old Christians," since as Jews they were related by blood to Christ Himself. When the *converso* bishop of Burgos, Alonso de Cartagena, prayed the Hail Mary, he would say with pride, "Holy Mary, Mother of God and my blood relative, pray for us sinners. . . ."

The expansion of *converso* wealth and power in Spain led to a backlash, particularly among aristocratic and middle-class Old Christians. They resented the arrogance of the *conversos* and envied their successes. Several tracts were written demonstrating that virtually every noble bloodline in Spain had been infiltrated by *conversos*. Anti-Semitic conspiracy theories abounded. The *conversos*, it was said, were part of an elaborate Jewish plot to take over the Spanish nobility and the Catholic Church, destroying both from within. The *conversos*, according to this logic, were not sincere Christians but secret Jews.

Modern scholarship has definitively shown that, like most conspiracy theories, this one was pure imagination. The vast majority of *conversos* were good Catholics who simply took pride in their Jewish heritage. Surprisingly, many modern authors—indeed, many Jewish authors—have embraced these anti-Semitic fantasies. It is common today to hear that the *conversos* really were secret Jews, struggling to keep their faith hidden under the tyranny of Catholicism. Even the American Heritage Dictionary describes *"converse"* as "a Spanish or Portuguese Jew who converted outwardly to Christianity in the late Middle Ages so as to avoid persecution or expulsion, though often continuing to practice Judaism in secret." This is simply false.

But the constant drumbeat of accusations convinced King Ferdinand and Queen Isabella that the matter of secret Jews should at least be investigated. Responding to their request, Pope Sixtus IV issued a bull on November 1, 1478, allowing the crown to form an inquisitorial tribunal consisting of two or three priests over the age of 40. As was now the custom, the monarchs would have complete authority over the inquisitors and the inquisition. Ferdinand, who had many Jews and *conversos* in his court, was not at first overly enthusiastic about the whole thing. Two years elapsed before he finally appointed two men. Thus began the Spanish Inquisition.

King Ferdinand seems to have believed that the inquiry would turn up little. He was wrong. A tinderbox of resentment and hatred exploded across Spain as the enemies of *conversos*—both Christian and Jewish—came out of the woodwork to denounce them. Score-settling and opportunism were the primary motivators. Nevertheless, the sheer volume of accusations overwhelmed the inquisitors. They asked for and received more assistants, but the larger the Inquisition became, the more accusations it received. At last even Ferdinand was convinced that the problem of secret Jews was real.

In this early stage of the Spanish Inquisition, Old Christians and Jews used the tribunals as a weapon against their *converso* enemies. Since the Inquisition's sole purpose was to investigate *conversos*, the Old Christians had nothing to fear from it. Their fidelity to the Catholic faith was not under investigation (although it was far from pure). As for the Jews, they were immune to the Inquisition. Remember, the purpose of an inquisition was to find and correct the lost sheep of Christ's flock. It had no jurisdiction over other flocks. Those who get their history from Mel Brooks's History of the World, Part I will perhaps be surprised to learn that all of those Jews enduring various tortures in the dungeons of the Spanish Inquisition are nothing more than a product of Brooks's fertile imagination. Spain's Jews had nothing to fear from the Spanish Inquisition.

In the early, rapidly expanding years, there was plenty of abuse and confusion. Most accused *conversos* were acquitted, but not all. Well-publicized burnings—often because of blatantly false testimony—justifiably frightened other *conversos*. Those with enemies often fled town before they could be denounced. Everywhere they looked, the inquisitors found more accusers. As the Inquisition expanded into Aragon, the hysteria levels reached new heights. Pope Sixtus IV attempted to put a stop to it. On April 18, 1482, he wrote to the bishops of Spain:

> In Aragon, Valencia, Mallorca, and Catalonia the Inquisition has for some time been moved not by zeal for the faith and the salvation of souls but by lust for wealth. Many true and faithful Christians, on the testimony of enemies, rivals, slaves, and other lower and even less proper persons, have without any legitimate proof been thrust into secular prisons, tortured and condemned as relapsed heretics, deprived of their goods and property and handed over to the secular arm to be executed, to the peril of souls, setting a pernicious example, and causing disgust to many.

Sixtus ordered the bishops to take a direct role in all future tribunals. They were to ensure that the Church's well-established norms of justice were respected. The accused were to have legal counsel and the right to appeal their case to Rome.

In the Middle Ages, the pope's commands would have been obeyed. But those days were gone. King Ferdinand was outraged when he heard of the letter. He wrote to Sixtus, openly suggesting that the pope had been bribed with converso gold:

> Things have been told me, Holy Father, which, if true, would seem to merit the greatest astonishment.... To these rumors, however, we have given no credence because they seem to be things which would in no way have been conceded by Your Holiness who has a duty to the Inquisition. But if by chance concessions have been made through the persistent and cunning persuasion of the *conversos*, I intend never to let them take effect. Take care therefore not to let the matter go further, and to revoke any concessions and entrust us with the care of this question.

That was the end of the papacy's role in the Spanish Inquisition. It would henceforth be an arm of the Spanish monarchy, separate from ecclesiastical authority. It is odd, then, that the Spanish Inquisition is so often today described as one of the Catholic Church's great sins. The Catholic Church as an institution had almost nothing to do with it.

In 1483 Ferdinand appointed Tomás de Torquemada as inquistor-general for most of Spain. It was Torquemada's job to establish rules of evidence and procedure for the Inquisition as well as to set up branches in major cities. Sixtus confirmed the appointment, hoping that it would bring some order to the situation.

Unfortunately, the problem only snowballed. This was a direct result of the methods employed by the early Spanish Inquisition, which strayed significantly from Church standards. When the inquisitors arrived in a particular area, they would announce an Edict of Grace. This was a 30-day period in which secret Jews could voluntarily come forward, confess their sin, and do penance. This was also a time for others with information about Christians practicing Judaism in secret to make it known to the tribunal. Those found guilty after the 30 days elapsed could be burned at the stake.

For *conversos*, then, the arrival of the Inquisition certainly focused the mind. They generally had plenty of enemies, any one of whom might decide to bear false witness. Or perhaps their cultural practices were sufficient for condemnation? Who knew? Most *conversos*, therefore, either fled or lined up to confess. Those who did neither risked an inquiry in which any kind of hearsay or evidence, no matter how old or suspicious, was acceptable.

Opposition in the hierarchy of the Catholic Church to the Spanish Inquisition only increased. Many churchmen pointed out that it was contrary to all accepted practices for heretics to be burned without instruction in the Faith. If the *conversos* were guilty at all, it was merely of ignorance, not willful heresy. Numerous clergy at the highest levels complained to Ferdinand. Opposition to the Spanish Inquisition also continued in Rome. Sixtus's successor, Innocent VIII, wrote twice to the king asking for greater compassion, mercy, and leniency for the *conversos*—but to no avail.

As the Spanish Inquisition picked up steam, those involved became increasingly convinced that Spain's Jews were actively seducing the *conversos* back into their old faith. It was a silly idea, no more real than the previous conspiracy theories. But Ferdinand and Isabella were influenced by it. Both of the monarchs had Jewish friends and confidants, but they also felt that their duty to their Christian subjects impelled them to remove the danger. Beginning in 1482, they expelled Jews from specific areas where the trouble seemed greatest. Over the next decade, though, they were under increasing pressure to remove the perceived threat. The Spanish Inquisition, it was argued, could never succeed in bringing the *conversos* back into the fold while the Jews undermined its work. Finally, on March 31, 1492, the monarchs issued an edict expelling all Jews from Spain.

Ferdinand and Isabella expected that their edict would result in the conversion of most of the remaining Jews in their kingdom. They were largely correct. Many Jews in high positions, including those in the royal court, accepted baptism immediately. In 1492 the Jewish population of Spain numbered about 80,000. About half were baptized and thereby kept their property and livelihoods. The rest departed, but many of them eventually returned to Spain, where they received baptism and had their property restored. As far as the Spanish Inquisition was concerned, the expulsion of the Jews meant that the caseload of *conversos* was now much greater.

The first 15 years of the Spanish Inquisition, under the direction of Torquemada, were the deadliest. Approximately 2,000 *conversos* were put to the flames. By 1500, however, the hysteria had calmed. Torquemada's successor, the cardinal archbishop of Toledo, Francisco Jiménez de Cisneros, worked hard to reform the Inquisition, removing bad apples and reforming procedures. Each tribunal was given two Dominican inquisitors, a legal adviser, a constable, a prosecutor, and a large number of assistants. With the exception of the two Dominicans, all of these were royal lay officials. The Spanish Inquisition was largely funded by confiscations, but these were not frequent or great. Indeed, even at its peak the Inquisition was always just making ends meet.

After the reforms, the Spanish Inquisition had very few critics. Staffed by well-educated legal professionals, it was one of the most efficient and compassionate judicial bodies in Europe. No major court in Europe executed fewer people than the Spanish Inquisition. This was a time, after all, when damaging shrubs in a public garden in London carried the death penalty. Across Europe, executions were everyday events. But not so with the Spanish Inquisition. In its 350-year lifespan only about 4,000 people were put to the stake. Compare that with the witch-hunts that raged across the rest of Catholic and Protestant

Europe, in which 60,000 people, mostly women, were roasted. Spain was spared this hysteria precisely because the Spanish Inquisition stopped it at the border. When the first accusations of witchcraft surfaced in northern Spain, the Inquisition sent its people to investigate. These trained legal scholars found no believable evidence for witches' Sabbaths, black magic, or baby roasting. It was also noted that those confessing to witchcraft had a curious inability to fly through keyholes. While Europeans were throwing women onto bonfires with abandon, the Spanish Inquisition slammed the door shut on this insanity. (For the record, the Roman Inquisition also kept the witch craze from infecting Italy.)

What about the dark dungeons and torture chambers? The Spanish Inquisition had jails, of course. But they were neither especially dark nor dungeon-like. Indeed, as far as prisons go, they were widely considered to be the best in Europe. There were even instances of criminals in Spain purposely blaspheming so as to be transferred to the Inquisition's prisons. Like all courts in Europe, the Spanish Inquisition used torture. But it did so much less often than other courts. Modern researchers have discovered that the Spanish Inquisition applied torture in only 2 percent of its cases. Each instance of torture was limited to a maximum of 15 minutes. In only 1 percent of the cases was torture applied twice and never for a third time.

The inescapable conclusion is that, by the standards of its time, the Spanish Inquisition was positively enlightened. That was the assessment of most Europeans until 1530. It was then that the Spanish Inquisition turned its attention away from the *conversos* and toward the new Protestant Reformation. The people of Spain and their monarchs were determined that Protestantism would not infiltrate their country as it had Germany and France. The Inquisition's methods did not change. Executions and torture remained rare. But its new target would forever change its image.

By the mid-16th century, Spain was the wealthiest and most powerful country in Europe. King Philip II saw himself and his countrymen as faithful defenders of the Catholic Church. Less wealthy and less powerful were Europe's Protestant areas, including the Netherlands, northern Germany, and England. But they did have a potent new weapon: the printing press. Although the Spanish defeated Protestants on the battlefield, they would lose the propaganda war. These were the years when the famous "Black Legend" of Spain was forged. Innumerable books and pamphlets poured from northern presses accusing the Spanish Empire of inhuman depravity and horrible atrocities in the New World. Opulent Spain was cast as a place of darkness, ignorance, and evil. Although modern scholars have long ago discarded the Black Legend, it still remains very much alive today. Quick: Think of a good conquistador.

Protestant propaganda that took aim at the Spanish Inquisition drew liberally from the Black Legend. But it had other sources as well. From the beginning of the Reformation, Protestants had difficulty explaining the 15-century gap between Christ's institution of His Church and the founding of the Protestant churches. Catholics naturally pointed out this problem, accusing Protestants of having created a new church separate from that of Christ. Protestants countered that their church was the one created by Christ but that it had been forced underground by the Catholic Church. Thus, just as the Roman Empire had persecuted Christians, so its successor, the Roman Catholic Church, continued to persecute them throughout the Middle Ages. Inconveniently, there were no Protestants in the Middle Ages, yet Protestant authors found them anyway in the guise of various medieval heresies. (They were underground, after all.)

In this light, the medieval Inquisition was nothing more than an attempt to crush the hidden, true church. The Spanish Inquisition, still active and extremely efficient at keeping Protestants out of Spain, was for Protestant writers merely the latest version of this persecution. Mix liberally with the Black Legend, and you have everything you need to produce tract after tract about the hideous and cruel Spanish Inquisition. And so they did.

The Spanish people loved their Inquisition. That is why it lasted for so long. It stood guard against error and heresy, protecting the faith of Spain and ensuring the favor of God. But the world was changing. In time, Spain's empire faded away. Wealth and power shifted to the north, in particular to France and England. By the late 17th century, new ideas of religious tolerance were bubbling across the coffeehouses and salons of Europe. Inquisitions, both Catholic and Protestant, withered. The Spanish stubbornly held on to theirs, and for that, they were ridiculed. French philosophers like Voltaire saw in Spain a model of the Middle Ages: weak, barbaric, superstitious. The Spanish Inquisition, already established as a bloodthirsty tool of religious persecution, was derided by Enlightenment thinkers as a brutal weapon of intolerance and ignorance. A new, fictional Spanish Inquisition had been constructed, designed by the enemies of Spain and the Catholic Church.

Because it was both professional and efficient, the Spanish Inquisition kept very good records. Vast archives are filled with them. These documents were kept secret, so there was no reason for scribes to do anything but accurately record every action of the Inquisition. They are a goldmine for modern historians who have plunged greedily into them. Thus far, the fruits of that research have made one thing abundantly clear—the myth of the Spanish Inquisition has nothing at all to do with the real thing.

Source: Thomas F. Madden. 2003. "The Truth about the Spanish Inquisition." *Crisis Magazine*, October. Reprinted with permission from InsideCatholic (www.insidecatholic.com).

Thomas F. Madden is Professor of History and Director of the Center for Medieval and Renaissance Studies at Saint Louis University. Dr. Madden's recent books include the *New Concise History of the Crusades, Empires of Trust,* and the award-winning *Enrico Dandolo and the Rise of Venice.* He has also written and lectured extensively on the ancient and medieval Mediterranean and the history of Christianity and Islam. Awards for his scholarship include the 2005 Otto Grundler Prize, awarded by the Medieval Institute, and the 2007 Haskins Medal, awarded by the Medieval Academy of America.

Chapter 9

The Protestant Reformation

The lack of unity among Christians is a monumental tragedy, a failure that all Christians have a duty to seek to rectify. Indeed, it is a scandal that undermines the efficacy of Christ's redeeming sacrifice for all mankind. Our Lord was clear in his desire for Christian unity and its importance in communicating to the world the Good News of the Gospel.

> I pray not only for them, but also for those who will believe in me through their word, so that they may all be one, as you, Father, are in me and I in you, that they also may be in us, that the world may believe that you sent me. And I have given them the glory you gave me, so that they may be one, as we are one, I in them and you in me, that they may be brought to perfection as one, that the world may know that you sent me, and that you loved them even as you loved me.[1]

The sad truth is that the Reformation was based primarily on misunderstandings and human weaknesses. The blame rests on both sides of the issue, reformers and the Church hierarchy. No objective reading of the facts could conclude that reform of some practices within the Church—as opposed to doctrines—was not needed. Unfortunately, the reformers threw out the proverbial baby with the bathwater. Indeed, Lutheran theologian David Yeago points out that human shortcomings were more instrumental in bringing about the split than serious theological disagreement.

---

[1] John 17: 20-23.

[W]e are no longer able to suppose that the Reformers discovered a radically new version of Christianity for which the old Church could not make room. On the reading I propose, the Reformation schism was brought about instead by contingent human choices in a confused historical context defined less by clear and principled theological argument (though that of course was present) than by a peculiar and distinctively sixteenth-century combination of overheated and ever-escalating polemics, cold-blooded Realpolitik, and fervid apocalyptic dreaming.[2]

In **"The Real Issues of the Reformation,"** James Hitchcock looks at the spirituality of sixteenth-century Europe to help us understand the conditions that made the Reformation possible.

> ➤ Few people at that time really understood the issue of "justification by faith alone," and it was probably not important to most of them.
> ➤ Most people saw the Church as an "oppressively intrusive institution."
> ➤ There was a loss of the "sacramental sense of reality," that is, the material and temporal as avenues to reach the spiritual and eternal.
> ➤ Many members of the hierarchy abused their positions to gain power and wealth.
> ➤ Many believers approached their faith in a ritualistic, mechanistic manner that bordered on superstition.
> ➤ The Church recognized the need for reform by 1500 and addressed it at the Fifth Lateran Council in 1517. However, this was too little too late.
> ➤ Unfortunately, the need for reform and a more profound interior spirituality led to a rejection of the sense of sacrament, the outward sign instituted by Christ to give grace.
> ➤ The Catholic Reformation brought about the needed reforms while preserving the doctrines and legitimate practices.

---

[2] David S. Yeago. 1996. "The Catholic Luther." *First Things* (61): 37-41 (March).

Further Reading

Hilaire Belloc. 1992. *How the Reformation Happened.* Rockford, Illinois: Tan Books.

Geoffrey Saint-Clair. 2001. "Who's Who in the Reformation." *Catholic Dossier* (7): 5 (September-October): 4-12.

The Real Issues of the Reformation

By James Hitchcock

Since the Second Vatican Council, the Reformation has been approached ecumenically, meaning that both Catholics and Protestants recognize legitimate concerns on each side of the sixteenth-century divide. Non-Catholic historians, for example, now commonly use the term Catholic Reformation instead of Counter Reformation, acknowledging that the forces of reform within the Church were not simply a reaction to the Protestant attack.

Ecumenism leads to an approach to the Reformation that is primarily doctrinal, which identifies the key theological issues that divided the Church in the sixteenth century, then expends great effort trying to understand and resolve them.

An informed person, asked what lay at the root of Martin Luther's theology, immediately answers, "Justification by faith alone." Logically, and in Luther's own mind, this is true. But it is questionable to what extent this was the actual driving force of the Reformation. The doctrine of justification is subtle indeed, provoking fierce arguments even among people who ostensibly share the same beliefs (Jesuits and Dominicans, Calvinists and Arminians). It is likely that relatively few people in the sixteenth century really understood the issue, much less was it the crucial question for most of them.

What then was? In broadest terms, the issues seem to have been the sense of the Church as an oppressively intrusive institution and, much more elusive, what might be defined as the loss of the sacramental sense of reality, of the awareness that the spiritual is mediated through the material, the eternal through the temporal.

The Church was intrusive in many ways. Probably the single most effective weapon the Reformers had was popular resentment of ecclesiastical financial exactions and of the bewildering forest of laws that accompanied them. (Part of the money collected from the preaching of the indulgences in Germany secretly went to a powerful archbishop, to pay for an exemption from the rule prohibiting a bishop from holding more than one see at a time.) The higher clergy possessed ostentatious power and wealth, and many orthodox reformers at the time pointed out that it was hard to see the apostolic fishermen in the mighty, often scandalously worldly, prince-bishops. This resentment, like the other reforming impulses of the time, was double-edged, inspiring both genuine reform (Cardinal Ximenz de Cisneros) and naked greed (Henry VIII's seizure of the monasteries).

Perhaps the best way of seeing the medieval Church is by analogy with modern architectural restoration. In 1500, the Church was a huge and complex structure with innumerable wings added over the centuries. Reformers, many of them quite orthodox, objected that behind all this it was difficult to discern the holy simplicity of the original Church.

Medieval piety was embodied in an extraordinarily comprehensive and effective system that penetrated every corner of human existence, providing religious meaning for every situation in life, from politics to illness and everything between. But thoughtful believers also wondered if their faith had not become much too formalistic, encouraging almost mechanical attitudes which bordered on, and sometimes crossed into, superstition; which encouraged people to believe that they could put themselves right with God simply by performing certain prescribed acts, without much concern for personal conversion.

Numerous late medieval reformers urged a simpler, more internalized approach to faith. As time went on, some such movements (Thomas à Kempis movement, for example) proved thoroughly Catholic; others metamorphosed into Protestantism. Still others (such as that of Erasmus of Rotterdam) remained ambiguous. By 1500, all thoughtful people understood that there was a need to reform, something which the Fifth Lateran Council of 1517 addressed too little and too late.

But the call for a greater interiority also revealed the second, only half-conscious issue of the day—the loss of the sacramental sense, the unease, often the overt hostility, to all outward manifestations of religion, the growing tendency to regard faith as a wholly interior and spiritual thing. At one end was the kind of piety that reveled in the complex network of rituals, images, indulgences, and relics, while at the other end were the spiritualist impulses that would end in movements like Quakerism. The Reformers fell somewhere in between, Luther close to the Catholic sense in some ways, Ulrich Zwingli the first Puritan. (To understand the Reformation it is more important to understand Zwinglian iconoclasm than Lutheran doctrine.)

History shows that orderly change is very difficult to achieve, and the tragedy of the sixteenth century was that valid, indeed imperative, calls for deeper interiorization of religion sometimes led to the wholesale rejection of the sacramental sense itself, epitomized in Zwingli's denial of the Real Presence, on the grounds that the infinite God could not be present in the finite elements of the Eucharist.

The Catholic Reformation, on the one hand, unflinchingly reaffirmed all disputed doctrines and practices. But tacitly it also accepted the legitimacy of some of the reformist criticisms. Attempts were made to counter popular superstitions through catechizing. Serious efforts were made to reform the structures of the Church so that it could be seen primarily as a spiritual entity. Above all, as in the work of St. Ignatius Loyola and the great Spanish mystics, it responded to that thirst for genuine interiority that has been characteristic of believers in every age.

Source: James Hitchcock. 2001. "The Real Issues of the Reformation." *Catholic Dossier* (7): 5 (September-October), 40-41. Reprinted with permission from James Hitchcock.

James Hitchcock earned a Ph.D. from Princeton University. He is a widely published author on many topics and Professor of History at St. Louis University. His books include *The Supreme Court and Religion in American Life*, two volumes (Princeton University Press, 2004); *The Recovery of the Sacred* (Ignatius Press, 1995); *Years of Crisis: Collected Essays, 1970-1983* (Ignatius Press, 1985); and *The Pope and the Jesuits: John Paul II and the New Order in the Society of Jesus* (National Committee of Catholic Laymen, 1984).

Chapter 10

Pope Pius XII and the Holocaust

The Holocaust will certainly be remembered as the most horrific event of the twentieth century. It is one of the primary examples cited of man's inhumanity to man. The reasons that the Holocaust occurred are many; they include hatred, anti-Semitism, and fear. While both Catholics and Protestants participated in the persecution of the Jews, many Christians—Catholics and Protestants—risked their lives to save Jews. Many Christians found themselves victims of the Nazis and perished in death camps.

After the war, Pope Pius XII was hailed as a hero for his role in saving thousands of Jews from certain death. Indeed, Israel's Foreign Minister, Golda Meir (later Prime Minister of Israel), telegraphed this message to the Vatican upon his death in 1958:

> When fearful martyrdom came to our people in the decade of Nazi terror, the voice of the Pope was raised for the victims. The life of our times was enriched by a voice speaking out on the great moral truths above the tumult of daily conflict. We mourn a great servant of peace.[1]

Yet, attempts have been made to rewrite history over the past forty years or to effectively smear the reputation of Pius XII. The numerous motives for these attempts include anti-Catholic sentiments held by disgruntled former Catholics and others.

---

[1] The source of this quote is Sir Martin Gilbert, *Hitler's Pope?*, a book review of David Dalin's "The Myth of Hitler's Pope: How Pope Pius XII Rescued Jews From the Nazis," *American Spectator,* July/August 2006. Sir Martin Gilbert, regarded by many as one of the world's leading authorities on World War II, is Winston Churchill's official biographer and the author of ten books on the Holocaust. This quote may also be found in many sources on the Internet.

In his article, **"Pius XII and the Jews: A Defense,"** David Dalin, a Jewish rabbi and an historian, presents a compelling defense.

> Despite the accusations of "silence" on the part of Pope Pius XII during the Holocaust, many Jewish leaders publicly thanked him for his efforts in saving many Jews.

> Although the Catholic Church may have missed opportunities to influence events, it is wrong to make Pius XII a target of moral outrage.

> Disaffected Catholics are using the Holocaust as a "club" against Catholic traditionalists.

> Several Jewish scholars have defended Pius XII in response to attacks in the past several years.

> The best historical evidence indicates that Pius XII was not silent about the Holocaust, and almost no one at the time thought he was.

> As Vatican secretary of state, Pius XII controlled Vatican Radio, which made pleas for prayers for the Jews being persecuted in Germany after the 1935 Nuremburg Legislation.

> *The New York Times* greeted his first encyclical, *Summi Pontificatus*, with the headline on October 28, 1939, "Pope Condemns Dictators, Treaty Violators, Racism."

> When Pius XII protested the deportation of Jews from France, *The New York Times* reported "Pope Is Said to Plead for Jews Listed for Removal from France."

> In retaliation, the Nazi government distributed a pamphlet calling Pius XII the "pro-Jewish pope."

> The Nazis criticized the Pope's 1942 Christmas message for standing up for the Jews.

> In October 1943, Pius XII instructed churches and convents in Italy to shelter Jews.

> Fascist documents published in 1998 revealed that the Nazis planned to seize St. Peter's basilica and massacre Pius XII and others in 1944.

> One scholar concluded in 1983, "[T]he picture that emerges is one of a group of intelligent and conscientious men, seeking to pursue the paths of peace and justice, at a time when these ideals were ruthlessly being rendered irrelevant in a world of 'total war.'"

Further Reading

Pierre Blett, S.J. 1999. *Pius XII and the Second World War: According to the Archives of the Vatican.* New York, New York, and Mahwah, New Jersey: Paulist Press.

Ralph McInerny. 2001. *The Defamation of Pius XII.* South Bend, Indiana: St. Augustine's Press.

Ronald J. Rychlak. 1998. "The Holy See vs. The Third Reich: Why Pope Pius XII Was Right." *New Oxford Review LXV* (9) (October).

Pius XII and the Jews: A Defense

By David G. Dalin

Even before Pius XII died in 1958, the charge that his papacy had been friendly to the Nazis was circulating in Europe, a piece of standard Communist agitprop against the West.

It sank for a few years under the flood of tributes, from Jews and gentiles alike, that followed the pope's death, only to bubble up again with the 1963 debut of *The Deputy*, a play by a left-wing German writer (and former member of the Hitler Youth) named Rolf Hochhuth.

The Deputy was fictional and highly polemical, claiming that Pius XII's concern for Vatican finances left him indifferent to the destruction of European Jewry. But Hochhuth's seven-hour play nonetheless received considerable notice, sparking a controversy that lasted through the 1960s. And now, more than thirty years later, that controversy has suddenly broken out again, for reasons not immediately clear.

Indeed, "broken out" doesn't describe the current torrent. In the last eighteen months, nine books that treat Pius XII have appeared: John Cornwell's *Hitler's Pope*, Pierre Blet's *Pius XII and the Second World War*, Garry Wills's *Papal Sin*, Margherita Marchione's *Pope Pius XII*, Ronald J. Rychlak's *Hitler, the War and the Pope*, Michael Phayer's *The Catholic Church and the Holocaust, 1930-1965*, Susan Zuccotti's *Under His Very Windows*, Ralph McInerny's *The Defamation of Pius XII*, and, most recently, James Carroll's *Constantine's Sword*.

Since four of these—the ones by Blet, Marchione, Rychlak, and McInerny—are defenses of the pope (and two, the books by Wills and Carroll, take up Pius only as part of a broad attack against Catholicism), the picture may look balanced. In fact, to read all nine is to conclude that Pius's defenders have the stronger case—with Rychlak's *Hitler, the War* and the Pope the best and most careful of the recent works, an elegant tome of serious, critical scholarship.

Still, it is the books vilifying the pope that have received most of the attention, particularly *Hitler's Pope*, a widely reviewed volume marketed with the announcement that Pius XII was "the most dangerous churchman in modern history," without whom "Hitler might never have . . . been able to press forward." The "silence" of the pope is becoming more and more firmly established as settled opinion in the

American media: "Pius XII's elevation of Catholic self-interest over Catholic conscience was the lowest point in modern Catholic history," the *New York Times* remarked, almost in passing, in a review last month of Carroll's *Constantine's Sword*.

Curiously, nearly everyone pressing this line today—from the ex-seminarians John Cornwell and Garry Wills to the ex-priest James Carroll—is a lapsed or angry Catholic. For Jewish leaders of a previous generation, the campaign against Pius XII would have been a source of shock. During and after the war, many well-known Jews—Albert Einstein, Golda Meir, Moshe Sharett, Rabbi Isaac Herzog, and innumerable others—publicly expressed their gratitude to Pius. In his 1967 book *Three Popes and the Jews,* the diplomat Pinchas Lapide (who served as Israeli consul in Milan and interviewed Italian Holocaust survivors) declared Pius XII "was instrumental in saving at least 700,000, but probably as many as 860,000 Jews from certain death at Nazi hands."

This is not to say that Eugenio Pacelli—the powerful churchman who served as nuncio in Bavaria and Germany from 1917 to 1929, then as Vatican secretary of state from 1930 to 1939, before becoming Pope Pius XII six months before World War II began—was as much a friend to the Jews as John Paul II has been. Nor is it to say that Pius was ultimately successful as a defender of Jews. Despite his desperate efforts to maintain peace, the war came, and, despite his protests against German atrocities, the slaughter of the Holocaust occurred. Even without benefit of hindsight, a careful study reveals that the Catholic Church missed opportunities to influence events, failed to credit fully the Nazis' intentions, and was infected in some of its members with a casual anti-Semitism that would countenance—and, in a few horrifying instances, affirm—the Nazi ideology.

But to make Pius XII a target of our moral outrage against the Nazis, and to count Catholicism among the institutions delegitimized by the horror of the Holocaust, reveals a failure of historical understanding. Almost none of the recent books about Pius XII and the Holocaust is actually about Pius XII and the Holocaust. Their real topic proves to be an intra-Catholic argument about the direction of the Church today, with the Holocaust simply the biggest club available for liberal Catholics to use against traditionalists.

A theological debate about the future of the papacy is obviously something in which non-Catholics should not involve themselves too deeply. But Jews, whatever their feelings about the Catholic Church, have a duty to reject any attempt to usurp the Holocaust and use it for partisan purposes in such a debate—particularly when the attempt disparages the testimony of Holocaust survivors and spreads to inappropriate figures the condemnation that belongs to Hitler and the Nazis.

The technique for recent attacks on Pius XII is simple. It requires only that favorable evidence be read in the worst light and treated to the strictest test, while unfavorable evidence is read in the best light and treated to no test.

So, for instance, when Cornwell sets out in *Hitler's Pope* to prove Pius an anti-Semite (an accusation even the pontiff's bitterest opponents have rarely leveled), he makes much of Pacelli's reference in a 1917 letter to the "Jewish cult"—as though for an Italian Catholic prelate born in 1876 the word "cult" had the same resonances it has in English today, and as though Cornwell himself does not casually refer to the Catholic cult of the Assumption and the cult of the Virgin Mary. (The most immediately helpful part of *Hitler, the War and the Pope* may be the thirty-page epilogue Rychlak devotes to demolishing this kind of argument in *Hitler's Pope.*)

The same pattern is played out in Susan Zuccotti's *Under His Very Windows.* For example: There exists testimony from a Good Samaritan priest that Bishop Giuseppe Nicolini of Assisi, holding a letter in his hand, declared that the pope had written to request help for Jews during the German roundup of Italian Jews in 1943. But because the priest did not actually read the letter, Zuccotti speculates that the bishop may have been deceiving him—and thus that this testimony should be rejected.

Compare this skeptical approach to evidence with her treatment, for example, of a 1967 interview in which the German diplomat Eitel F. Mollhausen said he had sent information to the Nazis' ambassador to the Vatican, Ernst von Weizsäcker, and "assumed" that Weizsäcker passed it on to Church "officials." Zuccotti takes this as unquestionable proof that the pope had direct foreknowledge of the German roundup. (A fair reading suggests Pius had heard rumors and raised them with the Nazi occupiers. Princess Enza Pignatelli Aragona reported that when she broke in on the pope with the news of the roundup early on the morning of October 16, 1943, his first words were: "But the Germans had promised not to touch the Jews!")

With this dual standard, recent writers have little trouble arriving at two pre-ordained conclusions. The first is that the Catholic Church must shoulder the blame for the Holocaust: "Pius XII was the most guilty," as Zuccotti puts it. And the second is that Catholicism's guilt is due to aspects of the Church that John Paul II now represents.

Indeed, in the concluding chapter of *Hitler's Pope* and throughout *Papal Sin* and *Constantine's Sword,* the parallel comes clear: John Paul's traditionalism is of a piece with Pius's alleged anti-Semitism; the Vatican's current stand on papal authority is in a direct line with complicity in the Nazis' extermination of the Jews. Faced with such monstrous moral equivalence and misuse of the Holocaust, how can we not object?

It is true that during the controversy over *The Deputy* and again during the Vatican's slow hearing of the case for his canonization (ongoing since 1965), Pius had Jewish detractors. In 1964, for example, Guenter Lewy produced *The Catholic Church and Nazi Germany,* and, in 1966, Saul Friedländer added *Pius XII and the Third Reich.* Both volumes claimed that Pius's anti-communism led him to support Hitler as a bulwark against the Russians.

As accurate information on Soviet atrocities has mounted since 1989, an obsession with Stalinism seems less foolish than it may have in the mid-1960s. But, in fact, the evidence has mounted as well that Pius accurately ranked the threats. In 1942, for example, he told a visitor, "The Communist danger does exist, but at this time the Nazi danger is more serious." He intervened with the American bishops to support lend-lease for the Soviets, and he explicitly refused to bless the Nazi invasion of Russia. (The charge of overheated anti-communism is nonetheless still alive: In *Constantine's Sword,* James Carroll attacks the 1933 concordat Hitler signed for Germany by asking, "Is it conceivable that Pacelli would have negotiated any such agreement with the Bolsheviks in Moscow?"—apparently not realizing that in the mid-1920s, Pacelli tried exactly that.)

In any case, Pius had his Jewish defenders as well. In addition to Lapide's *Three Popes and the Jews,* one might list *A Question of Judgment,* the 1963 pamphlet from the Anti-Defamation League's Joseph Lichten, and the excoriating reviews of Friedländer by Livia Rotkirchen, the historian of Slovakian Jewry at Yad Vashem. Jeno Levai, the great Hungarian historian, was so angered by accusations of papal silence that he wrote *Pius XII Was Not Silent* (published in English in 1968), with a powerful introduction by Robert M.W. Kempner, deputy chief U.S. prosecutor at Nuremberg.

In response to the new attacks on Pius, several Jewish scholars have spoken out over the last year. Sir Martin Gilbert told an interviewer that Pius deserves not blame but thanks. Michael Tagliacozzo, the leading authority on Roman Jews during the Holocaust, added, "I have a folder on my table in Israel entitled 'Calumnies Against Pius XII.' . . .Without him, many of our own would not be alive." Richard Breitman (the only historian authorized to study U.S. espionage files from World War II) noted that secret documents prove the extent to which "Hitler distrusted the Holy See because it hid Jews."

Still, Lapide's 1967 book remains the most influential work by a Jew on the topic, and in the thirty-four years since he wrote, much material has become available in the Vatican's archives and elsewhere. New oral-history centers have gathered an impressive body of interviews with Holocaust survivors, military chaplains, and Catholic civilians. Given the recent attacks, the time has come for a new defense of Pius—because, despite allegations to the contrary, the best historical evidence now confirms both that Pius XII was not silent and that almost no one at the time thought him so.

In January 1940, for instance, the pope issued instructions for Vatican Radio to reveal "the dreadful cruelties of uncivilized tyranny" the Nazis were inflicting on Jewish and Catholic Poles. Reporting the broadcast the following week, the Jewish Advocate of Boston praised it for what it was: an "outspoken denunciation of German atrocities in Nazi Poland, declaring they affronted the moral conscience of mankind." The *New York Times* editorialized: "Now the Vatican has spoken, with authority that cannot be questioned, and has confirmed the worst intimations of terror which have come out of the Polish darkness." In England, the Manchester Guardian hailed Vatican Radio as "tortured Poland's most powerful advocate."

Any fair and thorough reading of the evidence demonstrates that Pius XII was a persistent critic of Nazism. Consider just a few highlights of his opposition before the war:

Of the forty-four speeches Pacelli gave in Germany as papal nuncio between 1917 and 1929, forty denounced some aspect of the emerging Nazi ideology.

In March 1935, he wrote an open letter to the bishop of Cologne calling the Nazis "false prophets with the pride of Lucifer."

That same year, he assailed ideologies "possessed by the superstition of race and blood" to an enormous crowd of pilgrims at Lourdes. At Notre Dame in Paris two years later, he named Germany "that noble and powerful nation whom bad shepherds would lead astray into an ideology of race."

The Nazis were "diabolical," he told friends privately. Hitler "is completely obsessed," he said to his long-time secretary, Sister Pascalina. "All that is not of use to him, he destroys; . . . this man is capable of trampling on corpses." Meeting in 1935 with the heroic anti-Nazi Dietrich von Hildebrand, he declared, "There can be no possible reconciliation" between Christianity and Nazi racism; they were like "fire and water."

The year after Pacelli became secretary of state in 1930, Vatican Radio was established, essentially under his control. The Vatican newspaper *L'Osservatore Romano* had an uneven record, though it would improve as Pacelli gradually took charge (extensively reporting Kristallnacht in 1938, for example). But the radio station was always good—making such controversial broadcasts as the request that listeners pray for the persecuted Jews in Germany after the 1935 Nuremberg Legislation.

It was while Pacelli was his predecessor's chief adviser that Pius XI made the famous statement to a group of Belgian pilgrims in 1938 that "anti-Semitism is inadmissible; spiritually we are all Semites." And it was Pacelli who drafted Pius XI's encyclical *Mit Brennender Sorge,* "With Burning Concern," a condemnation of Germany among the harshest ever issued by the Holy See. Indeed, throughout the 1930s, Pacelli was widely lampooned in the Nazi press as Pius XI's "Jew-loving" cardinal, because of the more than fifty-five protests he sent the Germans as the Vatican secretary of state.

To these must be added highlights of Pius XII's actions during the war:

His first encyclical, *Summi Pontificatus,* rushed out in 1939 to beg for peace, was in part a declaration that the proper role of the papacy was to plead to both warring sides rather than to blame one. But it very pointedly quoted St. Paul—"there is neither Gentile nor Jew"—using the word "Jew" specifically in the context of rejecting racial ideology. The *New York Times* greeted the encyclical with a front-page headline on October 28, 1939: "Pope Condemns Dictators, Treaty Violators,

Racism." Allied airplanes dropped thousands of copies on Germany in an effort to raise anti-Nazi sentiment.

In 1939 and 1940, Pius acted as a secret intermediary between the German plotters against Hitler and the British. He would similarly risk warning the Allies about the impending German invasions of Holland, Belgium, and France.

In March 1940, Pius granted an audience to Joachim von Ribbentrop, the German foreign minister and the only high-ranking Nazi to bother visiting the Vatican. The Germans' understanding of Pius's position, at least, was clear: Ribbentrop chastised the pope for siding with the Allies. Whereupon Pius began reading from a long list of German atrocities. "In the burning words he spoke to Herr Ribbentrop," the *New York Times* reported on March 14, Pius "came to the defense of Jews in Germany and Poland."

When French bishops issued pastoral letters in 1942 attacking deportations, Pius sent his nuncio to protest to the Vichy government against "the inhuman arrests and deportations of Jews from the French-occupied zone to Silesia and parts of Russia." Vatican Radio commented on the bishops' letters six days in a row—at a time when listening to Vatican Radio was a crime in Germany and Poland for which some were put to death. ("Pope Is Said to Plead for Jews Listed for Removal from France," the *New York Times* headline read on August 6, 1942. "Vichy Seizes Jews; Pope Pius Ignored," the *Times* reported three weeks later.) In retaliation, in the fall of 1942, Goebbels's office distributed ten million copies of a pamphlet naming Pius XII as the "pro-Jewish pope" and explicitly citing his interventions in France.

In the summer of 1944, after the liberation of Rome but before the war's end, Pius told a group of Roman Jews who had come to thank him for his protection: "For centuries, Jews have been unjustly treated and despised. It is time they were treated with justice and humanity, God wills it and the Church wills it. St. Paul tells us that the Jews are our brothers. They should also be welcomed as friends."

As these and hundreds of other examples are disparaged, one by one, in recent books attacking Pius XII, the reader loses sight of the huge bulk of them, their cumulative effect that left no one, the Nazis least of all, in doubt about the pope's position.

A deeper examination reveals the consistent pattern. Writers like Cornwell and Zuccotti see the pope's 1941 Christmas address, for example, as notable primarily for its failure to use the language we would use today. But contemporary observers thought it quite explicit. In its editorial the following day, the *New York Times* declared, "The voice of Pius XII is a lonely voice in the silence and darkness enveloping Europe this Christmas. . . . In calling for a 'real new order' based on 'liberty, justice, and love,' . . . the pope put himself squarely against Hitlerism."

So, too, the pope's Christmas message the following year—in which he expressed his concern "for those hundreds of thousands who, without any fault of their own, sometimes only by reason of their nationality or race, are marked down for death or progressive extinction"—was widely understood to be a public condemnation of the Nazi extermination of the Jews. Indeed, the Germans themselves saw it as such: "His speech is one long attack on everything we stand for. . . . He is clearly speaking on behalf of the Jews. . . . He is virtually accusing the German people of injustice toward the Jews, and makes himself the mouthpiece of the Jewish war criminals," an internal Nazi analysis reads.

This Nazi awareness, moreover, had potentially dire consequences. There were ample precedents for the pope to fear an invasion: Napoleon had besieged the Vatican in 1809, capturing Pius VII at bayonet point; Pius IX fled Rome for his life after the assassination of his chancellor; and Leo XIII was driven into temporary exile in the late nineteenth century.

Still, Pius XII was "ready to let himself be deported to a concentration camp, rather than do anything against his conscience," Mussolini's foreign minister railed. Hitler spoke openly of entering the Vatican to "pack up that whole whoring rabble," and Pius knew of the various Nazi plans to kidnap him. Ernst von Weizsäcker has written that he regularly warned Vatican officials against provoking Berlin. The Nazi ambassador to Italy, Rudolf Rahn, similarly describes one of Hitler's kidnapping plots and the effort by German diplomats to prevent it. General Carlo Wolff testified to having received orders from Hitler in 1943 to "occupy as soon as possible the Vatican and Vatican City, secure the archives and the art treasures, which have a unique value, and transfer the pope, together with the Curia, for their protection, so that they cannot fall into the hands of the Allies and exert a political influence." Early in December 1943, Wolff managed to talk Hitler out of the plan.

In assessing what actions Pius XII might have taken, many (I among them) wish that explicit excommunications had been announced. The Catholic-born Nazis had already incurred automatic excommunication, for everything from failure to attend Mass to unconfessed murder to public repudiation of Christianity. And, as his writings and table-talk make clear, Hitler had ceased to consider himself a Catholic—indeed, considered himself an anti-Catholic—long before he came to power. But a papal declaration of excommunication might have done some good.

Then again, it might not. Don Luigi Sturzo, founder of the Christian Democratic movement in wartime Italy, pointed out that the last times "a nominal excommunication was pronounced against a head of state," neither Queen Elizabeth I nor Napoleon had changed policy. And there is reason to believe provocation would, as Margherita Marchione puts it, "have resulted in violent retaliation, the loss of many more Jewish lives, especially those then under the protection of the Church, and an intensification of the persecution of Catholics."

Holocaust survivors such as Marcus Melchior, the chief rabbi of Denmark, argued that "if the pope had spoken out, Hitler would probably have massacred more than six million Jews and perhaps ten times ten million Catholics, if he had the power to do so." Robert M.W. Kempner called upon his experience at the Nuremberg trials to say (in a letter to the editor after *Commentary* published an excerpt from Guenter Lewy in 1964), "Every propaganda move of the Catholic Church against Hitler's Reich would have been not only 'provoking suicide,' . . . but would have hastened the execution of still more Jews and priests."

This is hardly a speculative concern. A Dutch bishops' pastoral letter condemning "the unmerciful and unjust treatment meted out to Jews" was read in Holland's Catholic churches in July 1942. The well-intentioned letter—which declared that it was inspired by Pius XII—backfired. As Pinchas Lapide notes: "The saddest and most thought-provoking conclusion is that whilst the Catholic clergy in Holland protested more loudly, expressly, and frequently against Jewish persecutions than the religious hierarchy of any other Nazi-occupied country, more Jews—some 110,000 or 79 percent of the total—were deported from Holland to death camps."

Bishop Jean Bernard of Luxembourg, an inmate of Dachau from 1941 to 1942, notified the Vatican that "whenever protests were made, treatment of prisoners worsened immediately." Late in 1942, Archbishop Sapieha of Cracow and two other Polish bishops, having experienced the Nazis' savage reprisals, begged Pius not to publish his letters about conditions in Poland. Even Susan Zuccotti admits that in the case of the Roman Jews the pope "might well have been influenced by a concern for Jews in hiding and for their Catholic protectors."

One might ask, of course, what could have been worse than the mass murder of six million Jews? The answer is the slaughter of hundreds of thousands more. And it was toward saving those it could that the Vatican worked. The fate of Italian Jews has become a major topic of Pius's critics, the failure of Catholicism at its home supposedly demonstrating the hypocrisy of any modern papal claim to moral authority. (Notice, for example, Zuccotti's title: Under His Very Windows.) But the fact remains that while approximately 80 percent of European Jews perished during World War II, 80 percent of Italian Jews were saved.

In the months Rome was under German occupation, Pius XII instructed Italy's clergy to save lives by all means. (A neglected source for Pius's actions during this time is the 1965 memoir *But for the Grace of God*, by Monsignor J. Patrick Carroll-Abbing, who worked under Pius as a rescuer.) Beginning in October 1943, Pius asked churches and convents throughout Italy to shelter Jews. As a result—and despite the fact that Mussolini and the Fascists yielded to Hitler's demand for deportations—many Italian Catholics defied the German orders.

In Rome, 155 convents and monasteries sheltered some five thousand Jews. At least three thousand found refuge at the pope's summer residence at Castel Gandolfo. Sixty Jews lived for nine months at the Gregorian University, and many were sheltered in the cellar of the Pontifical Biblical Institute. Hundreds found sanctuary within the Vatican itself. Following Pius's instructions, individual Italian priests, monks, nuns, cardinals, and bishops were instrumental in preserving thousands of Jewish lives. Cardinal Boetto of Genoa saved at least eight hundred. The bishop of Assisi hid three hundred Jews for over two years. The bishop of Campagna and two of his relatives saved 961 more in Fiume.

Cardinal Pietro Palazzini, then assistant vice rector of the Seminario Romano, hid Michael Tagliacozzo and other Italian Jews at the seminary (which was Vatican property) for several months in 1943 and 1944. In 1985, Yad Vashem, Israel's Holocaust Memorial, honored the cardinal as a righteous gentile—and, in accepting the honor, Palazzini stressed that "the merit is entirely Pius XII's, who ordered us to do whatever we could to save the Jews from persecution." Some of the laity helped as well, and, in their testimony afterwards, consistently attributed their inspiration to the pope.

Again, the most eloquent testimony is the Nazis' own. Fascist documents published in 1998 (and summarized in Marchione's *Pope Pius XII)* speak of a German plan, dubbed "Rabat-Fohn," to be executed in January 1944. The plan called for the eighth division of the SS cavalry, disguised as Italians, to seize St. Peter's and "massacre Pius XII with the entire Vatican"—and specifically names "the papal protest in favor of the Jews" as the cause.

A similar story can be traced across Europe. There is room to argue that more ought to have been attempted by the Catholic Church—for the unanswerable facts remain that Hitler did come to power, World War II did occur, and six million Jews did die. But the place to begin that argument is with the truth that people of the time, Nazis and Jews alike, understood the pope to be the world's most prominent opponent of the Nazi ideology:

As early as December 1940, in an article in *Time* magazine, Albert Einstein paid tribute to Pius: "Only the Church stood squarely across the path of Hitler's campaign for suppressing the truth. I never had any special interest in the Church before, but now I feel a great affection and admiration because the Church alone has had the courage and persistence to stand for intellectual truth and moral freedom. I am forced thus to confess that what I once despised, I now praise unreservedly."

In 1943, Chaim Weizmann, who would become Israel's first president, wrote that "the Holy See is lending its powerful help wherever it can, to mitigate the fate of my persecuted co-religionists."

Moshe Sharett, Israel's second prime minister, met with Pius in the closing days of the war and "told him that my first duty was to thank him, and through him the Catholic Church, on behalf of the Jewish public for all they had done in the various countries to rescue Jews."

Rabbi Isaac Herzog, chief rabbi of Israel, sent a message in February 1944 declaring, "The people of Israel will never forget what His Holiness and his illustrious delegates, inspired by the eternal principles of religion, which form the very foundation of true civilization, are doing for our unfortunate brothers and sisters in the most tragic hour of our history, which is living proof of Divine Providence in this world."

In September 1945, Leon Kubowitzky, secretary general of the World Jewish Congress, personally thanked the pope for his interventions, and the World Jewish Congress donated $20,000 to Vatican charities "in recognition of the work of the Holy See in rescuing Jews from Fascist and Nazi persecutions."

In 1955, when Italy celebrated the tenth anniversary of its liberation, the Union of Italian Jewish Communities proclaimed April 17 a "Day of Gratitude" for the pope's wartime assistance.

On May 26, 1955, the Israeli Philharmonic Orchestra flew to Rome to give in the Vatican a special performance of Beethoven's Seventh Symphony—an expression of the State of Israel's enduring gratitude to the pope for help given the Jewish people during the Holocaust.

This last example is particularly significant. As a matter of state policy, the Israeli Philharmonic has never played the music of Richard Wagner, because of his well-known reputation as "Hitler's composer," the cultural patron saint of the Third Reich. During the 1950s especially, the Israeli public, hundreds of thousands of whom were Holocaust survivors, still viewed Wagner as a symbol of the Nazi regime. It is inconceivable that the Israeli government would have paid for the entire orchestra to travel to Rome to pay tribute to "Hitler's pope." On the contrary, the Israeli Philharmonic's unprecedented concert in the Vatican was a unique communal gesture of collective recognition for a great friend of the Jewish people.

Hundreds of other memorials could be cited. In her conclusion to *Under His Very Windows,* Susan Zuccotti dismisses—as wrong-headed, ill-informed, or even devious—the praise Pius XII received from Jewish leaders and scholars, as well as expressions of gratitude from the Jewish chaplains and Holocaust survivors who bore personal witness to the assistance of the pope.

That she does so is disturbing. To deny the legitimacy of their gratitude to Pius XII is tantamount to denying the credibility of their personal testimony and judgment about the Holocaust itself. "More than all others," recalled Elio Toaff, an Italian Jew who lived through the Holocaust and later became chief rabbi of Rome, "we had the opportunity of experiencing the great compassionate goodness and magnanimity of the pope during the unhappy years of the persecution and terror, when it seemed that for us there was no longer an escape."

But Zuccotti is not alone. There is a disturbing element in nearly all the current work on Pius. Except for Rychlak's *Hitler, the War and the Pope,* none of the recent books—from Cornwell's vicious attack in *Hitler's Pope* to McInerny's uncritical defense in *The Defamation of Pius XII*—is finally about the Holocaust. All are about using the sufferings of Jews fifty years ago to force changes upon the Catholic Church today.

It is this abuse of the Holocaust that must be rejected. A true account of Pius XII would arrive, I believe, at exactly the opposite to Cornwell's conclusion: Pius XII was not Hitler's pope, but the closest Jews had come to having a papal supporter—and at the moment when it mattered most.

Writing in Yad Vashem Studies in 1983, John S. Conway—the leading authority on the Vatican's eleven-volume *Acts and Documents of the Holy See During the Second World War*—concluded: "A close study of the many thousands of documents published in these volumes lends little support to the thesis that ecclesiastical self-preservation was the main motive behind the attitudes of the Vatican diplomats. Rather, the picture that emerges is one of a group of intelligent and conscientious men, seeking to pursue the paths of peace and justice, at a time when these ideals were ruthlessly being rendered irrelevant in a world of 'total war.'" These neglected volumes (which the English reader can find summarized in Pierre Blet's *Pius XII and the Second World War*) "will reveal ever more clearly and convincingly" as John Paul told a group of Jewish leaders in Miami in 1987—"how deeply Pius XII felt the tragedy of the Jewish people, and how hard and effectively he worked to assist them."

The Talmud teaches that "whosoever preserves one life, it is accounted to him by Scripture as if he had preserved a whole world." More than any other twentieth-century leader, Pius fulfilled this Talmudic dictum, when the fate of European Jewry was at stake. No other pope had been so widely praised by Jews—and they were not mistaken. Their gratitude, as well as that of the entire generation of Holocaust survivors, testifies that Pius XII was, genuinely and profoundly, a righteous gentile.

Source: David G. Dalin. 2001. "Pius XII and the Jews: A Defense." *The Weekly Standard* (006): 23 (February 26). Reprinted with permission from *The Weekly Standard.*

David Dalin holds the degrees of B.A. from the University of California at Berkeley, and M.A. and Ph.D. from Brandeis University, and he completed seminary studies at the Jewish Theological Seminary of America. He is Professor of History and Political Science at Ave Maria University in Florida. Dr. Dalin, an ordained rabbi, has written widely on the role of Jews in the political history of the United States. He is currently writing a book on the impact of Jews on the presidents of the United States. He has lectured widely on Pope Pius XII and the Jews in World War II and on the relationship of Pope John Paul II and the Jews.

Chapter 11

Sex Abuses by Catholic Priests

The scandal of priestly sex abuse that exploded several years ago has been a source of great sadness and outrage for all who love the Church. It is difficult to find a satisfactory excuse for why this happened and how it could have been allowed to persist over many years. Most people certainly agree that the Church must take the lead in ensuring that justice is carried out and that healing is pursued for all members of the Church, especially the victims. The most difficult goal will be to do what is right in a spirit of mercy and forgiveness.

Journalists asked the Holy Father, Pope Benedict XVI, about this scandal during his trip to the United States in April 2008. The Pope mentioned the great suffering these scandals have caused the Church and himself personally. He said he was ashamed and that the Church will do everything in its power to make sure this does not happen again.[1]

Much has been written about the scandal, and no doubt much more will be written. Many people will take advantage of this scandal to advance their own agenda for the Church, including changes in priestly celibacy, female priests, and the Church's moral teaching on sexuality. However, it is not the purpose of this chapter to address all the possible ways that disaffected Catholics might co-opt the sex abuse scandal.

While in no way exonerating members of the Church for their failings in this matter, it is important to understand that sexual abuse has not been strictly a Catholic issue. In fact, a 2004 report by the U.S. Department of Education estimated, based on a study of public school

[1] Pope Benedict XVI. 2008. Pre-Visit Papal Interview during the Flight to the United States, *L'Osservatore Romano*, April 15.

students, that "nearly 9.6 percent of students are targets of educator sexual misconduct sometime during their school career."[2]

The two articles that follow provide valuable perspectives on the scandal. They are particularly useful for faithful Catholics who love their Church despite its human flaws.

Philip Jenkins, in **"The Myth of the Pedophile Priest,"** makes clear that the nature of the problem is primarily one of homosexuality rather than pedophilia. He shows that the Catholic Church does not have a monopoly on sexual misconduct.

> ➤ Jenkins' research over 20 years shows that Catholic or other celibate clergy are no more likely to be involved in sexual misconduct than any other denomination or any non-clergy group.
> ➤ Based on a study conducted in the Chicago Archdiocese, only a very small percentage of priests over a forty-year period have been judged to have likely been guilty of sexual misconduct. The estimate is about 1.8 percent. (*Editor's note*: more recent research estimates the figure to be closer to 4 percent.)
> ➤ The vast majority of priestly sexual abuse cases do not constitute pedophilia, which is a psychiatric term for one having a sexual interest in children under the age of puberty. Rather, most involved sexual relations with a person under the age of sexual consent or sixteen or seventeen years old.
> ➤ Jenkins, a professor of history and religious studies and non-Catholic, provides this perspective to help people better understand the issue and protect innocent clergy from unjustified attacks.

In **"Don't Get Mad, Get Holy: Overcoming Evil with Good,"** Leon Suprenant, Jr., writes for members of the Catholic laity who are trying to make sense of it all. While recognizing the horror of the Church's sex abuse scandal and the damage it has done, he offers several suggestions for approaching the scandal and moving on as faithful Catholics.

---

[2] C. Shakeshaft. 2004. "Educator Sexual Misconduct: A Synthesis of the Literature." U.S. Department of Education, Washington, DC.

➤ The Church has a great need for holiness as a response to this challenge. Sanctity is not something exclusively for spiritual "superstars" like Mother Teresa. Ordinary people are also called to a life of holiness. We are the ones who will pull the Church out of this morass.

➤ We need a strong and informed faith so we can view the crisis with a supernatural outlook. Our faith will help us face persecution and ridicule.

➤ The Church needs holy priests, and we can support them with our prayers. Good priests are formed in families, and parents should pray for vocations among their children.

➤ The Church needs our financial support to thrive, and we need to be generous.

➤ Scandal does untold damage to those who give it and those who witness it. We need to be careful how we discuss the Church in our conversations.

➤ God has put us in the world to evangelize those with whom we come in contact. Pope John Paul II called for a "new evangelization" that laymen can carry out with their family, friends, neighbors, and colleagues. Our effectiveness will be enhanced if we are knowledgeable and if we are striving for holiness.

➤ Although some bishops failed to carry out their duties as shepherds of their flocks, we must not generalize and implicate all bishops. Our bishops are successors of the apostles and bear the authority of Christ. Nevertheless, the laity has the right to bring concerns to their bishops.

➤ All Catholics are called to be ambassadors of Christ's reconciliation, mercy, and healing.

Further Reading

Roger Landry. 2002. "Crisis of Saints." *This Rock* (13): 5 (May-June).

William Cardinal Levada. 2010. "*The New York Times* and Pope Benedict XVI: How It Looks to an American in the Vatican." Prefect of the Congregation for the Doctrine of the Faith, March 26.
http://www.vatican.va/resources/resources_card-levada2010_en.html.

The Myth of the Pedophile Priest

By Philip Jenkins

The Roman Catholic Church in the U.S. is currently going through one of the most traumatic periods in its long history. Every day, the news media have a new horror story to report, under some sensational headline: Newsweek, typically, is devoting its current front cover to "Sex, Shame and the Catholic Church: 80 Priests Accused of Child Abuse in Boston." Though the sex abuse cases have deep roots, the most recent scandals were detonated by the affair of Boston priest John J. Geoghan. Though his superiors had known for years of Geoghan's pedophile activities, he kept being transferred from parish to parish, regardless of the safety of the children in his care. The stigma of the Geoghan affair could last for decades, and some Catholics are declaring in their outrage that they can never trust their Church again.

No-one can deny that Boston church authorities committed dreadful errors, but at the same time, the story is not quite the simple tale of good and evil that it sometime appears. Hard though it may be to believe right now, the "pedophile priest" scandal is nothing like as sinister as it has been painted—or at least, it should not be used to launch blanket accusations against the Catholic Church as a whole.

We have often heard the phrase "pedophile priest" in recent weeks, and such individuals can exist: Father Geoghan was one such, as was the notorious Father James Porter a decade or so back. But as a description of a social problem, the term is wildly misleading. Crucially, Catholic priests and other clergy have nothing like a monopoly on sexual misconduct with minors. My research of cases over the past twenty years indicates no evidence whatever that Catholic or other celibate clergy are any more likely to be involved in misconduct or abuse than clergy of any other denomination—or indeed, than non-clergy. However determined the news media may be to see this whole affair as a crisis of celibacy, the charge is just unsupported. Literally every denomination and faith tradition has its share of abuse cases, and some of the worst involve non-Catholics. Every mainline Protestant denomination has had scandals aplenty, as have Pentecostals, Mormons, Jehovah's Witnesses, Jews, Buddhists, Hare Krishnas, and the list goes on. One Canadian Anglican (Episcopalian) diocese is currently on the verge of bankruptcy as a result of massive lawsuits caused by decades of systematic abuse, yet the Anglican church does not demand celibacy of its clergy. However much this statement contradicts conventional wisdom, the "pedophile priest" is not a Catholic specialty; yet when did we ever hear about "pedophile pastors"?

Just to find some solid numbers, how many Catholic clergy are involved in misconduct? We actually have some good information on this issue, since in the early 1990s, the Catholic archdiocese of Chicago undertook a bold and thorough self-study. The survey examined every priest who had served in the archdiocese over the previous forty years, some 2200 individuals, and re-opened every internal complaint ever made against these men. The standard of evidence applied was not legal proof that would stand up in a court of law, but just the consensus that a particular charge was probably justified. By this low standard, the survey found that about forty priests, about 1.8 percent of the whole, were probably guilty of misconduct with minors at some point in their careers. Put another way, no evidence existed against about 98 percent of parish clergy, the overwhelming majority of the group.[1] Since other organizations dealing with children have not undertaken such comprehensive studies, we have no idea whether the Catholic figure is better or worse than the rate for schoolteachers, residential home counselors, social workers, or scout-masters.

The Chicago study also found that of the 2200 priests, just one was a pedophile. Now, many people are confused about the distinction between a pedophile and a person guilty of sex with a minor, but the difference is very significant. The phrase "pedophile priests" conjures up nightmare images of the worst violation of innocence, callous molesters like Father Porter who assault children of six or seven years old. "Pedophilia" is a psychiatric term meaning sexual interest in children below the age of puberty. But the vast majority of clergy misconduct cases are nothing like this. The vast majority of instances

---

[1] *Editor's note*: More recent research covering the period 1950 to 2002 and a very broad geographic area in the United States estimates the figure at about 4 percent. See United State Conference of Catholic Bishops. 2004. "The Nature and Scope of the Problem of Sexual Abuse of Minors by Catholic Priests and Deacons in the United States," A Research Study Conducted by the John Jay College of Criminal Justice.

involve priests who have been sexually active with a person below the age of sexual consent, often sixteen or seventeen years old, or even older. An act of this sort is multiply wrong: it is probably criminal, and by common consent it is immoral and sinful; yet it does not have the utterly ruthless, exploitative, character of child molestation. In almost all cases too, with the older teenagers, there is an element of consent.

Also, the definition of "childhood" varies enormously between different societies. If an act of this sort occurred in most European countries, it would probably be legal, since the age of consent for boys is usually around fifteen. To take a specific example, when newspapers review recent cases of "pedophile priests," they commonly cite a case that occurred in California's Orange County, when a priest was charged with having consensual sex with a seventeen year old boy. Whatever the moral quality of such an act, most of us would not apply the term "child abuse" or "pedophilia." For this reason alone, we need to be cautious when we read about scores of priests being "accused of child abuse."

The age of the young person involved is also so important because different kinds of sexual misconduct respond differently to treatment, and church authorities need to respond differently. If a diocese knows a man is a pedophile, and ever again places him in a position where he has access to more children, that decision is simply wrong, and probably amounts to criminal neglect. But a priest who has a relationship with an older teenager is much more likely to respond to treatment, and it would be more understandable if some day the church placed him in a new parish, under careful supervision. The fact that Cardinal Law's regime in Boston seems to have blundered time and again does not mean that this is standard practice for all Catholic dioceses, still less that the church is engaged in some kind of conspiracy of silence to hide dangerous perverts.

I am in no sense soft on the issue of child abuse. Recently, I published an exposé of the trade in electronic child pornography, one of the absolute worst forms of exploitation, and my argument was that the police and FBI need to be pressured to act more strictly against this awful thing. My concern over the "pedophile priest" issue is not to defend evil clergy, or a sinful church (I cannot be called a Catholic apologist, since I am not even a Catholic). But I am worried that justified anger over a few awful cases might be turned into ill-focused attacks against innocent clergy. The story of clergy misconduct is bad enough without turning into an unpardonable outbreak of religious bigotry against the Catholic Church.

Source: Philip Jenkins. 2002. "The Myth of the Pedophile Priest." *Pittsburgh Post-Gazette*, March 3. Reprinted with permission of Philip Jenkins.

Philip Jenkins is Edwin Erle Sparks Professor of the Humanities at Pennsylvania State University. He works in several fields in both History and Religious Studies. His major current interests include the study of global Christianity, past and present; of new and emerging religious movements; and of twentieth-century U.S. history, chiefly post-1975. He has published more than twenty books that have been translated into twelve languages. Some recent titles include *The Next Christendom: The Rise of Global Christianity* (Oxford University Press, 2002); *Decade of Nightmares: The End of the 1960s and the Making of Eighties America* (Oxford University Press, 2006); and *The Lost History of Christianity* (HarperOne, 2008). His most recent book is *Jesus Wars* (HarperOne, 2010) on the Christological controversies of the fifth century.

Don't Get Mad, Get Holy:
Overcoming Evil With Good

by Leon Suprenant

The current clerical sex abuse scandal is a tragedy that has sent shock waves through the Catholic Church and American society. Catholic dioceses face many pastoral and legal challenges as they address the needs of victims while also developing policies to prevent such crimes from occurring in the future. Surely, as Pope John Paul II says, "The abuse which has caused this crisis is by every standard wrong and rightly considered a crime by society; it is also an appalling sin in the eyes of God."

This scandal has caused harm to the entire Church. Most obviously, there are the victims of the sex abuse themselves and their families, who so much need healing and love. The perpetrators of these crimes have caused tremendous physical and spiritual harm (cf. Mt.18:6-9) and have dire need of divine mercy, in addition to any medical treatment or criminal sanction. There are the many good and faithful priests and religious who suddenly find themselves the objects of suspicion, hatred, and perhaps even false charges. And then there is the larger Church, whose pastoral and missionary efforts have been compromised by the sins of a few of her members.

In addition to all this pain, there is also the considerable anger, frustration, betrayal, sadness, confusion, and outrage experienced by Catholics and non-Catholics alike over this crisis. These feelings are directed not only toward the perpetrators of these crimes but also toward a Church bureaucracy and ecclesial climate that would allow repeat offenders to remain in active ministry. The Holy Father affirms that "because of the great harm done by some priests and religious, the Church herself is viewed with distrust, and many are offended at the way in which the Church's leaders are perceived to have acted in this matter."

Further, many faithful Catholics are profoundly offended when the Church is unfairly vilified in the media and when opponents and critics of the Church capitalize on this opportunity to attack the Church and promote their own agendas in the process.

This position paper does not attempt to provide a comprehensive treatment of the spiritual, psychological, and sociological dimensions of this problem, nor does it examine the intra-ecclesial procedures that are being put in place to more effectively address claims of clerical misconduct in the future.

Rather, as a private association of lay Catholics, Catholics United for the Faith (CUF) desires in this position paper to provide sound, practical guidance to lay Catholics who desire to be faithful to Jesus Christ and His Church, notwithstanding the scandalous behavior of some of her members.

The size and gravity of the current clerical sex abuse scandal can lead to anger, discouragement, and a sense of powerlessness. Yet Our Lord promised to be with us until the end of the world, and He can—and does—bring about good from even the greatest evils when we put our trust in Him (cf. Rom. 8:28). In point of fact, there are many things we can do to be "part of the solution," to cooperate with divine grace to make a difference in this crisis. Therefore, we offer the following eight practical steps Catholic laity can take to help bring some good out of this unspeakable evil.

Holiness

In every age, and particularly during times of crisis, what the Church needs most is Saints—the example and intercession of holy men and women. "The saints have always been the source and origin of renewal in the most difficult moments in the Church's history" (Catechism, no. 828). In our time we've been blessed with Pope John Paul II and Mother Teresa—both celibates—whose holy lives bear effective, credible witness to the Gospel they proclaim.

But as Vatican II teaches, holiness is not just for Catholic "superstars" like the Pope but also for rank-and-file lay Catholics. Therefore, the first order of business must be a renewal of our own commitment to the Lord and His Body, the Church. We must commit ourselves to daily prayer and the sacramental life of the Church as the first—not last—resort.

Not without reason does our Lord counsel us to remove the planks from our own eyes before trying to remove splinters from others' eyes (cf. Mt. 7:3). Imagine there's a mishap on an airplane, and the craft begins losing cabin pressure. In the face of such a calamity, most of us would want to be courageous, to do the right thing and help as many of our fellow passengers as possible. Yet, if we don't use our own air mask first, in a matter of seconds we'll be of no use to anybody. We would be among the first casualties.

While there may be other righteous actions we can take, if we were only to devote ourselves to prayer, frequent reception of the sacraments of Confession and Holy Communion, weekly if not daily holy hours of reparation before the Blessed Sacrament, spiritual and corporal works of mercy; and other such activities out of love for Our Lord and a desire to help rebuild His Church, we would be providing the greatest service we can possibly give.

Faith

We should pray specifically for an increase of the virtue of faith (cf. Lk. 17:5). That language may be off-putting to some. After all, we either have faith or we don't, right? Yet we surely need to believe all that God has revealed through Christ and His Church with greater understanding, conviction, and joy.

Even more, the virtue of faith enables us to see the fullness of reality, with its natural and supernatural components. Faith enables us to see the divine amid the human. Jesus is not simply a good man, but the Second Person of the Blessed Trinity. Scripture is not just a collection of ancient human writings but also truly the work of the Holy Spirit. And the Church is not simply a human "institution" but also the Mystical Body of Christ and the means of salvation for the whole world.

It takes a strong faith to acknowledge an "apostolic" Church if the "apostle" in our midst fails in his duties. It takes a strong faith to accept a "holy" Church when we're constantly having the sins of her members—and even some of her leaders—rubbed in our faces.

We cannot deny the shortcomings and failures of members of the Church through the ages, including those that have been publicized in recent months. But we do need the virtue of faith to see the greater reality. The best way to grow in faith is to ask the Lord for this gift. Here is one popular Act of Faith that can be used to ask the Lord to increase our faith:

O my God, I firmly believe that you are one God in three divine Persons, Father, Son, and Holy Spirit. I believe that your divine Son became man and died for our sins, and that He will come to judge the living and the dead. I believe these and all the truths which the holy Catholic Church teaches, because You have revealed them, who can neither deceive nor be deceived. Amen.

Vocations

Vatican II clearly called upon all the faithful to beg the Lord of the harvest for more laborers in the vineyard (cf. Mt. 9:36-38), particularly for an increase of vocations to the priesthood and religious life. In a special way, this call goes out to families, which must be "incubators" of vocations in the Church (cf. *Catechism*, no. 1656). Parents must not exert pressure on their children when it comes to choosing a state in life, but rather they should encourage their children to follow Jesus and to accept with generosity whatever specific vocation the Lord has in store for them (cf. *Catechism*, nos. 2230, 2232).

Sadly, some parents do not want their children to become priests or religious. Yet the Catechism teaches: "Parents should welcome and respect with joy and thanksgiving the Lord's call to one of their children to follow him in virginity for the sake of the Kingdom in the consecrated life or in priestly ministry" (no. 2233).

If, however, our focus is only on the next generation of priests, then we're missing an increasingly significant aspect of our vocations effort. Many priests and religious feel the spiritual and material support of the faithful while they're in formation, but then they are ordained or take their final vows and then seemingly fall off the intercessory map. More than ever, all priests and religious need the prayers, support, and encouragement of all the Church.

In times past, a parish might have had three or four priests in residence. Now often there is usually just one, and increasingly he is serving two or more parishes. Further, with the latest scandals, all priests more than ever are the butt of jokes and subjected to derision and anti-Catholic venom. The Lord surely will bless efforts to support our beloved priests through our prayers and our friendship (cf. Mt. 10:40-42).

Church Support

Catholics have the duty of providing for the material needs of the Church, each according to his abilities (cf. *Catechism*, no. 2043; Code of Canon Law, canon 222). This can be a real stumbling block for some Catholics today, especially in dioceses where millions of dollars are being paid to settle sex abuse lawsuits.

First, it should be understood that funds donated in the weekly collection plate or to an annual diocesan campaign are not typically the source of the funds used when the diocese settles a lawsuit. Even so, the diocese should spell this out specifically for the faithful so that there is no misunderstanding as to how the settlements are being funded. Clearly, the Church's immense humanitarian, educational, parochial, and missionary activities are dependent upon the ongoing support of Catholics.

Even more, we must learn from the account of the widow's mite (Lk. 21:1-4). Her contribution was inconsequential, but she was held up for special praise because she gave what she had, not simply what she could spare.

In the Old Testament, Our Lord accuses those who refuse to tithe of stealing from Him (cf. Mal. 3:8). Surely lay people have the right to decide to which parishes, diocesan programs, religious communities, and apostolates they will contribute, and they will likely contribute their hard-earned money to those entities which they consider to be the best stewards of their offerings. But Our Lord and His Church are clear about our need to do what we can to support the Church.

"Generosity" literally means "full of giving life." Putting our time, talent, and treasure at the service of the Church is a reflection of the priority of Jesus Christ in our lives (cf. Mt. 6:24) and will help breathe new life in the Church in the new millennium.

Avoid Scandal

We have to be so careful today in terms of how we talk about the priesthood and contemporary issues facing the Church. Probably the harshest critics of the Church are former Catholics and those who still consider themselves Catholic but who oppose the Church on any number of issues.

It's very easy to find fault in the Church right now. People are rightly upset or disturbed. When we give verbal expression to these feelings, we may be just "letting off steam," and everything we say may well be true. But having part of the truth and needing to let off steam do not excuse making statements that will harm the faith of other Catholics whose faith perhaps is weaker, provide an unnecessary stumbling block for nonbelievers, and needlessly and perhaps even unfairly harm the reputations of others (cf. *Catechism*, no. 2477).

In place of the above, Scripture is very clear. We are told to say "only the things men need to hear, things that will help them" (Eph. 4:29). As St. Paul says, "Whatever is true, whatever is honorable, whatever is just, whatever is pure, whatever is lovely, whatever is gracious, if there is any excellence, if there is anything worthy of praise, think about these things" (Phil. 4:8).

Scandal involves inducing others to sin (cf. *Catechism*, nos. 2284-87). It's a type of spiritual murder. Are our comments regarding the Church being expressed in ways that will actually turn people against the Church? And if *giving* scandal is like spiritual murder, then *taking* scandal is akin to spiritual suicide. We must protect our own hearts, that we do not allow our own negative feelings about the real evils in some dioceses to fester and ultimately to lead us out of the Church.

In the business world there's a maxim that may help us take the right approach in this matter. Successful managers are able to "catch their employees doing something right" and in the process provide positive reinforcement for good behavior. In the spiritual realm, we likewise do well to "overcome evil with good" (Rom. 12:21).

There are holy people in the Church. There are many great stories of contemporary Christian heroes, not to mention the lives of saints through the centuries. There is much good going on in the Church on many different fronts, globally, nationally, and in our backyard. We need to acknowledge and publicize this truth.

This does not mean that we ignore the sins of Church members. As we discussed above, the Church is at once holy yet always in need of renewal and reform, and *charitably* correcting a sinner is a spiritual work of mercy.

Using an analogy, let us assume that a husband and wife are having marital problems, and the husband wants to do something about it. The first step would be for the husband to honestly acknowledge the nature and extent of the problem. He would try to work things out with his spouse, and no one would criticize him for seeking the help of others—marital counselors, spiritual advisors, friends and confidantes, and above all God Himself—to help remedy the problem.

However, if the husband were to begin to vilify his wife to his children, to neighbors, perhaps even to the press, we can say that regardless of the truth and frustration level behind his statements, he would only be hurting the situation. Notice that St. Joseph, when confronted with the apparent infidelity of his wife, determined to "divorce her *quietly*," without subjecting her to shame (Mt. 1:19).

As Catholics, we similarly have to distinguish between acknowledging the truth and taking restorative action from mere venting and causing greater division within the Church.

Engaging the World

The Holy Father has continually called for a "new evangelization" or a reevangelization of formerly Christian cultures. We should not confuse "new evangelization" with "easy evangelization," nor should we expect the seeds of a "new springtime of faith" to sprout without opposition, persecution, and, indeed, the blood of martyrs.

An integral part of the new evangelization entails a prudent engagement with the world. Catholic laity need to be holy and they need to be informed. The Catholic Church is frequently battered in the media. We can't run from the media, but neither should we accept the media's rules of engagement—rules that often preclude, among other things, the existence of God and an objective moral law. We need, with God's grace, to be smarter and more convincing, not more fearful, compromising, or inflammatory.

And all of us know people, many of whom were raised as Catholics, who have an inadequate understanding of the Christian faith generally, and who are inclined to accept uncritically whatever evil the media attributes to the Church. Being able to put such attacks in their proper light is an important form of apologetics, of being prepared to make a defense, with gentleness and reverence, of the abiding hope that is in us (cf. 1 Pet. 3:15).

Bishops

Both the enemies of the Church and many of those who wish to come to her defense tend to blame the bishops for any and all evils in the Church. Certainly the bishop is responsible for his particular church, or diocese, and throughout Church history, including in the present time, there have been bishops who have not been faithful to the sacred office entrusted to them. When such infidelity or malfeasance occurs, the Church suffers greatly.

Yet it is futile to envision a Church without bishops, as they are legitimate successors of the apostles who bear the authority of Christ (cf. *Catechism*, nos. 880, 886, 888). They are spiritual fathers in the Church.

One important teaching of Vatican II, which has also found its way into the current Code of Canon Law, is the laity's right to bring their concerns respectfully to their bishops (cf. Catechism, no. 907). Such a right should be exercised in a constructive way and not simply as a justification to attack or condemn. The faithful should encourage their bishops not only to take appropriate action in clerical sex abuse cases, but also in related issues to the extent they are relevant, such as seminary screening, ministry to homosexuals, classroom sex education in Catholic schools, and other such issues.

Ambassadors of Reconciliation

Regardless of our state in life, all of us as Christ's disciples are called to be ambassadors of His reconciliation, mercy, and healing:

All this is from God, who through Christ reconciled us to himself and gave us the ministry of reconciliation; that is, God was in Christ reconciling the world to Himself, not counting their trespasses against them, and entrusting to us the message of reconciliation. So we are ambassadors for Christ, God making his appeal through us. We beseech you on behalf of Christ, be reconciled to God (2 Cor. 5:18-20).

A lively sense of divine mercy is so needed today, and we need to be its instruments as well as its recipients. We must be ambassadors of reconciliation within the Church, afflicted as she is with dissent and scandal. Without in any way minimizing the need to bring criminals to justice, we need to forgive from the heart the perpetrators of the crimes that have been committed as well as those who have allowed such crimes to continue, all the while praying for their repentance and conversion.

We must be instruments of the Lord's healing and compassion to all those who have been directly harmed by abusive priests. We must repeatedly forgive those who have used the scandal as a pretext for attacking the Church and for furthering their own agendas, even as we peaceably answer their charges. And we need to be instruments of God's mercy and peace to all those we meet.

The current situation does not need more heat. Rather, it needs the light of Christ. May we be ambassadors of the light of Christ to a society that is frequently walking in darkness (cf. Mt. 4:12-17; 5:14-16).

In this time of tribulation, when there are such grievous wounds inflicted on the Body of Christ, we must pray much more fervently for the Church, for all victims, for our bishops, priests, and seminarians, that this great suffering may be for the purification of the Church, and that the necessary exposure of evil may have a medicinal effect. This should be a wake-up call also for each of us poor sinners. We too are at fault because of our lukewarmness.

We must do penance and make reparation for the offense against God. We already can see that Christ in His mercy is in the process of purifying His Bride the Church. We must pray unceasingly that Christ will have the final victory. This is the sentiment of our beloved Holy Father, who has said:

> We must be confident that this time of trial will bring a purification of the entire Catholic community, a purification that is urgently needed if the Church is to preach more effectively the Gospel of Jesus Christ in all its liberating force. Now you must ensure that where sin increased, grace will all the more abound (cf. Rom 5:20). So much pain, so much sorrow must lead to a holier priesthood, a holier episcopate, a holier Church.

God alone is the source of holiness, and it is to Him above all that we must turn for forgiveness, for healing, and for the grace to meet this challenge with uncompromising courage and harmony of purpose.

Source: Leon Suprenant. 2004. "Dealing With Scandals: Don't Get Mad, Get Holy." Catholics United for the Faith, April 2. Reprinted with permission from Catholics United for the Faith (www.cuf.org).

Leon Suprenant was President of Catholics United for the Faith and Emmaus Road Publishing, as well as publisher of *Lay Witness,* an award-winning magazine for lay Catholics. He was general editor with Scott Hahn of the best-selling book, *Catholic for a Reason: Scripture and the Mystery of the Family of God* (Emmaus Road). He is currently employed by The School of Faith in Kansas.

This essay is originally an excerpt from the "Position Paper of Catholics United for the Faith on the Current Clerical Sex Abuse Scandal," copyright 2002, Catholics United for the Faith. This edition of the essay, "Don't Get Mad; Get Holy," first appeared in *Shaken by Scandals,* edited by Paul Thigpen (Ann Arbor, Michigan: Servant Publications, 2002). Used with permission.

Part III.

⸺⸎⸺

Misunderstood Doctrines of the Church

Many Catholics misunderstand a number of Church doctrines. The misunderstanding stems largely from a lack of ongoing adult formation and religious education. Many of us stopped studying the tenets of our faith in the eighth or twelfth grade. As our intellectual sophistication advanced over the years, some of us simply left behind our adolescent understanding of the doctrines of the faith. Part III explains these doctrines, helps us understand why the Church teaches what it does, and explains their importance to our spiritual life.

Chapter 12

——⁂——

The Mass

Of all things Catholic, the Mass must be the most misunderstood by Protestants and the most underappreciated by Catholics. Many Protestants believe Catholics hold that Our Lord is crucified over and over again with each Mass offered. Rather, the Catholic Church teaches very clearly that Jesus died once on Calvary, but because God is not constrained by time and space, the sacrifice of the cross is perpetuated, re-presented to us, each time the holy Mass is offered.

Based on the frequency with which many Catholics avail themselves of this most sublime event, it is reasonable to conclude they fail to appreciate it. How could one embrace the truth of what the Mass really is, with the Real Presence of Jesus in the Eucharist, and casually opt out of opportunities to pray the Mass as often as possible?

The *Catechism of the Catholic Church* provides a beautiful explication of the Eucharist that should be read in its entirety and reflected upon. The Eucharist is "the source and summit of the Christian life." The entire spiritual good of the Church, Jesus Christ himself, is contained in it.[1]

The Mass is the perfect prayer, in which Christ offers himself to the Father for us individually and for his Church collectively. Should we not make every effort to pray the Mass better and attempt to learn more about it, struggle against distractions, and attend as often as possible? The three articles that follow will give us a better understanding of the Mass and help us to love it more deeply.

In **"Why Believe in the Real Presence of Christ in the Eucharist?,"** Stephen Gabriel provides three compelling reasons to believe in

---

[1] *Catechism of the Catholic Church.* 1997. 2nd ed., no. 1324. Vatican City: Libreria Editrice Vaticana.

the Real Presence: the testimony of St. John's Gospel, the testimony of the early Christians, and the teaching of Christ's Church.

> ➤ It is clear that Jesus meant what he said when he proclaimed that we must eat his flesh and drink his blood if we are to find eternal life.
> ➤ The people to whom he was speaking were repulsed by the notion of eating his flesh and drinking his blood. When they left him after hearing his words, Christ did not call them back to clarify that he was merely speaking metaphorically.
> ➤ The writings of St. Paul and the early Church Fathers make it clear that they believed that the Eucharist was Christ's body and blood.
> ➤ Our Lord gave his Church the authority to teach infallibly on matters of faith and morals, and his Church has always taught the Real Presence of Christ in the Eucharist.

Father William Saunders, in "**Is the Mass Really a Sacrifice?**," explains the sense in which the Mass is indeed a sacrifice, the same sacrifice that took place on Calvary over 2,000 years ago.

> ➤ Passages from Scripture should not be interpreted in isolation.
> ➤ The Church does not teach that Our Lord physically dies over and over again at the celebration of each Mass, but that the Mass participates in the everlasting sacrifice of Christ.
> ➤ The sacrifice of Our Lord on Calvary cannot be separated from surrounding events such as the Last Supper and the Resurrection. These form one saving event.
> ➤ God does not exist in time; he is eternal. For God, there is no past, present, or future. Although Christ's death occurred at a specific point in history, it remains an ever-present reality for us.
> ➤ At the Last Supper, Jesus said, "Do this in remembrance of me." Clearly, he wanted this sacramental mystery repeated for all time.
> ➤ Hence, the sacrifice of the cross and the sacrifice of the Mass are one and the same sacrifice. The sacrifice of the cross is represented to us at each Mass. The only difference is the unbloody manner in which it is offered.

In "**The Mass Explained**," Father Cormac Burke explains each part of the Mass.

➢ The most important aspect of the Mass is the action of Christ himself. It is his sacrifice, the same as the one that occurred on the cross 2,000 years ago.

➢ We love the Mass if we love Christ. When we go to Mass, we go to Calvary.

➢ Understanding and appreciating the Mass requires faith.

➢ The purposes of the Mass are adoration, thanksgiving, reparation, and petition.

➢ We offer ourselves to God in the presentation of the gifts.

➢ During the consecration, we should be attentive and offer many acts of faith, love, and adoration. We are on Calvary now!

➢ Holy Communion is a great gift from God. How eager we should be to receive Our Lord in the Holy Eucharist.

➢ In the Mass, Our Lord offers himself for us. In Holy Communion, he offers himself to us.

➢ It is important to take a little time after Mass to offer thanks to God for all he has given us, especially the Mass and Holy Communion.

Further Reading

Jason Shanks. 1999. "This Is a Hard Teaching: Why Christ Meant Literally What He Said About the Eucharist." *This Rock* (10:9) (September).

F.J. Sheed. 1981. "Eucharist and Mass." *Theology for Beginners*. Ann Arbor, Michigan: Servant Books.

Why Believe in the Real Presence of Christ in the Eucharist?

By Stephen Gabriel

Recent polls suggest that a large percentage of Catholics do not believe in the Real Presence of Christ in the Eucharist. In light of this skepticism, it may be helpful to review the doctrine, which has several sources. First, we believe in the Real Presence because Jesus, true God and true man, stated it in the Gospels. Second, we believe because the testimony of the early Christians affirms the doctrine. Third, we believe because Christ's Church has taught this belief for 2,000 years.

The Testimony of the Gospels

If we take as a given that a Christian believes the Gospels accurately report what Jesus actually did and taught, we will turn to the Gospels to find out what was written about the Real Presence of Christ in the Eucharist. The best source for such a discussion is Christ's Eucharistic discourse recorded in the sixth chapter of the Gospel of St. John.

I am the living bread that came down from heaven; whoever eats this bread will live forever; and the bread that I will give is my flesh for the life of the world."

The Jews quarreled among themselves, saying, "How can this man give us (his) flesh to eat?"

Jesus said to them, "Amen, amen, I say to you, unless you eat the flesh of the Son of Man and drink his blood, you do not have life within you. Whoever eats my flesh and drinks my blood has eternal life, and I will raise him on the last day. For my flesh is true food, and my blood is true drink. Whoever eats my flesh and drinks my blood remains in me and I in him. Just as the living Father sent me and I have life because of the Father, so also the one who feeds on me will have life because of me. This is the bread that came down from heaven. Unlike your ancestors who ate and still died, whoever eats this bread will live forever." These things he said while teaching in the synagogue in Capernaum. Then many of his disciples who were listening said, "This saying is hard; who can accept it?" (John 6: 51-60).

As a result of this, many (of) his disciples returned to their former way of life and no longer accompanied him (John 6: 66).

Jesus then said to the Twelve, "Do you also want to leave?" Simon Peter answered him, "Master, to whom shall we go? You have the words of eternal life. We have come to believe and are convinced that you are the Holy One of God" (John 6: 67-69).

Some argue that Jesus' words were metaphorical, that he did not mean that his disciples must literally eat his flesh and drink his blood. Jesus certainly used metaphor while teaching. He said, "I am the vine, you are the branches" (John 15: 5). However, when he said this, the crowd did not murmur or wonder how he could possibly call himself a vine and them branches. In the Eucharistic discourse, the crowd understood clearly what Jesus meant and they were repulsed by it. They responded, "This saying is hard; who can accept it?" And they stopped following him. Jesus did not attempt to stop them, did not explain that he was speaking metaphorically. In fact, he asked his Apostles if they would leave as well.

The full understanding of how they would obey his instructions was probably not clear to the Apostles until the Last Supper.

Then he took the bread, said the blessing, broke it, and gave it to them, saying, "This is my body, which will be given for you; do this in memory of me." And likewise the cup after they had eaten, saying, "This cup is the new covenant in my blood, which will be shed for you (Luke 22: 19-20).

Why, we might ask, if Jesus intended that the bread and wine be actually changed into his body and blood, didn't he change the appearance of the bread and wine and not just its substance? After all, he did change water into both the substance and appearance of wine at the wedding feast of Cana. We can't know for certain why Our Lord did what he did. Perhaps, knowing human nature, he understood just how difficult it would be for us to consume the Eucharist if it appeared as human flesh and human blood. Perhaps, he foresaw that we would reserve his precious body and blood in the tabernacle and if the Eucharist took on the accidents of flesh and blood, it would be difficult to preserve without becoming rancid, especially before the development of refrigeration. But, most likely he wanted us to have faith in the testimony of the Gospels, the Apostles and early Christians and his Church. Faith was most important to Our Lord. Jesus generally only cured those with faith. Remember his words to Thomas, "Have you come to believe because you have seen me? Blessed are those who have not seen and have believed" (John 20: 29).

The Testimony of the Early Christians

It is clear from the Gospel accounts that Jesus meant his words to be taken literally and that the people to whom Jesus was speaking believed he was being literal about the need to eat his flesh and drink his blood. There was no misunderstanding. Jesus' teaching that his followers must eat his flesh and drink his blood was not meant only for the people of his day. Because he came to save all mankind, past, present and future, he had to enable this sacrament to be perpetuated until the end of time. Accordingly, he instituted the priesthood at the Last Supper with his instruction, "Do this in memory of me."

Corroborating this view are the writings of St. Paul and the early Church Fathers.

> The cup of blessing that we bless, is it not a participation in the blood of Christ? The bread that we break, is it not a participation in the body of Christ? Because the loaf of bread is one, we, though many, are one body, for we all partake of the one loaf (1 Cor 10: 16-17).

> For I received from the Lord what I also handed on to you, that the Lord Jesus, on the night he was handed over, took bread, and, after he had given thanks, broke it and said, "This is my body that is for you. Do this in remembrance of me." In the same way also the cup, after supper, saying, "This cup is the new covenant in my blood. Do this, as often as you drink it, in remembrance of me." For as often as you eat this bread and drink the cup, you proclaim the death of the Lord until he comes. Therefore whoever eats the bread or drinks the cup of the Lord unworthily will have to answer for the body and blood of the Lord. A person should examine himself, and so eat the bread

and drink the cup. For anyone who eats and drinks without discerning the body, eats and drinks judgment on himself (1 Cor 11: 23-27).

Ample evidence in the writings of the early Church Fathers points to their belief in the Real Presence of Christ in the Eucharist from the very beginnings of Christianity. For example, St. Ignatius of Antioch, in his *Letter to the Smyrnaeans* (paragraph 6, circa 80-110 A.D.) refers to the Eucharist as "the flesh of our Savior Jesus Christ." St. Justin Martyr, in his *First Apology* (chapter 66, A.D. 148-155) called the "food consecrated by the Word of prayer . . . the flesh and blood of that incarnate Jesus." St. Irenaeus of Lyons, in *Against Heresies* (180 A.D.), referred to Christ's words declaring the cup and the bread to be His own blood and body.

This sampling of the evidence from early Christian writings confirms that belief in the Real Presence of Christ in the Eucharist was held by the early Church.[1] Of course, even in the early Church were some who would not accept this teaching. After all, "This saying is hard." Although it was unfortunate that some failed to believe in the Real Presence during the early days of the Church, it was a blessing for us because it led the Church leaders at the time to condemn the heresy and reiterate the consistent teaching of the Church. If there were no heresies then, we may not have the writings now of St. Ignatius and others confirming very clearly the Church's teaching on the matter.

The Teaching of Christ's Church

It is clear from scripture that Jesus established his Church with Peter as its head. He established a hierarchical Church with teaching authority.

And so I say to you, you are Peter, and upon this rock I will build my church, and the gates of the netherworld shall not prevail against it.

---

[1] Additional quotations of the early Christians indicating their belief in the Real Presence of Christ in the Eucharist are available on the website of The Real Presence Eucharistic Education and Adoration Association at http://www.therealpresence.org/eucharst/father/a5.html#bible. Another good source is Mike Aquilina. 2001. *The Mass of the Early Christians. Our Sunday Visitor* Publishing Division.

I will give you the keys to the kingdom of heaven. Whatever you bind on earth shall be bound in heaven; and whatever you loose on earth shall be loosed in heaven (Matt 16: 18-19).

It is obvious that Jesus did not intend for his Church fade away with the death of the Apostles. He expected that Peter would have a successor, indeed a series of successors, until the end of time.

Christ made it very clear that he wanted unity in his Church. Given the importance that Jesus put on faith throughout his public life, it is reasonable to conclude that the unity he desired for his Church was unity of faith, unity of belief. His prayer for unity during the Last Supper is both touching and revealing.

I pray not only for them, but also for those who will believe in me through their word, so that they may all be one, as you, Father, are in me and I in you, that they also may be in us, that the world may believe that you sent me. And I have given them the glory you gave me, so that they may be one, as we are one, I in them and you in me, that they may be brought to perfection as one, that the world may know that you sent me, and that you loved them even as you loved me (John 17: 20-23).

Jesus wanted unity in his Church as a witness to the truth, as a testimony to those who would come after his Apostles. He knew the only way to have unity in his Church was to establish a hierarchical structure with the authority to teach in his name. Without an authoritative teaching office and a visible head in Peter's successor, we would have just what we have today in the Christian world, a proliferation of beliefs, a lack of unity—indeed, a scandal for all to see!

The Church has always taught that Our Lord is present in the Eucharist—body, blood, soul, and divinity. However, the world was scandalized by corruption in the priesthood and the superficial practice of the faith in the 1500s, and rightly so. Reform was needed. Many reformers experienced a loss of the sense of sacrament as a result.[2] Unfortunately, the Protestant reformers wound up throwing out "the baby with the bath water" when they eliminated the sacraments—one way to get rid of corrupt priests. We can only hope that, with prayer

---

[2] James Hitchcock. 2001. "The Real Issues of the Reformation." *Catholic Dossier*, 40-41 (September–October).

and good will, the unity that Our Lord desired so much will be restored to his people.

Conclusion

For those Catholics (and Protestants for that matter) who hold that belief in the Real Presence of Christ in the Eucharist is a matter of interpretation, let us hope that they are not ignoring the evidence because "this saying is hard."

The Eucharist does indeed contain the Real Presence of Christ. The evidence is overwhelming. We have the evidence of the Gospels, which reports that Jesus and the people to whom he spoke took his words literally when he said they must eat his flesh and drink his blood. We have the evidence of the early Christians who gained nothing and risked everything by embracing this seemingly outrageous belief. And we have the evidence of centuries of teaching by the Church vested with the authority to teach in Christ's name so that we could be one as he and the Father are one.

Source: Stephen Gabriel writes from Falls Church, Virginia. He is the author of *To Be a Father* (Moorings Press, 2010) and *Speaking to the Heart: A Father's Guide to Growth in Virtue* (*Our Sunday Visitor*, 1999).

Is the Mass Really a Sacrifice?

by Rev. William Saunders, Ph.D.

Some people cite passages from St. Paul's letter to the Hebrews to support their view that the Mass could not be a sacrifice. The quote in question probably comes from chapter 9 of the Letter to the Hebrews, which addresses the sacrifice of Jesus. Verses 25-28 read, "Not that [Christ] might offer Himself there again and again, as the high priest enters year after year into the sanctuary with blood that is not his own; if that were so, He would have had to suffer death over and over from the creation of the world. But now He has appeared at the end of the ages to take away sins once for all by His sacrifice. Just as it is appointed that men die once, and after death be judged, so Christ was offered up once to take away the sins of many; He will appear a second time not to take away sin but to bring salvation to those who eagerly await Him."

Another passage from Hebrews is: "Unlike the other high priests, [Jesus] has no need to offer sacrifice day after day, first for His own sins and then for those of the people; He did that once for all when He offered Himself." (Hebrews 7:27) To isolate these verses from the rest of sacred Scripture and simply take them for face value would lead one to conclude that there could be no other sacrifice—Christ sacrificed Himself, it is over and done with, and that is it. Period. Such a view is myopic to say the least.

Please note that in no way do we as Catholics believe that Christ continues to be crucified physically or die a physical death in heaven over and over again. However, we do believe that the Mass does participate in the everlasting sacrifice of Christ.

First, one must not separate the sacrifice of our Lord on the cross from the events which surround it. The sacrifice of our Lord is inseparably linked to the Last Supper. Here Jesus took bread and wine. Looking to St. Matthew's text (26:26ff), He said over the bread, "Take this and eat it. This is My body"; and over the cup of wine, "This is My blood, the blood of the covenant, to be poured out on behalf of many for the forgiveness of sins."

The next day, on Good Friday, our Lord's body hung on the altar of the cross and His precious blood was spilt to wash away our sins and seal the everlasting, perfect covenant. The divine life our Lord offered and shared for our salvation in the sacrifice of Good Friday is the same offered and shared at the Last Supper. The Last Supper, the sacrifice of Good Friday and the Resurrection on Easter form one saving event.

Second, one must have a nuanced understanding of time. One must distinguish chronological time from kairotic time, as found in sacred Scripture. In the Bible, *chronos* refers to chronological time—past, present and future—specific deeds which have an end point. *Kairos*, or kairotic time, refers to God's eternal time, time of the present moment which recapitulates the entire past as well as contains the entire future. Therefore, while our Lord's saving event occurred chronologically around the year AD 30-33, in the kairotic sense of time it is an ever-present reality which touches our lives here and now. In the same sense, this is why through baptism we share now in the mystery of Christ's passion, death and resurrection, a chronological event that happened almost 1,965 years ago, but is still efficacious for us today.

With this in mind, we also remember that our Lord commanded, as recorded in the Gospel of St. Luke (22:14ff) and St. Paul's First Letter to the Corinthians (11:23ff), "Do this in remembrance of Me." Clearly our Lord wanted the faithful to repeat, to participate in and to share in this sacramental mystery. The Last Supper, which is inseparably linked to Good Friday (and the Resurrection), is perpetuated in the holy Mass for time eternal.

The Mass therefore is a memorial. In each of the Eucharistic prayers, the *anamnesis*, or memorial, follows the consecration, whereby we call to mind the passion, death, resurrection and ascension of our Lord. However, this memorial is not simply a recollection of past history in chronological time, but rather a liturgical proclamation of living history, of an event that continues to live and touch our lives now in that sense of kairotic time.

Just as good orthodox Jews truly live the Passover event when celebrating the Passover liturgy, plunging themselves into an event which occurred about 1,200 years before our Lord, we too live Christ's saving event in celebrating the Mass. The sacrifice which Christ made for our salvation remains an ever-present reality: "As often as the sacrifice of the cross by which 'Christ our Pasch is sacrificed' is celebrated on the altar, the work of our redemption is carried out" ("Lumen Gentium," No. 3). Therefore, the *Catechism* asserts, "The Eucharist is thus a sacrifice because it re-presents (makes present) the sacrifice of the cross, because it is a memorial and because it applies its fruit" (No. 1366).

Therefore, the actual sacrifice of Christ on the cross and the sacrifice of the Mass are inseparably united as one single sacrifice. The Council of Trent in response to Protestant objections decreed, "The victim is one and the same: the same now offers through the ministry of priests, who then offered Himself on the cross; only the manner of offering is different," and "In this divine sacrifice which is celebrated in the Mass, the same Christ who offered Himself once in a bloody manner on the altar of the cross is contained and is offered in an unbloody manner." For this reason, just as Christ washed away our sins with his blood on the altar of the cross, the sacrifice of the Mass is also truly propitiatory. The Lord grants grace and the gift of repentance. He pardons wrong-doings and sins (cf. Council of Trent, "Doctrine on the Most Holy Sacrifice of the Mass").

Moreover, the Mass involves the sacrifice of the whole Church. Together we offer our prayers, praise, thanksgiving, work, sufferings to our Lord and thereby join ourselves to His offering. The whole Church is united with the offering of Christ. This is why in the Eucharistic Prayers we remember the pope, the vicar of Christ; the bishop, shepherd of the local diocese; the clergy who minister *in persona Christi* to the faithful; the faithful living now, the deceased and the saints.

The "Constitution on the Sacred Liturgy" of the Second Vatican Council summed it up well: "At the Last Supper, on the night He was betrayed, our Savior instituted the Eucharistic sacrifice of His Body and Blood. This He did in order to perpetuate the sacrifice on the cross through the ages until He should come again, and so to entrust to His beloved spouse, the Church, a memorial of His death and resurrection: a sacrament of love, a sign of unity, a bond of charity, a paschal banquet in which Christ is consumed, the mind is filled with grace, and a pledge of future glory is given to us" (No. 47).

As we celebrate the liturgies of Holy Week, may we give thanks to our Lord for the beautiful, precious gift of the Mass and the holy Eucharist.

Source: Rev. William Saunders. 1995. "Is the Mass Really a Sacrifice?" *Arlington Catholic Herald*, April 13. Reprinted with permission from Rev. William Saunders.

Father William Saunders is Professor of Catechetics and Theology at Christendom College and pastor of Our Lady of Hope Parish in Potomac Falls, Virginia. This article is a "Straight Answers" column he wrote for the *Arlington Catholic Herald*. Father Saunders is also the author of *Straight Answers*, a book based on 100 of his columns and published by Cathedral Press in Baltimore, Maryland.

The Mass Explained

By Cormac Burke

To judge the "quality" of the Christian life of a community is always a difficult task, and perhaps a foolhardy one. There are so many factors that should be taken into account. And the most important of them are hidden!

Nevertheless, if the Holy Mass is the central act of our Catholic life, then Mass-going must surely remain one of the most indicative of these factors. With good reason therefore we consider the number of people coming to Mass, not only on Sundays but also very specially on weekdays. With even better reason we try to assess the "quality" of their participation in the Mass; their understanding of its nature and their application to their own lives of what it should mean for them. And we often think of the ways in which we can help them.

This is where our catechists on the Mass must come in: a constant catechesis, with big groups and small groups, with Sunday's congregations and very particularly with the weekday ones; a constant and simple catechesis that is not afraid to drive home the basic points by dint of repetition.

The following commentaries—one for each day of the month—were first prepared for school use, with the idea of repeating them once every two or three months. They can easily be adapted for use on a different basis. The person-to-person style is no doubt more suited to the spoken word or to be put down in writing, but it seemed preferable not to change it.

Christ's Action

The Holy Mass is the holiest thing we have here on earth. Why? Because it is the action of Christ. The main thing in the Mass is not what is read from the Holy Scriptures, even though this is the word of God and should be listened to as such. The main thing in the Mass is not what the priest preaches in his sermon or what the people do or sing. The main thing is what Christ does. And what does Christ do in the Holy Mass? He offers himself for us, as he offered himself on the

Cross. He sacrifices himself for us. That is why we say that the Mass is the same Sacrifice as that of the Cross renewed in an unbloody manner on the altar. On the altar just as on the Cross, Christ offers his body and blood for us. The difference is that on the Cross his body and blood were visible to the eyes of those who were present, while in the Mass they are hidden under the appearances of bread and wine. But they are really present. This is the great fact. In each Mass, Christ is really present and renews the Sacrifice of the Cross.

Love for the Mass

"A man who fails to love the Mass fails to love Christ."[1] To love the Mass is a guarantee for salvation. But to love the Mass does not mean just being present and no more. It means to be present with faith and devotion. It means to take part in the Mass, realizing what it is: the Sacrifice of the Cross renewed on the altar; and realizing that when we go to Mass, we go, as it were, to Calvary. And that we should be present there, like our Blessed Lady beside the Cross, in loving contemplation of Christ who offers himself lovingly for each one of us.

Faith

The Holy Eucharist is the "mystery of faith." Without faith, all you would see is bread and wine being offered, no more. Without faith, the most you could see in this is a gesture, a symbol, nothing more. With faith you know that at the moment of the Consecration—which is when the priest says, "This is my body," "This is the cup of my blood"— the bread and wine are changed into the body and blood of Jesus Christ who is then really present as God and as Man sacrificing himself for us on the altar as he sacrificed himself on the cross. If you come to Mass without faith, or with little faith you will easily get distracted and perhaps even bored. What a sad thing to get bored with Christ's sacrifice! Would we have been bored if we had been present at Calvary? If we hadn't faith, perhaps we would. Or at least we would have completely failed to understand what the death of that Man nailed to the cross really meant. You will only begin to understand the greatness of

---

[1] J. M. Escriva. *Christ is Passing By*, no. 92.

the Mass if you have faith. Stir up your faith. And then you will always be amazed at the Mass, you will realize that it is the greatest thing we possess here on earth.

The Purposes of the Mass

What else should you do, besides having a lot of faith, if you want to attend Holy Mass well? You should identify yourself with Christ. You should remember the Scriptures and have "the same mind" that he had on the cross (cf. Phil 2:5). The same mind which means the same purposes. What purposes did Jesus have on the cross? What was he concerned about? We can sum up his ends or purposes as four: to give glory to God the Father; to thank him; to make up for the sins of men; and to ask him for graces for us. If each time you go to Mass, you try to live at least one of these four purposes, you will attend Holy Mass well.

The First Purpose: Adoration

God is our Creator. He is the Lord of the whole world. We depend on him for everything. He is infinite, eternal, all-powerful. His infinite greatness and goodness ought to fill us with amazement and enthusiasm. When people get enthused about God, they want to praise him, they want to adore him. Jesus Christ, with his humanity, gave perfect glory to God the Father from the cross, and he continues to do so from the altar. If you unite yourself to him, you will be offering a perfect sacrifice of adoration and praise. Pay special attention to the *Gloria* and the *Sanctus*.

The Second Purpose: To Give Thanks

God is infinitely good. And all the good things we have, have come from him: life, family, sanctifying grace, faith, the sacraments, the gift of his Mother . . . And so many other natural and supernatural gifts. It is good to give thanks. The person who is too proud to say "Thank You" is not only ungrateful but is bound to end up being unhappy. Unite yourself to our Lord in the Mass, giving thanks, and you will see how you also become more optimistic as a result, because you will become more and more convinced of the goodness of God.

The Third Purpose: To Make Up for our Sins

Jesus is perfect God and perfect Man. He is all-holy. Therefore he has not and could not have been guilty of any sin. But, as the Holy Scriptures says, he took our sins on himself and made up for them. He did penance for us by dying on the cross. If we want to take part properly in the Holy Mass, we must be sorry for our sins. The person who is not sorry for his sins will never understand or love the Mass, nor will he ever really take part in it. But the person who comes to Mass with real sorrow for his sins, will draw from it great strength to fight against temptations and to realize that, despite his weaknesses, God loves him very much.

The penitential act—the "I confess"—that we all say together at the start of the Mass does not pardon mortal sins. Forgiveness of mortal sins has to be obtained in the sacrament of penance. It is also important to remember that a person who has committed a mortal sin cannot go to communion unless he goes to confession beforehand. But the penitential act, if it is said well, certainly helps to obtain pardon for present venial sins as well as to stir up new sorrow for past sins that have already been forgiven. In this way it helps us to purify ourselves and so to take better part in the Holy Mass.

The Fourth Purpose: Petition

Our God is a merciful and a very generous God. He longs to give. He wants to give us what is absolutely the best, what is the greatest gift imaginable: eternal life and all the help we need to make it ours. God wants to give. But he also wants to be asked: "Ask and you shall receive." That is why we ask with a prayer of petition. However, it is wise, when asking, to be able to back up our petition with some proof of special merit on our part. This is where we seem to run into a big difficulty. For when we look at ourselves, we see ourselves so full of defects and so lacking in merits that there seems to be no reason why God should ever heed our petitions. That is why we look to the merits of Christ, and to those of our Lady and the saints. That is why, if we are sensible, we unite our prayer to the prayer of Christ.

Christ's prayer is always effective because it is simply impossible that God the Father should not listen to the prayer of his beloved Son.

Jesus prayed for us on the cross. He continues praying for us on the altar. When we pray in the Holy Mass, therefore, and unite our prayers to that of Jesus, we can be sure that our requests will be heard by God the Father.

Readings

Holy Scripture is God's word. God speaks to us in the inspired books, so that we can know what we have to believe and what we have to do, in order to get to heaven. After each reading we say, "Thanks be to God." Why do we say this? Because it is a wonderful thing that God speaks to us, that he addresses his words to us in these holy books, pointing out to us the way to heaven. It is another marvelous proof of his love for us. That is why we thank him.

Gospel

The Gospels tell us of the life of Jesus Christ, true God and true Man. They tell us of the things he did and the words he spoke during his life here on earth. We stand—at attention, as it were—in order to listen to the Gospel. This should be a sign to others and a reminder to ourselves that we are ready and determined to put into practice what we are listening to. You will have noticed how, just before the priest begins to read the Gospel, he turns towards the altar or the tabernacle, bows down and prays. What he is doing is to ask God for grace to be able to proclaim the good news of the Gospel well. At that moment you too would do well to ask for grace to be able to listen to the Gospel joyfully, to understand it and to put it into practice.

Creed

This is said on Sundays and the bigger feasts. We declare our faith. Do we really believe in the things we say in the Creed? Of course! But do we realize how big these things are? We believe in God, who is Father, Son, and Holy Spirit, who is One and Three, who created us, who redeemed us by means of his Son, Jesus Christ, who sanctifies us, giving us a share in his own life—by means of grace, through the work of the Holy Spirit and that of the holy Church—who forgives us always

(always provided we are sorry and ask for his pardon), and who is determined to bring us to heaven. There are some people who live in a closed world, as if they were inside a tunnel.[2] Faith brings us out of the tunnel and lets us live in the wonderful world of God. To declare our faith, as we do in the Creed, is something that should fill us with wonder, thanks and joy.

Presentation of the Gifts

We have ended the liturgy of the word. Now we start the Eucharistic liturgy in which the main actions of the Mass take place. The Eucharistic liturgy is made up of three main parts: the presentation of the gifts, the Eucharistic prayer or Canon (with the consecration), and the communion. In the presentation of the gifts (or the offertory) the priest (and we with him) offers the hosts—some small particles of unleavened bread—and small quantity of wine. What he offers is really very little. We could say that it has practically no value. But, *it should represent us*. If you want to learn to take proper part in the Holy Mass, it is important that you learn to offer yourself and to offer all that is yours in this moment of the Mass.[3] Take your work, your studies, your needs, your struggle, and even your weaknesses. Take all of that and put it on the paten beside the hosts, those small pieces of bread. Put it in the chalice with the wine.

Jesus Christ is going to come to this altar within a few minutes. There are many ways in which he could have chosen to come. But he has wished to come by marvelously turning the bread and the wine into his own body and blood. He has wished to come by means of transubstantiation, by which something that we offer him, something that is ours, is changed into his body and blood, while of the bread and wine only the appearances remain. The bread and the wine are our gifts, our offering to God. They will be your gift and your offering if you make them yours, if you put yourself there, on the paten with the bread, in the chalice with the wine. If you let yourself get distracted at the moment when the priest is offering the gifts, then the bread and the wine will be other people's gifts, something that other people offer to God. But they won't be your gifts, because you have not offered them,

---

[2] J. M. Escriva. *The Way*, no. 575.

[3] Cf. Vatican II. *Presbyterorum Ordinis*, no. 5; *Lumen Gentium*, nos. 11 and 34.

you have not offered yourself with them. Now do you see how important it is not to get distracted at the moment of the offertory?

Presentation of the Gifts

We have seen how in the presentation of the gifts, we offer to God a little bread and wine. We have seen too that these offerings ought to represent us. In themselves they are things of little value, but our affection accompanies them. Now think of what is going to happen to these gifts of ours. At the moment of the consecration, God is going to change them into something divine: into himself. From bread and wine they become the body and blood of Jesus Christ, true God and true Man! Up to the moment of the consecration our offering to God has practically no value. From the moment on, it has infinite value! Doesn't this help you see the importance of offering yourself with the bread and the wine so that they represent your day, your life? If you do this you are participating in the Mass and God will gradually do with your life what he does with the bread and wine. He will gradually turn your life—your ordinary everyday life—into something with divine value in his eyes. Your life—your work, your rest, your sports, your friendships—if you associate it closely to the Holy Mass, will be a sanctified life, which means sanctified work, sanctified rest, sanctified sports, sanctified friendships. Unite yourself well to the Holy Mass.

Orate, Fratres

We have spoken of how we ought to offer ourselves on the paten with the bread, and in the chalice with the wine. You have probably noticed how the priest, before he offers the chalice, adds a few drops of water to the wine, the wine that will soon be turned into the blood of our Lord. These drops of water—which are dissolved in the wine and therefore also turn into the Blood of Christ—represent us and all that we offer to God with Christ. Consider what happens next. After offering the bread and wine, the priest turns to the people and invites them to pray "so that our sacrifice," he says—my sacrifice and yours—"may be acceptable to God the Father Almighty." Don't pass over this too lightly: the sacrifice of the Mass is Christ's action, Christ's sacrifice. But it is also the sacrifice of the priest and of the people. It is your sacrifice—if you have made it yours, if you have really put some part of yourself into this sacrifice.

Sanctus

The Preface introduces the Canon which is the central and most solemn part of the Holy Mass. At the end of the Preface we say the Sanctus: "Holy, holy, holy Lord God . . ." It is like a song or a shout of enthusiasm. Let us think for a moment what our God is like. He is all powerful (he can do anything). He is infinite Love (he loves us as no one else could ever love us). He is all goodness and truth and greatness (he became Man out of love for us; he died on the cross to redeem us; and then he overcame death by rising again).

All of this should fill us with gratitude and joy. And then, like the saints and the angels in heaven, we will grow really enthusiastic about our God, we will want to praise him, and we will repeat the "Holy, holy, holy" with faith and fervor.

Consecration

The most solemn moment of the Holy Mass is the consecration. Up to that moment what is on the altar is bread and wine. From the moment when the priest pronounces the words of the consecration"—This is my body"; "This is the cup of my blood"—what is on the altar is the body and blood of Jesus Christ. Of the bread and wine nothing remains except the appearances. But, under those appearances, God is really present. All of this is done by the power of God. Jesus Christ is God become Man and he can do anything. He can even change a little bread and wine into his own body and blood so that it can be our offering and sacrifice: and also, if we are fit to receive him, so that it can be our food.

The priest raises the host and the chalice. And we adore him. Appearances will not deceive us if we have faith. With the eyes of our body we only see bread. But with the eyes of faith—which is how the Christian soul sees—we see and recognize our Lord himself. Let us express our faith. You remember those words of Saint Thomas, "My Lord and my God." Many people repeat them quietly to themselves at the moment of the elevation. Thomas wished to see the glorious Body of the risen Jesus. Then he proclaimed his divinity. Our Lord said to him, "Thomas, you believe because you can see me. Happy are those who have not seen and yet believe." Let us proclaim our faith in the real presence of Jesus in the host, relying for proof on his infallible word.

Consecration—Communion

This is the moment of the Mass when we have to be most awake, putting heart and soul into many acts of faith and love and adoration. Because Christ is at last on the altar. There is no longer any bread or wine. By the miraculous process of transubstantiation all of it has been changed into the body and blood of Jesus Christ, God become Man. Our Lord is really present with his humanity and his divinity, offering himself for us on the altar just as he offered himself for us on the cross.

We are on Calvary. This is the "composition of place" that we should make in these moments. Christ is offering himself for us. We too should want to be beside him, like our Lady and Saint John who were beside him and kept him company on Calvary. Let us ask them to help us not to get distracted, to be present with faith, to realize what Jesus is doing as he offers himself on the altar for the whole humanity—to adore him, to thank him.

The Mass is never a private action. Even if very few people or only a single person accompanies the priest, the whole Church is present. "Priests fulfill their chief duty in the mystery of the Eucharistic sacrifice. In it the work of our redemption continues to be carried out. For this reason, priests are strongly urged to celebrate Mass every day, for even if the faithful are unable to be present, it is an act of Christ and the Church."[4] Let us be conscious of this presence of the whole Church which, of course, also includes the angels and the saints. They are present and adoring from the moment of the consecration. If we ask them, they will help us too, to be present in a spirit of reverence and adoration.

The Our Father

The Eucharistic Prayer or Canon is the central part of the Mass. Now the moment for communion is approaching. As we end the Canon

---

[4] Vatican II. *Presbyterorum Ordinis*, no. 13.

we begin our more immediate preparation for communion. And first of all we say the prayer that our Lord himself taught his disciples: "Taught by him, we dare to call God our Father—he is the Almighty who created heaven and earth, and he is a loving Father who waits for us to come back to him again and again, as the story of the prodigal son repeats itself in our lives."[5] The Our Father contains seven petitions. We would do well to meditate on each one of them as they cover all of our most important needs.

Preparation for Communion

"This is the Lamb of God . . . Lord, I am not worthy. . . . We are going to receive our Lord. On this earth, when we receive an important person, we bring out the best—lights, music, formal dress. How should we prepare to receive Christ into our soul? Have we ever thought about how we would behave if we could only receive him once in a lifetime?"[6] We are not worthy to have him enter even once into our house, into our poor soul. Yet he is so eager to enter there very often. What we can and ought to do is to ensure that however poor the house of our soul is, it is clean. We cannot receive our Lord with a dirty soul, with a soul dirtied by sin. If we ever stain ourselves with a serious sin, then we have to get cleaned in the sacrament of penance before going to communion. We are not worthy to receive our Lord. But we must never receive him unworthily with a mortal sin on our soul that has not been confessed. It would be like the kiss of Judas. It would mean betraying Christ, striking him, crucifying him all over again.

Communion

"Happy are those who are called to his supper." "If you do not eat the flesh of the Son of Man, you will not have life in you." "Anyone who eats this bread will live forever. . . ." We come to Mass because we have felt ourselves invited to accompany our Lord in his sacrifice—while he offers himself for us—and to offer ourselves with him. We come to Holy Mass, therefore, to take part in the sacrifice of Christ. When the moment of communion comes, we feel that our Lord continues to

---

[5] *Christ is Passing By*, no. 91.
[6] *Ibid.*

invite us. Now he is calling us to his supper where he offers himself to us to be the food of our souls. How hungry we should be to receive him!

The soul needs its nourishment even much more than the body. But we should not forget that while the appetite of the body is generally spontaneous (three or four times a day we *feel* like eating), the appetite of the soul is rather *reflexive* and *voluntary*: it is a consequence of faith. Stir up your faith in him who is hidden beneath the appearances of bread: "Lord, I recognize you." Stir up your faith in his promises: "Anyone who eats this bread will live forever." And your hunger for communion will increase from day to day.

We should be so eager to receive him! Holy Communion is the greatest gift we could be offered. And yet some people are not interested! They could go to communion frequently; but they don't. And there are others who don't go to communion because their weaknesses get the better of them. But why don't they go to confession first, and then to communion? And then they will get *strength*, precisely to resist those weaknesses! But since God not only knows this but loves us, he has given us a source of special strength, of divine strength, in the sacrament. How eager we ought to be to receive them, especially those two which we can receive often, confession and communion.

We should put so much love into how we receive him! Always with faith, and always with love. If you really have faith, if you realize what it is you receive, you will receive him with love, just as it is with love that he comes to you. He comes to you with love, and you *ought* to receive him with love. There is no *obligation* to go to communion frequently. But if you do go to communion, then there is an obligation to receive him with love and affection. It would be such a lack of reverence to receive our Lord in a routine way, without trying to make many acts of faith and of love.

Holy Mass: Self-giving

In the Mass, Christ offers himself for us. And in Holy Communion he offers himself to us. Think what this offering costs our Lord—his whole passion! The Mass asks us also for correspondence and self-giving. If we attend Mass with faith, it will be easier for us to give ourselves to God each day trying to fulfill his commandments with love. And it will also be easier for us to give ourselves generously to other people, in a constant effort to love them, to understand them, to make their lives happier.

Opening Prayer, Prayer over the Gifts, Prayer after Communion

In the Holy Mass we are praying constantly with Jesus and through Jesus. Remember, for instance, the prayer that we say before the readings, and those that come after the offertory and communion. We ask for different things. But what matters most is that we always ask "through Jesus Christ our Lord." It has been said that the only prayer which reaches heaven with full effect is that of Jesus. Therefore, when we pray through him in the Mass, we can be sure that our prayers reach God the Father and that he listens to them.

Mass: Presence of God

There are so many other small details in the Mass that we can learn from. One is the fact that time and again throughout the Mass the priest says to the people—he wishes them—"the Lord be with you," and the people return him the same wish. Could we wish someone anything better? The Lord is going to be with us during the whole of the Mass, and we should try to be with him. And then he will also be more with us—and we more with him during the rest of the day.

Sorrow for One's Sin

The Mass is a sacrifice offered for the forgiveness of sins. We would not have proper dispositions for taking part in the Mass if we were not aware of our sins and *sorry for* them. That is why, as soon as the Mass has begun, the priest invites each one of us to call our sins to mind. And all of us pray together, acknowledging that we have sinned through our own fault in our thoughts and words, in what have done and failed to do. If you are not sorry for your sins you will never attend Mass well. Think at the moment therefore about your sins and your acts of selfishness, and ask Blessed Mary ever Virgin, and all the angels and saints, to pray for you and help you to be very sorry for those faults of yours which, even if they are not very grave, nevertheless disfigure the soul.

Thanksgiving

Christ offers himself for us in the Holy Mass, and he offers himself to us in Holy Communion. To be present at Mass, and receive Holy Communion, is the greatest thing we can do here on earth. Here, on the altar, we receive the greatest benefits that God gives us on earth. Once Mass has ended it is only logical that we remain for a few minutes giving thanks to our Lord. To leave without giving thanks would be a sign of little consideration or little faith. "The fact that the sacred function . . . has come to an end, does not dispense him who has communicated from making his thanksgiving. On the contrary it is most fitting that after he has received Holy Communion and after the Mass is over he should collect his thoughts and, in close union with his Divine Master, pass such time as circumstances allow in devout and salutary conversation with him."[7]

Those moments, when one has received communion and the Mass has just ended, are the best moments to ask graces and favors from our Lord. He is so eager to give, but at the same time he wants us to ask. "Ask and you shall receive." Can there be any better moment for asking than when we are united with him, when he is inside us, brought there by his immense love towards each one of us? Don't waste those moments. Use them to pray for many things, for yourself, for your loved ones, for the Church, for the Pope, for souls everywhere, for the whole world. . . .

Source: Cormac Burke. 1981. "The Mass Explained." Manila: Sinag-Tala Publishers. Reprinted with permission from Cormac Burke.

A Professor of Modern Languages and a Doctor of Canon Law, as well as a civil lawyer and member of the Irish Bar, Cormac Burke was ordained a priest of the Opus Dei Prelature in 1955. After thirty years of pastoral and teaching work in Europe, North America, and Africa, he was appointed by Pope John Paul II as a Judge of the Roman Rota, the High Court of the Church. During his thirteen years at the Vatican, he also taught Anthropology at the Studium

---

[7] Pope Pius XII. *Mediator Dei,* no. 130.

Rotale, as well as Canon Law at the Pontifical University of the Holy Cross. Among his best known books are *Conscience and Freedom, Authority and Freedom in the Church,* and *Covenanted Happiness.* In 1999, he returned to Africa, where he teaches at Strathmore University, Nairobi, Kenya.

Chapter 13

The Sacrament of Confession

A common lament these days is that the lines for Communion are long but the lines for Confession are very short. Indeed, the sacrament of Confession seems to have fallen out of fashion—due, no doubt, to the loss of the sense of sin that many commentators have pointed out, including Pope John Paul II.

It is not unusual to hear lapsed Catholics complain that the Church put them on a "guilt trip." These people do not seem to realize the profound value of the feeling of guilt that we experience when we sin. Guilt is real. Guilt arises when a functioning conscience tells us we have done wrong. It is the first step toward repentance, forgiveness, and peace.

Some may think of the sacrament of Confession as sort of a "dumping ground" where sinners go to unburden themselves and then resume their sinful ways. However, this is not the case. We are forgiven our sins in the sacrament of Confession only when we are truly sorry and have the firm intention of avoiding those sins confessed. The goal of confession is a conversion of the heart.

We have all heard people say, "I can confess my sins directly to God." This is true! We can and we should confess our sins to God and express our profound sorrow to him in our prayers. However, this is not the way Our Lord prescribed for us to obtain forgiveness. Scripture makes it clear that Jesus gave the Apostles and (logically) their successors the power to forgive sins. He instituted the sacrament of Confession because he knew that we needed it. Can God forgive sins outside of the sacrament? Of course he can; God is not constrained by his sacraments. But it is his will that we confess to a priest in the sacrament as the normal manner of obtaining forgiveness. We ignore God's will in this matter at our own peril!

In **"Why Go to Confession?,"** Father William Saunders cites the Scriptural basis for the sacrament as well as the evidence that the early Church took Our Lord's words seriously and celebrated the sacrament.

> Our Lord entered the world to forgive sins, and he made clear that he wanted this ministry of reconciliation to continue after he ascended to the Father.

> On the day of his Resurrection, Jesus said, "Receive the Holy Spirit. If you forgive men's sins, they are forgiven them; if you hold them bound, they are held bound" (John 20: 21-23).

> St. Paul said, "God has reconciled us to Himself through Christ and has given us the ministry of reconciliation" (2 Cor 5:18).

> An early work written around 80 A.D., *The Didache* (or Teachings of the Twelve Apostles), makes it clear that penitents were to confess their sins prior to receiving Holy Communion.

> The writings of several early Church Fathers (Saints Cyprian, Ambrose, and Athanasius) refer to the practice of confessing one's sins.

> For those truly aspiring to a Christ-like life, regular Confession (every one or two months) is recommended. We should confess both sins of commission and sins of omission.

The late John Hardon, S.J., makes the case for frequent confession in **"The Spiritual and Psychological Value of Frequent Confession."**

> Although the practice of frequent Confession is a relatively recent development in the long history of the Church, it is evidence of the "genius of Catholic Christianity."

> All nine popes of the twentieth century have encouraged the practice of frequent confession.[1]

> The spiritual benefits of frequent confession have been enumerated by the modern popes.
>   • Self-knowledge is increased.
>   • Bad habits are corrected.
>   • Conscience is purified.
>   • The will is strengthened.
>   • Salutary self-control is attained.
>   • We become more sinless.

---

[1] Father Hardon's article was written prior to the pontificate of Benedict XVI. Pope Benedict XVI has also been a great proponent of frequent confession.

- We become more conformed to Jesus Christ.
- We become more submissive to the Holy Spirit.

➢ Confession also has psychological value.

➢ The sacrament contributes to the well-being of mind and gives us peace of soul.

➢ Psychologists report that a sense of guilt is a principle source of "disquiet of mind and disturbance of will." The forgiveness obtained in the sacrament of Confession addresses this sense of guilt directly.

➢ The more frequently we avail ourselves of the sacrament, the greater our depth of peace.

Further Reading

Benedict Baur. 1999. *Frequent Confession*. Princeton, New Jersey: Scepter Publishers.

Russell Shaw. 1986. *Why We Need Confession*. Huntington, Indiana: *Our Sunday Visitor* Books.

Why Go to Confession?

by Rev. William Saunders, Ph.D.

Jesus entered this world to forgive sins. Recall the words of our Lord: "God so loved the world that He gave His only Son, that whoever believes in Him may not die but may have eternal life" (Jn 3:16). During His public ministry, Jesus preached about the forgiveness of sins: remember the parables of the Prodigal Son (Lk 15:11ff) or the Lost Sheep (Lk 15:1ff), and His teaching that "There will likewise be more joy in heaven over one repentant sinner than over 99 righteous people who have no need to repent" (Lk 15:7). Jesus Himself forgave sins: remember the story of the woman caught in adultery (Jn 8:1ff) or the woman who washed His feet with her tears. (Lk 7:36ff) He also taught us to pray for forgiveness in the "Our Father:" "Forgive us our trespasses as we forgive those who trespass against us." His mission of reconciliation would climax in His passion, death and resurrection: Jesus suffered, died and rose to free us from sin and death.

However, Jesus never trivialized sin or rationalized it. No, for Jesus, sin is sin, a violation of love against God and neighbor.

However, in His divine mercy, Jesus called the sinner to realize the sin, to repent of it, and to be reconciled with God and neighbor.

Jesus wanted this ministry of reconciliation to continue. On the first Easter Sunday evening, Jesus appeared to His Apostles, "breathed on them," and said, "Receive the Holy Spirit. If you forgive men's sins, they are forgiven them; if you hold them bound, they are held bound." (Jn 20:21-23) Only twice in Sacred Scripture do we find God breathing into human beings. First, in the Genesis account of creation, God breathes the life of a soul into the man He has created. (Gen 2:7) Now, Jesus, the Son, breathes His life into His Apostles His priests, so that through them He will "breathe" life into the souls of contrite sinners. In this scene, Christ instituted the sacrament of penance and made His Apostles the ministers of it.

At the ascension, Jesus again charged His Apostles with this ministry: "Thus it is written that the Messiah must suffer and rise from the dead on the third day. In His name penance for the remission of sins is to be preached to all the nations, beginning at Jerusalem. You are witnesses of this (Lk 24:46ff). Clearly, Jesus came to forgive sins, He wanted that reconciliation to continue and He gave the Church a sacrament through which priests would continue to act as the ministers of this reconciliation.

Perhaps many Protestants do not see the need for confession because most Protestant denominations do not have sacraments or at least the understanding of sacraments as efficacious signs through which the Lord gives us grace. (However, traditional or "high" Episcopalians have confessions. The Lutherans also have a ritual for reconciliation.)

Nevertheless, we see this ministry of reconciliation lived out in the early Church. St. Paul wrote, "God has reconciled us to Himself through Christ and has given us the ministry of reconciliation" (2 Cor 5:18). The *Didache* (or *Teachings of the Twelve Apostles*), written about 80 AD, stated, "In the congregation you shall confess your transgressions" and "On the Lord's Day, come together and break bread . . . having confessed your transgressions that your sacrifice may be pure." St. Cyprian in his *De lapsis* concerning the reconciliation of Christians who had succumbed to offering pagan worship rather than face martyrdom, wrote, "Let each confess his sin while he is still in this world, while his confession can be received, while satisfaction and the forgiveness granted by the priests is acceptable to God." At this time of persecution, when local "parishes" were small, individuals publicly confessed their sins at the beginning of Mass (as mentioned in the *Didache)* and received absolution from the bishop or priest.

After the legalization of the Church by Constantine, the Church fathers continued to emphasize the importance of confession. St. Ambrose wrote, "It seemed impossible that sins should be forgiven through penance; Christ granted this power to the Apostles and from the Apostles it has been transmitted to the office of priests" (*De poenitentia*). Similarly, St. Athanasius asserted, "As the man whom the priest baptizes is enlightened by the grace of the Holy Ghost, so does he who in penance confesses his sins, receive through the priest forgiveness in virtue of the grace of Christ" (*Contra Novatus*). By the mid-400s and the pontificate of Leo I, private confession under the seal of secrecy becomes the norm to safeguard the reputation of the penitent and to attract others to the sacrament.

Therefore, we go to confession because it is a sacrament given to us by Christ, and it has always been a practice of the Church.

This sacrament is so important in our sharing in the life of Christ, the Church has even mandated its practice. To prevent laxity, the Fourth Lateran Council in 1215 required that "every faithful of either sex who has reached the age of discretion should at least once a year faithfully confess all his sins to his own priest. He should strive as far as possible to fulfill the penance imposed on him, and with reverence receive at least during Easter time the sacrament of the Eucharist." This rule is still a precept of the Church. The Council of Trent in 1551 in its *Doctrine on the Sacrament of Penance* asserted that since mortal sin "kills" the life of God in our souls, these sins must be confessed and absolved through the sacrament of penance (a principle repeated by Pope John Paul II in *Veritatis Splendor*). Trent also said "it is right and profitable" to confess venial sins.

We could end the answer here. However, regular confession is a healthy spiritual practice. Each sincere Catholic needs to periodically—every month or two—do a good examination of conscience holding himself to the standard of Christ. Each person should reflect on how well he has lived a "Christ-like life" by following the commandments and the teachings of the Church.

Perhaps one's failures are not so much commissions as they are omissions. For all of these, we bring our soul to the Lord and receive forgiveness. The healing grace of the sacrament of penance washes away sin and give us the strength to avoid that sin again. The more we love the Lord, the more we are aware of the smallest sins and the more we want to say, "I am sorry. Please forgive me." I am sure this is why Mother Teresa and Pope John Paul II go to confession weekly. As we continue our Easter celebration, may we take full advantage of this beautiful sacrament which draws us closer to the Lord.

Source: Rev. William Saunders. 1994. "Why Go to Confession?" *Arlington Catholic Herald*, April 7. Reprinted with permission from Rev. William Saunders.

Father William Saunders is Professor of Catechetics and Theology at Christendom College and pastor of Our Lady of Hope Parish in Potomac Falls, Virginia. The above article is a "Straight Answers" column he wrote for the *Arlington Catholic Herald*. Father Saunders is also the author of *Straight Answers*, a book based on 100 of his columns and published by Cathedral Press in Baltimore, Maryland.

The Spiritual and Psychological Value of Frequent Confession

by John A. Hardon, S.J.

The more frequently we receive the sacrament of Christ's mercy, the more grace is restored to our soul.

Judging by the drastic drop in confessions in countries like the United States, the false opinion is gaining ground that Confession is not to be received, or made, frequently. No doubt, one reason for this sad state of affairs is the prevalence of some wild theories about mortal sin. For example, the Fundamental Option theory claims that no mortal sin is committed unless a person totally rejects God. Who but the devil hates God? One adultery or one abortion is not a mortal sin. On these grounds, there are parishes in which almost no one goes to Confession.

Our focus in this conference, however, is more specific. We wish to emphasize the value of frequent Confession, where no conscious mortal sins are being confessed. We are speaking of the frequent, and therefore early confessions of children, as soon as they reach the age of reason—and let's make sure before they receive their First Holy Communion. We are speaking of the frequent confessions of youth, of married people, of those in declining years. We are with emphasis speaking of the frequent confessions of priests and religious, whose progress in sanctity is so closely bound up with their often receiving the sacrament of Penance.

Before going on, let me assure you that I am quite familiar with the present state of affairs in more than one diocese. People tell me it is becoming increasingly difficult to find a priest to hear your confession. You may have to make an appointment by telephone at the priest's convenience. You may have to meet a priest in person in the parlor and identify yourself before you go to Confession. You may have to listen to an unwelcome homily on not abusing the sacrament by having nothing except venial sins to confess, or be told to come back some other time, when you have something worthwhile to say.

Before going any further, I must tell you: choose your confessors carefully and wisely, and pray for those priests who seem unwilling to exercise this precious sacramental ministry as the Savior who ordained them wants it to be exercised, with prudence and kindness and the practice of Christ-like mercy.

The Church's Teaching

There is no doubt that the practice of frequent Confession in the absence of mortal sin is a relatively recent development in the Catholic Church. Such development under divine guidance is part of the genius of Catholic Christianity.

Consequently, those who frown on frequent Confession and go back to dusty volumes about the practice of Penance in the early Church are behind the times. They fail to realize that the Church is not a static organization, but the living and therefore developing Mystical Body of Christ. So what is wrong with the Church growing up?

The nine pontiffs of the present century have defended frequent Confession against, you guessed it, critics among the clergy.

Let me quote the words of Pope Pius XII. The quotation is long, but I do not hesitate saying it deserves to be memorized.

> It is true that venial sins may be expiated in many ways that are to be highly commended, but to ensure more rapid progress day by day in the practice of virtue we want the pious practice of frequent Confession which was introduced into the Church by the inspiration of the Holy Spirit to be earnestly advocated. By it genuine self-knowledge is increased, Christian humility grows, bad habits are corrected, spiritual neglect and tepidity are resisted, the conscience is purified, the will strengthened, a salutary self-control is attained, and grace is increased in virtue of the sacrament itself. Let those, therefore, among the younger clergy who make light of or lessen esteem for frequent Confession know what they are doing. What they are doing is alien to the spirit of Christ and disastrous for the Mystical Body of Christ.[1]

Then came the Second Vatican Council with widespread liturgical changes that are common knowledge. What may not be common knowledge, however, is that since the Council, Pope Paul VI authorized

---

[1] Pius XII. *Mystici Corporis Christi*, 88.

one of the most eloquent pleas in papal history for frequent reception of the sacrament of Penance. While recognizing that the immediate purpose of the sacrament is to remit grave sins, the new ritual emphasizes its salutary function also when mortal sins against God have not been committed. Once again, I quote in full.

> Frequent and reverent recourse to this sacrament, even when only venial sin is in question, is of great value. Frequent confession is not mere ritual repetition, nor is it merely a psychological exercise. Rather is it a constant effort to bring to perfection the grace of our Baptism so that as we carry about in our bodies the death of Jesus Christ who died, the life that Jesus Christ lives may be more and more manifested in us. In such confessions penitents, while indeed confessing venial sins, should be mainly concerned with becoming more deeply conformed to Christ, and more submissive to the voice of the Spirit.[2]

Pope John Paul II, in one document and speech after another, repeats the same message. He dares to say that those who discourage going to Confession because it produces a repressive mentality "are lying." He tells the faithful to receive this sacrament as often as possible. Why? Because "by this sacrament, we are renewed in fervor, strengthened in our resolutions, and supported by divine encouragement." How we need to hear these words in an age when discouragement, leading to despair, is almost the hallmark of the modern world.

Spiritual Value of Confession

Suppose we examine, and even number, the spiritual benefits of frequent Confession as identified by the modern popes.

Self-Knowledge Is Increased. How blind we are to our own failings and weaknesses. We are hawk-eyed in seeing the faults of others, but stone blind when it comes to our own. There is nothing in the world that we more need to grow in humility than to recognize how stupid and helpless we are in the face of temptation. How desperately we need God's grace to see ourselves as we really are.

---

[2] Paul VI. 1973. *Congregation of Divine Worship* (December 2).

Bad Habits Are Corrected. Another word for bad habits is "vices." These bad habits are acquired by the repetition of bad actions. We may have the habit of unkind words, or of selfish behavior, which may have taken years to acquire. On the natural level, it would take years to change these bad habits into the opposite virtues. But with the grace of the sacrament of Confession, we can overcome these vices in record time, beyond all human expectation.

Conscience Is Purified. We do not commonly speak of purifying the conscience. But we should. What is a pure conscience? A pure conscience is one that sees clearly, we may say instinctively, what should be done in a given situation and how to do it. The opposite of a pure conscience is a dull or insensitive conscience. People will do all kinds of evil, commit every kind of sin, without even realizing that they are doing wrong. The sacrament of Penance purifies our mind to recognize God's will in every circumstance of our lives, instantly and almost without reflection. How? By the action of the Holy Spirit, whose gift of counsel enlightens the mind to know exactly what the Lord wants us to do and how to do it the moment we are faced with a moral decision.

The Will Is Strengthened. We could spend not just a whole conference on this subject, but a semester course on the value of what I call "the sacrament of courage." Certainly, we all have a free will. But our natural inclination is to do our own will, to choose what we want and reject what we do not want. The very expression "pro-choice" has become a synonym for the culture of death in our society. Christ told us to love others as He has loved us, even to dying out of love for another person. The world is now telling us in the laws of most nations to murder innocent unborn children out of self-love.

Do we ever need to have our wills strengthened to resist our love of self and submit these wills to the will of God! I do not hesitate to say it is the single most desperate need as we come to the close of the twentieth century. The self has been literally deified. In one Western university after another, the philosophy of Immanuel Kant is the staple diet of the academic curriculum. At the root of Kantian morality is the principle of the autonomy of the will. My will is the basic and final norm of my conduct.

Did we ask whether we need the sacramental grace of Confession to strengthen our wills to submit to the will of God? In our age of self-idolatry, this grace is indispensable, dare I say, for the survival of Christianity.

Salutary Self-Control Is Attained. A standard English dictionary contains, by actual count, three hundred eighty terms beginning with the word "self." Among these are such terms as self-absorption, self-admiration, self-advancement, self-applause, self-approbation, self-assertion, self-assurance, to mention only the words with an "a" after the prefix "self."

To its credit, the dictionary defines self-control as "restraint exercised over one's own impulses, emotions, or desires."

But everything depends on what we mean by "restraint." All that we have so far said about the spontaneous tendency we have to satisfy our own desires brings out the importance of the Christian meaning of self-control.

Our faith tells us that we have a fallen human nature. Part of that nature is the loss of the gift of integrity that our first parents possessed before they had sinned. From the moment of our conception in our mother's womb, we already have the spontaneous tendency to desire what is pleasant and to run away from what is painful.

On these premises, self-control means the mastery of our impulses to conform to the mind and will of the Creator. Not everything we want is pleasing to Him, and not everything we dislike is contrary to His will. Self-control means mastering our thoughts and desires to correspond to the infinite mind and will of God.

That is why the Church, founded by the Incarnate God, is telling us to have frequent access to what Christ has instituted in the sacrament of Confession. We need the light which this sacrament assures us and the strength we so desperately need to surrender our "Selves" to the almighty Self from whom we came and for whom we were made.

We Become More Sinless. By the frequent and reverent reception of the sacrament of Penance, we make more perfect the justification we first received in Baptism. What does this mean? It means we become more and more sinless. Christ thereby exercises His saving redemption on our souls by cleansing us more and more and thus preparing us better and better for that kingdom of glory where nothing undefiled can enter and where only the sinless have a claim to enjoy the vision of the All-holy God. And who in his right mind would claim he or she is already sinless?

We Become More Conformed to Jesus Christ. We become more like Jesus Christ in the power to practice the virtues that characterized His visible life on earth. What virtues are they? We become more humble and better able to conquer our foolish and stubborn pride. And the very humiliation of telling our sins to another sinner is God's way of telling us, "If you confess, I will make you more humble." We become more patient in bearing with pain and enduring the people that God puts into our lives. Sometimes I think pain should have a masculine and feminine gender. Most of our suffering, most of the difficulties and problems and tribulations, that we have to endure on earth, if your lives are like mine, come from other people. And of course, we pay them the favor of being corresponding graces of tribulation in their lives. Through this sacrament we become more conformed to Jesus by becoming more prayerful in greater awareness of God's majesty and, therefore, our need to pay attention to God, and in greater awareness of our weakness and constant need for assistance from the Lord. This is one place where Jesus did not have to pray to overcome His sinful tendencies. Above all we become more loving in giving and giving and giving ourselves according to the divine will even as Jesus kept giving Himself to the will of His Father even to the last drop of His blood.

We Become More Submissive to the Holy Spirit. The Holy Spirit, dwelling in the depths of our hearts, is always speaking to us, but we are not always listening to Him. We are so busy with so many things, so preoccupied with ourselves, our interests and concerns, that He is often not only the unseen but, I am afraid, the unappreciated Guest in our souls. As John the Baptist said of the Savior to his contemporaries, "There is one in our midst whom we know not." And if we are going to be submissive to this Spirit of God, the first condition is that we are aware that there is a Spirit, that He has a voice and that He is talking. You do not listen to silence. And this is divine speech.

The Spirit of God wants nothing more than for us to pay attention to Him. Pay Him the courtesy, if you will, of recognizing that He is within us. The Spirit of God wants us to thank Him for all the good things He has given us. He wants us to keep asking Him. That is why He keeps creating problems. Those are divine signals. Did you know that? They are divine shouts, "Listen to me. Thanks. Thanks for at least looking at me. And except for the pain or sorrow or trial or temptation, knowing you," He tells us, "you would not even bother thinking of me.

Thanks! Now that you are awake, listen!" So we rub our eyes and say, "Yes, Lord."

But mainly the Holy Spirit wants us to be submissive to His will whether this be obedience to His commands when He tells us, "*Do this,*" or "*Do not do that,*" or when He gently invites us to do something more than we have to under penalty of sin, when He just whispers, "*Would you mind doing this?*" or "*Would you mind avoiding that?* Not because you have to, but because I would like you to show that you love me." All of this, and far more than human speech can describe, is available to us, so the Church of God tells us, by our frequent and reverent reception of the sacrament of Christ's peace.

Psychological Value of Confession

Frequent Confession has not only deep spiritual value as we have just seen. It is also immensely beneficial psychologically. In other words, the frequent reception of the sacrament of Penance contributes to the well-being of our mind. In one declarative sentence, it is a divinely instituted means of giving us peace of soul.

Remember what happened on Easter Sunday night. As described by St. Luke, "The doors were closed in the room where the disciples were, for fear of the Jews. Jesus came and stood among them. He said to them, 'Peace be with you,' and showed them His hands and His side. The disciples were filled with joy when they saw the Lord, and He said to them again, 'Peace be with you. As the Father sent me, so am I sending you.' After saying this, He breathed on them and said, 'Receive the Holy Spirit. For those whose sins you forgive, they are forgiven; for those whose sins you retain, they are retained'" (Jn 20:19-23).

As the Catholic Church teaches, by these words of the risen Savior, He instituted the sacrament of Confession. For twenty centuries, it has been called the sacrament of peace.

The principal source of conflict in the human spirit is the sense of guilt. Psychologists tell us, it is the mysterious feeling of guilt which lies at the root of most people's disquiet of mind and disturbance of will. On both levels, the sacrament of Confession is the Lord's great gift to His followers.

Peace of mind is the experience of knowing the truth. We all know that we are sinners. We also know that, as sinners, we have offended God and become estranged from His love in the measure of our sins.

How we need the assurance, based on faith, that this offended God is still pleased with us. When Christ tells us that there is greater joy in heaven over one sinner doing penance than over ninety-nine who are just, He is speaking of us who have deserved His rejection. The more often we receive His sacrament of mercy, the more deeply we are at peace.

Peace of heart is the experience of doing the will of God. There is no peace in doing what we want. I know whereof I speak when I say that, doing one's own will is hell on earth. God wants us to enjoy peace of heart. That is why He instituted the sacrament of Confession. The more frequently we confess our failings, no matter how minor they may seem to be, the more deeply peaceful we shall be. Why? Because if there is one thing that God wants us to admit, and keep admitting, it is that we are sinners who trust in His loving mercy.

There is some value in explaining what the Catholic Church understands by guilt. Guilt is the loss of God's grace. The more deeply we have sinned, the more guilt we incur. That is what mortal sin means. It is the supernatural death of the soul by the loss of sanctifying grace.

But all sin incurs guilt. Every sin we commit deprives us of more or less of the grace of God. The subjective experience that is called guilt is only the tip of an iceberg. Beneath the feeling of guilt is the objective fact that we have been deprived, however minimally, of God's friendship.

I like the statement of St. Thomas Aquinas who says, "The act of sin may pass, and yet the guilt remains."

The more frequently we receive the sacrament of Christ's mercy, the more grace is restored to our soul. We can experience the effect by growing in that peace of soul for which there is no substitute this side of heaven, realizing and not only knowing that, in spite of our sins, God loves us with that special love He reserves for repentant sinners.

Source: Father John A. Hardon. 1998. "The Spiritual and Psychological Value of Frequent Confession." Inter Mirifica. Reprinted with permission from *Inter Mirifica.*

Fr. John A. Hardon, S.J., (1914-2000) was a tireless apostle of the Catholic faith and the author of over twenty-five books, including *Catholic Prayer Book, The Catholic Catechism, Modern Catholic Dictionary, Pocket Catholic Dictionary, Pocket Catholic Catechism, Q & A Catholic Catechism, Treasury of Catholic Wisdom, Catholic Lifetime Reading Plan,* and many other books and hundreds of articles. Father Hardon was a close associate and advisor of Pope Paul VI, Pope John Paul II, and Mother Teresa and the Missionaries of Charity.

Chapter 14

Papacy and the Doctrine of Infallibility

Properly understood, Catholics see the papacy and the infallibility of the teaching office of the Church as wonderful gifts from God. Without them, the Church would not have been able to maintain the unity for which Our Lord so ardently prayed the night before he died.

Holy Father, keep them in your name that you have given me, so that they may be one just as we are (John 17: 11).

I pray not only for them, but also for those who will believe in me through their word, so that they may all be one, as you, Father, are in me and I in you, that they also may be in us, that the world may believe that you sent me. And I have given them the glory you gave me, so that they may be one, as we are one, I in them and you in me, that they may be brought to perfection as one, that the world may know that you sent me, and that you loved them even as you loved me (John 17: 20-23).

Without the papacy and its teaching authority, all of Christendom would resemble Protestantism, without a true teaching authority and with a proliferation of sects embracing different beliefs. Indeed, the sad reality is that the unity for which Christ prayed has been fractured by schism, the Protestant Reformation, and dissent within the Catholic Church. We all should pray for reconciliation, healing, and unity among Christians throughout the world.

Catholics believe that Jesus Christ established the papacy and that he appointed Peter to be the first Pope. This is clearly established in the Gospels and is supported by the writings of the early Fathers of the Church.

The doctrine of infallibility is widely misunderstood, even among Catholics. Although the doctrine was not officially defined until the First Vatican Council in 1870, it was held by Christians from the earliest days of the Church.

In **"The Petrine Principal: Faith of Our Fathers,"** Mike Aquilina shows that the ancient Church believed in the primacy of the papacy.

➤ The early Christians believed that the Popes were successors of Peter and held the same authority. This is clear from the first-century writings of St. Clement of Rome as well as those of the ancient Greek Church.

➤ When trouble arose, the Church Fathers appealed to the Pope for assistance.

➤ The writings of St. Jerome in 376 A.D. addressed Pope St. Damasus as the successor of the fisherman and other titles linking him to Peter.

➤ Great reverence for the papacy is found in ancient Christian culture and artifacts.

Pedro Rodriguez presents a comprehensive discussion of the papacy in **"The Primacy of the Pope in the Church."**

➤ Even non-Catholic Christian scholars are coming to the conclusion that the papacy has a necessary role at the center of Christianity.

➤ The organization of the Church is based on the will of Christ expressed through Sacred Scripture and Tradition.

➤ The apostolic college and the spirit of Christ are the two elements provided by Our Lord to minister to his people.

➤ The Church's hierarchy is not a socio-political phenomenon; rather, it stems from the will of Christ.

➤ Christ instituted the sacrament of Holy Orders to perpetuate his Church.

➤ The universal authority of the Pope, held since the beginning of Christianity, was proposed as a dogma of the faith by the Council of Florence in 1439.

➤ This authority is necessary to preserve the unity of faith.

➤ The primacy of the Pope comes from the very clear teaching of Scripture (Matthew 16: 16-18 and John 21: 15ff).

➤ The principles of the indefectibility and perpetuity of the Church require papal succession, that is, apostolic and papal succession is necessary if the Church is to last forever and maintain its unity as desired by Christ.

➤ The belief in apostolic and papal authority and succession can be found in the writings of the Church Fathers.

➤ The Pope is a bishop, the Bishop of Rome. His power concerns only matters related to the threefold mission of teaching, sanctifying, and leading the faithful to God.

➤ The primacy of Peter is a pastoral primacy, a primacy of love.

➤ The authority of the Pope relates, not only to matters of faith and morals, but also to discipline and government of the universal Church.

➤ The Pope has very wide power to enable him to serve the unity of the Church.

➤ The decisions of the Pope are final, and there is no tribunal to which one can appeal.

➤ Papal primacy is based on its historical institution by Christ and the actual presence of Christ today in the primatial acts of the Pope. The Pope "acts in the person of Christ."

➤ In his official actions, the Pope represents the whole Church and the college of bishops.

➤ The primacy of Peter is "the perpetual and visible center and foundation of the community of churches which is vivified by the Spirit of Christ."

In **"Pillar and Bulwark of the Truth: The Infallible Magisterium of the Catholic Church,"** Catholics United for the Faith provides an explanation of the Church's Magisterium—the teaching office of the Church—and its infallibility.

➤ Infallibility is a charism whereby the Holy Spirit protects the Magisterium from teaching errors in matters of faith and morals.

➤ The Church is infallible when it teaches definitively, whether through its extraordinary Magisterium or through the ordinary and universal Magisterium.

➤ Addressing the Apostles, Jesus made it clear that the Holy Spirit would teach them all things and bring to mind all his teachings (John 14:26).

➤ The papacy was established by Christ to ensure a reliable source of teaching and to maintain unity in his Church.

- ➢ The college of bishops has supreme and full authority only when it is in union with the Pope.
- ➢ Jesus said that the gates of hell would not prevail against his Church (Matt 16: 18-19). We have Christ's word that the Magisterium of the Church will be protected from teaching error.
- ➢ It is our faith in God that leads us to embrace the teachings of the Church as he said to his apostles, "[H]e who hears you hears me, and he who rejects you rejects me" (Luke 10:16).
- ➢ Two types of teaching require our full and irrevocable assent:
  - Divinely revealed teachings, that have their source in Scripture or Tradition and are part of the "deposit of faith"
  - Teachings that have been definitively pronounced.
- ➢ A third category of teaching calls for adherence with religious assent. These teachings, while not proposed definitively, are presented as true and sure. An example would be the recent teaching on the death penalty: it should not be used unless there is no other "way of defending human lives against an unjust aggressor."
- ➢ Infallible teaching is proposed by the Church in two ways: its extraordinary Magisterium, where it teaches solemnly, for example, when the pope speaks "ex cathedra" (from the chair) on a matter concerning faith or morals; and when the Pope and the bishops united to him solemnly define a teaching at an ecumenical council.
- ➢ The ordinary and universal Magisterium, the Pope and bishops united to him, teaches infallibly in the following situations:
  - The teaching is intended to be held definitively by the Pope and bishops.
  - Without issuing a solemn definition, the teaching confirms or reaffirms the Church's teachings at an ecumenical council.
  - The Pope confirms that a teaching is infallibly taught by the ordinary Magisterium—that it "has been constantly maintained and held by Tradition and transmitted by the ordinary, universal Magisterium." Examples of this include the recent reaffirmations by Pope John Paul II that priestly ordination is reserved to males and that the Church cannot condone artificial contraception.

Further Reading

"Papal Infallibility." Catholic.com.
    http://www.catholic.com/library/Papal_Infallibility.asp.

"Peter and the Papacy." Catholic.com.
    http://www.catholic.com/library/Peter_and_the_Papacy.asp.

Thomas Storck. "What Is the Magisterium?" IgnatiusInsight.com.
    http://www.ignatiusinsight.com/features2007/tstorck_magisterium_may0
    7.asp.

The Petrine Principal:
Faith of Our Fathers

by Mike Aquilina

The New Testament bears ample testimony to the ancient faith of the Roman Christians. Rome marks the final destination of the Acts of the Apostles. Rome was the postal address of the first of St. Paul's canonical letters.

And the ancient Romans treasured their heritage. They knew, with unerring Christian instinct, what the African Tertullian would say so eloquently in the third century: The blood of the martyrs is seed. If that is so, the Romans were blessed indeed to count among their martyrs the apostles Peter and Paul.

There is no legal document—not even a forged one—that names the successors of St. Peter as title-holders to the Church, bearers of the keys. But the ancient Christians required no other proof than the Scriptures and the apostolic tradition.

Writing probably in AD 69 (and surely no later than 96), St. Clement of Rome, the third successor of Peter, remonstrated the faraway congregation in Corinth, Greece. Clement could do this because he spoke with Peter's authority, which was granted by Christ Himself. As he concluded his letter, he urged the Corinthians to "render obedience unto the things written by us through the Holy Spirit." And they did. A century later, the Greek church still hallowed Clement's letter, as did other churches that counted it among the canonical scriptures and proclaimed its words in the liturgy.

Obedience to Christ in the person of His vicar: This is the common testimony of the Fathers. When the saints of East and West saw danger, they appealed to the pope. We find such pleas in the letters of St. Irenaeus (second century), St. Basil the Great (fourth century), St. John Chrysostom (early fifth century), and St. Cyril of Alexandria (mid-fifth century).

One and all, these were men with an encyclopedic knowledge of the Scriptures. So when they wished for an action that bore the authority of Jesus Christ, they knew where to send their petition. Sometimes they were disappointed by the papal response, but they maintained their faith in the papal office.

In the year 376, the greatest Scripture scholar in the ancient world, St. Jerome, addressed Pope St. Damasus I with a torrent of biblical seals of the papacy: "I speak with the successor of the fisherman and disciple of the Cross. Following none but Christ as my primate, I am united in communion with Your Beatitude—that is, with the chair of Peter. Upon that Rock I know the Church is built. Whosoever eats a lamb outside this house is profane. Whoever is not in Noah's ark will perish when the flood prevails."[1]

To be a Christian was—then as now—to obey Jesus Christ in the holy Scriptures.

Thus, to be a Christian was to obey Jesus Christ in his vicar, the pope.

This was not just the teaching of churchmen who had a vested interested in papal power. It was the faith of the congregations.

The Roman people passed down many traditions of Peter's ministry in their city. According to one story, during his imprisonment, the apostle preached to his jailers, who begged him for baptism. Finding insufficient water, Peter prayed and a pure spring bubbled up into the cell. Today we can see an ancient testimony to this story on the walls of the Catacomb of Commodilla. There, the early Christians portrayed Peter as a new Moses, striking a rock wall and drawing forth water.

But, again, reverence for the papacy wasn't just a Roman thing. A coffin in Arles, France, made around the same time, shows Christ handing on the Law to Peter.

Christ gave His Law to Peter with the grace of state. Peter passed it on to Linus, Linus to Cletus, Cletus to Clement, as John Paul passed it on to Benedict last April, while the whole world was watching.

Source: Mike Aquilina. 2006. "The Petrine Principal: Faith of Our Fathers." *Lay Witness Magazine* (March/April). Reprinted with permission from Mike Aquilina.

Mike Aquilina is author or editor of more than a dozen books on Catholic history, doctrine, and devotion. He is vice president of the St. Paul Center for

---

[1] This quotation from Jerome is from Thomas C. Lawler's translation of the saint's letters.

Biblical Theology in Steubenville, Ohio. He is co-host, with Scott Hahn, of "The Lamb's Supper" (2001), "Hail, Holy Queen" (2002), "First Comes Love" (2003), "Lord, Have Mercy" (2004), and "Swear to God" (2005)—all airing on the Eternal Word Television Network (EWTN). He also appears regularly as a panelist on "The Weekly Roman Observer," broadcast by Catholic Familyland Network. His career in publishing spans two decades, and hundreds of his articles have appeared in periodicals and journals in the United States and abroad.

The Primacy of the Pope in the Church

By Pedro Rodriguez

The well-known Lutheran scholar W. Pannenburg has this to say when asked about the Papacy: "Leaving aside for the moment the question whether the Papacy is of divine or human right, the need for a ministry of unity in the Church is so evident that negative Protestant attitudes ought no longer be adopted."[1] The statement on the question of authority in the Church agreed upon by Catholic and Anglican theologians at Venice in 1976 acknowledges a 'primatial authority' side by side with a "conciliar authority." The document then goes on to affirm that 'the only See which makes any claim to universal primacy and which has exercised and still exercises such "episcope" is the See of Rome, the city where Peter and Paul died. It seems appropriate that in any future union a universal primacy such as has been described should be held by that See."[2]

These two opinions reflect a state of mind which nowadays is quite widespread among non-Catholic Christians. Looking at things from very different points of view the conclusion is reached that in the Church there must be a world authority which is the source of unity. And it is further seen that in the history of Christianity such authority has only been claimed by the Roman Pontiff. Different scholars, some armed with reasons taken from the Bible, others appealing to Tradition, and still others arguing in terms of logical coherency, are coming to the same conclusion, namely, that the Papacy has an absolutely necessary role to play at the center of Christianity.

Obviously many of the statements and stances taken by non-Catholics regarding the Papacy only coincide partially with the teaching of the Catholic Church about the power and ministry of Peter's successor. But it is highly significant that as Dr. Pannenburg's paren-

---

Editor's Note: The author's use of quotation marks does not conform to common usage in the United States. The editor chose to retain the punctuation used in the original source document.

[1] W. Pannenburg. 1975. *Una Sancta* (30): 220-21.

[2] "Authority in the Church. A Statement on the Question of Authority: Its Nature, Exercise and Implication." 1976. Agreed by the Anglican-Roman Catholic International Commission Venice. London, CTS/SPCK, 1977, no.23.

thesis shows, Catholic dogmatic teaching that the primacy of the Pope belongs, by the will of Christ, to the fundamental structure of the Church is even now being discussed by non-Catholics. The reconsideration of the topic in sectors of the Anglican and evangelical churches (and the same could be said of the Orthodox churches) is in sharp contrast with the more usual neglect of the subject altogether. This is not the place to study the historical and spiritual reasons which have given rise to this new interest in the Papacy. It suffices to say that they show how much to the point were the words of a recent Catholic convert: "If God had not instituted the primacy of the Roman Pontiff we men would have had to invent it. . . ."

This new openness in Protestant circles is in sharp contrast too to the criticism leveled by some Catholics at the traditional teaching of the Church. Perhaps as a way of making it easier for our separated brethren to approach Rome one forgets far too frequently what Vatican Council II has said regarding ecumenical dialogue: 'It is essential that the doctrine be clearly presented in its entirety. Nothing is so foreign to the spirit of ecumenism as a false irenicism which harms the purity of Catholic doctrine and obscures its genuine and certain meaning.'[3] Accordingly it will be useful now to recall some central points of Catholic teaching regarding the authority of the Roman Pontiff, successor of St. Peter in the primacy of the universal Church.

The Will Of God Regarding His Church

Pope Leo XII gave us in his encyclical *Satis cognitum* (1896) a very clear guideline which must be borne in mind while studying the nature and fundamental structure of the Church: 'The origin of the Church and its whole constitution are matters determined by free will. Therefore, any judgment about them must be based on "factual history," and we should investigate, not the ways in which "it was possible" that there should be only one Church, but how "the founder fixed it" that there could only be one.'[4] There we have the whole question posed in correct terms. What counts are not more or less brilliant theories about

---

[3] "Decree on Ecumenism," no. 11.

[4] Dz. 3302. 1954. The emphases are in the original, A.A.S. 28 (1895/96, p.710. The Pope applies the principle to the particular case of the unity of the Church which he is dealing with in his encyclical letter.

the Church and her organization but the will of Christ, foundation stone and founder of the Church. In other words, the nature, origin and fundamental structure of the Church are known not by the intellectual skill and wisdom of her pastors and theologians, but by listening humbly to divine revelation—Sacred Scripture and Tradition—which witnesses to the foundational will of Christ. In this way, when the Church explains the mystery of herself and expounds it infallibly as a doctrine of faith she has the most well-founded confidence that all diligent and honest research in the sources of revelation—recognized as the Word of God—carried out by our separated Christian brethren cannot but substantiate the teachings of the Magisterium or, at least, point in the direction of them.

It is to Christ then that we must look and listen. "This is my beloved Son . . . Listen to Him" (Matt. 17:5). The guidelines of Pope Leo XIII must, in the words of Vatican Council II, preside over all ecumenical dialogue: "All are led to examine their own faithfulness to Christ's will for the Church."[5]

The following words of Pope Paul VI can serve as a short synthesis of the will of Christ for the constitution and makeup of his Church: "Christ promised and sent two elements to constitute his work, to extend in time and over all the world the kingdom founded by him and to make of redeemed mankind his Church, his mystical body, in expectation of his second and triumphal return at the end of the world. These elements are the apostolic college and the Spirit. The apostolic college works externally and objectively. It forms, one might say, the material body of the Church and gives her a visible and social structure. The Spirit works internally, within each person and within the community as a whole animating, vivifying and sanctifying. These two agents, namely the apostolic college whose successor is the sacred hierarchy, and the spirit of Christ, which makes the Church Christ's ordinary instrument in the ministry of the word and the sacraments, work together. On Pentecost morning they are seen in a marvelous harmony at the beginning of Christ's great work."[6]

For the remainder of this article we will be concerned with the first of these two elements.

---

[5] "Decree on Ecumenism," no. 4.
[6] Paul VI. 1964. "Address to Vatican Council II," September 14, A.A.S. (56), p. 807.

The Catholic Church teaches as a doctrine of faith that Christ gave the Church, in his apostles, a hierarchical structure of an episcopal nature and that within the hierarchy and the Church he established a primacy of authority in the successor of St. Peter.

Hierarchical Constitution of the Church

"All the faithful, from the Pope to the child who has just been baptized share in one and the same grace."[7] Nonetheless, when it is affirmed that the Church is a hierarchical society we are in substance saying that in spite of the 'radical or fundamental equality' which is to be found among the People of God, the Church has structures, features and differentiations by virtue of which she is a society in which there is a 'functional inequality.'[8] That is to say: not all the faithful have the same function or mission. For this reason Pope St. Pius X could say that "the Church is essentially an unequal society, that is, a society composed of two types of people: shepherds and sheep."[9]

This hierarchical structure is not the result of socio-political influences but stems from the will of Christ. This has been stated solemnly by both the Council of Trent and Vatican I,[10] but it is Vatican II which has given a detailed summary: "The Lord Jesus, having prayed at length to the Father, called to himself those whom he willed and appointed twelve to be with him, whom he might send to preach the kingdom of God (cf. Mark 3:13-19; Matthew 10:1-42). These apostles (cf. Luke 6:13) he constituted in the form of a college or permanent assembly, at the head of which he placed Peter, chosen from amongst them (cf. John 21:15-17). He sent them first of all to the children of Israel and then to all peoples (cf. Romans 1:16), so that, sharing in his power, they might make all peoples his disciples and sanctify and govern them (cf. Matthew 28:16-20; Mark 16:15; Luke 24:45-48; John 20:21-23) and thus spread the Church and, administering it under the guidance of the Lord, shepherd it all days until the end of the world (cf. Matthew 28:20)."[11]

---

[7] A. del Portillo. 1976. "Faithful and Laity in the Church," *Shannon*, p.19.
[8] "Ibidem," p. 22.
[9] St. Pius X. 1906. Encyclical, *Vehementer*, February 11, A.A.S. 3(9); 8.
[10] Dz. 1776 (66), 3051 (1821).
[11] "Decree on the Church," no.19.

Here we have the "hierarchical principle" of the Church established in the persons of the apostles. The Council goes on to say that this structure, which is of divine origin, is a constitutive part of the Church for all time, not just for the beginnings of the Church but for today as well. This is so, she says, by virtue of the "principle of apostolic succession." 'That divine mission, which was committed by Christ to the apostles, is destined to last until the end of the world (cf. Matthew 28:20), since the gospel, which they are charged to hand on, is, for the Church, the principle of all its life for all time. For that very reason the apostles were careful to appoint successors in this hierarchically constituted society."[12] The Council then explains in great detail and attentive to historical reality, to "factual history" in the words of Pope Leo XIII, how this transmission of authority and ministry was made 'to the bishops and their helpers, the priests and deacons.' This whole procedure, we are told, must be related to "the will of Christ": 'He willed that the successors (of the apostles), the bishops namely, should be the shepherds in his Church until the end of the world."[13] And finally, the Council solemnly declares: 'The sacred synod consequently teaches that the bishops have by divine institution taken the place of the apostles as pastors of the Church, in such wise that whoever despises them despises Christ and him who sent Christ (Luke 10:16).[14]

"This divinely instituted hierarchy, which is composed of bishops, priests and ministers"[15] received the mission which Christ had entrusted to his apostles. 'With priests and deacons as helpers, the bishops received the charge of the community, presiding in God's stead over the flock of which they are the shepherds, in that they are teachers of doctrine, ministers of sacred worship and holders of office in government."[16]

The sacrament of order is the way established by Christ for perpetuating in his Church this essential hierarchy[17] to which he has given the power of mission with its threefold office of teaching, sanctifying and ruling the faithful. 'The holders of office, who are invested with the

---

[12] "Ibidem," no. 20.

[13] "Ibidem," no. 18.

[14] "Ibidem," no. 20.

[15] Council of Trent, Session 23, c.6, Dz. 1776 (966).

[16] "Decree on the Church," no. 20.

[17] "Ibidem," no. 21 and 28.

sacred power, are, in fact, dedicated to promoting the interests of their brethren so that all who belong to the People of God, and are consequently endowed with true Christian dignity, may, through their free and well-ordered efforts towards a common goal, attain salvation."[18]

Primacy of the Roman Pontiff

The Church's teaching about the authority and ministry of the Pope within the Church places, also by the express will of Christ, that authority and ministry at the very center of her hierarchical structure. The universal authority of the Roman Pontiff, witnessed to throughout the history of Christianity and proposed as a dogma of faith by the Council of Florence in 1439,[19] was given a detailed dogmatic explanation by Vatican Council I in 1870 in its dogmatic constitution on the Church of Christ ("Pastor aeternus"). This document, in turn, was taken up and confirmed by Vatican Council II in 1964.

It is interesting to note that, before describing the content of this power and authority, Vatican I wished to underline its "purpose" and "meaning" in the Church according to "the will of Christ." This authority exists so that 'the episcopate might be one and undivided and that the whole multitude of believers might be preserved in unity of faith and communion by means of a well-organized priesthood.'[20] 'In order that the episcopate itself might be one and undivided he (Christ) put Peter at the head of the other apostles, and in him set up a lasting and visible source and foundation of the unity both of faith and communion.'[21]

Within this basic framework the Church has given her teaching on the primatial authority of the Roman Pontiff in three well defined points: 1. the institution of the primacy in the person of Peter the apostle, 2. the perpetuity of the primacy through the principle of succession, 3. the nature of this primatial power.

We will now study each of these three points in turn.

---

[18] "Ibidem," no. 18.
[19] Dz. 1307 (694).
[20] Dz. 3051 (1921).
[21] "Decree on the Church," no. 18.

1. Institution of the Primacy in the Person of the Apostle Peter

It is a matter of faith that the blessed apostle Peter "was constituted by Christ the Lord as the prince of all the apostles and the visible head of the whole Church militant" and "that he received immediately and directly from Jesus Christ our Lord not only a primacy of honor but a true and proper primacy of jurisdiction."[22] The Church affirms that this is witnessed to by "the testimony of the gospel"[23] and is the "very clear teaching of the Holy Scriptures."[24]

The scriptural texts brought forward by the Council are the two following very well-known passages: a) this first is known as the "text of the promise": "Blessed are you Simon, son of Jonah, because it was not flesh and blood that revealed this to you but my Father who is in heaven. And now I say to you: You are Peter and on this rock I will build my Church and the gates of hell will not prevail against it. I will give you the keys of the kingdom of heaven. And whatever you loose on earth will be loosed in heaven" (Matthew 16:16-18); b) the second is known as the "fulfillment text": "Feed my lambs, feed my sheep" (John 21:15ff).

An analysis of other numerous texts of the New Testament would show what precisely was the will of Christ regarding the humble fisherman from Galilee, how Peter afterwards exercised his primacy, and how conscious the other apostles and the first Christians were that Simon was at the head of the mission which Christ had entrusted to them all.[25]

2. The Successor of Peter: Perpetuity of the Primacy in the Bishop of Rome

As regards this point the dogmatic teaching of the Church runs as follows: "It is according to the institution of Christ our Lord himself,

---

[22] Dz. 3055 (1823).
[23] Dz. 3053 (1822).
[24] Dz. 3054 (1822).
[25] Cf. for example L. Bouyer, "L'Eglise de Dieu, Corps de Christ, et Temple de l'Espirit," Paris, 1970, pp. 460-468. 'The evangelists were convinced that the function of Peter in the early Church was in no way the result of an outstanding personality, but of a "formal disposition of Christ" and therefore, of a charism corresponding to a particular situation' (p.462).

that is, by divine law, that St. Peter has perpetual successors in the primacy over the whole Church" and that "the Roman Pontiff is the successor of St. Peter in that primacy."[26]

A. "The Principle of Succession"

What we saw earlier for the hierarchy of the Church in general we see again but this time applied to the Pope, namely, on the one hand the "principle" of succession as a truth of faith, and, on the other, the "fact" of the succession as it is found in the bishop of Rome. When speaking of the primacy of Peter, Vatican I appealed to the texts of Holy Scripture which established it. Now, when speaking of the succession, the Council, and in this it will be followed almost a century later by Vatican II,[27] proceeds not directly from Sacred Scripture but from the principle of indefectibility and perpetuity in the Church. Since by the will of Christ the Church has to last until the end of time so too must the principle and foundation of unity given by Christ last.

And so theology finds the succession in the primacy of Peter affirmed implicitly in the word of Christ to Simon (Matthew 16:16-18 and John 21:15ff).

Tradition gives the all important argument, namely the consciousness that the Church has always held that the primacy was preserved in the person of the bishop of Rome. As an example of this Tradition these words spoken by the Pope's legate at the Council of Ephesus in 431 will suffice: "No one doubts; in fact, it is obvious to all ages that the holy and most blessed Peter, head and prince of the apostles, the pillar of faith, and the foundation of the Catholic Church received the keys of the kingdom from our Lord Jesus Christ, the savior and redeemer of the human race. Nor does anyone doubt that the power of forgiving and retaining sins was also given to this same Peter who, in his successors, lives and exercises judgment even to this time and forever."[28]

As far back as the second century St. Irenaeus of Lyons, when studying the criteria for sound teaching had recourse to the apostolic succession and in particular "to the great church, the oldest and best known of all, founded and established in Rome by the glorious apostles Peter and Paul. . . . All other churches ought to be in agreement with

---

[26] Dz. 3058. 1825.

[27] Cf. reference no. 12.

[28] D 112 and Dz. 3056. 1824.

this church because of her more powerful authority . . . for in her is preserved the tradition which comes from the apostles."[29]

B. "The Succession and the Plans of God"

The truth is that it would have been very "comfortable," from the point of view of theological argumentation, if the text from St. Matthew which is so often quoted ran along these lines: "And to you and your successors I give the keys of the kingdom of heaven. . . .' The same could be said about other important texts on the hierarchical constitution of the Church in general, e.g. 'Go, therefore, you and your successors, make disciples of all the nations . . . as my Father has sent me so I send you and your successors. . . .'"

But it is easy to see that this way of speaking would be foreign to the way Jesus refers to his work of redemption and to his Church, for he speaks in a prophetic and symbolic way. It has been said, not without a dash of humor, that it is a good thing that the Gospel of St. Matthew has not named the successors of Peter, for if it had, there would surely be people to see this as one more reason to reject the authenticity of the gospel itself.

Perhaps the most striking element in the context of this gospel for understanding the silence of Jesus about the succession in the apostolic college is his constant decision to keep hidden from the apostles and from the rest of men, the "day of the Lord," the parousia, the end point of salvation history whose imminence he always leaves open: "Stay awake, because you do not know either the day or the hour" (Matthew 25:13).

3. The Nature of the Papal Primacy

Chapter 3 of the dogmatic constitution on the Church of Vatican Council I ("Pastor aeternus") is the principal document of the Magisterium about the content and nature of the primatial power of the Roman Pontiff. Chapter 4 is a development and defining of one particular characteristic of this primatial power, namely the Pope's supreme teaching authority, i.e. when the Pope speaks "ex cathedra" he teaches the doctrine of the faith infallibly. The Magisterium of the Roman Pontiff is one of the chief elements of his primatial authority.

1

---

[29] St. Irenaeus, "Adversus haereses," III, 3, 2.

A. "Primacy of Jurisdiction"

The primacy spoken about by Vatican I is a primacy of jurisdiction. The word jurisdiction underlines the binding power of the authority which Christ has conferred on the Pope in the Church. It demands obedience of all the faithful. It is in opposition to a primacy of honor ("Primus inter pares") and to a primacy of direction which might be endowed with the power of advising and guiding, but not with the power of commanding.[30] The word, as is obvious, has its roots in judicial language. But what is defined by the Council transcends judicial categories and can be understood more fully in the light of the properties which the Council assigns to the primatial power of the Pope.[31]

The Pope's power is

i) "universal": it extends to the whole Church, i.e. to all the members of the Church (pastors and faithful) as to all the various matters which can arise;

ii) "ordinary": it is not extraordinary, which would mean that it can be used only in exceptional circumstances; nor is it delegated, that is, it belongs inherently to the office of Pope and is not delegated to him by someone else;

iii) "supreme": meaning that it is not subordinated to any other authority[32];

iv) "full": it takes in all questions which might arise in the life of the Church, and does so from every point of view;

v) "immediate": it need not be exercised through intermediaries and where necessary can have the most practical applications.

---

[30] Dz. 3064. 1831.

[31] Dz. 3064. 1831.

[32] Vatican Council I, the theologians tell us, made this affirmation in a positive, not an exclusive way, for the episcopal college, with the Pope at its head, also has full and supreme power in the Church (cf. "Decree on the Church", no. 22) and in this sense has a power equal to the Pope's power.

B. "Bishop of the Catholic Church"

The authority of the Pope is truly episcopal.[33] This feature is very important because it connects the juridical terminology in which the aforementioned properties are expressed, with the sacramental and ministerial meaning which the term "episcop," has in the New Testament. The Pope is indeed a bishop, and his power has an episcopal character and a pastoral purpose. It is not concerned with human or political matters but is rather a power for fulfilling the threefold mission of teaching, sanctifying and leading to God the flock of Christ. For this reason Pope Paul VI delighted in calling himself "Bishop of the Catholic Church" and under this title he signed the various documents of Vatican II. Undoubtedly he is bishop of Rome, and not of Dublin or Cologne, but as bishop of Rome he is also Pope, successor to Peter, and has, over all the Church (over all diocese and all members of the Church), the office which is proper to a bishop.[34]

A study of this truly episcopal power is the simplest way of understanding more deeply the nature of papal authority. The apostle Peter, he who was charged by Christ with looking after the flock, is he who has the most vivid awareness that his ministry is to be a mere instrument in the hands of Christ, head of the Church. "The primacy of Peter in leading and serving the Christian people was going to be a pastoral primacy, a primacy of love. The nature and efficacy of the pastoral function of the apostolic primacy would be based on the undying love of Peter for Jesus."[35] Accordingly it is Peter who encourages the shepherds of the Church to exercise their ministry with their eyes fixed on Christ, so that "when the chief shepherd appears you will be given the crown of unfading glory" (1 Peter 5:4). The work of bishops consists in making it easy for the faithful, and for all men, to turn, not to the shepherds of the Church, but "to the shepherd and guardian of your souls" (Christ) (1 Peter 2:25).

Christ is the Shepherd; Christ is the Bishop. This is Peter's message because when Jesus promised him the primacy Peter heard him speak of "my" Church, not "your" Church. All bishops, with Peter at their head, are "vicars", that is, they take the place of Christ on earth. To

---

[33] Dz. 3060. 1827.

[34] The power of the Pope is not to be thought of as standing in the way of the power of the bishops, each in his own diocese; cf. Dz. 3061 (1827).

[35] Paul VI. 1967. "Address," March 29.

enable them to fulfill their mission of service he conferred on them the necessary power.

C. "Power and Service of Peter"

Frequently nowadays, and rightly so, because it is based on Scripture and Tradition, we speak of the mission of the Pope and the bishops as a ministry, as a service. Indeed, they are there to serve. 'The office which the Lord has committed to the pastors of his people is, in the strict sense of the term, a service, which is called very expressively in Sacred Scripture, a "diakonia" or ministry.'[36] One of the titles proper to the Pope himself is 'servant of the servants of God.' The term service cannot be understood as a divesting themselves of the authority which is theirs by right, opposing service to power. That would be a most unbiblical and untraditional way of understanding the word ministry. The Pope and the bishops can only render to the Church the service God wants from them if they exercise their power, which is of divine origin and only they have. If they were not to use their power, they would be unable to serve; they would be of no use. Now all of us Christians ought to serve one another as Christ loved us and served us. But bishops, besides being counted among the faithful themselves, are pastors and must serve their brethren and children through the use of their pastoral power. Such service demands humility ("The greatest among you must be your servant", Matt. 31:11) and fortitude ("The Holy Spirit has made you overseers to feed the Church of God", Acts 20:28). St. Leo the Great, paraphrasing the words of Jesus, put it like this: 'You are a Rock, Simon. Rather, I am the unshakeable Rock, I am the Cornerstone which unites what was separated. I am the Foundation and no one can lay any other. And yet, you Simon, you also are a Rock because I am going to give you my strength, in such a way that by this sharing, the power which is only mine will be common to you and to me.'[37]

D. "Unity: Reason for Primacy"

Vatican Council I affirmed that the authority of the Pope, and the resulting obligation to obey him, took in 'not only matters that pertain to the faith and morals, but also matters that pertain to discipline and

---

[36] "Decree on the Church," no. 24.
[37] St. Leo the Great. "Sermon III on the Nativity."

government of the Church throughout the whole world.'[38] It is what we call universal power (applicable, it is clearly understood, to ecclesiastical matters only). The power which the Pope receives from Christ has its own internal statutes and lays upon the successor of St. Peter a very grave moral obligation.

Earlier on I referred to this service on behalf of the unity of the Church. The Pope has a very wide power in order to be able to serve in a supreme way the unity of the Church. He must use his authority whenever it is required and in the way it is required so as to serve the unity of faith and communion in the Church. Not to use it could constitute a serious fault; and to hinder its exercise is to hinder the supreme way which Christ has instituted for keeping his Church one.[39] On the other hand, if the Pope were to intervene with his supreme authority where it was not needed he would be making use of the power conferred on him by Christ in a way contrary to the meaning of that power which, in the whole Church, is "for building up, not pulling down (2 Cor. 10:8) and is 'for us men and for our salvation.' In the ministry of the Pope to build up and save is to care for the unity of faith and of communion among pastors and faithful.

E. "The Pope, Vicar of Christ"

The primacy of the Pope is a mystery in the economy of salvation. And to this mystery belong those internal statutes just previously spoken about. "In his chief ministry the Pope is obliged by the objective rules of faithfulness which derive from the revealed word of God, from the fundamental constitution of the Church and by Tradition."[40] He has the necessary divine assistance to carry out his office. But this does not relieve him of a very grave responsibility before Christ whom God "has appointed to judge everyone, alive or dead" (Acts 10:42). It demands of the holder of the office of bishop of the Catholic Church humility, prudence and holiness and of the faithful continual prayer to God for the head of the Church on earth.

However, and this is important, on earth there is no external tribunal, neither in the Church nor in civil society to which one can

---

[38] DZ. 3060. 1827.
[39] For this reason Vatican I affirmed the right of the Pope to communicate freely with the bishops and faithful of the whole Church, cf. Dz. 3062 (1829).
[40] Cardinal Seper. 1969. "Introductory Address to the Synod of Bishops.

appeal against his decisions. The Pope must look for advice, take the steps which prudence demands in the delicate function of governing the Church, listen to the opinion of his brother bishops, etc., but "the judgment of the apostolic See, whose authority is unsurpassed, is not subject to review by anyone, nor is anyone allowed to pass judgment on his decisions. Therefore, those who say that it is permitted to appeal to an ecumenical council from the decisions of the Roman Pontiff (as to an authority superior to the Roman Pontiff) are far from the straight path of truth."[41]

We reach here, perhaps, the nerve center of all teaching about the primacy. It is what most brings out the fact that we are faced with a "mystery of faith" and not with "an organizational factor" in the Church ascertainable by the natural light of human reason. But it also brings us to take our stance on what is the ultimate basis of the whole mystery, a basis which is centered on Christ himself. The basis of the primacy is, on the one hand, its historical institution by Christ, but on the other it is the actual presence "today" of Christ in the primatial acts of the Pope. 'The relation of the primacy to Christ is not only historical-causal, but also actual-causal, for in the activity of the Pope, Christ himself is audible and visible. Of the Pope it can truly be said: "He acts in the person of Christ".'[42] With theological wisdom, St. Catherine of Siena called the Pope the 'gentle Christ on earth' but at the same time, conscious of the moral responsibility of the Pope, she urged him to exercise with fortitude his 'service of unity' in the Church, that is to say, to be faithful to his most important mission.

From the time when St. Clement of Rome intervened in the affairs of the church of Corinth to reestablish peace in that troubled community down to our own days with its contemporary methods for governing the universal Church, the Roman Pontiffs have been the instruments willed by Christ for maintaining unity among the bishops and for keeping the multitude of the faithful, that is to say, the Church, in a unity of faith and communion. The ways of exercising the primacy have varied with time, but its substance does not change for it is immutable. Accordingly the primacy cannot be watered down in the wake of "Episcopalian" or "democratic" ideals.

---

[41] 1830. Dz. 3063.

[42] M. Schmaus. 1960. "Teologia Dogmatica, VI. La Iglesia." Madrid, p. 462.

'When the Pope acts in virtue of his office he represents at one and the same time the whole Church and the entire body of bishops. But one cannot deduce from this that he receives his power from the community of believers or from the bishops. On the contrary, he receives it from Christ.'[43] 'The Pope,' writes Cardinal Ratzinger, "is not just someone who speaks in the name of the bishops, a kind of mouthpiece they give themselves and which is there to do their bidding. The Pope is where he is, with a direct responsibility before God, to take the place of the Lord, and to ensure the unity of the word and work of Christ, in the same way as Christ gave Peter that same function within the community of the Twelve."[44]

F. "Unity of Christians around the Pope"

On one occasion Pope Paul VI said that he viewed "the charism of the primacy in the Church, given by Christ himself to Peter, whose humble successor I am, more as an office to be exercised than as a right."[45] This way of seeing things coincides with the attitude which Christians ought to have and which was expressed by Msgr. Escriva de Balaguer: Christians must "work, not as subject to an authority, but with the piety of children, with the love of those who feel themselves to be and are members of the body of Christ."[46] Behind this spirituality of love for the Pope lies the deep conviction that his authority cannot be done away with. "Do not tire of preaching love and full obedience to the Holy Father. Even if his office had not been instituted by Jesus Christ my head tells me that a strong central authority—that of the Holy See—would be needed to induce those who are in disagreement with the Church and who blunder about to act reasonably. But over and beyond these logical reasons there is the will of God who has wanted to have a Vicar on earth and to assist him infallibly with his Holy Spirit."[47]

In the words of Pope Paul VI to the Council Fathers: "If our apostolic office obliges us to put up signposts, to define terms, to lay down

---

[43] G. Philips. 1967. "L'Eglise et son mystere au IIe Concile du Vatican." Paris, p. 297.

[44] J. Ratzinger. 1969. "Das neue Volk Gottes," Dusseldorf, p. 169.

[45] Paul VI. 1969. "Address," October 27, A.A.S. 61, p. 728.

[46] J. Escriva de Balaguer. 1965.

[47] "Idem," 1943.

guidelines and modes for the exercise of episcopal power it is—you know well—for the good of the entire Church and for the unity of the Church. The need for guidelines and direction is all the more necessary as the catholic unity spreads, as she faces graver danger, as the needs of the Christian people become more pressing in different historical circumstances and, we could add, as the means of communication become more sophisticated."[48]

Behind the theology of the successor of Peter there is always the communion, the unity of the Church in the midst of her variety. According to divine revelation this is the formal meaning of the primacy of Peter: to be the perpetual and visible center and foundation of the community of Churches which is vivified by the Spirit of Christ. This is what, in a turbulent crisis of faith and unity, is felt by many who are outside the boat of Peter. Those of us who through the grace of God sail in Christ's boat have the grave responsibility not to defraud that hope.

Source: Pedro Rodriguez. 1981. "The Primacy of the Pope in the Church." *Catholic Position Papers,* September. Reprinted with permission from Pedro Rodriguez.

Father Pedro Rodriguez is a theologian who specializes in church studies or ecclesiology. He has written dozens of books and articles on theology. He is a priest of the prelature of Opus Dei. He teaches at the University of Navarra in Pamplona, Spain, and was the dean of theology for many years.

---

[48] Paul VI, "o. c."

Pillar and Bulwark of the Truth: The Infallible Magisterium of the Catholic Church

By *Catholics United for the Faith*

What is the Magisterium? How should the faithful respond to the Magisterium? What is the charism of infallibility? How is that charism exercised by the Church?

The Magisterium is the Church's teaching office established by Jesus Christ to "guard what has been entrusted" (1 Tim. 6:20). The Magisterium, in service to the Word of God, authentically interprets the Word, whether in Scripture or in the form of Tradition. The Magisterium is exercised by the Pope and the bishops in union with him. Because Christ has instituted the Magisterium to communicate His saving truth, the faithful should respond in docility and joy to the Church's teaching out of love for Christ.

Infallibility is a charism whereby the Holy Spirit protects the Magisterium from teaching error on matters of faith and morals. The Church exercises this charism when she teaches *definitively*, whether in a solemn manner (i.e., through the extraordinary Magisterium) or through the ordinary and universal Magisterium.

Discussion

Jesus sent the Holy Spirit to guide His Church into all truth. The Holy Spirit teaches the Church "all things," bringing to mind everything that Christ first taught His apostles (cf. Jn. 14:26). That is why Jesus can say, regarding His apostles and their bishop successors, "He who receives you receives me" (Mt. 10:40). Chosen by Christ, they exercise the Church's Magisterium or teaching office. Christ sends His apostles and their successors as the Father sent Him-with "all authority in heaven and on earth" (Mt. 28:18).

To provide a sure source of teaching and to maintain unity in the Church, Christ established the papacy with supreme authority in the Church. The Pope's office is one of succession from Peter and is marked by the authority of "the keys of the kingdom of heaven" (cf. Mt. 16:18-19;

Is. 22:15-25). As the Second Vatican Council reminds us, "the Roman Pontiff, by reason of his office as Vicar of Christ, and as pastor of the entire Church, has full, supreme, and universal power over the whole Church, a power which he can always exercise unhindered" (*Lumen Gentium*, no. 22). Thus, only in union with the Pope does the college or body of bishops have supreme and full authority over the universal Church (*ibid.*).

Jesus did not leave His people vulnerable to the doctrinal whims of competing leaders. Rather, He built the Church on the solid foundation of the apostles (cf. Eph. 2:19-20). He gave the Church His Holy Spirit, the Paraclete, to enable her to be "the pillar and bulwark of the truth" (1 Tim. 3:15). Despite the cultural winds that have blown through the ages, the faithful have always had a visible, easily identifiable magisterial "rock" on which they could safely stand in all seasons. As the *Catechism* provides, quoting Vatican II:

> The task of giving an authentic interpretation of the Word of God, whether in its written form or in the form of Tradition, *has been entrusted to the living, teaching office of the Church alone.* Its authority in this matter is exercised in the name of Jesus Christ" [*Dei Verbum*, no. 10]. This means that the task of interpretation has been entrusted to the bishops in communion with the successor of Peter, the Bishop of Rome (no. 85, emphasis added).

Jesus declared that the gates of hell would never prevail against His Church (cf. Mt. 16:18-19). This protection from evil includes protecting the Magisterium from teaching error. Regardless of who the Pope and bishops in union with him may be at a particular time in Church history, the faithful have Christ's Word that the Holy Spirit will guide His Magisterium in preserving and teaching the truth.

Faith Seeking Understanding

Some Catholics will not assent to a particular teaching unless the Church has demonstrated to their satisfaction that the teaching is true. Some go so far to reserve the right to overrule any magisterial pronouncement with a judgment of conscience. In doing so, they erroneously apply the Church's teaching on conscience, in essence arguing that every Church teaching is subject to their approval. Faith is not mere agreement, but a humble submission to God's authority. Thus the *Catechism* says: "Faith is first of all a personal adherence of man to God. At the same time, and inseparably, it is a *free assent to the whole truth that God has revealed*" (no. 150, original emphasis).

Such assent presupposes a joyful obedience to God as He reveals Himself and His saving truth. "To obey (from the Latin *ob-audire*, to "hear or listen to") in faith is to submit freely to the word that has been heard, because its truth is guaranteed by God, who is Truth itself" (Catechism, no. 144). As Jesus said, "He who hears you hears me, and he who rejects you rejects me" (Luke. 10:16). Catholics assent to the Church's teachings out of faith in God, who has invested the Magisterium, the servant of His Word, with His authority:

> What moves us to believe is not the fact that revealed truths appear as true and intelligible in the light of our natural reason: we believe "because of the authority of God himself who reveals them, who can neither deceive nor be deceived. . . ." (*Catechism*, no. 156, footnotes omitted).

Unfortunately, some seek teachers "to suit their own likings, and will turn away from listening to the truth and wander into myths" (2 Tim. 4:3). Faith, not our own preferences or likings, is what leads us to truth. Because of God's faithfulness, because of the certainty that comes with His divine light, Catholics can joyfully echo the words of John Henry Cardinal Newman when the temptation to withhold assent is put before them: "Ten thousand difficulties do not make one doubt" (Catechism, no. 157, footnote omitted). "Mindful of Christ's words to his apostles: 'He who hears you, hears me' [Lk. 10:16], the faithful receive with docility the teachings and directives that their pastors give them in different forms" (*Catechism*, no. 87).

You Better Believe It

Despite the Church's teaching on faith and assent, some Catholics think that they only have to assent to "*ex cathedra*" and other "solemnly defined" teachings, maintaining that only these are guaranteed to be infallible by the Holy Spirit. As a result, they shortchange themselves, minimizing the wealth of the Church's teachings. Rather, the Church has three basic types of teaching, all of which require the assent of the faithful. The first consists of "divinely revealed" teachings, those which God has imparted to His Church through Scripture and Tradition and which are thus part of the "deposit of faith" (*Catechism*, nos. 84; 2033). These teachings require the assent of faith, based on the authority of God's Word. One is guilty of heresy if he denies such teachings (cf. *Catechism*, no. 2089).

The second category consists of those teachings on which the Church has definitively pronounced. These teachings require an assent of faith, but it is based on faith in the Holy Spirit's assistance to the Magisterium and on the related doctrine of infallibility, which the Catechism's glossary defines thus: "the gift of the Holy Spirit whereby the pastors of the Church, the pope and the bishops in union with him, can *definitively* proclaim a doctrine of faith or morals for the belief of the faithful. . . ." (emphasis added). As the Code of Canon Law provides, "anyone who rejects propositions which are to be held definitively sets himself against the teaching of the Catholic Church" (Canon 750 §2).[1] While not part of the deposit of faith, these teachings are "required for the holy keeping and faithful exposition of the deposit of faith" (Canon 750 §2).

Teachings in these first two categories require full and irrevocable assent. As the *Catechism* explains, they are taught infallibly:

> The supreme degree of participation in the authority of Christ is ensured by the charism of *infallibility*. This infallibility extends as far as does the deposit of divine Revelation; it also extends to all those elements of doctrine, including morals, without which the saving truths of the faith cannot be preserved, explained, or observed (no. 2035, original emphasis).

Thus, these two categories of teachings, infallibly proposed, are equal in scope to ("is coextensive with") the deposit of revelation. There is a third category of teachings that "leads to a better understanding of Revelation in matters of faith and morals" (*Catechism*, no. 892). These teachings illuminate understanding, helping revelation to bear fruit. While not definitively proposed, they are presented as true or sure. The Magisterium receives divine assistance in proposing these teachings, to

---

[1] Pope John Paul II amended the Code of Canon Law, adding Canon 750 §2, through his 1998 decree *Ad Tuendam Fidem* (*To Protect the Faith*).

which the faithful "'are to adhere to it with religious assent" which, though distinct from the assent of faith, is nonetheless an extension of it" (*Catechism*, no. 892, footnote omitted). An example would be the Church's recent teaching that the death penalty should not be administered unless "this is the only possible way of effectively defending human lives against the unjust aggressor" (*Catechism*, no. 2267).

High Definition

Thus, there are three types of teachings that require our assent, two of which are proposed infallibly. How does the Magisterium propose teaching infallibly? There are two ways: through the extraordinary Magisterium and through the ordinary and universal Magisterium.

The "extraordinary Magisterium" is so named because it issues solemn or formal pronouncements on relatively rare occasions. The extraordinary Magisterium pronounces infallibly through two types of solemn definitions. The first type of definition is by a Pope alone when he speaks *"ex cathedra"*—"from the chair" of Peter—that is, when "acting in the office of shepherd and teacher of all Christians, he defines, by virtue of his supreme apostolic authority, a doctrine concerning faith and morals to be held by the universal Church."[2] Examples include the dogmatic definitions regarding Mary's Immaculate Conception (Pope Pius IX, 1854) and Assumption into heaven (Pope Pius XII, 1950).

The second type of definition occurs when the Pope and the bishops in union with him solemnly define a teaching at an "ecumenical" or "general" council—a council whose teachings are binding on the whole Church (cf. canon 750 §2). Examples include the various solemn definitions made at the Council of Trent, including on the Mass, the sacraments, justification, and indulgences.

Some Catholics mistakenly try to limit infallibility to only those teachings that are solemnly defined. They cite a section of canon law, "no doctrine is understood to be infallibly defined unless this is mani-

---

[2] Vatican I, Dogmatic Constitution on the Church of Christ, chapter 4; as cited in J. Neuner, S.J., and J. Dupuis. 1996. *The Christian Faith: In the Doctrinal Documents of the Catholic Church*—Sixth Revised and Enlarged Edition. New York: Alba House, no. 839, 297-98.

festly demonstrated" (canon 749 § 2). This section, however, does not limit infallibility to solemn definitions. Instead, it prohibits placing a doctrine on the level of a solemn definition unless it can be shown to be so. A doctrine itself, however, may be infallible on another level. As Vatican II, the *Catechism,* and the Code of Canon Law all affirm, *any* definitively proposed teaching enjoys the charism of infallibility, not simply those which are solemnly defined.

The ordinary and universal Magisterium is the normal or usual means by which the Pope and the bishops in union with him infallibly propose teachings to the whole Church. It is exercised when the Pope and bishops agree that a particular doctrine is to be held definitively, and is typically carried out when the bishops are dispersed throughout the world in their respective dioceses. The ordinary and universal Magisterium also teaches infallibly when, without issuing a solemn definition, it definitively confirms or reaffirms the Church's teachings at an ecumenical council, e.g., through a dogmatic constitution.

If a teaching is taught by the ordinary and universal Magisterium, it is necessarily definitive and therefore infallible. However, controversies sometimes arise as to whether a particular doctrine is in fact a teaching of the ordinary and universal Magisterium. On such occasions, the Pope can definitively confirm or reaffirm that a particular doctrine is indeed infallibly taught by that Magisterium. In such cases, the Pope does not make an *ex cathedra* pronouncement. Rather, he infallibly and definitively pronounces that a doctrine "has been constantly maintained and held by Tradition and transmitted by the ordinary, universal Magisterium."[3]

The definitive character of such papal pronouncements is rooted in the very Tradition they confirm. Thus, the infallibility of these reaffirmations follows in part from the infallibility of previous teachings they affirm. As Archbishop Tarcisio Bertone, the secretary of the Congregation for the Doctrine of the Faith, has explained, "a papal pronouncement of confirmation enjoys the same infallibility as the teaching of the ordinary, universal Magisterium. . . ."[4] These definitive pronouncements provide a more concrete way of knowing that a doctrine has been proposed infallibly.

---

[3] Archbishop Tarcisio Bertone, 1997. *L'Osservatore Romano* (Weekly English Edition), January 29, 6.
[4] Ibid.

Pope John Paul II's definitive pronouncement that only men can be ordained to the ministerial priesthood is a recent example of an infallible papal confirmation. He made his pronouncement in his 1994 apostolic letter *Ordinatio Sacerdotalis* (*On Reserving Priestly Ordination to Men Alone*):

> [T]hat priestly ordination is to be reserved to men alone has been preserved by the constant and universal Tradition of the Church and firmly taught by the Magisterium in its more recent documents. . . . Wherefore, in order that all doubt may be removed regarding a matter of great importance, a matter which pertains to the Church's divine constitution itself, in virtue of my ministry of confirming the brethren (cf. Lk. 22:32), I declare that the Church has no authority whatsoever to confer priestly ordination on women and that this judgment is to be definitively held by all the Church's faithful (no. 4).

Ordinatio Sacerdotalis is a good example of a definitive papal pronouncement that confirms or reaffirms a teaching of the ordinary and universal Magisterium. The Pope states that the teaching regarding priestly ordination is "the constant and universal Tradition of the Church." He thus definitively identifies the teaching as magisterial. The Holy Father then definitively states that his pronouncement is a confirmation ("in virtue of my ministry of confirming the brethren"). Finally, affirming that he is acting to remove all doubt on the matter, the Pope adds that his "judgment is to be definitively held by all the Church's faithful."

Another example of how a Pope can definitively pronounce without an *ex cathedra* statement concerns contraception. In 1930, the Anglican Church broke with longstanding Christian Tradition and taught that contraception could be allowed in some "difficult" cases. In response, Pope Pius XI issued that same year his encyclical *Casti Connubii* (*On Christian Marriage*). Speaking "in token" of the Church's "divine ambassadorship," Pius XI reaffirmed that this teaching belonged to "the uninterrupted Christian Tradition," proclaiming anew that "any use whatsoever of matrimony exercised in such a way that the act is deliberately frustrated in its natural power to generate life is an offense against the law of God and of nature. . . ." (no. 56).

Pius XI's definitive pronouncement illustrates that the issue of contraception was definitively settled long before Pope Paul VI's 1968 encyclical *Humanae Vitae*, which itself affirms that same "uninterrupted Christian Tradition." Other recent examples include John Paul II's definitive pronouncements regarding abortion, murder, and euthanasia in his 1995 encyclical *Evangelium Vitae* (*The Gospel of Life*).

Christ has provided the Magisterium as a great gift to His Church, so that the faithful may give free and grateful assent to the saving truth God has revealed to His Church. The Magisterium enables the faithful to live God's truth in the abundantly fruitful manner He intended. When the Magisterium pronounces definitively on a matter of faith or morals, the Holy Spirit ensures that the Church will not teach erroneously. The Church can pronounce infallibly through the extraordinary Magisterium as well as through the ordinary and universal Magisterium. He who hears and obeys the Church hears and obeys her founder, Jesus Christ. And, as Jesus promised, "If you continue in my word, you are truly my disciples, and you will know the truth, and the truth will make you free" (Jn. 8:31-32).

Source: Catholics United for the Faith. "Pillar and Bulwark of the Truth: The Infallible Magisterium of the Catholic Church." *Faith Facts*, Catholics United for the Faith. (www.cuf.org). Reprinted with the permission of Catholic United for the Faith.

Chapter 15

Marian Devotion

Devotion to the Blessed Virgin Mary is as old as Christianity itself. Without Mary, there would be no Christianity. Pope John Paul II points out that the Church honors Mary with special reverence for several reasons. First, she believed Gabriel, God's messenger, when she was told she would conceive and bear a son. Second, she was perfectly faithful to the person and mission of Jesus, her Son. Third, she is Mother of the Father's Son through the power of the Holy Spirit.[1]

Mary, the masterpiece of God's grace, was the first great Christian teacher. What more could be added to her instructions at the wedding feast of Cana, "Do whatever he tells you" (John 2:5)? The Church teaches that devotion to Mary is a pathway to her Son, Jesus.

Unfortunately, many of our Protestant friends have grave misgivings about Catholics' devotion to the Blessed Mother. Mark Shea, a Catholic convert and former Evangelical Protestant, explains why these misgivings are misplaced in "**The Mother of the Son: The Case for Marian Devotion.**"

- ➤ Mary's life is a referred life, that is, it draws its importance from the Son to whom she gave birth. Without Jesus, Mary would be of little interest to us. Without Mary, there would be no Jesus.
- ➤ Indeed, Protestants sing the praises of St. Paul, the great Apostle of the Gentiles. Yet, they flinch at the thought of singing the praises of Mary, whose virtue, obedience, fidelity, and cooperation with God were instrumental in our redemption.
- ➤ Scripture itself declares in Mary's Magnificat, "My soul magnifies the Lord . . . From this day all generations will call me blessed" (Luke 1: 46-49). This is a solid Scriptural basis for honoring Mary.

---

[1] John Paul II. 1987. Encyclical Letter, *Mother of the Redeemer*, no. 142 (March 25).

➢ Shea argues that much of the difference between Catholics and Protestants in this regard is cultural, not theological. Evangelicals have a more masculine culture, while the Catholic culture is more feminine. Hence, Protestants are attracted to the hyperactive adventurer Paul, while Catholics are more prone to identify with the "Great Icon of Contemplative Prayer," the Blessed Virgin.

➢ Luke likens Mary to the Ark of the Covenant by saying that during the Annunciation the Holy Spirit "overshadowed" her as the Spirit of God overshadowed the tent containing the Ark of the Covenant in the Old Testament.

➢ The woman in the book of Revelation has always been interpreted as Mary.

➢ Marian dogmas, theological truths taught about Mary, communicate some essential truth about Jesus, the nature of the Church, or the nature of the human person.

Further Reading

John A. Hardon, S.J. "The Blessed Virgin in the History of Christianity." IngnatiusInsight.com.

James Hitchcock. "Misgivings About Mary." IgnatiusInsight.com.

Dwight Longenecker. 2003. "How to Explain Mary to a Sola Scriptura Protestant." *This Rock* (14):1 (January).

The Mother of the Son:
The Case for Marian Devotion

By Mark Shea

It has to be one of the strangest things in the world: So many Christians who love Jesus with all their hearts recoil in fear at the mention of His mother's name, while many who do love her find themselves tongue-tied when asked to explain why.

Most of the issues people have with Mary are really issues about something else. "Where is the Assumption of Mary in the Bible?" isn't really a question about Mary. It's a question about the validity of Sacred Tradition and the authority of the Church.

"Why should I pray to Mary?" isn't really about Mary, either. It's actually a question about the relationship of the living and the dead in Christ. "Do Catholics worship Mary?" isn't a question about Mary. It's concerned more with whether or not Catholics countenance idolatry and what the word "honor" means. And curiously enough, all these and many more objections both pay homage to and completely overlook the central truth about Mary that the Catholic Church labors to help us see: that her life, in its entirety, is a referred life.

Mary would, after all, be of absolutely no consequence to us if not for her Son. It is because she is the mother of Jesus Christ that she matters to the world at all. If He hadn't been born, you never would have heard of her. John, with characteristic economy of expression, captures this referred life in her own words: "Do whatever He tells you" (John 2:5). And, of course, if this were all the Church had to say about her, Evangelicals would be more than happy to let her refer us to Jesus and be done with it. What baffles so many non-Catholics is the Church's tendency to keep referring us to her. *Ad Iesum per Mariam!* we say, to which many non-Catholics nervously respond, "Isn't Christianity supposed to be about a relationship with Jesus Christ? Why do Catholics honor Mary so much?"

Sublime Neglect

As an Evangelical, that question sounded reasonable—right up until another question began to bother me: If Catholics honor Mary too much, exactly how do we Evangelicals honor her "just enough"? For the reality was that my native Evangelicalism recoiled from any and all mention of Mary.

This was odd. After all, Evangelicals could talk all day about Paul and never feel we were "worshiping" him or giving him "too much honor." We rightly understood that God's word comes to us through St. Paul, and there's no conflict between the two (even though Paul exhibits more character flaws than Mary).

Yet the slightest mention of Mary by a Catholic immediately brought a flood of warnings, hesitations, scrutinies of her lack of faith (allegedly demonstrated in Mark 3:21), and even assertions that Jesus was less pleased with her than He was with His disciples (because He called her "Woman," not "Mom"; and because He commended His own disciples as "my brother and sister and mother" [Mark 3:35]). And all this was despite the fact that not just God's word (e.g. the Magnificat), but God's Word, came to us through Mary (John 1:14). As Evangelicals we could say, "If not for Paul, the gospel would never have reached the Gentiles." But we froze up if somebody argued that, "If not for Mary, the gospel would never have reached the earth." Suddenly, a flurry of highly speculative claims about how "God would simply have chosen somebody else!" would fill the air, as though Mary was a mere incubation unit, completely interchangeable with any other woman on earth. "No Paul, no gospel for the Gentiles" made perfect sense. But "No Mary, no incarnation, no death, no resurrection, no salvation for the world" was just too extreme.

Indeed, from Evangelical piety and preaching as it is actually practiced, one could be forgiven for getting the sense that Jesus didn't really even like His mother (like a teenager irritated because Mom just doesn't understand him). Having "Mary Is No Big Deal" hammered home whenever her name was raised tended to give you the feeling that—after her brief photo-op for the Hallmark Christmas card industry—Jesus was glad to spend time away from the family in the Temple discussing higher things. The position in Evangelicalism was more or less that we should do likewise and not lavish any attention on the mother who was too dim to understand who He was and whom He "rebuked" by saying, "Why were you looking for me? Did you not know that I must be in my Father's house?"

And so, our claims to honor her "just enough" effectively boiled down to paying no shred of positive attention to her beyond singing "round yon Virgin, mother and Child" each Christmas. The rest of the time it was either complete neglect or jittery assurances of her unimportance and dark warnings not to over-emphasize the woman of whom inspired Scripture said, "From this day all generations will call me blessed."

It was a startling paradigm shift to realize we treated her so allergically—and one that, I have since noticed, isn't unusual for converts. Dale Ahlquist, president of the American Chesterton Society, told me once that when he was still hanging back from the Church because of Mary, a blunt priest he knew asked him, "Do you believe her soul magnifies the Lord? It's right there in Scripture." Ahlquist reflexively answered back, "Of course I do! I know the Bible!" But even as he replied he was thinking to himself, "I never really thought of that before." It can be a disorienting experience.

But, in fact, it is right there in the Bible. Her soul magnifies the Lord, and from that day to this all generations have called her blessed. So why, when we Evangelicals looked at Jesus, did we never look at Him through the divinely appointed magnifying glass? Why were we so edgy about calling her "blessed" and giving her any honor? That realization was my first clue that it was, perhaps, Catholics who were simply being normal and human in honoring Mary, while we Evangelicals were more like teetotalers fretting that far too much wine was being drunk at the wedding in Cana.

The Cultural Obstacles

Part of the problem, I came to realize, was that Evangelical fears about Mary are visceral and not entirely theological. Indeed, much of the conflict between Catholics and Evangelicals is cultural, not theological. Evangelical culture (whether you're a man or a woman) is overwhelmingly masculine, while Catholic culture (again, whether you're a man or a woman) is powerfully feminine. And the two groups often mistake their cultural differences for theological ones.

The Catholic approach tends to be body-centered, Eucharistic, and contemplative. Prayer, in Catholic culture, is primarily for seeking union with God. Evangelical approaches to God tend to be centered on Scripture, verbal articulation of belief, mission, and the Spirit working in power. Prayer, in such a culture, is primarily for getting things done. Both are legitimate Christian ways of approaching the gospel. Indeed, they should both be part of the Catholic approach to the gospel. But because of these unconscious differences, Evangelicals and Catholics often clash about culture while they think they're debating theology. The feminine spirituality of the Catholic can regard the masculine Evangelical approach as shallow, noisy, and utilitarian, lacking an interior life. Meanwhile, Catholic piety can be seen by Evangelicals as cold, dead, ritualistic, biblically ignorant, and cut off from real life. Thus, Evangelicals frequently criticize the Catholic life as a retreat from reality into rituals and rote prayers.

Not surprisingly, the heroes of the two camps are (for Evangelicals) the Great Human Dynamo of Apostolic Energy, St. Paul; and (for Catholics) the Great Icon of Contemplative Prayer Issuing in Incarnation, the Blessed Virgin Mary. As an Evangelical, I found Paul much easier to appreciate, since he was "biblical"—he wrote much of the New Testament, after all. You could talk about Paul since he'd left such a significant paper trail. Not so with Mary. Apart from the Magnificat and a couple remarks here and there—plus, of course, the infancy narratives—she didn't appear to occupy nearly as much psychic space for the authors of the New Testament as she did for Catholics. Marian devotion looked like a mountain of piety built on a molehill of Scripture.

Looks, however, can be deceiving. For as I got to know the Bible better, it became obvious to me that the authors of Scripture were not nearly as jittery about Mary as my native Evangelicalism. Furthermore, they accorded to her honors that looked a great deal more Catholic than Evangelical.

Luke, for instance, likens her to the Ark of the Covenant in recording that the Holy Spirit "overshadowed" her. The same word in Greek is used to describe the way the Shekinah (glory of God) overshadowed the tabernacle in Luke 1:35. Likewise, John makes the same connection between Mary and the Ark of the Covenant when he announces in Revelation 11:19-12:2:

Then God's temple in heaven was opened, and the ark of his covenant was seen within his temple; and there were flashes of lightning,
voices, peals of thunder, an earthquake, and heavy hail. And a great
portent appeared in heaven, a woman clothed with the sun, with the
moon under her feet, and on her head a crown of twelve stars; she
was with child and she cried out in her pangs of birth, in anguish for
delivery.

The chapter goes on to describe the woman as giving birth to a
male child who rules the nations with an iron scepter and who is
almost devoured by a great red dragon.

As an Evangelical, my own tradition found it remarkably easy to
detect bar codes, Soviet helicopters, the European Common Market,
and the Beatles encoded into the narrative of Revelation. But when
Catholics suggested that the woman of Revelation might have something to do with the Blessed Virgin occupying a place of cosmic
importance in the grand scheme of things, this was dismissed as
incredible. Everyone knew that the woman of Revelation was really the
symbolic Virgin Daughter of Zion giving birth to the Church. A Jewish
girl who stood at the pinnacle of the Old Covenant, summed up the
entirety of Israel's mission, and gave flesh to the Head of the Church
saying, "Behold, I am the handmaid of the Lord; let it be to me according to your word"—what could she possibly have to do with those
images? Why, that would suggest that she was the Virgin Daughter of
Zion and the Flower of her People, the Model Disciple, the Icon of the
Church, the Mother of Jesus and of all those who are united with Him
by faith and. . . . Come to think of it, Scripture was looking rather
Catholic after all.

The Heart of Marian Doctrine

That was the revolutionary thought that made it possible for me to
press on, as a new Catholic, to find out what the Church was trying to
get at with her Marian teaching. In coming to understand this, it
seemed to me, I'd come a long way toward understanding why Mary
figures so prominently, not merely in the heads, but in the hearts of
Catholics.

The first question that arises, of course, is, "Why Marian dogma at all?" Why not just dogmas about Christ and let Catholics think what they like about Mary? Why bind consciences here?

The answer is that Catholics do think what they like—not only about Mary, but about lots of things. And sometimes they think deeply erroneous things. When they do, and that thought imperils some revealed truth to the point it threatens the integrity of the Church's witness, the Church will, from time to time, define its doctrine more precisely. This is a process that's already at work in the New Testament (cf. Acts 15), and it continues until the return of Christ.

So, for instance, in the fifth century there arose (yet again) the question of just who Jesus is. It was a question repeated throughout antiquity and, in this case, an answer to the question was proposed by the Nestorians. They argued that the mortal man Jesus and the Logos, or Second Person of the Trinity, were more or less two persons occupying the same head. For this reason, they insisted that Mary could not be acclaimed (as she had been popularly acclaimed for a very long time) as Theotokos, or "God bearer." Instead, she should only be called Christo-tokos, or "Christ bearer." She was, they insisted, the Mother of Jesus, not of God.

The problem with this was that it threatened the very witness of the Church and could even lead logically to the notion that there were two Sons of God, the man Jesus and the Logos who was sharing a room with Him in His head. In short, it was a doorway to theological chaos over one of the most basic truths of the Faith: that the Word became flesh, died, and rose for our sins.

So the Church formulated its response. First, Jesus Christ is not two persons occupying the same head. He is one person possessing two natures, human and divine, joined in a hypostatic union. Second, it was appropriate to therefore call Mary Theotokos because she's the Mother of the God-Man. When the God-Man had His friends over for lunch, He didn't introduce Mary saying, "This is the mother of my human nature." He said, "This is my mother."

Why did the Church do this? Because, once again, Mary points to Jesus. The dogma of the Theotokos is a commentary on Jesus, a sort of "hedge" around the truth about Jesus articulated by the Church. Just as Nestorianism had tried to attack the orthodox teaching of Christ through Mary (by forbidding the veneration of her as Theotokos), now the Church protected that teaching about Christ by making Theotokos a dogma. That is a vital key to understanding Marian dogmas: They're always about some vital truth concerning Jesus, the nature of the Church, or the nature of the human person.

This is evident, for instance, in the definition of Mary as a Perpetual Virgin (promulgated in 553 at the Council of Constantinople). This tradition isn't so much explicitly attested as reflected in the biblical narrative. Yes, we must grant that the biblical narrative is ambiguous in that it speaks of Jesus' "brothers" (but does it mean "siblings" or merely "relatives"?). However, other aspects of the biblical narrative strongly suggest she remained a virgin.

For instance, Mary reacts with astonishment at the news that she, a woman betrothed, will bear a son. If you are at a wedding shower and tell the bride-to-be, "You're going to have cute kids," and she responds, "How can that be?," you can only conclude one of two things: she either doesn't know about the birds and the bees, or she's taken a vow of virginity. In short, the promise of a child is an odd thing for a betrothed woman to be amazed about . . . unless, of course, she'd already decided to remain a virgin even after marriage.

Likewise, Joseph reacts with fear at the thought of taking Mary as a wife. Why fear? Modernity assumes it was because he thought her guilty of adultery, but the typical view in antiquity understood the text to mean he was afraid of her sanctity—as a pious Jew would be afraid to touch the Ark of the Covenant. After all, think of what Mary told him about the angel's words: "The Holy Spirit will come upon you, and the power of the Most High will overshadow you; therefore the Child to be born will be called holy, the Son of God."

I'm not even a pious Jew, but with words like that echoing in my ears about my wife, I'd find it easy to believe that Joseph, knowing what he did about his wife, would have chosen celibacy.

"But nothing is sure, based on the text alone. It's still ambiguous," says the critic. Right. The biblical text alone doesn't supply an unambiguous answer to this or a myriad of other questions, including "Is the Holy Spirit God?," "How do you contract a valid marriage?," and "Can you be a polygamist?" But the Tradition of the Church in union with the biblical text does supply an answer: Mary had no other children, a fact so commonly known throughout the early Church that when Jerome attacks Helvidius for suggesting otherwise, nobody makes a peep. In a Church quite capable of tearing itself to pieces over distinctions between homoousious and homoiousious, you hear the sound of crickets in response to Jerome, punctuated with the sound of other Fathers singing hymns to "Mary, Ever-Virgin." The early Church took it for granted and thought Helvidius as credible as Dan Brown.

But why a dogma about it? Because, again, Mary's life is a referred life. Her virginity, like Christ's, speaks of her total consecration to God and of our call as Christians to be totally consecrated as well. Her virginity is not a stunt or a magic trick to make the arrival of the Messiah extra-strange. It is, rather, a sign to the Church and of the Church. And that matters for precisely the reason I'd thought it did not matter when I was an Evangelical: because Christianity is indeed supposed to be about a relationship with Jesus Christ. But a relationship necessarily involves more than one person.

What it comes down to is this: Jesus can do a world of wonderful things, but there is something even Jesus cannot do—He cannot model for us what it looks like to be a disciple of Jesus. Only a disciple of Jesus can do that. And the first and best model of the disciple of Jesus is the one who said and lived "Yes!" to God, spontaneously and without even the benefit of years of training or the necessity of being knocked off a horse and blinded. And she continues to do so right through the agony of watching her Son die and the ecstasy of knowing Him raised again.

This is why the Church, like the Gospels, has always called Mary our Mother: because Mom is the best model for training children. The command to call her "Mother" comes, of course, from Jesus Himself. John doesn't record the words "Behold your mother" (John 19:27) because he thought his readers might be curious about domestic arrangements for childless Jewish widows. Rather, as with everything else John writes, "These are written that you may believe that Jesus is the Christ, the Son of God, and that believing you may have life in His name" (John 20:31). In other words, he doesn't record everything about Jesus, only those things that have a significant theological meaning. This includes Christ's words to the Beloved Disciple. For the Beloved Disciple is you and not merely John. Mary is your mother and you are her child. And so we are to look to her as mother and imitate her as she imitates Christ.

Defeating Destructive Ideologies

This brings us to the last two (and intimately related) Marian dogmas. Given that Marian dogma is always a commentary on Christ and His Church, what is the Church saying in its dogmatic teaching that (1) Mary was preserved at the moment of her conception from the stain of all sin, both original and actual; and (2) Mary was assumed bodily into heaven at the end of her earthly existence?

The great crisis that faced the Church in the 19th century (when the Holy Spirit, doing His job of leading the Church into all truth, led the Church to promulgate the dogma of the Immaculate Conception) was the rise of several ideologies—still very much with us—that called into question the origins and dignity of the human person. Darwin said the human person was an unusually clever piece of meat whose origins were as accidental as a pig's nose. Marx said humans were mere ingredients in a vast economic historical process. Laissez-faire capitalism saw people as natural resources to be exploited and thrown away when they lost their value. Eugenics said human dignity rested on "fitness." Much of Protestantism declared humans "totally depraved," while much of the Enlightenment held up the myth of human innocence, the "noble savage," and the notion of human perfectibility through reason. Racial theory advanced the notion that the key to human dignity was the shape of your skull, the color of your skin, and your membership in the Aryan or Teutonic tribe. Freud announced that your illusion of human dignity was just a veil over fathomless depths of unconscious processes largely centering in the groin or emerging out of issues with Mom and Dad.

All these ideologies—and many others—had in common the degrading rejection of human beings as creatures made in the image of God and intended for union with God (and the consequent subjection of the human person to some sort of creature). In contrast to them all, the Church, in holding up the icon of Mary Immaculate, held up an icon of both our true origin and our true dignity. That she was sinless was a teaching as old as the hills in the Church, which had hailed her as Kecharitomene, or "full of grace," since the time of Luke and saluted her as Panagia, or "all-holy," since the early centuries of the Church. So then why did the Holy Spirit move the Church to develop and focus this immemorial teaching more clearly?

Because what needed to be said loud and clear was that we were made in the image of God and that our fallenness, though very real, does not name or define us: Jesus Christ does. We are not mere animals; statistical averages; cogs in a machine; sophisticated primordial ooze; or a jangling set of complexes, appetites, tribal totems, Aryan supermen, naturally virtuous savages, or totally depraved Mr. Hydes. We were made by God, for God. Therefore sin, though normal, is not natural and doesn't constitute our humanity. And the proof of it was Mary, who was preserved from sin and yet was more human than the lot of us. She wasn't autonomously innocent, as though she could make it without God. She was the biggest recipient of grace in the universe, a grace that made her, in a famous phrase, "younger than sin." Because of it, she was free to be what Irenaeus described as "the glory of God": a human being fully alive. And as she is, so can the grace of Christ make us.

The 19th-century ideologies didn't, however, remain in libraries and classrooms. In the 20th century, they were enacted by the powers of state, science, business, entertainment, education, and the military into programs that bore abundant fruit in such enterprises as global and regional wars, the Holocaust, the great famines, the killing fields, the "great leap forward," the sexual revolution, and the culture of death, which is still reaping a rich bounty of spiritual and physical destruction. In short, as the 19th-century philosophies assaulted the dignity and origin of the human person, so the working out of those philosophies on the ground in the 20th century assaulted the dignity and destiny of the human person.

So what did the Holy Spirit do? Once again, in 1950, in the middle of a century that witnessed the biggest assault on the human person and on the family that the world has ever seen, the Church again held up Mary as an icon of who we really are and who we are meant to become by promulgating the doctrine of the assumption of Mary. Just as the immaculate conception held Mary up as the icon of the divine dignity of our origins, so the Church, in teaching "that the Immaculate Mother of God, the ever Virgin Mary, having completed the course of her earthly life, was assumed body and soul into heavenly glory," was now holding her up as the icon of the divine dignity of our destiny.

The Church is repeating, in effect, that the God who loves the world does not will that our fate be the oven, the mass grave, the abortuary, the anonymity of the factory, the brothel, the cubicle, or the street. The proper end of our life is supposed to be for us, as it already is for her, the ecstatic glory of complete union with the Triune God in eternity. Once again, God shows us something vital about our relationship to Himself through her, His greatest saint.

And that, in the end, is the point of Marian devotion and theology. Through Our Lady, we see Jesus Christ reflected in the eyes of His greatest saint. But we also see "what are the riches of his glorious inheritance in the saints, and what is the immeasurable greatness of his power in us who believe, according to the working of his great might" (Ephesians 1:18-19). For what He has already done for her, He will one day do also in us.

Source: Mark Shea. 2004. "The Mother of the Son: The Case for Marian Devotion." *Crisis* (December). Reprinted with permission from InsideCatholic (www.insidecatholic.com).

Mark Shea is Senior Content Editor for Catholic Exchange. He is an awarding-winning columnist, contributing a weekly feature to *Inside Catholic* and "Connecting the Dots" to the *National Catholic Register*, as well as numerous articles to many other magazines. Mark is the author of *Making Senses Out of Scripture: Reading the Bible as the First Christians Did* (Basilica, San Diego, 2001), *By What Authority?: An Evangelical Discovers Catholic Tradition* (Our Sunday Visitor, Huntington, Indiana, 1996), and *This Is My Body: An Evangelical Discovers the Real Presence* (Christendom, Front Royal, Virginia, 1993).

Chapter 16

Women and the Church

Women have always had a crucial role in the Church, beginning with Mary, the mother of Our Lord and the other holy women who remained faithful to Jesus and accompanied him in his final agony on Calvary. Women were also vital collaborators of St. Paul in the evangelization of the Gentiles, a fact clearly documented in his Epistles. Nevertheless, critics of the Church perpetuate the notion that women are, in some way, second-class citizens in the Church because they cannot be ordained to the ministerial priesthood.

Throughout history, the dignity of women clearly has not been acknowledged as it should have been, nor have women been treated with the respect they deserve. Pope John Paul II spoke to this unfortunate truth in his *Letter to Women* and apologized for the role any member of the Church played in undermining the true dignity of women.

Despite the disadvantages that women experienced throughout history, they have made monumental contributions to the Church and society. John Paul II refers to the "genius of woman" when pointing out the various great women who made such a profound difference in the history of the Church.[1]

Christopher Kaczor, in "**Does the Catholic Church Hate Women?**," provides a refreshingly balanced discussion of how the Church has treated women. He exposes some warts, but on balance he shows how the Church helped women shed the shackles of oppression and promoted women as equal to men in dignity.

➢ Not all members of the Church have followed Christ in their treatment of women throughout history, as John Paul II acknowledges.

---

[1] Pope John Paul II. 1995. *Letter to Women*, no. 11, June 29.

➤ The failure of Christians to follow Christ is not limited to wrongdoing against women. Indeed, the victimization of women has been perpetrated by many groups, not only Catholics.

➤ Christians separate themselves from Christ and his Church to the extent that they sin and commit acts of injustice.

➤ Christian theology, at times influenced by personal sin and the prevailing culture, has failed to express the true dignity of women. Some Christian thinkers and even Fathers of the Church adopted the unenlightened thinking of their era with regard to women.

➤ St. Thomas Aquinas taught, "[T]he male sex is more noble than the female." But, he also taught that in marriage a husband and wife were equals.

➤ Jesus' teaching against divorce established Christianity as the only religion in history to embrace strict monogamy, greatly benefitting women who were usually left impoverished by divorce.

➤ The high esteem with which the early Church held them no doubt contributed to Christianity's attractiveness to women, who converted in significant numbers.

➤ The passage from Ephesians that calls wives to be subject to their husbands should be read in context. St. Paul calls for a mutual subjection of husband and wife. Indeed, he calls husbands to love their wives with the sacrificial love that Christ has for his Church.

➤ In reserving the priesthood to men, the Church is merely following the example of Christ, who selected only men to be priests.

➤ The priesthood is not a position of power, but of service, love, and sacrifice.

➤ A clerical view holds that only priests have "full and active participation" in the Church. This erroneous view suggests that the Blessed Virgin Mary, Mother Teresa, St. Thomas More, and St. Francis of Assisi did not participate fully in Church life because they were not priests.

➤ The Second Vatican Council taught that *all* men and women are called to holiness; lay Catholic men and women can and should participate actively in the Church.

Some view the priesthood as a sort of male club, a reflection of the sociological and cultural values of Our Lord's time. But, the Church has made it clear that reserving the ministerial priesthood to men is based solely on theological considerations. Pope John Paul II has declared that "the Church has no authority whatsoever to confer priestly ordination on women" and that his "judgment is to be definitively held by all the Church's faithful."[2]

Joyce Little, in **"Ordination of Women,"** explains the theology behind the Church's teaching that only men may be ordained to the priesthood.

> ➤ The exclusion of women from the priesthood is based on the actions of Christ and the Tradition of the Church.
> ➤ The priesthood is a sacramental office, not merely a job or function. Priests act *in persona Christi* (in the Person of Christ) as the head and bridegroom of the Church.
> ➤ Two teachings of the Church are keys to understanding the male priesthood: the Trinity and the human person's creation in the image of God as male and female.
> ➤ We are created in the image of God as persons ordered to and dependent upon one another in the non-interchangeable relations of husband and wife. The male is created to become bridegroom, the female to become bride.
> ➤ Our imaging of God is bound up with sexual differentiation and marital union.
> ➤ The New Covenant is not just Jesus Christ, but precisely the marital union of Christ the bridegroom with his bride the Church.
> ➤ Christ's reservation of the priesthood to men is connected with the fact that the priest receives a share in the priesthood of Christ and is called to act in the Person of Christ the bridegroom, which is the specifically male relation.
> ➤ The restriction of the priesthood to men in no way suggests that women are inferior to men. In fact, *Genesis* makes clear the equality of men and women.

Further Reading

Joanna Bogle. 1997. "Catholic Women—A Case of Oppression?" *This Rock* (8): May 5).

Michael Novak. 1993. "Women, Ordination, and Angels." *First Things* (April).

---

[2] John Paul II. 1994. *Ordinatio Sacerdotalis*, May 22.

Does the Catholic Church Hate Women?

By Christopher Kaczor

The Catholic Church is subjected to a great deal of suspicion, if not outright scorn, when it comes to its treatment of women. Does the Church treat women as "second class"? In short, does the Catholic Church hate women? Few people would put the question that strongly, yet many believe the answer is "yes."

As evidence, they point to sexist quotations from Church Fathers and sexist interpretations of Scripture. Even Scripture contains "subordination" passages, such as "Let wives also be subject in everything to their husbands" (Eph. 5:24). Moreover, the Catholic Church is also well-known for its opposition to abortion and contraception, which many believe are the keys to women's sexual and economic freedom. Finally, only men can be ordained priests. Isn't that clear evidence of discrimination? As one slogan puts it: "If women are good enough to be baptized, why aren't they good enough to be ordained?"

We're a Church of Sinners

Unfortunately, members of the Church have not always followed Christ as closely as they should with respect to the treatment of women, and this lends credence to the accusations. As Pope John Paul II confessed, many members of the Church, including some in the hierarchy, have acted—and sometimes still act—in ways that fail to express the equality of man and woman. As John Paul wrote:

> And if objective blame [for offenses against the dignity of women], especially in particular historical contexts, has belonged to not just a few members of the Church, for this I am truly sorry. May this regret be transformed, on the part of the whole Church, into a renewed commitment of fidelity to the gospel vision. When it comes to setting women free from every kind of exploitation and domination, the gospel contains an ever relevant message that goes back to the attitude of Jesus Christ himself. Transcending the established norms of his own culture, Jesus treated women with openness, respect, acceptance, and tenderness. In this way he honored the dignity that women have always possessed according to God's plan and in his

love. As we look to Christ at the end of this second millennium, it is natural to ask ourselves: How much of his message has been heard and acted upon? *(Letter to Women 3).*

The situation today is better than it once was, but sexual and physical abuse of women still occurs, as does unjust discrimination and the failure to recognize talents.

Of course, failing in Christian discipleship is not limited to wrongdoing against the dignity of women—baptism does not remove the believer from the temptations and weaknesses endured by all of humanity. Moreover, it is not only Catholics who victimize, and it is not only women who are victimized. As Robert Burns wrote, "Man's inhumanity to man makes thousands mourn." Cruel and unfeeling behavior stretches beyond Cain and Abel to Adam's blaming of Eve.

But such shortcomings do not reflect what the Church is called to be. Sins against young and old, black and white, male and female are characteristic of all people. What is characteristic of Christians, though, is the imitation of Christ. The degree to which someone does not imitate Christ is the degree to which that person fails to be fully Christian. There is a long list of "Catholic" murderers. But when a Catholic commits murder, he separates himself from Christ, and therefore from the body of Christ, the Church.

Theologians Sometimes Fail

In addition to the sad but real failings of Catholics to live up to their calling in their treatment of women, Christian theology has also fallen short in this regard. Personal sin undoubtedly plays a role in the corruption of theology, but the cultural context must also be considered. Christianity arose in an environment of female inequality. Greek philosophy, as well as Hebrew sources, are rife with misogynistic judgments. It is not surprising that the Church Fathers sometimes adopted these attitudes without critical reflection—and some academics have been quick to interpret passages in the least charitable light. John Paul II continues in his *Letter to Women:*

> Unfortunately, we are heirs to a history that has conditioned us to a remarkable extent. In every time and place, this conditioning has been an obstacle to the progress of women. Women's dignity has of-

ten been unacknowledged and their prerogatives misrepresented; they have often been relegated to the margins of society and even reduced to servitude. This has prevented women from truly being themselves, and it has resulted in a spiritual impoverishment of humanity. Certainly it is no easy task to assign the blame for this, considering the many kinds of cultural conditioning that down the centuries have shaped ways of thinking and acting *(LW 3)*.

Just as Christian thinkers will sometimes uncritically adopt the scientific outlook of the day, so, too, in the social realm. Hence, Fathers of the Church and great scholastic doctors not only at times uncritically repeat the sexist truisms inherited from the secular culture of their day but sometimes interpret the theological tradition in light of those assumptions. The same attitudes and judgments can also inform the reading of Scripture.

Therefore, the theology of the Church sometimes stands in need of correction. If revelation is really from God, then nothing revealed can be false or lacking in justice or goodness. But the same does not hold true for any individual's interpretation of revelation, even a saintly and learned individual. The development of doctrine leads to a greater understanding of revelation in part by sorting out what actually pertains to revelation from what only seems to.

From Sublime to Repellent

Among all the sublime thought of great Christian theologians, we occasionally come across something repellent. For example, St. Thomas Aquinas, following the sexist views of his time, held:

The male sex is more noble than the female, and for this reason he [Jesus] took human nature in the male sex *(Summa Theologiae* III:31:4 ad 1*)*.

At the same time, Aquinas believed that the female sex should not be despised on this account, since Christ took his flesh from a woman. In other passages, too, Thomas shows an awareness of the equality of men and women recognized by Christ:

If a husband were permitted to abandon his wife, the society of husband and wife would not be an association of equals but, instead, a sort of slavery on the part of the wife *(Summa contra Gentiles III:124:[4])*.

In fact, Thomas used the idea of equality in marital friendship to argue against polygamy and in favor of an unconditional love between husband and wife:

The greater the friendship is, the more solid and long lasting it will be. Now there seems to be the greatest friendship between husband and wife, for they are united not only in the act of fleshly union, which produces a certain gentle association even among beasts, but also in the partnership of the whole range of domestic activity. Consequently, as an indication of this, man must even "leave his father and mother" for the sake of his wife as it is said in Genesis (2:24).

Furthermore, Aquinas believed that the fact that Eve was made from Adam's rib indicates that she was not above him (as she might be had she been created from Adam's head) nor below him, like a slave (as she might be had she arisen from his feet). She comes from his side, indicating that she is a partner and companion. These statements of the equality of man and women—not the statement of male superiority—were new and radical. The specifically Christian attitude toward women—not the pre-existing pagan attitude—was new and radical. It has taken some time, though, for the wheat to be separated from the chaff.

Equal-Opportunity Moral Code

As it still does today, divorce in the ancient world left many women in dire economic and social straits. At the time of Christ, Mosaic law allowed a husband to leave his wife, but a wife could not leave her husband. Jesus' prohibition of divorce established Christianity as the only religion in the history of the world to call its members to strict monogamy:

Whoever divorces his wife and marries another, commits adultery against her; and if she divorces her husband and marries another, she commits adultery (Mark 10:11–12).

This teaching of Jesus protected women, for, according to Church Father Gregory of Nazianz:

The majority of men are ill-disposed to chastity and their laws are unequal and irregular. For what was the reason they restrained the woman but indulged the man, and that a woman who practices evil against her husband's bed is an adulteress and the penalties of the law severe, but if the husband commits fornication against his wife, he has no account to give? I do not accept this legislation. I do not approve this custom *(Oration 37:6)*.

By establishing one moral code obligatory on men and women alike, Christianity fostered a lasting commitment of unconditional covenantal love, protecting the family structure and putting the sexes on an equal footing.

What Women Really Thought

Apparently the justice of Christian morality offered a refreshing perspective to women in the ancient world accustomed to husbands who cheated and left at will. The number of women who converted to Christianity in the early centuries after Christ indicates that women were attracted to this new way of life. Indeed, they were among the most zealous converts and defenders of the faith:

Christianity seems to have been especially successful among women. It was often through the wives that it penetrated the upper classes of society in the first instance. Christians believed in the equality of men and women before God and found in the New Testament commands that husbands should treat their wives with such consideration and love as Christ manifested for his Church. Christian teaching about the sanctity of marriage offered a powerful safeguard to married women (Henry Chadwick, *The Early Church*, Penguin, 58–59).

Many women today do feel alienated from the Church for a variety of reasons, but it is often because they disagree with the Church's basic beliefs about the meaning of life, the nature of human happiness, and the interaction of the divine and the human.

Is Scripture Misogynistic?

But what should be made of subordination passages in Scripture, such as "Let wives also be subject in everything to their husbands" (Eph. 5:24)? This appears to contradict the idea that Christianity views the sexes as equal. Pope John Paul II's answer was:

> The author knows that this way of speaking, so profoundly rooted in the customs and religious traditions of the time, is to be understood and carried out in a new way: as a "mutual subjection out of reverence for Christ" (*Mulieris Dignitatem* 24; cf. Eph. 5:21).

Discussing the bond of marriage as it exists after the taint of original sin, John Paul states:

> The matrimonial union requires respect for and perfection of the true personal subjectivity of both of them. The woman cannot be made the object of dominion and male possession *(MD 10).*

That husband and wife are to be subject to one another is reinforced in the next verse of the original passage cited: "Husbands, love your wives, as Christ loved the Church and gave himself up for her" (Eph. 5:25). This injunction transforms the potentially selfish orientation of male love into a form of intense self-sacrificial service. Subordination is mutual, but the admonition is given to husbands, perhaps because they need it more. What is implied, then, is not general female inferiority but general female superiority in the order that most matters eschatologically—the order of charity.

It's Not about Power

The reservation of priestly ordination to men is perhaps the sorest spot among contemporary critics of the Catholic Church's treatment of women. Many people understandably believe that the Church feels that women are less holy, less intellectually capable, less pastorally sensitive, or less capable of leadership than men. It is true that medieval theologians defended male priestly ordination with just such arguments, but the reservation in and of itself does not imply the inferiority of women. As the *Catechism of the Catholic Church* recalls, Christ himself established what constitutes the sacraments. The Church, in obedience to the Lord, is free only to follow what Christ has ordained.

Baptism must make use of water and not sand. This does not imply that sand is in and of itself less than water; indeed, those lost at sea need sand much more than they need water. The Eucharist must make use of bread and wine and not sausage and beer, even in Germany, where presumably those celebrating the Eucharist would prefer a meal of sausage and beer to one of bread and wine. Similarly, the Church teaches that Christ established that the proper recipient of the sacrament of holy orders is a baptized male; similarly, this in no way implies that men are better than women. The teaching itself does not imply in any way inferiority on the part of women.

Some theologians have even speculated that one reason for the reservation of priestly orders to males could be that men are typically worse people than women. Most murderers, rapists, thieves, and scoundrels of the highest order are men. It is, therefore, men and not women who are in particular need of models of self-sacrificial service and love. A priest is one who gives sacrifice, and the sacrifice is not only something he does but something he is:

> We who have received the sacrament of orders call ourselves "priests." The author does not recall any priest ever having said that "I was ordained a victim." And yet, was not Christ the Priest, a Victim? Did he not come to die? He did not offer a lamb, a bullock, or doves; he never offered anything except himself. "He gave himself up on our behalf, a sacrifice breathing out a fragrance as he offered it to God" (Eph. 5:2). . . . So we have a mutilated concept of our priesthood if we envisage it apart from making ourselves victims in the prolongation of his Incarnation (Fulton J. Sheen, *The Priest Is Not His Own*, McGraw-Hill, 2).

The priesthood is misconstrued in terms of domination, power, and exultation; it is properly understood in terms of service, love, and sacrifice, and there are more than enough opportunities for both men and women to exercise these offices outside of the priesthood.

Full and Active Participation

It is almost always assumed by advocates of women's ordination that the "full and active participation" in the Church called for by the Second Vatican Council (*Sacrosanctum Concilium* 14) requires priestly ordination. The view that only priests are called to holiness or to important roles or to "full and active" participation in the Church is often called clericalism, an idea rejected by the Council. The lay person can participate actively and fully in the Church—as a lay person. The Spirit bestows different gifts on different people. As the first letter to the Corinthians indicates, just as the human body has different members and each member a different purpose, so, too, the various parts of the body of Christ—successors to the apostles, prophets, teachers, healers, helpers, administrators—are all essential, valuable, and vital (cf. 1 Cor. 12:4–30).

The clericalist view implies that Mother Teresa, St. Thomas More, St. Francis of Assisi, and the Virgin Mary did not fully participate in the Church because they were not priests.

Of course, the ordination question is much more complicated and involved. But having read the literature extensively, I know of no argument in any contemporary source defending the reservation of priestly ordination to men that invokes the idea that men are better, holier, smarter, more worthy, more pastorally sensitive, or superior in any talent to women. I have also never read a critique of the Church's teaching that did not explicitly or implicitly rely on clericalist assumptions.

The myth of Catholic misogyny is well addressed in terms of the practical care the Church offers to women (and men) throughout the world. Has any institution educated more women? Fed more women? Clothed more women? Rescued more female infants from death? Offered more assistance or medical care to mothers and their born and unborn children? Members of the Church have undoubtedly behaved badly, but no less have members of the Church undoubtedly behaved well, heroically well. When they have done so, they have been even more fully incorporated into the mystical body of Christ whose Head came to serve all, love all, and save all, and in whose image—as God—he created both male and female.

Source: "Does the Catholic Church Hate Women?" 2006. *This Rock* (17): 3 (March). Reprinted with permission from Christopher Kaczor.

Christopher Kaczor is Associate Professor in the Department of Philosophy in the Bellarmine College of Liberal Arts at Loyola Marymount University in Los Angeles. He graduated from the Honors Program of Boston College and holds an M.M.S. and a Ph.D. from the University of Notre Dame. He is the author or coauthor of seven books, including *Thomas Aquinas on the Cardinal Virtues: Edited and Explained for Everyone* (Sapientia Press of Ave Maria University, 2009) and *Thomas Aquinas on Faith Hope and Love: Edited and Explained for Everyone* (Sapientia Press of Ave Maria University, 2008). Dr. Kaczor has been interviewed on issues of ethics, philosophy, and religion for newspapers and radio stations across the country, as well as on television on EWTN, ABC, NBC, Fox, CBS, MSNBC, and *The Today Show*.

Ordination of Women

By Joyce A. Little

In the history of the Church, the ordained priesthood has consistently been restricted to men. This restriction has been understood as reflecting the mind of Christ, who chose only men to be his Apostles. The exclusion of women, therefore, is rooted in the action of Christ and sustained in the Tradition of the Church. Clearly, why this should be so is based on the fact that the priesthood is a *sacramental office*, not just a job or function, because priests are ordained to act *in persona Christi* (in the Person of Christ) as the head and bridegroom of the Church. In order, however, to understand the significance of the relationship of Christ and the Church as bridegroom and bride, we must understand two other teachings of the Church, first, that of the Trinity, and second, that of man's creation in the image of God as male and female.

The Lesson of the Trinity

When we say that God is Trinity, we mean that God is one substance and three Persons—Father, Son, and Holy Spirit. These three Persons are subsistent *relations*. The Father is the relation of paternity (or fatherhood), the Son the relation of filiation (or sonship), the Holy Spirit the relation of passive spiration—"spiration" because he is spirated by the Father and the Son, "passive" because he does not do the spirating himself but is spirated by them. To be a person in the Trinity, therefore, is to be a relation.

These three Persons are also mutually *dependent* upon one another and mutually *ordered* to one another. The Father is Father because he has a Son, and he is ordered to the Son as Father. The Son is Son because he has a Father, and is ordered to the Father as Son. The Holy Spirit is Spirit because he is spirated by the Father and the Son, and is ordered to the Father and the Son as the One spirated by them. These Persons are therefore *noninterchangeable*. The Father, for example, cannot be the Son or Holy Spirit and cannot therefore do any of those things appropriate to filiation or spiration. (As one God, of course God can do all things capable of being done.) In short, the Trinity reveals to us that to be a person is to be in a dependent, ordered, noninterchangeable relation to another person or other persons.

Human beings, according to Revelation, are made in the image of God as male and female (Gn 1:27). They are made not just as male and female, however, but also as gifts to one another in the marital union of husband and wife (Gn 2:24). In other words, human beings are created to image God as *persons ordered to and dependent upon one another in the noninterchangeable relations of husband and wife.* The male is created to become bridegroom, the female to become bride. Although the Trinitarian implications of man's creation in the image of God are not apparent until the revelation given in Christ that God is Trinity, the Genesis text makes it clear that our imaging of God is bound up with sexual differentiation and marital union.

The New Covenant not only reveals the triune character of God but also reaffirms, in the order of salvation, the marital order of creation, for the New Covenant is not just Jesus Christ, but precisely the marital union of Christ the bridegroom with his bride the Church. This union is the "great mystery," or "great sacrament," of salvation. Indeed, the author of Ephesians links this marital union with the original marital ordering of creation (Eph 5: 31-31). Not only is Christ the Son of God, enjoying by virtue of his divinity a dependent, ordered, noninterchangeable relationship with the Father and Holy Spirit, he also is the bridegroom of the Church, enjoying by virtue of his humanity a dependent, ordered, noninterchangeable relationship with his bride the Church. We might, therefore, suppose that Christ is male not because God is male (there is no gender in God) but because he is *the relation of bridegroom*, which only a male can be. As Pope John Paul II has pointed out: "Christ has entered this history and remains in it as the Bridegroom who 'has given himself'" (*On the Dignity and Vocation of Women, Mulieris Dignitatem*, 25).

"In the Person of Christ"

That Christ reserved the ordained priesthood for men is, therefore, bound up with the fact that the priest receives a share in the priesthood of Christ and is called to act in the Person of Christ the bridegroom, which is the specifically male relation.

Pope John Paul II has declared that "the Church has no authority whatsoever to confer priestly ordination on women and . . . this judgment is to be definitively held by all the Church's faithful"; this is, he adds, "a matter of great importance . . . which pertains to the Church's divine constitution itself" (*Ordinatio Sacerdotalis*, 4). He is referring here to the holiness or integrity of the Church and her structures. The reservation of the ordained priesthood to men is one of the unchangeable structures of the Church because it is holy or good in itself, reflecting the mind of Christ, who reaffirms the order of creation within the order of salvation. The male priesthood is bound up with the very integrity of that order. The Church's teaching in this matter was reaffirmed yet again by the Congregation for the Doctrine of the Faith in a *Responsum* of November 18, 1995.

Two final considerations. First, the restriction of the priesthood to men does not mean that women are inferior to men. The Genesis text that makes clear the noninterchangeable character of male and female as the image of God also, and just as clearly, reveals their equality. "Here too [Gn 1:27] we find the first statement of the equal dignity of man and woman; both, in equal measure, are person. Their constitution, with the specific dignity which derives from it, defines 'from the beginning' the qualities of the common good of humanity, in every dimension and circumstance of life. To this common good both man and woman make their specific contribution. Hence one can discover, at the very origins of human society, the qualities of communion and of complementarity" (Pope John Paul II, *Letter to Families*, 6).

The persons of the human community are equal in their humanity, just as the Persons of the divine communion are equal in their divinity.

Second, the ordained priesthood exists to serve the royal priesthood, that priesthood of all the faithful received at Baptism. In relation to her members, as well as in relation to Christ, the Church has a feminine character, and every one of us is entrusted at Baptism to the Church as mother. By the same token, every one of us is entrusted at conception to a woman as mother. We might therefore ask ourselves the question that John Paul II raises regarding the significance of women in relation to the royal priesthood: "If the human being is entrusted by God to women in a particular way, does not this mean that *Christ looks to them for the accomplishment of the 'royal priesthood'* (1 pt 2:9), which is the treasure he has given to every individual?" (*Mulieris Dignitatem*, 30).

Joyce A. Little taught theology at the University of St. Thomas, Houston. Previously, she taught at Marquette University, where she received her doctorate in theology. Her books are *Toward a Thomist Methodology* (Edwin Mellen Press, 1988) and *The Church and the Culture War* (Ignatius Press, 1995). She also has written articles and reviews for numerous publications and has lectured widely.

Chapter 17

Is There Salvation Outside the Church?

"Outside the Church there is no salvation." This ancient teaching of the Church is based on Scripture. Our Lord proclaimed, "I am the way, the truth, and the life; no one comes to the Father, but by me." (John 14:6). Peter stated clearly, "There is salvation in no one else, for there is no other name under heaven given among men by which we must be saved" (Acts: 4: 12).

The Catholic Church reiterates this teaching, stating that "[T]he Church is the one Mediator and the unique way of salvation." Christ himself taught clearly and consistently the absolute need for faith and baptism.[1]

Although the Church continues to teach this fundamental truth, her understanding of its full meaning has developed over time. The Church acknowledges that non-Catholic Christians are, in a certain sense, part of the Church.[2]

It is God's will that all be saved. He even invites those who, through no fault of their own, have not embraced the faith of Christ.[3] Affirming the necessity of Baptism, the Church teaches that, since God knows the most interior dispositions of his creatures and understands the longing of their hearts, he provides a path to heaven for those who "would have desired Baptism explicitly if they had known its necessity."[4]

---

[1] "Dogmatic Constitution on the Church." 1964. *Lumen Gentium*.
[2] *Catechism of the Catholic Church*. 1997. no. 838. Vatican City: Libreria Editrice Vaticana.
[3] "Dogmatic Constitution on the Church." 1964. *Lumen Gentium*, 16.
[4] *Catechism of the Catholic Church*. 1997. no. 1260. Vatican City: Libreria Editrice Vaticana.

In **"Who Can Be Saved?,"** Cardinal Dulles traces the development of the Church's understanding of "outside the Church there is no salvation."

> Early Christian thinkers held that those who lived before Christ's time could be saved by virtue of their good life and, in the case of the prophets and patriarchs of Israel, their longing for the Savior.

> No doctrine, however, held that pagans could be saved after the Gospel was preached.

> Gregory of Nyssa and John Chrysostom, among others, taught that in the Christian era only Christians could be saved.

> The Council of Florence (1442) taught that pagans, Jews, schismatics, and heretics could not be saved. However, some medieval theologians cited 1 Tim. 2:4, which says that God "desires all men to be saved and come to the knowledge of the truth" to question this teaching.

> The discovery of the New World in the sixteenth and seventeenth centuries led to a major theological development as evidence emerged that the people of these lands had never heard of the Gospel of Christ.

> Some theologians held that an "implicit faith in Christ" by the unevangelized could be sufficient to attain salvation.

> In the mid-nineteenth century, Pope Pius IX stated that those who were invincibly ignorant of Christianity and lived according to the natural law could be saved. Still, he reaffirmed that no one could be saved outside the Catholic Church. He did not explain how or in what sense these righteous non-Christians were in the Church.

> Pius XII, in *Mystici Corporis*, advanced the notion of adherence to the Church through implicit desire.

> The Second Vatican Council, in its "Dogmatic Constitution on the Church," explains how non-Catholics, non-Christians, and even atheists can be saved through the elements of salvation and truth that subsist in the Catholic Church.

> This, of course, does not suggest that missionary activity and evangelization are not important as those who have not heard the Gospel message are more vulnerable to a life of hopelessness in a world without God.

> The Church provides many aids to salvation and sanctification that are unavailable to those outside the Church.

> ➢ Dulles cautions, "We cannot take it for granted that everyone is seeking the truth and is prepared to submit to it when found. Some, perhaps many, resist the grace of God and reject the signs given to them. They are not on the road to salvation at all. In such cases, the fault is not God's but theirs. The references to future punishment in the gospels cannot be written off as empty threats."

Further Reading

Ray Ryland. 2005. "No Salvation Outside the Church," *This Rock* (16): 10 (December).

Mark P. Shea. 2004. "Can Non-Catholics Be Saved?" *Crisis Magazine* (October).

Peter Stravinskas. 1998. "Can Outsiders Be Insiders?" *Envoy* (September/October).

Who Can Be Saved?

by Avery Cardinal Dulles

Nothing is more striking in the New Testament than the confidence with which it proclaims the saving power of belief in Christ. Almost every page confronts us with a decision of eternal consequence: Will we follow Christ or the rulers of this world? The gospel is, according to Paul, "the power of God for salvation to everyone who has faith" (Rom. 1:16). The apostles and their associates are convinced that in Jesus they have encountered the Lord of Life and that he has brought them into the way that leads to everlasting blessedness. By personal faith in him and by baptism in his name, Christians have passed from darkness to light, from error to truth, and from sin to holiness.

Paul is the outstanding herald of salvation through faith. To the Romans he writes, "If you confess with your lips that Jesus is Lord and believe in your heart that God raised him from the dead, you will be saved" (Rom. 10:9). Faith, for him, is inseparable from baptism, the sacrament of faith. By baptism, the Christian is immersed in the death of Christ so as to be raised with him to newness of life (Rom. 6:3-4

The Book of Acts shows the apostles preaching faith in Christ as the way to salvation. Those who believe the testimony of Peter on the first Pentecost ask him what they must do to be saved. He replies that they must be baptized in the name of Jesus Christ for the forgiveness of their sins and thereby save themselves from the present crooked generation (Acts 2:37-40). When Peter and John are asked by the Jewish religious authorities by what authority they are preaching and performing miracles, they reply that they are acting in the name of Jesus Christ and that "there is no other name under heaven given among men by which we must be saved" (Acts 4:12). Paul and his associates bring the gospel first of all to the Jews because it is the fulfillment of the Old Testament promises. When the Jews in large numbers reject the message, Paul and Barnabas announce that they are turning to the Gentiles in order to bring salvation to the uttermost parts of the earth (Acts 13:46-47).

A few chapters later in Acts, we see Paul and Silas in prison at Philippi. When their jailer asks them, "What must I do to be saved?" they reply, "Believe in the Lord Jesus and you will be saved." The jailer and his family at once accept baptism and rejoice in their newfound faith (Acts 16:30-34).

The same doctrine of salvation permeates the other books of the New Testament. Mark's gospel ends with this missionary charge: "Go into all the world and preach the gospel to the whole of creation. He who believes and is baptized will be saved; but he who does not believe will be condemned" (Mark 16:15-16).

John in his gospel speaks no less clearly. Jesus at one point declares that those who hear his word and believe in him do not remain in darkness, whereas those who reject him will be judged on the last day (John 12:44-50). At the Last Supper, Jesus tells the Twelve, "This is eternal life, that they may know thee, the only true God, and Jesus Christ whom thou hast sent" (John 17:3). John concludes the body of his gospel with the statement that he has written his account "so that you may believe that Jesus is the Christ and that believing you may have life in his name" (John 20:31).

From these and many other texts, I draw the conclusion that, according to the primary Christian documents, salvation comes through personal faith in Jesus Christ, followed and signified by sacramental baptism.

The New Testament is almost silent about the eternal fate of those to whom the gospel has not been preached. It seems apparent that those who became believers did not think they had been on the road to salvation before they heard the gospel. In his sermon at Athens, Paul says that in times past God overlooked the ignorance of the pagans, but he does not say that these pagans were saved. In the first chapter of Romans, Paul says that the Gentiles have come to a knowledge of God by reasoning from the created world, but that they are guilty because by their wickedness they have suppressed the truth and fallen into idolatry. In the second chapter of Romans, Paul indicates that Gentiles who are obedient to the biddings of conscience can be excused for their unbelief, but he indicates that they fall into many sins. He concludes that "all have sinned and fall short" of true righteousness (Rom. 3:23). For justification, Paul asserts, both Jews and Gentiles must rely on faith in Jesus Christ, who expiated the sins of the world on the cross.

Animated by vibrant faith in Christ the Savior, the Christian Church was able to conquer the Roman Empire. The converts were convinced that in embracing Christianity they were escaping from the darkness of sin and superstition and entering into the realm of salvation. For them, Christianity was the true religion, the faith that saves. It would not have occurred to them that any other faith could save them.

Christian theologians, however, soon had to face the question whether anyone could be saved without Christian faith. They did not give a wholly negative answer. They agreed that the patriarchs and prophets of Israel, because they looked forward in faith and hope to the Savior, could be saved by adhering in advance to him who was to come.

The apologists of the second and third centuries made similar concessions with regard to certain Greek philosophers. The prologue to John's gospel taught that the eternal Word enlightens all men who come into the world. Justin Martyr speculated that philosophers such as Socrates and Heraclitus had lived according to the Word of God, the Logos who was to become incarnate in Christ, and they could therefore be reckoned as being in some way Christians. Irenaeus, Clement of Alexandria, and Origen held that the Wisdom of God gave graces to people of every generation, both Greeks and barbarians.

The saving grace of which these theologians were speaking, however, was given only to pagans who lived before the time of Christ. It was given by the Word of God who was to become incarnate in Jesus Christ. There was no doctrine that pagans could be saved since the promulgation of the gospel without embracing the Christian faith.

Origen and Cyprian, in the third century, formulated the maxim that has come down to us in the words *Extra ecclesiam nulla salus*—"Outside the Church, no salvation." They spoke these words with heretics and schismatics primarily in view, but they do not appear to have been any more optimistic about the prospects of salvation for pagans. Assuming that the gospel had been promulgated everywhere, writers of the high patristic age considered that, in the Christian era, Christians alone could be saved. In the East, this view is represented by Gregory of Nyssa and John Chrysostom. The view attributed to Origen that hell would in the end be evacuated and that all the damned would eventually be saved was condemned in the sixth century.

In the West, following Ambrose and others, Augustine taught that, because faith comes by hearing, those who had never heard the gospel would be denied salvation. They would be eternally punished for original sin as well as for any personal sins they had committed. Augustine's disciple Fulgentius of Ruspe exhorted his readers to "firmly hold and by no means doubt that not only all pagans, but also all Jews, and all heretics and schismatics who are outside the Catholic Church, will go to the eternal fire that was prepared for the devil and his angels."

The views of Augustine and Fulgentius remained dominant in the Christian West throughout the Middle Ages. The Fourth Lateran Council (1215) reaffirmed the formula "Outside the Church, no salvation," as did Pope Boniface VIII in 1302. At the end of the Middle Ages, the Council of Florence (1442) repeated the formulation of Fulgentius to the effect that no pagan, Jew, schismatic, or heretic could be saved.

On one point the medieval theologians diverged from rigid Augustinianism. On the basis of certain passages in the New Testament, they held that God seriously wills that all may be saved. They could cite the statement of Peter before the household of Cornelius: "Truly I perceive that God shows no partiality, but in every nation anyone who fears him and does what is right is acceptable to him" (Acts 10:34-35). The First Letter to Timothy, moreover, declares that God "desires all men to be saved and come to the knowledge of the truth" (1 Tim. 2:4). These assurances made for a certain tension in Catholic teaching on salvation. If faith in Christ was necessary for salvation, how could salvation be within reach of those who had no opportunity to learn about Christ?

Thomas Aquinas, in dealing with this problem, took his departure from the axiom that there was no salvation outside the Church. To be inside the Church, he held, it was not enough to have faith in the existence of God and in divine providence, which would have sufficed before the coming of Christ. God now required explicit faith in the mysteries of the Trinity and the Incarnation. In two of his early works (*De Veritate* and *Commentary on Romans*), he discusses the hypothetical case of a man brought up in the wilderness, where the gospel was totally unknown. If this man lived an upright life with the help of the graces given him, Thomas reasoned, God would make it possible for him to become a Christian believer, either through an inner illumination or by sending a missionary to him. Thomas referred to the biblical example of the centurion Cornelius, who received the visitation of an angel before being evangelized and baptized by Peter (Acts 10). In his *Summa Theologiae*, however, Thomas omits any reference to miraculous instruction; he goes back to the Augustinian theory that those who had never heard the gospel would be eternally punished for original sin as well as their personal sins.

A major theological development occurred in the sixteenth and seventeenth centuries. The voyages of discovery had by this time disclosed that there were large populations in North and South America, Africa, and Asia who had lived since the time of Christ and had never had access to the preaching of the gospel. The missionaries found no sign that even the most upright among these peoples had learned the mysteries of the Trinity and the Incarnation by interior inspirations or angelic visitations.

Luther, Calvin, and the Jansenists professed the strict Augustinian doctrine that God did not will to save everyone, but the majority of Catholic theologians rejected the idea that God had consigned all these unevangelized persons to hell without giving them any possibility of salvation. A series of theologians proposed more hopeful theories that they took to be compatible with Scripture and Catholic tradition.

The Dominican Melchior Cano argued that these populations were in a situation no different from that of the pre-Christian pagans praised by Justin and others. They could be justified in this life (but not saved in the life to come) by implicit faith in the Christian mysteries. Another Dominican, Domingo de Soto, went further, holding that, for the unevangelized, implicit faith in Christ would be sufficient for salvation itself. Their contemporary, Albert Pighius, held that for these unevangelized persons the only faith required would be that mentioned in Hebrews 11:6: "Without faith it is impossible to please him. For whoever would draw near to God must believe that he exists and that he rewards those who seek him." They could therefore be saved by general revelation and grace even though no missionary came to evangelize them.

The Jesuit Francisco Suarez, following these pioneers, argued for the sufficiency of implicit faith in the Trinity and the Incarnation, together with an implicit desire for baptism on the part of the unevangelized. Juan de Lugo agreed, but he added that such persons could not be saved if they had committed serious sins, unless they obtained forgiveness by an act of perfect contrition.

In the mid-nineteenth century, the Jesuits of the Gregorian University followed in the tradition of Suarez and de Lugo, with certain modifications. Pope Pius IX incorporated some of their ideas in two important statements in 1854 and 1863. In the first, he said that, while no one can be saved outside the Church, God would not punish people for their ignorance of the true faith if their ignorance was invincible. In the second statement, Pius went further. He declared that persons invincibly ignorant of the Christian religion who observed the natural law and were ready to obey God would be able to attain eternal life, thanks to the workings of divine grace within them. In the same letter, the pope reaffirmed that no one could be saved outside the Catholic Church. He did not explain in what sense such persons were, or would come to be, in the Church. He could have meant that they would receive the further grace needed to join the Church, but nothing in his language suggests this. More probably he thought that such persons would be joined to the Church by implicit desire, as some theologians were teaching by his time.

In 1943, Pius XII did take this further step. In his encyclical on the Mystical Body, *Mystici Corporis,* he distinguished between two ways of belonging to the Church: in actual fact (*in re*) or by desire (*in voto*). Those who belonged *in voto,* however, were not really members. They were ordered to the Church by the dynamism of grace itself, which related them to the Church in such a way that they were in some sense in it. The two kinds of relationship, however, were not equally conducive to salvation. Those adhering to the Church by desire could not have a sure hope of salvation because they lacked many spiritual gifts and helps available only to those visibly incorporated in the true Church.

Mystici Corporis represents a forward step in its doctrine of adherence to the Church through implicit desire. From an ecumenical point of view, that encyclical is deficient, since it does not distinguish between the status of non-Christians and non-Catholic Christians. The next important document came from the Holy Office in its letter to Cardinal Cushing of Boston in 1949. The letter pointed out—in opposition to Father Leonard Feeney, S.J., and his associates at St. Benedict Center—that, although the Catholic Church was a necessary means for salvation, one could belong to it not only by actual membership but by also desire, even an unconscious desire. If that desire was accompanied by faith and perfect charity, it could lead to eternal salvation.

Neither the encyclical *Mystici Corporis* nor the letter of the Holy Office specified the nature of the faith required for *in voto* status. Did the authors mean that the virtue of faith or the inclination to believe would suffice, or did they require actual faith in God and divine providence, or actual faith in the Trinity and the Incarnation?

The Second Vatican Council, in its "Dogmatic Constitution on the Church" and its "Decree on Ecumenism," made some significant departures from the teaching of Pius XII. It avoided the term *member* and said nothing of an unconscious desire for incorporation in the

Church. It taught that the Catholic Church was the all-embracing organ of salvation and was equipped with the fullness of means of salvation. Other Christian churches and communities possessed certain elements of sanctification and truth that were, however, derived from the one Church of Christ that subsists in the Catholic Church today. For this reason, God could use them as instruments of salvation. God had, however, made the Catholic Church necessary for salvation, and all who were aware of this had a serious obligation to enter the Church in order to be saved. God uses the Catholic Church not only for the redemption of her own members but also as an instrument for the redemption of all. Her witness and prayers, together with the eucharistic sacrifice, have an efficacy that goes out to the whole world.

In several important texts, Vatican II took up the question of the salvation of non-Christians. Although they were related to the Church in various ways, they were not incorporated in her. God's universal salvific will, it taught, means that he gives non-Christians, including even atheists, sufficient help to be saved. Whoever sincerely seeks God and, with his grace, follows the dictates of conscience is on the path to salvation. The Holy Spirit, in a manner known only to God, makes it possible for each and every person to be associated with the Paschal mystery. "God, in ways known to himself, can lead those inculpably ignorant of the gospel to that faith without which it is impossible to please him." The council did not indicate whether it is necessary for salvation to come to explicit Christian faith before death, but the texts give the impression that implicit faith may suffice.

Vatican II left open the question whether non-Christian religions contain revelation and are means that can lead their adherents to salvation. It did say, however, that other religions contain elements of truth and goodness, that they reflect rays of the truth that enlightens all men, and that they can serve as preparations for the gospel. Christian missionary activity serves to heal, ennoble, and perfect the seeds of truth and goodness that God has sown among non-Christian peoples, to the glory of God and the spiritual benefit of those evangelized.

While repeatedly insisting that Christ is the one mediator of salvation, Vatican II shows forth a generally hopeful view of the prospects of non-Christians for salvation. Its hopefulness, however, is not unqualified: "Rather often, men, deceived by the evil one, have become caught up in futile reasoning and have exchanged the truth of God for a lie, serving the creature rather than the Creator. Or, some there are who,

living and dying in a world without God, are subject to utter hopeless-
ness." The missionary activity of the Church is urgent for bringing such
persons to salvation.

After the council, Paul VI (in his pastoral exhortation "Evangelization in the Modern World") and John Paul II (in his encyclical
Redemptoris Missio) interpreted the teaching of Vatican II in relation to
certain problems and theological trends arising since the council. Both
popes were on guard against political and liberation theology, which
would seem to equate salvation with formation of a just society on
earth and against certain styles of religious pluralism, which would
attribute independent salvific value to non-Christian religions. In 2000,
toward the end of John Paul's pontificate, the Congregation for the
Doctrine of the Faith issued the declaration *Dominus Iesus*, which
emphatically taught that all grace and salvation must come through
Jesus Christ, the one mediator.

Wisely, in my opinion, the popes and councils have avoided talk
about implicit faith, a term that is vague and ambiguous. They do speak
of persons who are sincerely seeking for the truth and of others who
have found it in Christ. They make it clear that sufficient grace is
offered to all and that God will not turn away those who do everything
within their power to find God and live according to his law. We may
count on him to lead such persons to the faith needed for salvation.

One of the most interesting developments in post-conciliar theology has been Karl Rahner's idea of "anonymous Christians." He taught
that God offers his grace to everyone and reveals himself in the interior
offer of grace. Grace, moreover, is always mediated through Christ and
tends to bring its recipients into union with him. Those who accept and
live by the grace offered to them, even though they have never heard of
Christ and the gospel, may be called anonymous Christians.

Although Rahner denied that his theory undermined the importance of missionary activity, it was widely understood as depriving
missions of their salvific importance. Some readers of his works understood him as teaching that the unevangelized could possess the whole
of Christianity except the name. Saving faith, thus understood, would
be a subjective attitude without any specifiable content. In that case,
the message of the gospel would have little to do with salvation.

The history of the doctrine of salvation through faith has gone
through a number of stages since the High Middle Ages. Using the New
Testament as their basic text, the Church Fathers regarded faith in

Christ and baptism as essential for salvation. On the basis of his study of the New Testament and Augustine, Thomas Aquinas held that explicit belief in the Trinity and the Incarnation was necessary for everyone who lived since the time of Christ, but he granted that in earlier times it was sufficient to believe explicitly in the existence and providence of God.

In the sixteenth century, theologians speculated that the unevangelized were in the same condition as pre-Christians and were not held to believe explicitly in Christ until the gospel was credibly preached to them. Pius IX and the Second Vatican Council taught that all who followed their conscience, with the help of the grace given to them, would be led to that faith that was necessary for them to be saved. During and after the council, Karl Rahner maintained that saving faith could be had without any definite belief in Christ or even in God.

We seem to have come full circle from the teaching of Paul and the New Testament that belief in the message of Christ is the source of salvation. Reflecting on this development, one can see certain gains and certain losses. The New Testament and the theology of the first millennium give little hope for the salvation of those who, since the time of Christ, have had no chance of hearing the gospel. If God has a serious salvific will for all, this lacuna needed to be filled, as it has been by theological speculation and church teaching since the sixteenth century. Modern theology, preoccupied with the salvation of non-Christians, has tended to neglect the importance of explicit belief in Christ, so strongly emphasized in the first centuries. It should not be impossible, however, to reconcile the two perspectives.

Scripture itself assures us that God has never left himself without a witness to any nation (Acts 14:17). His testimonies are marks of his saving dispensations toward all. The inner testimony of every human conscience bears witness to God as lawgiver, judge, and vindicator. In ancient times, the Jewish Scriptures drew on literature that came from Babylon, Egypt, and Greece. The Book of Wisdom and Paul's Letter to the Romans speak of God manifesting his power and divinity through his works in nature. The religions generally promote prayer and sacrifice as ways of winning God's favor. The traditions of all peoples contain elements of truth imbedded in their cultures, myths, and religious practices. These sound elements derive from God, who speaks to all his children through inward testimony and outward signs.

The universal evidences of the divine, under the leading of grace, can give rise to a rudimentary faith that leans forward in hope and expectation to further manifestations of God's merciful love and of his guidance for our lives. By welcoming the signs already given and placing their hope in God's redeeming love, persons who have not heard the tidings of the gospel may nevertheless be on the road to salvation. If they are faithful to the grace given them, they may have good hope of receiving the truth and blessedness for which they yearn.

The search, however, is no substitute for finding. To be blessed in this life, one must find the pearl of great price, the treasure hidden in the field, which is worth buying at the cost of everything one possesses. To Christians has been revealed the mystery hidden from past ages, which the patriarchs and prophets longed to know. By entering through baptism into the mystery of the cross and the Resurrection, Christians undergo a radical transformation that sets them unequivocally on the road to salvation. Only after conversion to explicit faith can one join the community that is nourished by the Word of God and the sacraments. These gifts of God, prayerfully received, enable the faithful to grow into ever greater union with Christ.

In Christ's Church, therefore, we have many aids to salvation and sanctification that are not available elsewhere. Cardinal Newman expressed the situation admirably in one of his early sermons:

> The prerogative of Christians consists in the possession, not of exclusive knowledge and spiritual aid, but of gifts high and peculiar; and though the manifestation of the Divine character in the Incarnation is a singular and inestimable benefit, yet its absence is supplied in a degree, not only in the inspired record of Moses, but even, with more or less strength, in those various traditions concerning Divine Providences and Dispositions which are scattered through the heathen mythologies.

We cannot take it for granted that everyone is seeking the truth and is prepared to submit to it when found. Some, perhaps many, resist the grace of God and reject the signs given to them. They are not on the road to salvation at all. In such cases, the fault is not God's but theirs. The references to future punishment in the gospels cannot be written off as empty threats. As Paul says, God is not mocked (Gal. 6:7).

We may conclude with certitude that God makes it possible for the unevangelized to attain the goal of their searching. How that happens is known to God alone, as Vatican II twice declares. We know only that their search is not in vain. "Seek, and you will find," says the Lord (Matt. 7:7). If non-Christians are praying to an unknown God, it may be for us to help them find the one they worship in ignorance. God wants everyone to come to the truth. Perhaps some will reach the goal of their searching only at the moment of death. Who knows what transpires secretly in their consciousness at that solemn moment? We have no evidence that death is a moment of revelation, but it could be, especially for those in pursuit of the truth of God.

Meanwhile, it is the responsibility of believers to help these seekers by word and by example. Whoever receives the gift of revealed truth has the obligation to share it with others. Christian faith is normally transmitted by testimony. Believers are called to be God's witnesses to the ends of the earth.

Who, then, can be saved? Catholics can be saved if they believe the Word of God as taught by the Church and if they obey the commandments. Other Christians can be saved if they submit their lives to Christ and join the community where they think he wills to be found. Jews can be saved if they look forward in hope to the Messiah and try to ascertain whether God's promise has been fulfilled. Adherents of other religions can be saved if, with the help of grace, they sincerely seek God and strive to do his will. Even atheists can be saved if they worship God under some other name and place their lives at the service of truth and justice. God's saving grace, channeled through Christ the one Mediator, leaves no one unassisted. But that same grace brings obligations to all who receive it. They must not receive the grace of God in vain. Much will be demanded of those to whom much is given.

Source: Avery Cardinal Dulles, S.J., 2008. "Who Can Be Saved?" *First Things* (180): 17-22 (February). Reprinted with permission from *First Things*.

Avery Cardinal Dulles, S.J. (1918–2008) held the Laurence J. McGinley Chair in Religion and Society at Fordham University, New York. The author of over 750 articles on theological topics, Cardinal Dulles published twenty-three books, including *The History of Apologetics*, (revised edition, Wipf and Stock Publishers, Eugene, Oregon, 2005 and *Magisterium: Teacher and Guardian of the Faith* (Ignatius Press, San Francisco, 2007). This essay is adapted from the Laurence J. McGinley Lecture delivered on November 7, 2007.

Chapter 18

Purgatory

Contrary to popular belief, the notion of Purgatory is not a creation of the Catholic Church. The Jews believed in a time of purification after death before the Christian era (2 Macc 12:43-45), and there are New Testament references to the need for purification in the afterlife (for example, Matt 12:32). The Fathers of the Church, such as St. Gregory the Great (c. 540–604) and St. John Chrysostom (c. 347–407), also taught that souls unprepared for heaven spend a time of purification so as to be fit to behold God's face in the beatific vision.

The existence of Purgatory should be a great source of hope for all people who recognize that they are weak and sinful souls, struggling toward perfection but falling short. God, in his mercy, has provided us a way to prepare ourselves to enter into his presence.

Mark Shea, in **"Purgatory? Where Is That in the Bible?,"** makes the case that the doctrine on Purgatory makes sense and is based on Scripture.

- ➤ Scripture teaches that we are to be purified of all that is sinful or unclean (Psalm 51:7-10 and 1 John 3: 2-3).
- ➤ Sanctification is the process of purification from sin. Purgatory completes this process for those who died in the state of grace but do not yet perfectly conform to the image of Christ (Rom 8:29).
- ➤ God wants so much that we be happy with him in heaven that if we do not complete the process of sanctification in this life, he does it for us in Purgatory.
- ➤ Although our sins are forgiven, their effects remain. In justice, reparation must be made either in this life or the next.

➢ We are all called by God to become saints. If we are "basically good" but not saints, we are still not fit to be in God's presence. To stand in the presence of God, our hearts must be changed.

➢ Our Lord said that we "must be perfect, as your heavenly Father is perfect" (Matt 5:48), that is, we are called to participate in the divine nature (2 Peter 1:4). God will enable those who have not reached this state before death to be cleansed in Purgatory.

➢ Although the term *Purgatory* came to be after the time of the apostles, this is also true for the terms *Trinity, Christianity, Second Coming*, and *Bible*. The idea of Purgatory existed prior to Christ's birth.

➢ About 150 years before Christ, Judas Maccabeus prayed for the dead and asked forgiveness for their sins (2 Macc 12:43-45). This practice was known as *kaddish* and was observed by the Jews of Jesus' time.

➢ Several New Testament passages refer to the need for purification after death (for example, Matt 5:21-26 and Matt 12: 32).

Further Reading

Regis Martin. 1997. "Purgatory." *Our Sunday Visitor's Encyclopedia of Catholic Doctrine*, pp. 550-52. Huntington, Indiana: *Our Sunday Visitor* Publishing Division.

Anthony Zimmerman. "Purgatory: Service Shop for Heaven." IgnatiusInsight.com. http://www.ignatiusinsight.com/features2006/zimmerman_purgatory_oct06.asp.

Purgatory? Where Is *That* in the Bible?

By Mark P. Shea

Few doctrines of the Catholic faith are more misunderstood than purgatory, yet few make more sense—or are more biblical—when rightly understood.

Some people think the Church teaches purgatory is a second chance where deceased souls headed for hell get a shot at working their way to heaven. Others have the notion that Catholics think purgatory is necessary in order for souls to supplement Christ's grace with their own good deeds. Nearly all who misunderstand the doctrine imagine it was unknown in the time of Christ, is unmentioned in Scripture, and crept into the Church in later centuries due to the influence of superstition.

All these notions are untrue. The Church's actual teaching is much more surprising, commonsensical, human, and biblical than the various non-Catholic theories about it. Surprising because the whole of the gospel is a surprise. Commonsensical because it dovetails perfectly with what God calls us to be and do. Human because it offers us the opportunity and the grace to become fully human as Christ is. And biblical because purgatory has solid roots in Scripture.

What Is Purgatory, Anyway? The word purgatory is derived from the Latin purgatio, which means "cleansing" or "purifying." Just as gold is purged of dross in the refining process, so Scripture teaches that we are to be purified of all that is sinful or unclean. For instance, Psalm 51:7-10 reads:

> Purge me with hyssop, and I shall be clean;
> wash me, and I shall be whiter than snow.
> Fill me with joy and gladness;
> let the bones which thou hast broken rejoice.
> Hide thy face from my sins,
> and blot out all my iniquities.
> Create in me a clean heart, O God,
> and put a new and right spirit within me.

Likewise, John writes, "Beloved, we are God's children now; it does not yet appear what we shall be, but we know that when he appears we shall be like him, for we shall see him as he is. And every one who thus hopes in him purifies himself as he is pure" (1 John 3:2–3).

In this life, the process of purification from sin is called sanctification. Purgatory is the culmination of that process by which a human being who has died in the grace of God is made completely full of the life of the Blessed Trinity and perfectly "conformed to the image of Christ" (Rom. 8:29).

When Does Sanctification Start and End?

Sanctification starts the moment a human being surrenders to Jesus. Jesus welcomes anyone who comes to him by faith (John 3:16). But he welcomes us in order to transform us (Rom. 12:2). Therefore our relationship with Jesus is a cooperative struggle in which his Holy Spirit helps us fulfill the promise of holiness planted in our hearts in baptism. This process is described by Peter, who writes, "By his great mercy we have been born anew to a living hope through the resurrection of Jesus Christ from the dead, and to an inheritance which is imperishable, undefiled, and unfading, kept in heaven for you, who by God's power are guarded through faith for a salvation ready to be revealed in the last time. In this you rejoice, though now for a little while you may have to suffer various trials, so that the genuineness of your faith, more precious than gold which though perishable is tested by fire, may redound to praise and glory and honor at the revelation of Jesus Christ" (1 Pet. 1:3–7).

Sanctification will continue, according to Paul, until "he who began a good work in you will bring it to completion at the day of Jesus Christ" (Phil. 1:6). In short, God will not rest until we are completely blessed and happy. If the process is not finished when we die, then God completes it in purgatory. That is why purgatory is not a second chance. All the souls in purgatory are assured of seeing God's face. They simply do not yet see it fully.

Peter's Mention of Suffering Sounds Ominous. Isn't the Christian Life Supposed to Be about Victory?

That's a bit like saying the athletic life is supposed to be about trophies instead of training. Trophies, as Paul notes, are awarded at the end of the race (2 Tim. 4:8). Purgatory does indeed involve pain, as does the extensive training that precedes a race. But pain is not the point of purgatory. The healing joy and ecstasy of heaven are.

As Job says, "Man is born to trouble as the sparks fly upward" (Job 5:7). Our Lord never promised a painless existence. Rather, he promised a *joyful* one in which nothing—not even pain and death—is wasted, and everything is redeemed and turned into glory. What is notable about the Christian life is not its lack of suffering but the grace that Christ gives us to suffer pain unto life and even unto joy.

What's "Pain unto Life"?

The opposite of damnation unto death. In baptism (and confession), the guilt of sin is forgiven and friendship with God is restored by the grace of Christ. But the fact that sin is forgiven does not mean that sin ceases to have effects on us and on those around us. God's forgiveness does not mean all bad habits are miraculously repealed, and the people we hurt are suddenly restored to perfect emotional and spiritual health simply because we are believers. Instead the Church says, in effect, "If you break someone's window in a hissy fit and repent, you shall certainly be forgiven. But you must still pay for the window and do something about that nasty temper." You must, in the words of Paul, "work out your own salvation with fear and trembling; for God is at work in you, both to will and to work for his good pleasure" (Phil. 2:12–13).

This is why Jesus commended Zacchaeus for paying back the money he stole, even though his sin of theft was forgiven (Luke 19:1–10). This is why repentant murderers must stay in jail, and repentant addicts must go on struggling against their cravings. Forgiven sin continues to have effects both on the sinner and on those against whom he sinned. The difference is that, with grace, these struggles do not have the effect of hardening sinners in their sin, but of liberating them from it. As Paul says, "Godly grief produces a repentance that leads to salvation and brings no regret, but worldly grief produces death" (2 Cor. 7:10).

What's the Point of Sanctification and Purgatory if You Are Basically a Good Person? Wouldn't a God of Love Accept Us as We Are?

Suppose someone said, "Einstein was basically a good scientist" or "Bach was basically a good musician" or "Joe DiMaggio was basically a good ballplayer." Doesn't this strike you as weak? When we say that someone is "basically good" we are really saying, "Despite their mediocrity, they have some good qualities." That is why nobody says Bach or Einstein or DiMaggio was "basically good" at what they did. They were special.

You are special too. Paul tells us "we are [God's] workmanship, created in Christ Jesus for good works, which God prepared beforehand, that we should walk in them." The term "workmanship" is translated from the Greek word *poiema* (from which we get the word *poem*). We are literally God's works of art, created in order to manifest fully the life of Christ in the world. Our destiny in Christ is not to be "basically good" but to be saints and "partakers in the glory that is to be revealed" (1 Pet. 5:1).

This being so, it is not enough to say that God accepts us as we are—though he certainly does that as well. We must recognize that he accepts us *for a purpose*: namely, to make us participants in his glory. For this to happen, there must be a change, not merely of our address from earth to heaven, but of our hearts from "basically good" to "holy." We must not merely go to heaven, we must *become* heavenly to be at home there, just as Christ is.

Isn't it Blasphemous To Talk of Being "Just as Christ is"?

It would be blasphemous to talk that way if we did so on our own. Adam and Eve fell for the serpent's suggestion that they should try on their own steam to "be like God, knowing good and evil" (Gen. 3:5). The irony is that, had they remained with God in trust, they would have found that God desired to *give* them what they tried to steal. According to Peter, God desires that we become "participants in the divine nature" (2 Pet. 1:4). That is why Jesus tells us we "must be perfect, as your heavenly Father is perfect" (Matt. 5:48)—in other words, we should "be like God."

Indeed, everything Satan tricked our first parents into trying to steal was just a cheap imitation of what God actually wills us to have. Wisdom, knowledge, power, love, true riches, assurance about the future, and even communion with the whole body of Christ both living and dead—these are our proper heritage in Christ (Eph. 1:18–19; 3:14–21). But to inherit these things is not merely to be forgiven, it is to be Christ-*like*. Desiring forgiveness without desiring inner transformation is like "cleansing the outside of the cup and of the plate, but inside they are full of extortion and rapacity" (Matt. 23:25). To be Christlike, we must be changed as well as forgiven.

How on Earth Can Anybody Do *That*?

Nobody on earth can—on his own, that is. If we are to meet God— much less participate in his divine nature—it is necessary for the Author to write himself into the characters' world, since the characters cannot get into the Author's world.

That is what God did: He wrote himself into this world by becoming human while remaining God. He became a character in his own story. Because of this, we can now ask for help from the only person who is both fully human and fully God, the only one who is both of heaven and of earth: Jesus Christ (John 3:31). If anyone professes faith in Jesus Christ and is baptized, the Lord promises, "My Father will love him, and we will come to him and make our home with him" (John 14:23).

In short, we are dependent upon the grace and love of God in Christ to enter our souls and change us. That is why Paul tells us, "For by grace you have been saved through faith; and this is not your own doing, it is the gift of God—not because of works, lest any man should boast" (Eph. 3:8-9). In faith and baptism our sins are forgiven, and we are given a share in the life of God that we never could have achieved on our own power. And that life, the moment it enters our souls, begins to change us.

If Baptism and Faith in Christ Give Us God's Grace, Why Is Sanctification Necessary?

Because baptism is grace, not magic. Grace is the "imperishable seed" of God's life given us by him (1 Pet. 1:23). But the seed must grow, as our Lord taught (Matt. 13:1–32). It does not, as some have claimed, cover our sins like snow on a dunghill. It is rather a means of transforming us in our inner being.

Consider Israel. In Exodus we read the story of how God got Israel out of slavery. But in the book of Numbers we also read about how, in order for the Israelites to be ready for the Promised Land (which is an image of our heavenly destiny), they had to undergo a series of chastisements to heal them of their idolatry and disobedience. They, not just their circumstances, had to be changed.

God does indeed cover and forgive our sins (Rom. 4:7). But that is not the end of the story. The soothing of the salve on a wound is a blessed thing. But more blessed still is the healing the salve promotes. In the same way, God's grace "covers" our sin, but also gives us the medicine of discipline, to heal our souls and make us more like Christ.

Such discipline respects us by operating through our *cooperation* with God's grace. This is why James tells not non-Christians but baptized and faithful believers, "Draw near to God and he will draw near to you. Cleanse your hands, you sinners, and purify your hearts, you men of double mind" (Jas. 4:8). James is aware that the forgiveness given in baptism is the beginning, not the end, of sanctification, which is intended by God to turn each and every one of into glorious saints.

How Can You Die "in God's Grace and Friendship" yet Be Imperfectly Purified?

The same way we can live in God's grace and friendship yet be imperfectly purified. Every day we struggle with the reality of sin in our lives. We do things we are ashamed of and reproach ourselves for. Every day we struggle to overcome not just sinful acts but habits of sin. Yet every day God welcomes us, loves us, and gives us grace to become a little bit more like Jesus than we were before—if we only repent.

This is possible because there is a difference between mortal sin and venial sin. The latter can hurt our relationship with God—like a bad cut hurts the body—but not, like the former, kill that relationship, like a bullet to the heart kills the body. To drive that point home, John tells us, "All wrongdoing is sin, but there is sin which is not mortal" (1 John 5:17). For such "non-mortal" sin John gives us the key to healing: prayer. This is why he says, "If any one sees his brother committing what is not a mortal sin, he will ask, and God will give him life for those whose sin is not mortal" (1 John 5:16).

It is also important to recognize that not every sin means a person is a monster of evil who has utterly rejected God, nor that every impurity in the soul means that a person who dies impure is bound for hell. Many people go to their graves *struggling* with sin. This struggling is a pretty good sign that one is still seeking the grace of God and has not severed one's relationship with him. That is also why the Church prays for those who died without finishing their process of becoming saints. Purgatory is a monument to hope.

But Aren't the Dead Supposed To Go Straight to Heaven?

If the dead are not fully heavenly, not fully prepared for a life of total love and self-giving at the hour of their death, how could they yet enjoy perfect happiness in heaven any more than the Israelites could love God completely when they were still tainted with the slavish minds and hearts of Egypt?

This is not to say those in purgatory are not sharing in the life of God. On the contrary, the dead in Christ are very much alive. Christ himself taught this when he told the Sadducees, "Have you not read what was said to you by God, 'I am the God of Abraham, and the God of Isaac, and the God of Jacob'? He is not God of the dead, but of the living" (Matt. 22:31–32). Further, he demonstrated that the dead in Christ are alive by permitting Moses to appear—alive—to the apostles on the Mount of Transfiguration (Matt. 17:3).

But not all the dead in Christ are fully ready—solidly built enough, we might say—for the intense, endless, ecstatic joy of heaven, since not all the dead die in perfect union with God. In Christ, we have been given a solid foundation of grace like a house built on rock (Matt. 7:24). But it happens every day that we try to build on the foundation with our own agendas, ideas, fears, and superstitions, often mixed in with the genuine building materials given us by the Divine Contractor. We often don't know what is wrong with the house of God we are building. We only have the vague sense that it is rather drafty and is not exactly the "mansion" Jesus spoke of.

Paul tells us what will become of the low-grade materials we attempt to use: "Now if any one builds on the foundation with gold, silver, precious stones, wood, hay, stubble—each man's work will become manifest; for the Day will disclose it, because it will be revealed with fire, and the fire will test what sort of work each one has done. . . . If any man's work is burned up, he will suffer loss, though he himself will be saved, but only as through fire" (1 Cor. 3: 12–13, 15). Purgatory is the process whereby we "lose" the last hindrances to perfect happiness with God.

Wasn't Purgatory Unheard of in Scripture and only Invented in the Dark Ages?

The term *purgatory* arose after the time of the apostles, as did the terms *Trinity, Christianity, Second Coming,* and *Bible.* But the *idea* of purgatory was already present before Jesus was born. We find a Jewish hero named Judas Maccabeus, about a century and a half before Jesus, praying for the dead and specifically asking they be forgiven their sins after they have died (2 Macc. 12:43–45). This practice, known as the *kaddish,* was well established among Jews in Jesus' own time. (Jews have historically believed, and many still believe, that the souls of the faithful departed undergo a period of purification which may be aided by the prayers and charity of the living. The Kaddish Foundation is a modern example of this ancient belief in action.)

Likewise, we find the New Testament frequently assuming the existence of purgatory. Jesus, during his time in the grave, is said by Peter to have "preached to the spirits in prison, who formerly did not obey" (1 Pet. 3: 18–20). Similarly, Jesus teaches that certain sins—notably unforgiveness—will be liable to judgment and imprisonment in the next. But he also implies this punishment is not necessarily eternal: "Truly I say to you, you will never get out until you have paid the last penny" (Matt. 5:21–26). Such imagery fits neither heaven—where there are no prisons—nor hell, where there is neither repentance nor "getting out" and therefore no point in preaching. It does, however, fit purgatory.

Jesus also implies the existence of purgatory or "forgiveness in the age to come" when he tells his disciples, "Whoever says a word against the Son of Man will be forgiven; but whoever speaks against the Holy Spirit will not be forgiven, either in this age or in the age to come" (Matt. 12:32). The Church after Jesus did not, therefore, "invent" purgatory. On the contrary, it simply repeated and clarified what Jesus and the apostles had taught them concerning the promise of hope for the afterlife.

What Does Purgatory Mean for Us Today?

It means what it has always meant: hope. Purgatory is the assurance that there will, in the end, be absolutely nothing to dim the mirror of our lives from reflecting the glory of God. We who have been captive to sin for so long will be released. Moreover, as sharers in the life of Christ, we have an extraordinary promise from him. For he tells us, "Truly, truly, I say to you, he who believes in me will also do the works that I do; and greater works than these will he do, because I go to the Father" (John 14:12).

In other words, we not only receive grace *from* him, we do his works of grace *with* him, for we are "fellow workers" with Christ (1 Cor. 3:9). This means among other things that, as he prays for us, so we can pray for one another with his power and authority. And such prayers can be made not only for the living but for the dead as well. We can, therefore, help those in purgatory who are still being purified, just as we can help those on earth—by our prayers and offerings of love, especially in the Mass.

As Paul tells us, "We, though many, are one body in Christ, and individually members one of another" (Rom. 12:5). That unity with God and with each other is not severed by death. We can continue to pray for those who have died with the hope of Christ that our prayers will be of real help to them as we "bear one another's burdens, and so fulfill the law of Christ" (Gal. 6:2).

Source: Mark P. Shea. 2001. "Purgatory? Where Is That in the Bible?" *This Rock* (12): 3. Reprinted with permission from Mark Shea.

Mark Shea is Senior Content Editor for Catholic Exchange. He is an awarding-winning columnist, contributing a weekly feature to *Inside Catholic* and "Connecting the Dots" to the *National Catholic Register*, as well as numerous articles to many other magazines. Mark is the author of *Making Senses Out of Scripture: Reading the Bible as the First Christians Did* (Basilica, San Diego, 2001), *By What Authority?: An Evangelical Discovers Catholic Tradition* (Our Sunday Visitor, Huntington, Indiana, 1996), and *This Is My Body: An Evangelical Discovers the Real Presence* (Christendom, Front Royal, Virginia, 1993).

Chapter 19

Indulgences

Indulgences are another proof of the infinite mercy of God, who wants all his people to be happy with him in heaven. The abuses associated with the sale of indulgences prior to the Protestant Reformation have given indulgences a bad name. Many regard them as remnants of the Church's past with no real relevance in the modern world. However, the Church still grants indulgences and they are, indeed, still relevant to a world of sinners who are struggling to overcome their weaknesses and seeking to see God in the next life.

What is an indulgence? *The Catechism of the Catholic Church* defines an indulgence as "a remission before God of the temporal punishment due to sins whose guilt has already been forgiven, which the faithful Christian who is duly disposed gains under certain prescribed conditions through the action of the Church which, as the minister of redemption, dispenses and applies with authority the treasury of the satisfactions of Christ and the saints."[1]

The Church teaches that in the Communion of Saints is a bond of charity among the Church Triumphant (those in heaven), the Church Militant (those still living), and the Church Suffering (those in Purgatory). Consequently, we can offer indulgences to aid those in Purgatory and lessen in some way their suffering.

We can gain indulgences through the power of the Church, which was granted the power of binding and loosing by Christ himself. Indulgences are generally associated with certain prayers, acts of charity, or other pious acts under certain conditions.

---

[1] *Catechism of the Catholic Church.* 1997. no. 1471. Vatican City: Libreria Editrice Vaticana.

In **"Indulgences,"** Catholics United for the Faith explains indulgences and the basis for the Church's power and authority to dispense them.

> - The Church dispenses indulgences when she "applies with authority the treasury of the satisfaction won by Christ and the saints."
> - Indulgences are either partial or plenary in that they remove either part or all of the temporal punishment, respectively, due to the sins we have committed. We must be properly disposed to receive an indulgence.
> - We can receive indulgences, if we are in the state of grace, for our own benefit or for souls in Purgatory.
> - Sin has both eternal and temporal consequences. Although we may be forgiven and spared the eternal consequences of our sin, we must atone to repair the damage done.
> - St. Paul taught that we participate in some manner in the redemptive suffering of Christ (Col. 1:24).
> - Jesus gave the Church the power to bind and loose on earth, and the granting of indulgences is an expression of this power.
> - We find ample evidence in Scripture of the temporal consequences of sin, even after forgiveness.
> - Purgatory is a "place" of purification, and indulgences help reduce the "time" of suffering in Purgatory due to our sins.
> - Conditions for obtaining indulgences include:
>   - The person gaining the indulgence must be free from mortal sin when the prescribed actions are completed.
>   - He must have the intention of gaining the indulgence.
>   - He must fulfill any additional specific conditions associated with the specific indulgence.
> - To obtain a plenary indulgence, one must:
>   - Complete the prescribed act.
>   - Be free from attachment to any sin, including venial sin.
>   - Receive the Sacrament of Penance within a week of performing the prescribed act.
>   - Receive Holy Communion within a week of performing the prescribed act.
>   - Pray for the intentions of the Pope within a week of performing the prescribed act.
> - Indulgences help the penitent:
>   - Recognize his sinfulness and the great mercy of God.

- Understand his need to participate in his redemption (Phil. 2:12-13; cf. Col 1:24).
- Understand the true nature of justification, which involves being *made* clean (cf. Rev. 21:27).

Further Reading

James Akin. 1994. "A Primer on Indulgences." *This Rock* (5): 11 (November).

Christopher M. Buckner. 1997. "Indulgences." *Our Sunday Visitor's Encyclopedia of Catholic Doctrine*, pp. 328-32. Huntington, Indiana: *Our Sunday Visitor* Publishing Division.

Pope Paul VI. 1967. *Indulgentiarum Doctrina* (Apostolic *Constitution on Indulgences*), January 1.

Indulgences

By Catholics United for the Faith

What is an indulgence? How do you obtain them? For whom can an indulgence be gained?

An indulgence remits temporal punishment[1] or consequences due to sins for which we have already been forgiven. The Church dispenses indulgences when, as a minister of Christ's Redemption, "she dispenses and applies with authority the treasury of the satisfaction won by Christ and the saints."[2] We gain an indulgence when we are properly disposed and perform prescribed penitential actions. Indulgences are either partial or plenary, so named because they remove either part (partial) or all (plenary) of the temporal punishment due to actual sin.[3] Through God's grace and the intercession of the saints, indulgences magnify the power of our penitential actions, remitting the temporal consequences of some or all of our sins.

Christians living on earth and in the state of grace can obtain indulgences, and they may do so only for themselves or a deceased member of the Body of Christ.

Discussion: To understand the Church's teaching on indulgences, one needs to understand the doctrine of binding and loosing. In

---

[1] When we speak in this FAITH FACT of canceling or satisfying the "temporal punishment" due because of our sins, we refer to atoning for or repairing the wrong done to God and the Body of Christ, the Church. Receiving an indulgence does not exempt a person from undergoing the temporal punishment of society, i.e., repairing the wrong to society through such actions as restitution of property and doing time in prison. However, given the proper spiritual disposition, our penitential actions to society can also have the salutary effect of atoning for our sins to God and the Church.

[2] Paul VI. Apostolic Constitution, *Indulgentarium Doctrina*, Norm 1.

[3] Ibid., Norm 2; cf. Norm 3. See also, *Catechism of the Catholic Church*, 1471. It is also crucial to say "actual" sin, because there are consequences from original sin, including death and suffering, which cannot be remitted or avoided (*Catechism*, no. 405).

addition, the teachings on justification, communion of saints and purgatory are intimately connected with the teaching on indulgences; to understand one fully requires and enables an understanding of the others.[4]

When we sin, there are both eternal and temporal consequences. Through the ministry of forgiveness, the eternal consequences of sin—namely, hell—are remitted simultaneously with the guilt of sin. Temporal consequences remain, requiring one to atone for or repair the wrongs we have committed. Atonement serves as a teaching device for the sinner to learn discipline according to the mind of Christ. Penance disciplines our human nature, repairs the wrongs and lessens the temporal consequences of sin.

Adam's original sin broke man's communion with God (*Catechism of the Catholic Church*, nos. 402-06). Christ died and rose from the dead to reestablish and greatly improve this communion (*Catechism*, no. 412), so that we might be freed from all consequences of sin:

> For, if while we were enemies we were reconciled to God by the death of His Son, much more, now that we are reconciled, shall we be saved by His life. Not only so, but we also rejoice in God through whom we have now received our reconciliation (Rom. 5:10-11).

Justification is the process by which we are reconciled to God (Titus 3:3-8), partake of God's nature (2 Pet. 1:4) and become "new creations" (2 Cor. 5:17). Scripture attests that justification not only involves the redemptive act of Christ's death, but also the continued sacrifices of the People of God, the Church (Jas. 2:14-24).[5] As St. Paul puts it, "Now I rejoice in my sufferings for your sake, and in my flesh I complete what is lacking in Christ's afflictions for the sake of His body, that is, the Church" (Col. 1:24). This is not because the objective redemption that Christ merited for us is insufficient, but because we must all personally participate in that redemption here and now, in our own lifetimes. The Catholic teachings on justification, the communion of saints, indulgences, and purgatory help explain Colossians 1:24.

---

[4] Faith Facts on these topics are available from CUF; see details at the end of this Faith Fact.

[5] For a more thorough discussion on the issue of justification, see our Faith Fact entitled "It 'Works' for Me: The Church's Teaching on Justification."

Christ established the Church to mediate His salvation, and He promised that the gates of hell would not prevail against it (Mt. 16:18-19). To minister this salvation, Christ gave St. Peter, the other apostles and their successor popes and bishops the power to mediate His forgiveness and merits. Jesus told Peter: "I will give you the keys of the kingdom of heaven, and whatever you bind on earth shall be bound in heaven, and whatever you loose on earth shall be loosed in heaven" (Mt. 16:18-19). The granting of indulgences is an expression of this power to bind and loose.

If we recognize that God works through the Church to freely remit the eternal consequences of our sin through forgiveness, it shouldn't be difficult to accept that He can do similarly regarding less significant—though still important—temporal consequences through indulgences.

The principle of temporal consequences remaining after forgiveness has strong roots in scripture. God forgave Adam and Eve but, because of their sin, temporal punishments remain, including that the earth would labor against man's efforts to bring forth fruit rather than submitting to him; women would labor in pain to bear children; and, most significant, men and women would suffer death (Gen. 3:16-20). Although Christ overcame the power of sin, the temporal consequences of Adam's sin remain.[6] When the Israelites balked at the Jordan and refused to enter the Promised Land, Moses interceded so that God would not destroy them all. Because of Moses' prayer, God forgave the Israelites but caused them to wander for 40 years and die in the desert as reparation for their sins.[7] The stories of David and Bathsheba (2 Sam. 11-12:25), David and the census (2 Sam. 24) and Hezekiah (2 Kgs. 20; 2 Chr. 32:24-31) also reflect the principle that temporal consequences of sins remain after forgiveness.

Acts of penance include prayer, fasting and charity. Rooted strongly in Scripture, the greatest of these is charity.[8] Through acts of penance, we discipline ourselves to live in a godly manner, that we might be conformed to Christ. As Scripture attests, "Then your light shall break forth like the dawn, and your wound shall quickly be

---

[6] *Catechism*, no. 405.

[7] Num. 14:1-38.

[8] Tobit 4:5-11; Prov. 19:17; Is.58:1-8 1 Pet. 5:7-8; James 5:16-20.

healed; your vindication shall go before you, and the glory of the Lord shall be your rear guard."[9]

As God teaches us, the prayers and good works of one, when offered on behalf of another, atones for sins:

> My brethren, if any one among you wanders from the truth and some one brings him back, let him know that whoever brings back a sinner from the error of his way will save his soul from death and will cover a multitude for sins (Jas. 5:19-20).

This exchange of graces is one example of the communion of saints. "In this wonderful exchange, holiness of one profits others, well beyond the harm that the sin of one could cause others (cf. Rom. 5:20). Thus recourse to the communion of saints lets the contrite sinner be more promptly and efficaciously purified of the punishments for sin."[10]

> We . . . call these spiritual goods of the communion of saints the Church's treasury, which is "not the sum total of the material goods which have accumulated during the course of the centuries. On the contrary the 'treasury of the Church' is the infinite value, which can never be exhausted, which Christ's merits have before God."[11]

In exercising her authority to bind and loose, the Church uses indulgences as a means to lessen the temporal consequences of sin and apply the effects of penance. As noted, one obtains an indulgence after having received forgiveness and performing the prescribed acts of penance.

If one dies without having repented of sin, as Scripture teaches, he suffers eternal damnation (Mt. 25:41-46; Rev. 2:5; Rev. 20:11-15). If he dies after having repented, but not having repaired his wrongs, he must be purified before entering heaven. Purgatory is the place of this purgation.[12] Indulgences lessen the temporal punishment for sin and apply the merits of penance more efficaciously.

To obtain an indulgence, certain general conditions apply. One may obtain indulgences for oneself or for souls in purgatory. Indul-

---

[9] Is. 58:8.
[10] *Catechism of the Catholic Church*, no. 1475.
[11] Ibid., no. 1476.
[12] Rev. 3:18; 22:12. See also our Faith Fact on Purgatory.

gences cannot be gained for other persons who are living on earth. In order to receive the indulgence, the person seeking an indulgence must be free from mortal sin at the completion of the prescribed actions. He must have the intention of gaining the indulgence. A general intention of gaining this grace is sufficient, and a person should renew this intention on a regular basis. Finally, there is a condition of accuracy. Individual indulgences have particular conditions that must be met in order to receive the indulgence. If there is a great deviation from the specified conditions of the indulgence, the indulgence is not obtained.

As noted, the Church recognizes two kinds of indulgences, partial and plenary. A partial indulgence removes some of the temporal consequences due for past sins. A plenary indulgence removes all temporal punishment incurred by sins.

To obtain a plenary indulgence, one must complete five requirements: 1) completion of the prescribed act itself; 2) be free from the attachment to any sin, even venial; 3) receive absolution through the Sacrament of Reconciliation; 4) receive the most Holy Eucharist; 5) pray for the intentions of the Holy Father.[13] Even if a person is not conscious of grave sin, he must go to Confession. Though the last three conditions may be fulfilled within one week of performing the prescribed act, it is fitting to receive Communion and pray for the Pope's intentions on the same day that the prescribed work is completed.[14]

Generally, one may acquire a plenary indulgence once in a single day. However, one can obtain a plenary indulgence for the moment of death, even if another plenary indulgence has already been acquired on the same day.[15] A partial indulgence may be acquired once a day, unless otherwise expressly indicated.[16]

Some people argue that the guidelines governing indulgences are meant to bind legalistically; **just the opposite is true**, for they help the penitent to realize better: 1) his sinfulness and God's great mercy regarding that sinfulness; 2) his God-ordained need to participate in his redemption (Phil. 2:12-13; cf. Col. 1:24); and 3) the true nature of justification, which involves not simply being declared clean but actually being made clean (cf. Rev. 21:27).

---

[13] *Enchiridion of Indulgences*, norm. 26.
[14] Ibid., norm 27.
[15] Ibid., norm 24.
[16] Ibid.

Although the terminology differs, the principles used by the Catholic Church to understand and apply indulgences reflect a universal understanding of natural law and justice. If a man is caught stealing money from a convenient store, the money is returned and the man is put on trial. If he is sincere in his desire for reform and pleads guilty, he will probably receive a lesser sentence than otherwise. While in jail, if he acts with good behavior, he could receive parole much more quickly and easily. In fact, our legal system promotes such clemency to encourage good behavior and genuine reform.

Protestants also apply these principles in their family lives. Though children admit a wrong, it remains necessary to discipline them, at least mildly, lest they continue to do wrong (Prov. 13:24; 23:13-14). If no consequences follow bad behavior, a child will presume clemency and never be disciplined in right living. Further, Protestants also encourage the use of societal justice, as outlined in the example above describing the thief's imprisonment. The use of indulgences in the Catholic Church is simply a recognition of this natural law principle of atonement.

Source: Catholics United for the Faith. "Indulgences." *Faith Facts*. http://www.cuf.org. Reprinted with the permission of Catholic United for the Faith.

Part IV.

·····⊶⊶⊶·····

Moral Teachings of the Church

Christ gave us the Church to guide us to the truth and to be a reliable interpreter of the moral law. The challenges we face come from within and without. Our fallen nature disposes us to sin and to rationalization of our immoral behavior. We live in a complex world where ideas and moral values are communicated around the globe in minutes. Biotechnology and medical knowledge are advancing quickly. The limits of what we can do seem to have no bounds. However, what we *can* do should not govern our actions. Rather, we should be guided by what we *ought* to do, based on sound principles grounded in the moral law. Part IV addresses the most hotly debated moral issues we encounter in our daily lives and explains clearly what the Church teaches and why.

Chapter 20

Natural Law

The notion that a natural law governs our behavior and determines what is morally right and wrong is a pre-Christian concept that has been embraced by a broad spectrum of cultures over a period of centuries, indeed millennia.[1] In its discussion of the natural moral law, the *Catechism of the Catholic Church* cites the Roman philosopher and statesman Cicero, lending credence to the view that natural law is written on the heart of everyone and can be known by unaided reason.

> For there is a true law: right reason. It is in conformity with nature, is diffused among all men, and is immutable and eternal; its orders summon to duty; its prohibitions turn away from offense. . . . To re-place it with a contrary law is a sacrilege; failure to apply even one of its provisions is forbidden; no one can abrogate it entirely.[2]

The belief that there is a natural law is not a product of any formal religion. Rather, it is a concept that springs from the quest throughout the ages to understand the nature of the human person.

Patrick Lee, in **"Natural Law,"** presents a theory of natural law and explains why it is, in fact, a "law," and unchangeable.

➤ We can know the basic principles of natural law through the use of our reason alone without relying on Divine Revelation.
➤ We are bound by natural moral law irrespective of prevailing civil or even Church laws.

---

[1] C.S. Lewis, 1980. *Mere Christianity*, 6. San Francisco: Harper.
[2] Cicero, *De re publica* III, 22, 33.

➢ Transgressions against the natural law such as stealing, lying, fornication, or contraception are wrong, not because the Church teaches that they are wrong, but because they violate natural law.

➢ A theory of natural law holds that because human beings have a particular nature, they are perfected by certain activities—knowledge, aesthetic experience, friendship—and diminished by others—sickness, ignorance, and broken relationships.

➢ We are called to embrace those things that perfect us and avoid those things that impede our perfection.

➢ Choices we make that are consistent with those goods leading to our perfection and that of others are morally good. Choices that are at odds with the attainment of perfection of ourselves or others are morally wrong.

➢ Natural moral law provides an objective standard for morality.

➢ Moral norms are directives from our Creator. They are not adhered to simply because they are reasonable. They are established to enable us to reach the perfection that is part of God's plan for us.

➢ The natural law is not simply the natural ends of the various powers associated with human nature. Rather, "it is this love of the real fulfillment of human persons, not the restriction of given patterns in human nature, which is decisive for the moral criterion."

➢ Hence, contraception is wrong because it perverts the essence of the conjugal act by separating its unitive from its procreative aspect and thwarts the latter.

➢ The natural moral law is not simply a set of moral norms that are conditioned by the society in which we live. Careful consideration of those goods by which human beings are perfected—such as life, friendship, and knowledge—are common to all cultures and times.

In **"The Revenge of Conscience,"** J. Budziszewski argues that the conscience is a powerful force that, when ignored or suppressed, leads to moral decline as a natural consequence. His reasoning leading to his conclusions is compelling.

➢ Our society's moral decline seems to be accelerating. The reason relates to the power of our conscience as a force that cannot be fully suppressed.

➢ Our conscience springs from the natural law that is written on the hearts of all human beings. We can come to know the precepts of natural law through the use of reason.

> ➤ The moral decline in society is not because we do not know right from wrong, but because we do know and we are "in denial."

> ➤ "The suppression of conscience is more violent and explosive than its mere weakening would be" because suppression only distorts and redirects its force, leading to further wrongdoing.

> ➤ "Even when suppressed, the knowledge of guilt always produces objective needs, including confession, atonement, reconciliation, and justification."

> ➤ The need for reconciliation, while suppressing the conscience, requires the transformation of society so it will not stand in judgment. The results are seen in such areas as efforts to change laws and infiltrate schools.

> ➤ The need for justification becomes rationalization and leads to undermining other moral norms to make room for the first wrong. For example, knowing that sex belongs in marriage, in order to justify having sex outside marriage one reinvents the concept of marriage to be compatible with the desired activity.

> ➤ Despite the fact that modern science points to the humanity of the unborn baby, advocates of abortion justify it by denying the humanity of the unwanted unborn baby. This rationalization opens the door to all kinds of atrocities.

> ➤ Conscience has its revenge. We suppress it at our own peril.

> ➤ The denial of conscience is like the compression of a spring; it is more likely to spring in moral collapse than remain compressed.

> ➤ The violation of natural law generally is accompanied by adverse consequences that can motivate us to obey the natural law. Hangovers follow drunkenness; sexual promiscuity leads to disease or pregnancy.

> ➤ The disciplinary effects of violating natural law, however, are frequently diminished by two factors. First is a delay in the implementation of the discipline. Second is the creation of social practices that help us evade the natural consequences of violating natural law.

> ➤ Frequently, delaying the natural consequences of immoral behavior only exacerbates the final consequences.

Further Reading

J. Budziszewski. 1997. *Written on the Heart: The Case for Natural Law.* Downers Grove, Illinois: InterVarsity Press.

Catechism of the Catholic Church. 1997. "The Moral Law." nos. 1950–1960. Vatican City: Libreria Editrice Vaticana.

James V. Schall, S.J. 2007. "Pope Benedict XVI on Natural Law." IgnatiusInsight.com, March 16.

Natural Law

By Patrick Lee

In his Letter to the Romans, St. Paul says that those who have not heard of the law of Moses, the Ten Commandments, still know what is right and wrong, because "what the law requires is written on their hearts" (Rom 2:15). This knowledge of what is right and wrong, somehow written on our hearts, has traditionally been referred to as the natural moral law.

Natural law can be considered on many levels. It is, first of all, the objective standard for what is morally right or wrong, which human beings can know, at least to a certain extent (its basic principles), without appealing to Divine Revelation. Moreover, it is the standard by which certain actions are right and other actions are wrong for all human beings, Catholic or not, and indeed Christian or not.

For example, the Church teaches that having babies, pursuing health, pursuing truth and aesthetic experience, are good to do, whereas contraception, intentionally killing innocent human persons, lying or deliberate obfuscation of truth, are in themselves morally wrong. The first types of actions are morally good and the second types of actions are morally bad, independently or whether they are prescribed or prohibited by any civil laws or enacted Church laws. And they are so for all people, whether they have accepted Revelation or not.

Hence moral truths, which are part of the natural moral law, are quite different from changeable rules enacted by a society, whether that society be a civil society or the Church. Eating meat on Friday used to be wrong for Catholics, not because it was thought to be against the natural moral law, but only because it was against a Church law or rule, a rule that has of course changed (except in Lent). On the other hand, things like stealing, lying, fornication, adultery, and contraception are acts that are against, not Church rules, but the natural moral law. They are not wrong because the Church said they were wrong; rather, the Church teaches that they are wrong because they are wrong, and they always *were* wrong, even before the Church taught so (i.e., before the Church was founded). Thus, the rightness or wrongness of certain actions is independent of cultural or individual viewpoints, but is in some way based on human nature itself. This is why the standard of moral right and wrong is called the *natural* moral law.

What has been said so far is part of Catholic teaching. However, Catholic thinkers do not all agree on how to explain what has been said; there are various accounts of exactly how human nature provides the standard for what is morally right and wrong. What follows is one understanding of that.

A Theory of Natural Law

Human beings are things of a certain kind—that is, they have a definite nature. Because of the kind of thing they are, because of their nature, they are perfected by certain objects or activities and diminished by other conditions. Thus, all human beings are perfected by life and health (since they are living, bodily beings, animals); knowledge and aesthetic experience (since they have the capacity for intelligence); play and skillful performance (since as animals with reason they can transform what is naturally given); self-integration, friendship, moral goodness itself, religion and marriage (since they are complex and have various capacities to form relationships). On the other hand, the diminishing of these objects or activities is objectively bad for human beings: It is true for all human beings that sickness, death, ignorance, broken relationships, and so on are bad and to be avoided or remedied.

Through experience and insight into our experiences, we come to recognize that life, knowledge, friendship, and so on would be good to realize, that they are worth pursuing both for ourselves and for other human persons. Thus, when we begin to deliberate about what to do, we understand that life, knowledge, friendship, and so on are to be pursued and that their opposites are to be avoided (cf. Pope John Paul II, *The Splendor of Truth, Veritatis Splendor*, 48-50).

In understanding these goods, we understand what we can be, what would be truly perfective of us as human persons, and thus part of what God is calling us to be, since God wills our fulfillment. These fundamental goods also provide an objective standard for what is right and what is wrong. "It is in the light of the dignity of the human person—dignity which must be affirmed for its own sake—that reason grasps the specific moral value of certain goods towards which the person is naturally inclined" (*Veritatis Splendor*, 48). For, while every choice is for the sake of one or more of these goods or for some aspect of it, nevertheless we can choose either in a way that is open to all of these goods or in a way that thwarts or unduly neglects some. So, choices in line with a love and appreciation of all of these goods, both in ourselves and in all other people, are morally upright and loving choices; but choices that in some way suppress a love and appreciation of any of these goods, whether in ourselves or in others, restrict our love and resist God's directives to the fulfillment of his plan, and are morally wrong. Thus the natural moral law is summed up in the directive to love God and love our neighbor as ourselves (Mt 22:37-40; Gal 5: 14; Vatican Council II, Pastoral Constitution on the Church in the Modern World, *Gaudium et Spes*, 16).

One might say that the natural law is the nature of the human person or that it is the basic moral truths themselves, based on the nature of the human person, which prescribe pursuit and respect for what is really perfective of human beings and proscribe violating or neglecting any of those goods of persons. One could also identify the natural moral law with human reason, insofar as it naturally apprehends those basic moral truths (cf. CCC 1955). In any case, the natural moral law provides an objective standard by which to determine what is right and wrong. Choices that respect every fundamental human good are morally right; choices that violate or unduly neglect a basic human good are morally wrong.

Why Natural "Law"?

Why is this standard called natural *law*? To understand this is to see that moral norms have a greater impact or significance than they would if they only specified what is reasonable. Moral norms are also directives from the Creator, the ruler of the universe. By pursuing and respecting what is truly perfective of ourselves and of other persons, we are cooperating with God's plan for his creation.

God created, not in order to fulfill some need of his, for he is perfect in his own being, but out of generosity, to communicate goodness to others. Moreover, God creates wisely, and so he has a definite plan. The plan is to communicate goodness to others. Part of that plan is for human creatures, human persons to attain the perfection of good to which God directs them in their natures. Sub-personal creatures exist for the sake of human persons, and through human persons they also will share in the attainment of God's plan.

Our human nature (which points us to our natural perfection or to the fundamental human goods) and our reason (by which we understand that these goods are to be pursued) are both created by God. Thus, our nature and our reason together are directives from God, ordering (orienting) us to our good and to the attainment of part of God's plan. Following St. Thomas Aquinas, the *Catechism of the Catholic Church* defines law in general—a definition of law that will apply to any type of law, whether it be civil law, Church law, or some other law—as "a rule of conduct enacted by competent authority for the sake of the common good" (*CCC* 1951). Since God is the ruler of the whole universe, and God created our reason and human nature, those basic moral truths are rightly called natural moral law.

One can see at once that this law is by no means a mere abstract code, based on an abstract human nature. Rather, natural law refers to the basic human goods. Thus, rightly understood, natural law is personalistic: It prescribes love of and respect for every human person. The basic goods—life, knowledge, skillful performance, friendship, self-integration, and so on—are just the various aspects of the being and full-being of persons. To love someone means to will what is truly good for him or her; and to will what is truly good for human persons is to will them, and actively pursue, their true fulfillment.

The natural moral law provides the basis for absolute moral norms. Since the natural moral law is the basic moral truth that we should respect every basic good, every intrinsic aspect, of human persons, it follows that choices which inevitably close one's will to some basic human good, either in oneself or in another, are always morally wrong, no matter what the circumstances and no matter the consequences one expects to follow.

A perennial misunderstanding of the natural moral law is to think of it as being nothing more than the natural teleologies (ends) of the various parts or powers of human nature. Indeed, some thinkers have argued that the Church's positions on sexual ethics, and especially on contraception, were tied to "physicalism" or "naturalism." This is the view that the criterion for what is morally right or wrong is merely the natural pattern of man's potentialities, so that certain acts are wrong simply because they are not in line with or frustrate the natural direction of this or that given power. (However, sometimes the word "naturalism" is used in a different sense, to mean any ethical theory holding that morality is in *any* way based on human nature. In this sense of the term, naturalism is not a bad thing; in fact, it is a synonym for natural moral law.)

On the physicalist or naturalist view, contraception would be wrong simply because it goes against the natural teleology of man's sexual power. However, the natural moral law need not be understood in such an impersonalist way. The moral criterion, as we have explained it above, is not the patterns found in human nature as given, but the real goods to which human beings are naturally inclined—goods that are no less than the intrinsic aspects of the full-being of human persons. Thus, it is true that the natural moral law is in some way based on the natural teleologies found in human beings; but this is so only in the sense that choices respectful of every aspect of human persons must be respectful of the real goods that constitute their full being. On the other hand, it is this love of the real fulfillment of human persons, not the restriction of given patterns in human nature, that is decisive for the moral criterion.

The two points were expressed succinctly by the Congregation for the Doctrine of the Faith in a document on respect for human life from which Pope John Paul quotes in the 1993 encyclical *Veritatis Splendor*: "The natural moral law expresses and lays down the purposes, rights and duties which are based upon the bodily and spiritual nature of the human person. Therefore this law cannot be thought of as simply a set of norms on the biological level; rather it must be defined as the rational order whereby man is called by the Creator to direct and regulate his life and actions and in particular to make use of his own body" (50). For example, contraception is wrong not because it goes against a natural teleology—indeed, acting against a natural teleology is not necessarily wrong—but because it involves a choice that sets one's will against new human life and closes one to the fulfillment of personal communion. It rewrites the meaning of the conjugal act, as it were, separating its unitive from its procreative aspect, with a will set against the latter.

What Is Changeable and What Is Not?

Sometimes it is objected that the idea of a natural moral law that transcends cultures is outdated, that this "classical view" must give way to the new "historically-minded consciousness." Some people argue that to believe there is an unchanging natural moral law is to imagine that there is some unchanging core of human persons called their "human nature," whereas in fact everything we can understand is historically conditioned. What, then, is changeable and what is not in the natural law?

When we think about an actual example of a basic human good, this problem turns out to be far less serious than it first appears. It has been true for all human beings in all times and in all cultures that knowledge would be a good thing for them and that health would be a good thing for them. No human being in any time or in any culture has been such that knowledge or health or friendship would not be good things, would not build up or perfect him or her. When one goes down the list of basic human goods one finds that the same is true for all.

Furthermore, there could not *be* a human being, an animal with reason and free will (the basic capacities for reasoning and freely choosing), who was not perfected by life, health, knowledge, friendship, and so on. There is a necessary connection between being an animal with reason and free will—a human being—and having the potentialities for life, health, knowledge, and the rest. That is, it is necessarily the case that every human being, no matter in what time or culture, is a being who would be fulfilled in these various ways. And so it is necessarily the case that every human being should pursue and respect these basic human goods, while the basic moral truths prescribing their pursuit are true for all cultures and all times. These parts of the natural moral law are unchangeable. Many of the conclusions derived from these basic moral truths are changeable, and there are various ways, according to different cultures and times, of pursuing and protecting the basic human good. But basic goods themselves are common to all cultures.

Source: Patrick Lee. 1997. "Natural Law." In Russell Shaw, ed., *Our Sunday Visitor's Encyclopedia of Catholic Doctrine*, pp. 463-466. Our Sunday Visitor Publishing Division, Our Sunday Visitor, Inc., Huntington, Indiana. The permission to reproduce copyrighted materials for use was extended by Our Sunday Visitor, 200 Noll Plaza, Huntington, Indiana, 46750; 1-800-348-2440. website: www.osv.com. No other use of this material is authorized.

Patrick Lee is the John N. and Jamie D. McAleer Professor of Bioethics and Director of the Institute of Bioethics at Franciscan University of Steubenville, Ohio. He is known nationally as a keynote speaker and author on contemporary ethics, especially on marriage and the value of human life. Lee attended University of Dallas, receiving a B.A. in 1974. He received an M.A. in philosophy from Niagara University in 1977, and a Ph.D. in philosophy from Marquette University in 1980. His books include *Body-Self Dualism in Contemporary Ethics and Politics* (Cambridge University Press, 2008) with Dr. Robert P. George of Princeton University, and *Abortion and Unborn Human Life* (Catholic University of America Press, 1996).

The Revenge of Conscience

by J. Budziszewski

I

Things are getting worse very quickly now. The list of what we are required to approve is growing ever longer. Consider just the domain of sexual practice. First we were to approve sex before marriage, then without marriage, now against marriage. First with one, then with a series, now with a crowd. First with the other sex, then with the same. First between adults, then between children, then between adults and children. The last item has not been added yet, but will be soon: you can tell from the change in language, just as you can tell the approach of winter from the change in the color of leaves. As any sin passes through its stages from temptation, to toleration, to approval, its name is first euphemized, then avoided, then forgotten. A colleague tells me that some of his fellow legal scholars call child molestation "intergenerational intimacy": that's euphemism. A good-hearted editor tried to talk me out of using the term "sodomy": that's avoidance. My students don't know the word "fornication" at all: that's forgetfulness.

The pattern is repeated in the house of death. First we were to approve of killing unborn babies, then babies in process of birth; next came newborns with physical defects, now newborns in perfect health. Nobel-prize laureate James Watson proposes that parents of newborns be granted a grace period during which they may have their babies killed, and in 1994 a committee of the American Medical Association proposed harvesting organs from some sick babies even before they die. First we were to approve of suicide, then to approve of assisting it. Now we are to approve of a requirement to assist it, for, as Ernest van den Haag has argued, it is "unwarranted" for doctors not to kill patients who seek death. First we were to approve of killing the sick and unconscious, then of killing the conscious and consenting. Now we are to approve of killing the conscious and protesting, for in the United States, doctors starved and dehydrated stroke patient Marjorie Nighbert to death despite her pleading "I'm hungry," "I'm thirsty," "Please feed me," and "I want food." Such cases are only to be expected when food and water are now often classified as optional treatments rather than humane care; we have not long to go before joining the Netherlands, where involuntary euthanasia is common. Dutch physician and author Bert Keizer has described his response when a nursing home resident choked on her food: he shot her full of morphine and waited for her to die. Such a deed by a doctor in the land that resisted the Nazis.

Why do things get worse so fast? Of course we have names for the process, like "collapse," "decay," and "slippery slope." By conjuring images—a stricken house, a gangrenous limb, a sliding talus—they make us feel we understand. Now, I am no enemy to word-pictures, but a civilization is not really a house, a limb, or a heap of rocks; it cannot literally fall in, rot, or skid out from underfoot. Images can only illustrate an explanation; they cannot substitute for one. So why do things get worse so fast? It would be well to know, in case the process can be arrested.

The usual explanation is that conscience is weakened by neglect. Once a wrong is done, the next wrong comes more easily. On this view conscience is mainly a restraint, a resistance, a passive barrier. It doesn't so much drive us on as hold us back, and when persistently attacked, the restraining wall gets thinner and thinner and finally disappears. Often this explanation is combined with another: that conscience comes from culture, that it is built up in us from outside. In this view the heart is malleable. We don't clearly know what is right and wrong, and when our teachers change the lessons, our consciences change their contents. What once we deemed wrong, we deem right; what once we deemed right, we deem wrong.

There is something to these explanations, but neither can account for the sheer dynamism of wickedness—for the fact that we aren't gently wafted into the abyss but violently propel ourselves into it. Nor, as I will show, can either one account for the peculiar quality of our present moral confusion.

I suggest a different explanation. Conscience is not a passive barrier but an active force; though it can hold us back, it can also drive us on. Moreover, conscience comes not from without but from within: though culture can trim the fringes, the core cannot be changed. The reason things get worse so fast must somehow lie not in the weakness of conscience but in its strength, not in its shapelessness but in its shape.

II

Whether paradoxical or not, the view of conscience I defend is nothing new; its roots are ancient. In one of the tragedies of Sophocles, the woman Antigone seeks to give her dead brother a proper burial, but is forbidden by the king because her brother was an enemy of the state. She replies to the tyrant that there is another law higher than the state's, and that she will follow it because of its divine authority. Not even the king may require anyone to violate it. Moreover, it requires not only forbearance from evil but active pursuit of the good: in this case, doing the honors for her brother.

Antigone's claim that this higher law has divine authority can easily be misunderstood, because the Greeks did not have a tradition of verbal revelation. The mythical hero Perseus had never climbed any Mount Sinai; the fabled god Zeus had never announced any Ten Commandments. So, although the law of which Antigone speaks somehow has divine authority, she has not learned it by reading something like a Bible, with moral rules delivered by the gods. Nor is she merely voicing the customs of the tribe—at least not if we are to believe Aristotle, who seems a safer authority on the Greeks than our contemporary skeptics. Instead she seems to be speaking of principles that everyone with a normal mind knows by means of conscience. She seems to be speaking of a law written on the heart—of what philosophers would later call the natural law.

Now by contrast with the pagan Greeks, Jews and Christians do have a tradition of verbal revelation. Moses did climb the mountain, God did announce the commandments. One might think, then, that Jews and Christians wouldn't have a natural law tradition because they wouldn't need it. But just the opposite is true. The idea of a law written on the heart is far stronger and more consistent among Jews, and especially Christians, than it was among the pagans. In fact, the very phrase "law written on the heart" is biblical; it comes from the New Testament book of Romans. Judaism calls the natural law the Noahide Commandments because of a rabbinic legend that God had given certain general rules to all the descendants of Noah—that is, all human beings—long before he made His special covenant with the descendants of Abraham. In similar fashion, Christianity distinguishes between "general revelation," which every human being receives, and "special revelation," which is transmitted by witnesses and recorded only in the Bible. General revelation makes us aware of God's existence and requirements so that we can't help knowing that we have a problem with sin. Special revelation goes further by telling us how to solve that problem.

The natural law is unconsciously presupposed—even when consciously denied—by modern secular thinkers, too. We can see the presupposition at work whenever we listen in on ethical debate. Consider, for example, the secular ethic of utilitarianism, which holds that the morally right action is always the one that brings about the greatest possible total happiness. Arguments against utilitarianism by other secularists often proceed by showing that the doctrine yields conclusions contrary to our most deeply held moral intuitions. For instance, it isn't hard to imagine circumstances in which murdering an innocent man might make all the others much happier than they were before. Utilitarianism, seeking the greatest possible total happiness, would require us to murder the fellow; nevertheless we don't, because we perceive that murder is plain wrong. So instead of discarding the man, we discard the theory. Here is the point: such an argument against utilitarianism stakes everything on a pre-philosophical intuition about the heinousness of murder. Unless there is a law written on the heart, it is hard to imagine where this intuition comes from.

The best short summary of the traditional, natural law understanding of conscience was given by Thomas Aquinas when he said that the core principles of the moral law are the same for all "both as to rectitude and as to knowledge"—in other words, that they are not only right for all but known to all. Nor is it true, as some suppose, that he was referring only to such formal principles as "good is to be done," for he speaks for the greater part of the tradition when he expressly includes such precepts as "Honor thy father and thy mother," "Thou shalt not kill," and "Thou shalt not steal." These, he says, are matters which "the natural reason of every man, of its own accord and at once, judges to be done or not to be done." To be sure, not every moral principle is part of the core, but all moral principles are at least derived from it, if not by pure deduction (killing is wrong and poison kills, so poisoning is wrong), then with the help of prudence (wrongdoers should be punished, but the appropriate punishment depends on circumstances). Our knowledge of derived principles such as "Rise up before the hoary head" may be weakened by neglect and erased by culture, but our knowledge of the core principles is ineffaceable. These are the laws we can't not know.

Ranged against this view are two others. One simply denies that the core principles are right for all; the other admits they are right for all, but denies they are known to all. The former, of course, is relativism. I call the latter mere moral realism—with emphasis on "mere" because natural law is realistic, too, but more so.

Not much need be said here about relativism. It is not an explanation of our decline, but a symptom of it. The reason it cannot be an explanation is that it finds nothing to explain. To the question "Why do things get worse so fast?" it can only return "They don't get worse, only different."

Mere moral realism is a much more plausible opponent, because by admitting the moral law it acknowledges the problem. Things are getting worse quickly—plainly because there isn't anything we "can't not know." *Everything* in conscience can be weakened by neglect and erased by culture. Now if mere moral realists are right, then although the problem of moral decline may begin in volition, it dwells in cognition: it may begin as a defect of will, but ends as a defect of knowledge. We may have started by neglecting what we knew, but we have now gone so far that we really don't know it any more. What is the result? That our contemporary ignorance of right and wrong is genuine. We really don't know the truth, but we are honestly searching for it—trying to see on a foggy night—doing the best that we can. In a sense, we are blameless for our deeds, for we don't know any better.

All this sounds persuasive, yet it is precisely what the older tradition, the natural law tradition, denies. We do know better; we are not doing the best we can. The problem of moral decline is volitional, not cognitive; it has little to do with knowledge. By and large we do know right from wrong, but wish we didn't. We only make believe we are searching for truth—so that we can do wrong, condone wrong, or suppress our remorse for having done wrong in the past.

If the traditional view is true, then our decline is owed not to moral ignorance but to moral suppression. We aren't untutored, but "in denial." We don't lack moral knowledge; we hold it down.

III

Offhand it seems as though believing in a law we "can't not know" would make it harder, not easier, to explain why things are so quickly getting worse. If the moral law really is carved on the heart, wouldn't it be hard to ignore? On the other hand, if it is merely penciled in as the mere moral realists say-well!

But this is merely picture thinking again. Carving and penciling are but metaphors, and more than metaphors are necessary to show why the suppression of conscience is more violent and explosive than its mere weakening would be. First let us consider a few facts that ought to arouse our suspicion—facts about the precise kind of moral confusion we suffer, or say we suffer.

Consider this tissue of contradictions: Most who call abortion wrong call it killing. Most who call it killing say it kills a baby. Most who call it killing a baby decline to prohibit it altogether. Most who decline to prohibit it think it should be restricted. More and more people favor restrictions. Yet greater and greater numbers of people have had or have been involved in abortions.

Or this one: Most adults are worried about teenage sex. Yet rather than telling kids to wait until marriage, most tell kids to wait until they are "older," as we are. Most say that premarital sex between consenting adults is a normal expression of natural desires. Yet hardly any are comfortable telling anyone, especially their own children, how many people they have slept with themselves.

Or this one: Accessories to suicide often write about the act; they produce page after page to show why it is right. Yet a large part of what they write about is guilt. Author George E. Delury, jailed for poisoning and suffocating his wife, says in his written account of the affair that his guilt feelings were so strong they were "almost physical."

As to the first example, if abortion kills a baby then it ought to be banned to everyone; why allow it? But if it doesn't kill a baby it is hard to see why we should be uneasy about it at all; why restrict it? We restrict what we allow because we know it is wrong but don't want to give it up; we feed our hearts scraps in hopes of hushing them, as cooks quiet their kitchen puppies.

As to the second example, sexual promiscuity has exactly the same bad consequences among adults as it has among teenagers. But if it is just an innocent pleasure, then why not talk it up? Swinging is no longer a novelty; the sexual revolution is now gray with age. If shame persists, the only possible explanation is that guilt persists as well.

The third example speaks for itself. Delury calls the very strength of his feelings a proof that they did not express "moral" guilt, merely the "dissonance" resulting from violation of an instinctual block inherited from our primate ancestors. We might paraphrase his theory, "the stronger the guilt, the less it matters."

Clearly, whatever our problem may be, it isn't that conscience is weak. We may be confused, but we aren't confused that way. It isn't that we don't know the truth, but that we tell ourselves something different.

<h1 style="text-align:center">IV</h1>

If the law written on the heart can be repressed, then we cannot count on it to restrain us from doing wrong; that much is obvious. I have made the more paradoxical claim that repressing it hurls us into further wrong. Holding conscience down doesn't deprive it of its force; it merely distorts and redirects that force. We are speaking of something less like the erosion of an earthen dike so that it fails to hold the water back, than like the compression of a powerful spring so that it buckles to the side.

Here is how it works. Guilt, guilty knowledge, and guilty feelings are not the same thing; men and women can have the knowledge without the feelings, and they can have the feelings without the fact. Even when suppressed, however, the knowledge of guilt always produces certain objective needs, which make their own demand for satisfaction irrespective of the state of the feelings. These needs include confession, atonement, reconciliation, and justification.

Now when guilt is acknowledged, the guilty deed can be repented so that these four needs can be genuinely satisfied. But when the guilty knowledge is suppressed, they can only be displaced. That is what generates the impulse to further wrong. Taking the four needs one by one, let's see how this happens.

The need to confess arises from transgression against what we know, at some level, to be truth. I have already commented on the tendency of accessories to suicide to write about their acts. Besides George Delury, who killed his wife, we may mention Timothy E. Quill, who prescribed lethal pills for his patient, and Andrew Solomon, who participated in the death of his mother. Solomon, for instance, writes in the *New Yorker* that "the act of speaking or writing about your involvement is, inevitably, a plea for absolution." Many readers will remember the full-page signature advertisements feminists took out in the early days of the abortion movement, telling the world that they had killed their own unborn children. At first it seems baffling that the sacrament of confession can be inverted to serve the ends of advocacy. Only by recognizing the power of suppressed conscience can this paradox be understood.

The need to atone arises from the knowledge of a debt that must somehow be paid. One would think such knowledge would always lead directly to repentance, but the counselors whom I have interviewed tell a different story. One woman learned during her pregnancy that her husband had been unfaithful to her. He wanted the child, so to punish him for betrayal she had an abortion. The trauma of killing was even greater than the trauma of his treachery, because this time she was to blame. What was her response? She aborted the next child, too; in her words, "I wanted to be able to hate myself more for what I did to the first baby." By trying to atone without repenting, she was driven to repeat the sin.

The need for reconciliation arises from the fact that guilt cuts us off from God and man. Without repentance, intimacy must be simulated precisely by sharing with others in the guilty act. Leo Tolstoy knew this. In *Anna Karenina* there comes a time when the lovers' mutual guiltiness is their only remaining bond. But the phenomenon is hardly restricted to cases of marital infidelity. Andrew Solomon says that he, his brothers, and his father are united by the "weird legacy" of their implication in his mother's death, and quotes a nurse who participated in her own mother's death as telling him, "I know some people will have trouble with my saying this but it was the most intimate time I've ever had with anyone." Herbert Hendin comments in a book on the Dutch affair with euthanasia, "The feeling that participation in death permits an intimacy that they are otherwise unable to achieve permeates euthanasia stories and draws patients and doctors to euthanasia." And no wonder. Violation of a basic human bond is so terrible that the burdened conscience must instantly establish an abnormal one to compensate; the very gravity of the transgression invests the new bond with a sense of profound significance. Naturally some will find it attractive.

The reconciliation need has a public dimension, too. Isolated from the community of moral judgment, transgressors strive to gather a substitute around themselves. They don't sin privately; they recruit. The more ambitious among them go further. Refusing to go to the mountain, they require the mountain to come to them: society must be transformed so that it no longer stands in awful judgment. So it is that they change the laws, infiltrate the schools, and create intrusive social-welfare bureaucracies.

Finally we come to the need for justification, which requires more detailed attention. Unhooked from justice, justification becomes rationalization, which is a more dangerous game than it seems. The problem is that the ordinances written on the heart all hang together. They depend on each other in such a way that we cannot suppress one except by rearranging all the others. A few cases will be sufficient to show how this happens.

Consider sexual promiscuity. The official line is that modern people don't take sex outside marriage seriously any longer; mere moral realists say this is because we no longer realize the wrong of it. I maintain that we do know it is wrong but pretend that we don't. Of course one must be careful to distinguish between the core laws of sex, the ones we can't not know, and the derived ones, which we can not know. For example, though true and reasonable, the superiority of monogamous to polygamous marriage is probably not part of the core. On the other hand, no human society has ever held that the sexual powers may be exercised by anyone with anyone, and the recognized norm is a durable and culturally protected covenant between man and woman with the intention of procreation. Casual shack-ups and one-night stands don't qualify.

Because we can't not know that sex belongs with marriage, when we separate them we cover our guilty knowledge with rationalizations. In any particular culture, particular rationalizations may be just as strongly protected as marriage; the difference is that while the rationalizations vary from culture to culture, the core does not. At least in our culture, such sexual self-deceptions are more common among women than men. I don't think this is because the female conscience is stronger (or weaker) than the male. However, sex outside marriage exposes the woman to greater risk, so whereas the man must fool only his conscience, she must fool both her conscience and her self-interest. If she does insist on doing wrong, she has twice as much reason to rationalize.

One common rationalization is to say "No" while acting "Yes" in order to tell oneself afterward "I didn't go along." William Gairdner reports that according to one rape crisis counselor, many of the women who call her do so not to report that they have been raped, but to ask whether they were raped. If they have to ask, of course, they probably haven't been; they are merely dealing with their ambivalence by throwing the blame for their decisions on their partners. But this is a serious matter. Denial leads to the further wrong of false witness.

Another tactic is inventing private definitions of marriage. Quite a few people "think of themselves as married" although they have no covenant at all; some even fortify the delusion with "moving-in ceremonies" featuring happy words without promises. Unfortunately, people who "think of themselves as married" not only refuse the obligations of real marriage but demand all of its cultural privileges; because rationalization is so much work, they require other people to support them in it. Such demands make the cultural protection of real marriage more difficult.

Yet another ruse is to admit that sex belongs with marriage but to fudge the nature of the connection. By this reasoning I tell myself that sex is okay because I am going to marry my partner, because I want my partner to marry me, or because I have to find out if we could be happy married. An even more dangerous fudge is to divide the form of marriage from its substance—to say "we don't need promises because we're in love." The implication, of course, is that those who do need promises love impurely; that those who don't marry are more truly married than those who do.

This last rationalization is even more difficult to maintain than most. Love, after all, is a permanent and unqualified commitment to the true good of the other person, and the native tongue of commitment is precisely promises. To work, therefore, this ruse requires another: having deceived oneself about the nature of marriage, one must now deceive oneself about the nature of love. The usual way of doing so is to mix up love with the romantic feelings that characteristically accompany it, and call them "intimacy." If only we have these feelings, we tell ourselves, we may have sex. That is to say, we may have sex-if we feel like it.

Here is where things really become interesting, because if the criterion of being as-good-as-married is sexual feelings, then obviously nobody who has sexual feelings may be prevented from marrying. So homosexuals must also be able to "marry"; their unions, too, should have cultural protection. At this point suppressed conscience strikes another blow, reminding us that marriage is linked with procreation. But now we are in a box. We cannot say "therefore homosexuals cannot marry," because that would strike against the whole teetering structure of rationalizations. Therefore we decree that having been made marriageable, homosexuals must be made procreative; the barren field must seem to bloom. There is, after all, artificial insemination. And there is adoption. So it comes to pass that children are given as a right to those from whom they were once protected as a duty. The normalization of perversion is complete.

V

When ordinary rationalization fails, people revert to other modes of suppression. We often see this when an unmarried young woman becomes pregnant. Suddenly her conscience discovers itself; though she was not ashamed to lift her skirts, she is suddenly ashamed to show her swelling belly. What can she do? Well, she can have an abortion; she can revert to the mode of suppression called "getting rid of the evidence." Once again conscience multiplies transgressions. But she finds that the new transgression is no solution to the old one; in fact now she has something even more difficult to rationalize.

Think what is necessary to justify abortion. Because we can't not know that it is wrong to deliberately kill human beings, there are only four options. We must deny that the act is deliberate, deny that it kills, deny that its victims are human, or deny that wrong must not be done. The last option is literally nonsense. That something must not be done is what it means for it to be wrong; to deny that wrong may not be done is merely to say "wrong is not wrong," or "what must not be done may be done." The first option is hardly promising either. Abortion does not just happen; it must be performed. Its proponents not only admit there is a "choice," they boast of it. As to the second option, if it was ever promising, it is no longer. Millions of women have viewed sonograms of their babies kicking, sucking their thumbs, and turning somersaults; whatever these little ones are, they are busily alive. Even most feminists have given up calling the baby a "blood clot" or describing abortion as the "extraction of menses."

The only option even barely left is number three: to deny the humanity of the victims. It is at this point that the machinery slips out of control. For the only way to make option three work is to ignore biological nature, which tells us that from conception onward the child is as human as you or me (does anyone imagine that a dog is growing in there?)—and invent another criterion of humanity, one that makes it a matter of degree. Some of us must turn out more human, others less. This is a dicey business even for abortionists. It hardly needs to be said that no one has been able to come up with a criterion that makes babies in the womb less human but leaves everyone else as he was; the teeth of the moral gears are too finely set for that.

Consider, for instance, the criteria of "personhood" and "deliberative rationality." According to the former, one is more or less human according to whether he is more or less a person; according to the latter, he is more or less a person according to whether he is more or less able to act with mature and thoughtful purpose. Unborn babies turn out to be killable because they cannot act maturely; they are less than fully persons, and so less than fully human. In fact, they must be killed when the interests of those who are more fully human require it. Therefore, not only may their mothers abort, but it would be wrong to stop the mothers from doing so. But look where else this drives us. Doesn't maturity also fall short among children, teenagers, and many adults? Then aren't they also less than fully persons-and if less than fully persons, then less than fully humans? Clearly so, hence they too must yield to the interests of the more fully human; all that remains is to sort us all out. No, the progression is too extreme! People are not that logical! Ah, but they are more logical than they know; they are only logical slowly. The implication they do not grasp today they may grasp in thirty years; if they do not grasp it even then, their children will. It is happening already. Look around.

So conscience has its revenge. We can't not know the preciousness of human life—therefore, if we tell ourselves that humanity is a matter of degree, we can't help holding those who are more human more precious than those who are less. The urge to justify abortion drives us inexorably to a system of moral castes more pitiless than anything the East has devised. Of course we can fiddle with the grading criteria: consciousness, self-awareness, and contribution to society have been proposed; racial purity has been tried. No such tinkering avails to change the character of our deeds. If we will a caste system, then we shall have one; if we will that some shall have their way, then in time there shall be a nobility of Those Who Have Their Way. All that our fiddling with the criteria achieves is a rearrangement of the castes.

Need we wonder why, then, having started on our babies, we now want to kill our grandparents? Sin ramifies. It is fertile, fissiparous, and parasitic, always in search of new kingdoms to corrupt. It breeds. But just as a virus cannot reproduce except by commandeering the machinery of a cell, sin cannot reproduce except by taking over the machinery of conscience. Not a gear, not a wheel is destroyed, but they are all set turning in different directions than their wont. Evil must rationalize, and that is its weakness. But it can, and that is its strength.

VI

We've seen that although conscience works in everyone, it doesn't restrain everyone. In all of us some of the time, in some of us all of the time, its fearsome energy merely "multiplies transgressions." Bent backwards by denial, it is more likely to catalyze moral collapse than hold it back.

But conscience is not the only expression of the natural law in human nature. Thomas Aquinas defined law as a form of discipline that compels through fear of punishment. In the case of human law, punishment means suffering the civil consequences of violation; in the case of natural law it means suffering the natural consequences of violation. If I cut myself, I bleed. If I get drunk, I have a hangover. If I sleep with many women, I lose the power to care for anyone, and sow pregnancies, pain, and suspicion.

Unfortunately, the disciplinary effect of natural consequences is diminished in at least two ways. These two diminishers are the main reason why the discipline takes so long, so that the best that can be hoped for in most cultures is a pendulum swing between moral laxity and moral strictness.

The first diminisher is a simple time lag: not every consequence of violating the natural law strikes immediately. Some results make themselves felt only after several generations, and by that time people are so deeply sunk in denial that even more pain is necessary to bring them to their senses. A good example of a long-term consequence is the increase of venereal disease. When I was a boy we all knew about syphilis and gonorrhea, but because of penicillin they were supposed to be on the way out. Today the two horrors are becoming antibiotic-resistant, and AIDS, herpes, chlamydia, genital warts, human papilloma virus, and more than a dozen other sexually transmitted diseases, most of them formerly rare, are ravaging the population. Other long-term consequences of violating the laws of sex are poverty, because single women have no one to help them raise their children; crime, because boys grow into adolescence without a father's influence; and child abuse, because although spouses tend to greet babies with joy, live-ins tend to greet them with jealousy and resentment. Each generation is less able to maintain families than the one before. Truly the iniquities of the fathers—and mothers—are visited upon the children and the children's children to the third and fourth generation.

The second diminisher comes from us: "Dreaming of systems so perfect that no one will need to be good," we exert our ingenuity to escape from the natural consequences of breaking the natural law. Not all social practices have this effect. For instance, threatening drunk drivers with legal penalties supplements the discipline of natural consequences rather than undermining it. Nor is the effect always intended. We don't devise social insurance programs in order to encourage improvidence, though they do have this result. It isn't even always wrong. It would be abominable to refuse treatment to a lifelong smoker with emphysema, even though he may have been buoyed in his habit by the confidence that the doctors would save him. But to act with the *purpose* of compensating for immorality is always wrong, as when we set up secondary school clinics to dispense pills and condoms to teenagers.

Here is an axiom: We cannot alter human nature, physical, emotional, or spiritual. A corollary is that no matter how cleverly devised, our contrivances never do succeed in canceling out the natural consequences of breaking the natural law. At best they delay them, and for several reasons they can even make them worse. In the first place they alter incentives: People with ready access to pills and condoms see less reason to be abstinent. In the second place they encourage wishful thinking: Most people grossly exaggerate their effectiveness in preventing disease and pregnancy and completely ignore the risks. In the third place they reverse the force of example: Before long the practice of abstinence erodes even among people who don't take precautions.

Finally they transform thought: Members of the contraceptive culture think liberty from the natural consequences of their decisions is somehow owed to them.

There comes a time when even the law shares their view. In *Planned Parenthood v. Casey*, which reauthorized the private use of lethal violence against life in the womb, the Supreme Court admitted that its original abortion ruling might have been wrong, but upheld it anyway. As it explained, "For two decades of economic and social developments, people have organized their intimate relationships and made choices that define their views of themselves and their places in society in reliance on the availability of abortion in the event that contraception should fail. . . . An entire generation has come of age free to assume [this] concept of liberty." To put the thought more simply, what we did has separated sex from responsibility for resulting life for so long that to change the rules on people now would be unfair.

Naught avails; our efforts to thwart the law of natural consequences merely make the penalty more crushing when it comes. The only question is whether our culture will be able to survive the return stroke of the piston.

To survive what is bearing down on us, we must learn four hard lessons: to acknowledge the natural law as a true and universal morality; to be on guard against our own attempts to overwrite it with new laws that are really rationalizations for wrong; to fear the natural consequences of its violation, recognizing their inexorability; and to forbear from all further attempts to compensate for immorality, returning on the path that brought us to this place.

Unfortunately, the condition of human beings since before recorded history is that we don't want to learn hard lessons. We would rather remain in denial. What power can break through such a barrier?

The only Power that ever has. Thomas Aquinas writes that when a nation suffers tyranny, those who enthroned the tyrant may first try to remove him, then call upon the emperor for help. When these human means fail, they should consider their sins and pray. We are now so thoroughly under the tyranny of our vices that it would be difficult for us to recognize an external tyrant at all. By our own hands we enthroned them: our strength no longer suffices for their removal: they have suspended the senate of right reason and the assembly of the virtues: the emperor, our will, is held hostage: and it is time to pray.

Nothing new can be written on the heart, but nothing needs to be; all we need is the grace of God to see what is already there. We don't want to read the letters, because they burn; but they do burn, so at last we must read them. This is why the nation can repent. This is why the plague can be arrested. This is why the culture of death can be redeemed. "For I know my transgressions, and my sin is ever before thee . . . a broken and contrite heart, O God, thou wilt not despise."

Source: J. Budziszewski. 1998. "The Revenge of Conscience," *First Things 84: 21-27* (June/July). Reprinted with permission from *First Things*.

J. Budziszewski is Professor of Government and Philosophy at the University of Texas. He specializes in political philosophy, ethical philosophy, and the interaction of religion with philosophy. Among his research interests are classical natural law, virtue ethics, moral self deception, and the problem of toleration. His books include *Written on the Heart: The Case for Natural Law* (InterVarsity, 1997); *The Revenge of Conscience: Politics and the Fall of Man* (Spence, 1999); *What We Can't Not Know: A Guide* (Spence, 2003); *Evangelicals in the Public Square: Four Formative Voices* (Baker Academic, 2006); *Natural Law for Lawyers* (Blackstone Fellowship, 2006); and *The Line Through the Heart: Natural Law as Fact, Theory, and Sign of Contradiction* (Intercollegiate Studies Institute Press, 2009). An earlier version of this article was published in William D. Gairdner, ed., *After Liberalism* (Stoddart, 1998).

Chapter 21

Contraception

The Church's moral teaching on artificial contraception is among the most difficult, if not *the* most difficult, to embrace. It combines the powerful force of the human sex drive with the practical fact that the fruits of that force (children) have a direct and profound impact on our lives. Indeed, despite the joys and satisfaction, parenthood is also frequently accompanied by a certain amount of hardship. Simply put, it is not easy raising a family of any size. Without a supernatural outlook and the grace of God, married couples would find it difficult to accept this teaching and the sacrifices that go with it.

The Church recognizes and appreciates the challenges of family life and does not take lightly the struggles associated with it. But, it is obliged to teach the truth and this teaching is nothing more than the natural law, something the Church has no authority to change. The Church teaches that our fertility is a gift from God and an end of marriage. A child "springs from the very heart of that mutual giving, as its fruit and fulfillment." It is necessary that every marriage act be open to the procreation of human life due to the "inseparable connection" between the unitive and procreative significance inherent to the marriage act.[1]

The Church does not expect married couples to have as many children as they possibly can. However, it does expect them to be generous, and as it is said, "God will not be outdone in generosity." For serious reasons, couples can utilize methods of natural family planning to put

---

[1] *Catechism of the Catholic Church.* 1997. no. 2366. Vatican City: Libreria Editrice Vaticana.

space between the birth of children.[2] The *Catechism of the Catholic Church* cites Pope John Paul II's *Familiaris Consortio* in explaining that contraception is morally wrong because it violates the fundamental truth and essence of the conjugal act.[3]

The advent of the birth control pill in the 1960s and the confusion over its morality led to the issuance of the encyclical letter, *Humanae Vitae*, by Pope Paul VI in 1968. The Pope's reiteration of the Church's teaching on contraception was not welcomed by many sectors of the Church, and dissent was fairly widespread. Nevertheless, this teaching has withstood the test of time and the world is reaping the bitter fruit of its rejection of this teaching and the profound insights provided by Pope Paul VI.

In **"Married Love and Contraception,"** Father Cormac Burke explains why contraception is inherently immoral. He delves deeply into the nature of marriage and the meaning of the conjugal act to help us understand why contraception is a serious violation of the natural law.

➤ In *Humanae Vitae*, Pope Paul VI confirms that contraception is immoral because of the "inseparable connection, established by God . . . between the unitive significance and the procreative significance which are both inherent to the marriage act."

➤ Burke asserts that contraception not only removes the procreative aspect of the marriage act, but "destroys its power to signify love: the love and union proper to marriage."

➤ The pleasure associated with marital intercourse is transient and not integral to the significance of the act, which is lasting.

➤ The marital act is the most intense expression of love and union because it is "an offer and acceptance, an exchange of something that uniquely represents the gift of oneself and the union of two selves."

➤ To give one's seed to another (this applies to both husbands and wives) is the greatest expression of one's desire to give himself or herself. It is giving to another what one will give to no other. It is

---

[2] *Catechism of the Catholic Church*. 1997. no. 2370. Vatican City: Libreria Editrice Vaticana.

[3] John Paul II. 1981. *Familiaris Consortio*, November 22.

expressing a desire to merge with the other and yield a new "you-and-me."

➢ The uniqueness of the marital relationship and union is the sharing of a power rather than the sharing of a sensation.

➢ By using artificial contraception, both persons in the couple rejects a part of the other—fertility. "They reject part of their mutual love: its power to be fruitful."

➢ "Love may somehow be present in their contraceptive relationship; conjugal love is not expressed by it."

➢ The distinctive knowledge that a husband and wife communicate to each other is "the knowledge of each other's integral human condition as spouse." Each reveals himself or herself to the other and surrenders to the other as husband and wife.

➢ "Only in procreative intercourse do the spouses exchange true 'knowledge' of one another, do they truly speak humanly and intelligibly to one another; do they truly reveal themselves to one another in their full human actuality and potential. Each offers, and each accepts, full spousal knowledge of the other."

➢ Sexual love involves the whole male and female person, both body and spirit. This love is falsified if the body and spirit say different things.

➢ The use of contraception in marriage is the same as saying, "I don't want all you offer me." "I prefer a sterile you." Even if both agree to this "radical human and sexual devaluation," they are not saved from the unfortunate effects it will have on their love and their happiness.

➢ "Contraception represents such a refusal to let oneself be known that it simply is not real carnal knowledge."

➢ Contraception in marriage has the effect of thwarting self-fulfillment in marriage.

➢ God is love and his love is creative. Man, made in the image of God, is also meant to love as God loves. He is meant to be creative.

➢ A couple in love wants to do something "original" together. What could be more original than a child that is the result of their union and their love?

➢ The strength of the sexual appetite reflects deep personalist needs. It reflects a deep longing for sexual union because we each have "a deep longing for all that is involved in true sexuality: self-giving, self-complementarity, self-realization, self-perpetuation, in spousal union with another."

➤ "If continuous and growing sexual frustration is a main consequence of contraception, this is also because the contraceptive mentality deprives the very strength of the sexual urge of its real meaning and purpose, and then tries to find full sexual experience and satisfaction in what is basically little more than a physical release."

Some forty years after the issuance of *Humanae Vitae,* we can see how prophetic Pope Paul VI was in warning us of the likely consequences of society adopting a contraceptive mentality. In "**The Vindication of *Humanae Vitae*,**" Mary Eberstadt chronicles the unfortunate modern day fulfillment of these prophecies.

➤ Despite the obvious damage that contraception has wrought in our society, the Church's teaching continues to be criticized as out of date, divisive, and controversial.

➤ Some secular scholars have linked many of today's social scourges to the widespread adoption of artificial contraception.

➤ Nobel Prize-winning economist George Akerlof has linked the sexual revolution facilitated by contraceptive technology to increased illegitimacy and abortion, as well as to the decrease in marriage and married fatherhood for men, leading to increased substance abuse, incarceration, and arrests.

➤ Akerlof also found an undeniable connection between a lower propensity to marry and the rise in poverty and social pathology.

➤ The adverse effects that divorce and single parenthood have on children and society have been widely documented.

➤ Some scholars have linked the rise in divorce rates to the contraceptive revolution itself.

➤ Sociologist Lionel Tiger has linked the sexual revolution to a host of societal problems—the breakdown of families, female impoverishment, trouble in the relationship between the sexes, single motherhood, and abortion.

➤ The doomsday population explosion warnings so popular in the sixties and seventies have proven utterly fallacious. Indeed, quite the opposite is true—a global birth dearth is a growing threat to the economic well-being of humanity in years to come.

➢ The current one-child policy of China and the Indian government's attempts to coerce its citizens to use contraception in the mid-seventies give credence to Pope Paul's warnings that may have seemed farfetched at the time.

➢ To the prediction that contraception would lead to greater "marital infidelity and a general lowering of moral standards," need we say more?

➢ Feminist literature gives testimony to the sexual discontent and grievances existing among women toward men.

➢ The loss of the sacredness of sex has lead to the scourge of pornography, which has undermined the intimacy of marital union and done violence to what is intended to be an exclusive act of self-giving.

➢ The Anglican Church's acceptance of contraception for married couples at the Lambeth Conference in 1930 led to the virtual implosion of the Episcopal Church. Nevertheless, some Protestants are re-thinking the contraception issue.

➢ The shortage of priests and the recent priestly sex scandals are likely related to the contraceptive mentality embraced by many Catholic married people.

➢ "If Paul VI was right about so many of the consequences deriving from contraception, it is because he was right about contraception itself."

Further Reading

Pope Paul VI. 1968. Encyclical Letter, *Humanae Vitae*, July 25.

Janet Smith. "Contraception: Why Not?" http://www.janetsmith.excerptsofinri.com.

Married Love and Contraception

By Cormac Burke

There is a modern argument for conjugal contraception which claims to speak in personalist terms, and which could be summarized as follows. The marriage act has two functions: a biological or procreative function, and a spiritual-unitive function. However, while it is only potentially a procreative act, it is actually and in itself a love act: it truly expresses conjugal love and unites husband and wife. Now, while contraception frustrates the biological or procreative potential of the marital act, it fully respects it's spiritual and unitive function; in fact it facilitates it by removing tensions or fears capable of impairing the expression of love in married intercourse. In other words—this position claims—while contraception suspends or nullifies the procreative aspect of marital intercourse, it leaves its unitive aspect intact.

Until quite recently, the argument presented by Christian moralists against artificial birth-control has mainly been that the sexual act is naturally designed for procreation, and it is wrong to frustrate this design because it is wrong to interfere with man's natural functions. Many persons are not altogether convinced by this argument, which does seem open to rather elementary objections. After all, we do interfere with other natural functions, for instance when we use earplugs or hold our nose, etc., and no one has ever argued that to do so is morally wrong. Why then should it be wrong to interfere for good reasons with the procreational aspect of marital intercourse? The defenders of contraception in any case, dismiss this traditional argument as mere "biologism"; as an understanding of the marital act that fails to go beyond its biological function or possible biological consequences, and ignores its spiritual function, i.e. its function in signifying and effecting the union of the spouses.

Those who advance this defense of marital contraception—couched in apparently personalist terms—feel they are on strong and positive ground. If we are to offer an effective answer and show the radical defectiveness of this position, I suggest that we too need to develop a personalist argument, based on a true personalist understanding of sex and marriage.

The contraceptive argument outlined is evidently built on an essential thesis: that the procreative and the unitive aspects of the marital act are separable, i.e. that the procreative aspect can be nullified without this in any way vitiating the conjugal act or making it less a unique expression of true marital love and union.

This thesis is of course explicitly rejected by the Church. The main reason why contraception is unacceptable to a Christian conscience is, as Pope Paul VI put it in *Humanae Vitae*, the "inseparable connection, established by God . . . between the unitive significance and the procreative significance which are both inherent to the marriage act" (HV 12).

Paul VI affirmed this inseparable connection. He did not however go on to explain why these two aspects of the marital act are in fact so inseparably connected, or why this connection is such that it is the very ground of the moral evaluation of the act. Perhaps serene reflection, matured by the ongoing debate of more than 20 years, can enable us to discover the reasons why this is so: why the connection between the two aspects of the act is in fact such that the destruction of its procreative reference necessarily destroys it's unitive and personalist significance. In other words, if one deliberately destroys the power of the conjugal act to give life, one necessarily destroys its power to signify love: the love and union proper to marriage.

The Marital Act as an Act of Union

Why is the act of intercourse called the conjugal act? Why is it regarded as the most distinctive expression of marital love and self-giving? Why is this act—which is but a passing and fleeting thing—particularly regarded as an act of union? After all, people in love express their love and desire to be united in many ways: sending letters, exchanging looks or presents, holding hands. . . . What makes the sexual act unique? Why does this act unite the spouses in a way that no other act does? What is it that makes it not just a physical experience but a love experience?

Is it the special pleasure attaching to it? Is the unitive meaning of the conjugal act contained just in the sensation, however intense, that it can produce? If intercourse unites two people simply because it gives special pleasure, then it would seem that one or other of the spouses could at times find a more meaningful union outside marriage than within it. It would follow too that sex without pleasure becomes meaningless, and that sex with pleasure, even homosexual sex, becomes meaningful.

No. The conjugal act may or may not be accompanied by pleasure; but the meaning of the act does not consist in its pleasure. The pleasure provided by marital intercourse may be intense, but it is transient. The significance of marital intercourse is also intense, and it is not transient; it lasts.

Why should the marital act be more significant than any other expression of affection between the spouses? Why should it be a more intense expression of love and union? Surely because of what happens in that marital encounter, which is not just a touch, not a mere sensation, however intense, but a communication, an offer and acceptance, an exchange of something that uniquely represents the gift of oneself and the union of two selves.

Here, of course, it should not be forgotten that while two persons in love want to give themselves to one another, to be united to one another, this desire of theirs remains humanly speaking on a purely volitional level. They can bind themselves to one another, but they cannot actually give themselves. The greatest expression of a person's desire to give himself is to give the seed of himself.[1] Giving one's seed is much more significant, and in particular is much more real, than giving one's heart. "I am yours, I give you my heart; here, take it," remains mere poetry, to which no physical gesture can give true body. But, "I am yours; I give you my seed; here, take it," is not poetry, it is love. It is conjugal love embodied in a unique and privileged physical action whereby intimacy is expressed—"I give you what I give no one"—and union is achieved: "Take what I have to give. This will be a new me. United to you, to what you have to give—to your seed—this will be a new 'you-and-me,' fruit of our mutual knowledge and love." In human terms, this is the closest one can come to giving one's self conjugally and to accepting the conjugal self-gift of another, and so achieving spousal union.

---

[1] *Seed* is here intended to refer equally to the male or the female generative element.

Therefore, what makes marital intercourse express a unique relationship and union is not the sharing of a sensation but the sharing of a
power: of an extraordinary life-related, creative physical sexual power.
In a true conjugal relationship, each spouse says to the other: "I accept
you as somebody like no one else in my life. You will be unique to me
and I to you. You and you alone will be my husband; you alone will be
my wife. And the proof of your uniqueness to me is the fact that with
you—and with you alone—am I prepared to share this God-given life-
oriented power."

In this consists the singular quality of intercourse. Other physical
expressions of affection do not go beyond the level of a mere gesture;
they remain a symbol of the union desired. But the conjugal act is not a
mere symbol. In true marital intercourse, something real has been
exchanged, with a full gift and acceptance of conjugal masculinity and
femininity. And there remains, as witness to their conjugal relationship
and the intimacy of their conjugal union, the husband's seed in the
wife's body.[2]

Now if one deliberately nullifies the life-orientation of the conjugal
act, one destroys its essential power to signify union. Contraception in
fact turns the marital act into self-deception or into a lie: "I love you so
much that with you, and with you alone, I am ready to share this most
unique power. . . ." But—what unique power? In contraceptive sex, no
unique power is being shared, except a power to produce pleasure. But
then the uniqueness of the marital act is reduced to pleasure. Its
significance is gone.

Contraceptive intercourse is an exercise in meaninglessness. It
could perhaps be compared to going through the actions of singing
without letting any sound of music pass one's lips.

Some of us can remember the love-duets of Jeanette McDonald
and Nelson Eddy, two popular singing stars of the early "talkies." How
absurd if they had sung silent duets: going through the motions of
singing, but not allowing their vocal chords to produce an intelligible
sound: just meaningless reverberations . . .; a hurry or a flurry of

---

[2] In this way, in fact, the uniqueness of the decision to marry a particular
person is reaffirmed in each marital act. By every single act of true intercourse,
each spouse is confirmed in the unique status of being husband or wife to the
other.

movement signifying nothing. Contraceptive intercourse is very much like that. Contraceptive spouses involve each other in bodily movements, but their "body language" is not truly human (The "language of the body" is of course a key expression in Pope John Paul II's writings on sexuality and marriage). They refuse to let their bodies communicate sexually and intelligibly with one another. They go through the motions of a love-song; but there is no song.

Contraception is in fact not just an action without meaning; it is an action that contradicts the essential meaning which true conjugal intercourse should have as signifying total and unconditional self-donation ("Contraception contradicts the truth of conjugal love," Pope John Paul II, Address, September 17, 1983). Instead of accepting each other totally, contraceptive spouses reject of each other in part, because fertility is part of each of them. They reject part of their mutual love: its power to be fruitful. . . .

A couple may say: we do not want our love to be fruitful. But if that is so, there is an inherent contradiction in their trying to express their love by means of an act which, of its nature, implies fruitful love; and there is even more of a contradiction if, when they engage in the act, they deliberately destroy the fertility-orientation from which precisely derives its capacity to express the uniqueness of their love.

In true marital union, husband and wife are meant to experience the vibration of human vitality in its very source.[3] In the case of contraceptive "union," the spouses experience sensation, but it is drained of real vitality.

The anti-life effect of contraception does not stop at the "No" which it addresses to the possible fruit of love. It tends to take the very life out of love itself. Within the hard logic of contraception, anti-life

---

[3] This still remains true even in cases where, for some reason or another, the spouses cannot have children. Their union in such cases, just as their union during the wife's pregnancy, draws its deepest meaning from the fact that both their conjugal act and the intention behind it are "open to life," even though no life can actually result from the act. It is their basic openness to life which gives the act its meaning and dignity. Just as the absence of this openness is what undermines the dignity and meaning of the act when the spouses, without serious reasons, deliberately limit their marital intercourse to the infertile periods.

becomes anti-love. Its devitalizing effect devastates love, threatening it with early ageing and premature death.

At this point it is good to anticipate the possible criticism that our argument so far is based on an incomplete disjunction, inasmuch as it seems to affirm that the conjugal act is either procreative or else merely hedonistic. . . . Can contraceptive spouses not counter this with the sincere affirmation that, in their intercourse, they are not merely seeking pleasure; they are also experiencing and expressing love for one another?

Let us clarify our position on this particular point. We are not affirming that contraceptive spouses may not love each other in their intercourse, nor—insofar as they are not prepared to have such intercourse with a third person—that it does not express a certain uniqueness in their relationship. Our thesis is that it does not express conjugal uniqueness. Love may somehow be present in their contraceptive relationship; conjugal love is not expressed by it. Conjugal love may in fact soon find itself threatened by it. Contraceptive spouses are constantly haunted by the suspicion that the act in which they share could indeed be, for each one of them, a privileged giving of pleasure, but could also be a mere selfish taking of pleasure. It is logical that their love-making be troubled by a sense of falseness or hollowness, for they are attempting to found the uniqueness of the spousal relationship on an act of pleasure that tends ultimately to close each one of them sterilely in on himself or herself, and they are refusing to found that relationship on the truly unique conjugal dimension of loving co-creativity capable, in its vitality, of opening each of them out not merely to one another but to the whole of life and creation.

Sexual Love and Sexual Knowledge

The mutual and exclusive self-donation of the marriage act consists in its being the gift and acceptance of something unique. Now this something unique is not just the seed (this indeed could be "biologism"), but the fullness of the sexuality of each spouse.

It was in the context of its not being good for man to be alone that God made him sexual. He created man in a duality—male and female—with the potential to become a trinity. The differences between the sexes speak therefore of a divine plan of complementarity, of self-completion and self-fulfillment, also through self-perpetuation.

It is not good for man to be alone because man, on his own, cannot fulfill himself; he needs others. He especially needs another: a companion, a spouse. Union with a spouse, giving oneself to a spouse—sexual and marital union in self-donation—are normally a condition of human growth and fulfillment.

Marriage, then, is a means of fulfillment through union. Husband and wife are united in mutual knowledge and love, a love which is not just spiritual but also bodily; and a knowledge supporting their love which is likewise not mere speculative or intellectual knowledge; it is bodily knowledge as well. Their marital love is also meant to be based on carnal knowledge; this is fully human and fully logical. How significant it is that the Bible, in the original Hebrew, refers to marital intercourse in terms of man and woman "knowing" each other. Adam, Genesis says, knew Eve, his wife. What comment can we make on this equivalence which the Bible draws between conjugal intercourse and mutual knowledge?

What is the distinctive knowledge that husband and wife communicate to one another? It is the knowledge of each other's integral human condition as spouse. Each "discloses" a most intimate secret to the other: the secret of his or her personal sexuality. Each is revealed to the other truly as spouse and comes to know the other in the uniqueness of that spousal self-revelation and self-gift. Each one lets himself or herself be known by the other, and surrenders to the other, precisely as husband or wife.

Nothing can undermine a marriage so much as the refusal to fully know and accept one's spouse or to let oneself be fully known by him or her. Marriage is constantly endangered by the possibility of one spouse holding something back from the other; keeping some knowledge to oneself that he or she does not want the other to possess.[4] This can occur on all levels of interpersonal communication: physical as well as spiritual.

In many modern marriages, there is something in the spouses, and between the spouses, that each does not want to know, does not want

---

[4] Obviously we are not referring here to those occasions in which, out of justice to a third party, one of the spouses is under an obligation to observe some secret, e.g. of a professional nature. Fulfillment of such an obligation is in no way a violation of the rights of married intimacy.

to face up to, wants to avoid: and this something is their sexuality. As a result, since they will not allow each other full mutual carnal knowledge, they do not truly know each other sexually or humanly or spousally. This places their married love under a tremendous existential tension that can tear it apart.

In true marital intercourse each spouse renounces protective self-possession, so as to fully possess and be fully possessed by the other. This fullness of true sexual gift and possession is only achieved in marital intercourse open to life. Only in procreative intercourse do the spouses exchange true "knowledge" of one another, do they truly speak humanly and intelligibly to one another; do they truly reveal themselves to one another in their full human actuality and potential. Each offers, and each accepts, full spousal knowledge of the other.

In the body language of intercourse, each spouse utters a word of love that is both a "self-expression"—an image of each one's self—as well as an expression of his or her longing for the other. These two words of love meet, and are fused in one. And, as this new unified word of love takes on flesh, God shapes it into a person—the child: the incarnation of the husband's and wife's sexual knowledge of one another and sexual love for one another.

In contraception, the spouses will not let the word—which their sexuality longs to utter—take flesh. They will not even truly speak the word to each other. They remain humanly impotent in the face of love; sexually dumb and carnally speechless before one another.

Sexual love is a love of the whole male or female person, body and spirit. Love is falsified if body and spirit do not say the same thing. This happens in contraception. The bodily act speaks of a presence of love or of a degree of love that is denied by the spirit. The body says, "I love you totally", whereas the spirit says, "I love you reservedly." The body says, "I seek you"; the spirit says, "I will not accept you, not all of you."

Contraceptive intercourse falls below mere pantomime. It is disfigured body-language; it expresses a rejection of the other. By it, each says: "I do not want to know you as my husband or my wife; I am not prepared to recognize you as my spouse. I want something from you, but not your sexuality; and if I have something to give to you, something I will let you take, it is not my sexuality."[5]

---

[5] If it is not sexuality that each spouse in contraceptive intercourse gives to or takes from the other, what does each one in fact actually take or give? In what

This enables us to develop a point we touched on earlier. The negation that a contraceptive couple are involved in is not directed just towards children, or just towards life, or just towards the world. They address a negation directly towards one another. "I prefer a sterile you", is equivalent to saying, "I don't want all you offer me. I have calculated the measure of my love, and it is not big enough for that; it is not able to take all of you. I want a "you" cut down to the size of my love. . . ." The fact that both spouses may concur in accepting a cut-rate version of each other does not save their love or their lives—or their possibilities of happiness—from the effects of such radical human and sexual devaluation.

Normal conjugal intercourse fully asserts masculinity and femininity. The man asserts himself as man and husband, and the woman equally asserts herself as woman and wife. In contraceptive intercourse, only a maimed sexuality is asserted. In the truest sense sexuality is not asserted at all. Contraception represents such a refusal to let oneself be known that it simply is not real carnal knowledge. A deep human truth underlies the theological and juridic principle that contraceptive sex does not consummate marriage.

Contraceptive intercourse, then, is not real sexual intercourse at all. That is why the disjunctives offered by this whole matter are insufficiently expressed by saying that if intercourse is contraceptive, then it is merely hedonistic. This may or may not be true. What is true—at a much deeper level—is that if intercourse is contraceptive, then it is not sexual. In contraception there is an "intercourse" of sensation, but no real sexual knowledge or sexual love, no true sexual revelation of self or sexual communication of self or sexual gift of self. The choice of contraception is in fact the rejection of sexuality. The warping of the sexual instinct from which modern society seems to suffer represents not so much an excess of sex, as a lack of true human sexuality.

---

might be termed the better cases, it is a form of love—divorced from sexuality. In other cases, it is merely pleasure, also—be it noted—divorced from sexuality. In one case or the other, contraceptive spouses always deny themselves sexuality. Their marriage, deprived of a true sexual relationship, suffers in consequence.

True conjugal intercourse unites. Contraception separates, and the separation works right along the line. It not only separates sex from procreation, it also separates sex from love. It separates pleasure from meaning, and body from mind. Ultimately and surely, it separates wife from husband and husband from wife.

Contraceptive couples who stop to reflect realize that their marriage is troubled by some deep malaise. The alienations they are experiencing are a sign as well as a consequence of the grave violation of the moral order involved in contraception. Only a resolute effort to break with contraceptive practices can heal the sickness affecting their married life. This is why the teaching of *Humanae Vitae* as well as subsequent papal Magisterium on the matter, far from being a blind adherence to an outdated posture, represent a totally clear-sighted defense of the innate dignity and true meaning of human and spousal sexuality.

Why Does Only Procreative Sex Fulfill?

Our argument so far is that contraceptive marital sex does not achieve any true personalist end. It does not bring about self-fulfillment in marriage, but rather prevents and frustrates it. But—one may still ask—does it follow that open-to-life marital sex alone leads to the self-fulfillment of the spouses? I think it does; and the reason lies in the very nature of love (cf. *Covenanted Happiness*, pp. 38-47). Love is creative. God's love (if we may put it this way) "drove" Him to create. Man's love, made in the image of God's, is also meant to create. If it deliberately does not do so, it frustrates itself. Love between two persons makes them want to do things together. While this is true of friendship in general, it has a singular application to the love between spouses. A couple truly in love want to do things together; if possible, they want to do something "original" together. Nothing is more original to a couple in love than their child: the image and fruit of their love and their union. That is why "the marital thing" is to have children; and other things, as substitutes, do not satisfy conjugal love.

Procreative intercourse fulfils also because only in such intercourse are the spouses open to all the possibilities of their mutual love: ready to be enriched and fulfilled not only by what it offers to them, but also by what it demands of them.

Further, procreative intercourse fulfils because it expresses the human person's desire for self-perpetuation. It expresses it and does not contradict it, as contraception does. It is only on life-wishes, not on death-wishes, that love can thrive. When a normal married couple have a child, they pass their child joyfully to each other. If their child dies, there is no joy, there are tears, as they pass its dead body to one another. Spouses should weep over a contraceptive act: a barren, desolate act which rejects the life that is meant to keep love alive, and would kill the life their love naturally seeks to give origin to. There may be physical satisfaction, but there can be no joy in passing dead seed; or in passing living seed only to kill it.

The vitality of sensation in sexual intercourse should correspond to a vitality of meaning (remembering—as we have said—that sensation is not meaning). The very explosiveness of sexual pleasure suggests the greatness of the creativity of sex. In each conjugal act, there should be something of the magnificence—of the scope and power—of Michelangelo's Creation in the Sistine Chapel in Rome. . . . But it is the dynamism not just of a sensation, but of an event: of something that happens, of a communication of life.

A lack of true sexual awareness characterizes the act if the intensity of pleasure does not serve to stir a fully conscious understanding of the greatness of the conjugal experience: I am committing myself—my creative life-giving power—not just to another person, but to the whole of creation: to history, to mankind, to the purposes and design of God. In each act of conjugal union, teaches Pope John Paul II, "there is renewed, in a way, the mystery of creation in all its original depth and vital power" (General Audience, November 21, 1979: Insegnamenti di Giovanni Paolo II, II, 2 [1979], p. 1215).

A last point should be made. The whole question we are considering is of course tremendously complicated precisely by the strength of the sexual instinct. Nevertheless, the very strength of this instinct should itself be a pointer towards an adequate understanding of sexuality. Elementary commonsense says that the power of the sexual urge must correspond to deep human aspirations or needs. It has of course been traditional to explain the sexual urge in cosmic or demographic terms: just as we have a food appetite to maintain the life of the individual, so we have a sex appetite to maintain the life of the species. This explanation makes sense—as far as it goes. However, it clearly does not go far enough. The sex appetite—the strength of the sex appetite—surely corresponds not only to cosmic or collectivist needs, but also to personalist needs. If man and woman feel a deep longing for sexual union, it is also because they have—each one personally has—a deep longing for all that is involved in true sexuality: self-giving, self-complementarity, self-realization, self-perpetuation, in spousal union with another.

The experience of such complete spousal sexuality is filled with many-facetted pleasure, in which the simple physical satisfaction of a mere sense instinct is accompanied and enriched by the personalist satisfaction of the much deeper and stronger longings involved in sex, and not marred and soured by their frustration. If continuous and growing sexual frustration is a main consequence of contraception, this is also because the contraceptive mentality deprives the very strength of the sexual urge of its real meaning and purpose, and then tries to find full sexual experience and satisfaction in what is basically little more than a physical release.

Source: Cormac Burke. 1998. "Married Love and Contraception." *Osservatore Romano* (English ed.), October 10. Reprinted with permission from Cormac Burke.

A Professor of Modern Languages and Doctor in Canon Law, as well as a civil lawyer and member of the Irish Bar, Cormac Burke was ordained a priest of the Opus Dei Prelature in 1955. After thirty years of pastoral and teaching work in Europe, North America, and Africa, Pope John Paul II appointed him a Judge of the Roman Rota, the High Court of the Church. During his thirteen years at the Vatican, he also taught anthropology at the "Studium Rotale," as well as Canon Law at the Pontifical University of the Holy Cross. Among his best known books are *Conscience and Freedom* (Sinag-Tala, 1992), *Authority and Freedom in the Church* (Ignatius Press, 1988), and *Covenanted Happiness* (Scepter Publishers, 1999). In 1999, he returned to Africa, where he has continued to teach at Strathmore University, Nairobi, Kenya.

The Vindication of *Humanae Vitae*

By Mary Eberstadt

I

That *Humanae Vitae* and related Catholic teachings about sexual morality are laughingstocks in all the best places is not exactly news. Even in the benighted precincts of believers, where information from the outside world is known to travel exceedingly slowly, everybody grasps that this is one doctrine the world loves to hate. During Benedict XVI's April visit to the United States, hardly a story in the secular press failed to mention the teachings of *Humanae Vitae*, usually alongside adjectives like "divisive" and "controversial" and "outdated." In fact, if there's anything on earth that unites the Church's adversaries—all of them except for the Muslims, anyway—the teaching against contraception is probably it.

To many people, both today and when the encyclical was promulgated on July 25, 1968, the notion simply defies understanding. Consenting adults, told not to use birth control? Preposterous. Third World parents deprived access to contraception and abortion? Positively criminal. A ban on condoms when there's a risk of contracting AIDS? Beneath contempt.

"The execration of the world," in philosopher G.E.M. Anscombe's phrase, was what Paul VI incurred with that document—to which the years since 1968 have added plenty of just plain ridicule. Hasn't everyone heard Monty Python's send-up song "Every Sperm Is Sacred"? Or heard the jokes? "You no play-a the game, you no make-a the rules." And "What do you call the rhythm method? *Vatican roulette.*" And "What do you call a woman who uses the rhythm method? *Mommy.*"

As everyone also knows, it's not only the Church's self-declared adversaries who go in for this sort of sport. So, too, do many American and European Catholics—specifically, the ones often called dissenting or cafeteria Catholics, and who more accurately might be dubbed the "Catholic Otherwise Faithful." *I may be Catholic, but I'm not a maniac about it,* runs their unofficial subtext—meaning: *I'm happy to take credit for enlightened Catholic positions on the death penalty/social justice/civil rights, but of course I don't believe in those archaic teachings about divorce/homosexuality/and above all birth control.*

Thus FOX News host Sean Hannity, for example, describes himself to viewers as a "good" and "devout" Catholic—one who happens to believe, as he has also said on the air, that "contraception is good." He was challenged on his show in 2007 by Father Tom Euteneuer of Human Life International, who observed that such a position emanating from a public figure technically fulfilled the requirements for something called heresy. And Hannity reacted as many others have when stopped in the cafeteria line. He objected that the issue of contraception was "superfluous" compared to others; he asked what right the priest had to tell him what to do ("judge not lest you be judged," Hannity instructed); and he expressed shock at the thought that *anyone* might deprive him of taking Communion just because he was deciding for himself what it means to be Catholic.

And so we have a microcosm of the current fate of *Humanae Vitae* and all it represents in the American Church—and, for that matter, in what is left of the advanced Western one, too. With each passing year, it seems safe to assume, fewer priests can be found to explain the teaching, fewer parishioners to obey it, and fewer educated people to avoid rolling their eyes at the idea that anyone in 2008 could possibly be so antiquarian as to hold any opinion about contraceptive sex—any, that is, other than its full-throttle celebration as the chief liberation of our time.

And in just that apparent consensus about the ridiculousness of it all, amid all those ashes scattered over a Christian teaching stretching back two millennia, arises a fascinating and in fact exceedingly amusing modern morality tale—amusing, at least, to those who take their humor dark.

"He that sitteth in the heavens shall laugh," the Psalmist promises, specifically in a passage about enjoying vindication over one's adversaries. If that is so, then the racket on this fortieth anniversary must be prodigious. Four decades later, not only have the document's signature predictions been ratified in empirical force, but they have been ratified as few predictions ever are: in ways its authors could not possibly have foreseen, including by information that did not exist when the document was written, by scholars and others with no interest whatever in its teaching, and indeed even inadvertently, and in more ways than one, by many proud public adversaries of the Church.

Forty years later, there are more than enough ironies, both secular and religious, to make one swear there's a humorist in heaven.

II

Let's begin by meditating upon what might be called the first of the secular ironies now evident: *Humanae Vitae's* specific predictions about what the world would look like if artificial contraception became widespread. The encyclical warned of four resulting trends: a general lowering of moral standards throughout society; a rise in infidelity; a lessening of respect for women by men; and the coercive use of reproductive technologies by governments.

In the years since *Humanae Vitae's* appearance, numerous distinguished Catholic thinkers have argued, using a variety of evidence, that each of these predictions has been borne out by the social facts. One thinks, for example, of Monsignor George A. Kelly in his 1978 "Bitter Pill the Catholic Community Swallowed" and of the many contributions of Janet E. Smith, including *Humanae Vitae: A Generation Later* and the edited volume *Why Humanae Vitae Was Right: A Reader*.

And therein lies an irony within an irony. Although it is largely *Catholic* thinkers who have connected the latest empirical evidence to the defense of *Humanae Vitae's* predictions, during those same forty years most of the experts actually *producing* the empirical evidence have been social scientists operating in the secular realm. As sociologist W. Bradford Wilcox emphasized in a 2005 essay: "The leading scholars who have tackled these topics are not Christians, and most of them are not political or social conservatives. They are, rather, honest social scientists willing to follow the data wherever it may lead."

Consider, as Wilcox does, the Nobel Prize-winning economist George Akerlof. In a well-known 1996 article in the *Quarterly Journal of Economics*, Akerlof explained in the language of modern economics why the sexual revolution—contrary to common prediction, especially prediction by those in and out of the Church who wanted the teaching on birth control changed—had led to an increase in both illegitimacy and abortion. In another work published in the *Economic Journal* ten years ago, he traced the empirical connections between the decrease in marriage and married fatherhood for men—both clear consequences of the contraceptive revolution—and the simultaneous increase in behaviors to which single men appear more prone: substance abuse, incarceration, and arrests, to name just three.

Along the way, Akerlof found a strong connection between the diminishment of marriage on the one hand and the rise in poverty and social pathology on the other. He explained his findings in nontechnical terms in *Slate* magazine: "Although doubt will always remain about what causes a change in social custom, the technology-shock theory does fit the facts. The new reproductive technology was adopted quickly, and on a massive scale. Marital and fertility patterns changed with similar drama, at about the same time."

To these examples of secular social science confirming what Catholic thinkers had predicted, one might add many more demonstrating the negative effects on children and society. The groundbreaking work that Daniel Patrick Moynihan did in 1965, on the black family, is an example—along with the critical research of psychologist Judith Wallerstein over several decades on the impact of divorce on children; Barbara Dafoe Whitehead's well-known work on the outcomes of single parenthood for children; Sara McLanahan and Gary Sandefur's seminal book, *Growing Up with a Single Parent*; and David Blankenhorn's *Fatherless America*, another lengthy summarization of the bad empirical news about family breakup.

Numerous other books followed this path of analyzing the benefits of marriage, including James Q. Wilson's *The Marriage Problem*, Linda Waite and Maggie Gallagher's *The Case for Marriage*, Kay Hymowitz's *Marriage and Caste in America*, and Elizabeth Marquardt's recent *Between Two Worlds: The Inner Lives of Children of Divorce*. To this list could be added many more examples of how the data have grown and grown to support the proposition that the sexual revolution has been resulting in disaster for large swaths of the country—a proposition further honed by whole decades of examination of the relation between public welfare and family dysfunction (particularly in the pages of the decidedly not-Catholic *Public Interest* magazine). Still other seminal works have observed that private actions, notably post-revolution sexual habits, were having massive public consequences; Charles Murray's *Losing Ground* and Francis Fukuyama's *The Great Disruption* come especially to mind.

All this is to say that, beginning just before the appearance of *Humanae Vitae*, an academic and intellectual rethinking began that can no longer be ignored—one whose accumulation of empirical evidence points to the deleterious effects of the sexual revolution on many adults and children. And even in the occasional effort to draw a happy face on current trends, there is no glossing over what are still historically high rates of family breakup and unwed motherhood. For example, in "Crime, Drugs, Welfare—and Other Good News," a recent and somewhat contrarian article in *Commentary*, Peter Wehner and Yuval Levin applauded the fact that various measures of social disaster and dysfunction seem to be improving from previous lows, including, among others, violent crime and property crime, and teen alcohol and tobacco use. Even they had to note that "some of the most vital social indicators of all—those regarding the condition and strength of the American family—have so far refused to turn upward."

In sum, although a few apologists such as Stephanie Coontz still insist otherwise, just about everyone else in possession of the evidence acknowledges that the sexual revolution has weakened family ties, and that family ties (the presence of a biologically related mother and father in the home) have turned out to be important indicators of child well-being—and more, that the broken home is not just a problem for individuals but also for society. Some scholars, moreover, further link these problems to the contraceptive revolution itself.

Consider the work of maverick sociobiologist Lionel Tiger. Hardly a cat's-paw of the pope—he describes religion as "a toxic issue"—Tiger has repeatedly emphasized the centrality of the sexual revolution to today's unique problems. *The Decline of Males*, his 1999 book, was particularly controversial among feminists for its argument that female contraceptives had altered the balance between the sexes in disturbing new ways (especially by taking from men any say in whether they could have children).

Equally eyebrow-raising is his linking of contraception to the breakdown of families, female impoverishment, trouble in the relationship between the sexes, and single motherhood. Tiger has further argued—as *Humanae Vitae* did not explicitly, though other works of Catholic theology have—for a causal link between contraception and abortion, stating outright that "with effective contraception controlled by women, there are still more abortions than ever. . . . Contraception causes abortion."

Who could deny that the predictions of *Humanae Vitae* and, by extension, of Catholic moral theology have been ratified with data and arguments that did not even exist in 1968? But now comes the question that just keeps on giving. Has this dramatic reappraisal of the empirically known universe led to any secular reappraisals, however grudging, that Paul VI may have gotten something right after all? The answer is manifestly that it has not. And this is only the beginning of the dissonance that surrounds us in 2008.

III

Just as empirical evidence has proved that the sexual revolution has had disastrous effects on children and families, so the past forty years have destroyed the mantle called "science" that *Humanae Vitae*'s detractors once wrapped round themselves. In particular, the doomsday population science so popular and influential during the era in which *Humanae Vitae* appeared has been repeatedly demolished.

Born from Thomas Robert Malthus' famous late-eighteenth-century *Essay on Population*, this was the novel view that humanity itself amounted to a kind of scourge or pollution whose pressure on fellow members would lead to catastrophe. Though rooted in other times and places, Malthusianism of one particular variety was fully in bloom in America by the early 1960s. In fact, *Humanae Vitae* appeared two months before the most successful popularization of Malthusian thinking yet, Paul R. Ehrlich's *The Population Bomb*—which opened with the words: "The battle to feed all of humanity is over. In the 1970s and 1980s hundreds of millions of people will starve to death in spite of any crash programs embarked upon now."

If, as George Weigel has suggested, 1968 was absolutely the worst moment for *Humanae Vitae* to appear, it could not have been a better one for Ehrlich to advance his apocalyptic thesis. An entomologist who specialized in butterflies, Ehrlich found an American public, including a generation of Catholics, extraordinarily receptive to his direst thoughts about humanity.

This was the wave that *The Population Bomb* caught on its way to becoming one of the bestsellers of recent times. Of course, many people with no metaphysics whatsoever were drawn to Ehrlich's doom-mongering. But for restless Catholics, in particular, the overpopulation scare was attractive—for if overpopulation were the problem, the solution was obvious: *Tell the Church to lift the ban on birth control.*

It is less than coincidental that the high-mindedness of saving the planet dovetailed perfectly with a more self-interested outcome, the freer pursuit of sexuality via the Pill. Dissenting Catholics had special reasons to stress the "science of overpopulation," and so they did. In the name of a higher morality, their argument went, birth control could be defended as the lesser of two evils (a position argued by the dissenter Charles Curran, among others).

Less than half a century later, these preoccupations with overwhelming birth rates appear as pseudo-scientific as phrenology. Actually, that may be unfair to phrenology. For the overpopulation literature has not only been abandoned by thinkers for more improved science; it has actually been so thoroughly proved false that today's cutting-edge theory worries about precisely the *opposite*: a "dearth birth" that is "graying" the advanced world.

In fact, so discredited has the overpopulation science become that this year Columbia University historian Matthew Connelly could publish *Fatal Misconception: The Struggle to Control World Population* and garner a starred review in *Publishers Weekly*—all in service of what is probably the single best demolition of the population arguments that some hoped would undermine church teaching. This is all the more satisfying a ratification because Connelly is so conscientious in establishing his own personal antagonism toward the Catholic Church (at one point asserting without even a footnote that natural family planning "still fails most couples who try it").

Fatal Misconception is decisive proof that the spectacle of overpopulation, which was used to browbeat the Vatican in the name of science, was a grotesque error all along. First, Connelly argues, the population-control movement was wrong as a matter of fact: "The two strongest claims population controllers make for their long-term historical contribution" are "that they raised Asia out of poverty and helped keep our planet habitable." Both of these, he demonstrates, are false.

Even more devastating is Connelly's demolition of the claim to moral high ground that the overpopulation alarmists made. For population science was not only failing to help people, Connelly argues, but also actively *harming* some of them—and in a way that summoned some of the baser episodes of recent historical memory:

> The great tragedy of population control, the fatal misconception, was to think that one could know other people's interests better than they knew it themselves. . . . The essence of population control, whether it targeted migrants, the "unfit," or families that seemed either too big or too small, was to make rules for other people without having to answer to them. It appealed to people with power because, with the spread of emancipatory movements, it began to appear easier and more profitable to control populations than to control territory. That is why opponents were essentially correct in viewing it as another chapter in the unfinished business of imperialism.

The forty years since *Humanae Vitae* appeared have also vindicated the encyclical's fear that governments would use the new contraceptive technology coercively. The outstanding example, of course, is the Chinese government's long-running "one-child policy," replete with forced abortions, public trackings of menstrual cycles, family flight, increased female infanticide, sterilization, and other assaults too numerous even to begin cataloguing here—in fact, so numerous that they are now widely, if often grudgingly, acknowledged as wrongs even by international human-rights bureaucracies. Lesser-known examples include the Indian government's foray into coercive use of contraception in the "emergency" of 1976 and 1977, and the Indonesian government's practice in the 1970s and 1980s of the bullying implantation of IUDs and Norplant.

Should governments come to "regard this as necessary," *Humanae Vitae* warned, "they may even impose their use on everyone." As with the unintended affirmation by social science, will anyone within the ranks of the population revisionists now give credit where credit is due?

IV

Perhaps the most mocked of *Humanae Vitae*'s predictions was its claim that separating sex from procreation would deform relations between the sexes and "open wide the way for marital infidelity and a general lowering of moral standards." Today, when advertisements for sex scream from every billboard and webpage, and every teen idol is sooner or later revealed topless or worse online, some might wonder what further proof could possibly be offered.

But to leave matters there would be to miss something important. The critical point is, one might say, not so much the proof as the pudding it's in. And it would be hard to get more ironic than having these particular predictions of *Humanae Vitae* vindicated by perhaps the most unlikely—to say nothing of unwilling—witness of all: modern feminism.

Yet that is exactly what has happened since 1968. From Betty Friedan and Gloria Steinem to Andrea Dworkin and Germaine Greer on up through Susan Faludi and Naomi Wolf, feminist literature has been a remarkably consistent and uninterrupted cacophony of grievance, recrimination, and sexual discontent. In that forty-year record, we find, as nowhere else, personal testimony of what the sexual revolution has done to womankind.

Consider just what we have been told by the endless books on the topic over the years. If feminists married and had children, they lamented it. If they failed to marry or have children, they lamented that, too. If they worked outside the home and also tended their children, they complained about how hard that was. If they worked outside the home and didn't tend their children, they excoriated anyone who thought they should. And running through all this literature is a more or less constant invective about the unreliability and disrespect of men.

The signature metaphors of feminism say everything we need to know about how happy liberation has been making these women: the suburban home as concentration camp, men as rapists, children as intolerable burdens, fetuses as parasites, and so on. These are the sounds of liberation? Even the vaunted right to abortion, both claimed and exercised at extraordinary rates, did not seem to mitigate the misery of millions of these women after the sexual revolution.

Coming full circle, feminist and *Vanity Fair* contributor Leslie Bennetts recently published a book urging women to protect themselves financially and otherwise from dependence on men, including from men deserting them later in life. Mothers cannot afford to stay home with their children, she argues, because they cannot trust their men not to leave them. (One of her subjects calls desertion and divorce "the slaughter of the lambs.") Like-minded feminist Linda Hirschman penned a ferocious and widely read manifesto in 2005 urging, among other bitter "solutions," that women protect themselves by adopting—in effect—a voluntary one-child policy. (She argued that a second child often necessitates a move to the suburbs, which puts the office and work-friendly conveniences further away).

Beneath all the pathos, the subtext remains the same: Woman's chief adversary is Unreliable Man, who does not understand her sexual and romantic needs and who walks off time and again at the first sashay of a younger thing. What are all these but the generic cries of a woman who thinks that men are "disregarding her physical and emotional equilibrium" and "no longer considering her as his partner whom he should surround with care and affection"?

Perhaps the most compelling case made for traditional marriage lately was not on the cover of, say, Catholic World Report but in the devoutly secular Atlantic. The 2008 article "Marry Him!" by Lori Gottlieb—a single mother who conceived her only child with donor sperm rather than miss out on motherhood as she has on marriage—is a frank and excruciatingly personal look into some of the sexual revolution's lonelier venues, including the creation of children by anonymous or absent sperm donors, the utter corrosiveness of taking a consumerist approach to romance, and the miserable effects of advancing age on one's sexual marketability.

Gottlieb writes as one who played by all the feminist rules, only to realize too late that she'd been had. Beneath the zippy language, the article runs on an engine of mourning. Admitting how much she covets the husbands of her friends, if only for the wistful relief of having someone else help with the childcare, Gottlieb advises: "Those of us who choose not to settle in hopes of finding a soul mate later are almost like teenagers who believe they're invulnerable to dying in a drunk-driving accident. We lose sight of our mortality. We forget that we, too, will age and become less alluring. And even if some men do find us engaging, and they're ready to have a family, they'll likely decide to marry someone younger with whom they can have their own biological children. Which is all the more reason to settle before settling is no longer an option."

To these and other examples of how feminist-minded writers have become inadvertent witnesses for the prosecution of the sexual revolution, we might add recent public reflection on the Pill's bastard child, ubiquitous pornography.

"The onslaught of porn," one social observer wrote, "is responsible for deadening male libido in relation to real women, and leading men to see fewer and fewer women as 'porn-worthy.'" Further, "sexual appetite has become like the relationship between agribusiness, processed foods, supersize portions, and obesity. . . . If your appetite is stimulated and fed by poor-quality material, it takes more junk to fill you up. People are not closer because of porn but further apart; people are not more turned on in their daily lives but less so." And perhaps most shocking of all, this—which with just a little tweaking could easily have appeared in *Humanae Vitae* itself: "The power and charge of sex are maintained when there is some sacredness to it, when it is not on tap all the time."

This was not some religious antiquarian. It was Naomi Wolf—Third Wave feminist and author of such works as The Beauty Myth and Promiscuities, which are apparently dedicated to proving that women can tomcat, too. Yet she is now just one of many out there giving testimony, unconscious though it may be, to some of the funny things that happened after the Pill freed everybody from sexual slavery once and for all.

That there is no auxiliary literature of grievance for men—who, for the most part, just don't seem to feel they have as much to grieve about in this new world order—is something else that *Humanae Vitae* and a few other retrograde types saw coming in the wake of the revolution. As the saying goes, and as many people did not stop to ask at the time, cui bono? Forty years later, the evidence is in. As Archbishop Charles J. Chaput of Denver observed on *Humanae Vitae's* thirtieth anniversary in 1998, "Contraception has released males—to a historically unprecedented degree—from responsibility for their sexual aggression." Will any feminist who by 2008 disagrees with that statement please stand up?

V

The adversaries of *Humanae Vitae* also could not have foreseen one important historical development that in retrospect would appear to undermine their demands that the Catholic Church change with the times: the widespread Protestant collapse, particularly the continuing implosion of the Episcopal Church and the other branches of Anglicanism. It is about as clear as any historical chain can get that this implosion is a direct consequence of the famous Lambeth Conference in 1930, at which the Anglicans abandoned the longstanding Christian position on contraception. If a church cannot tell its flock "what to do with my body," as the saying goes, with regard to contraception, then other uses of that body will quickly prove to be similarly off-limits to ecclesiastical authority.

It makes perfect if unfortunate sense, then, that the Anglicans are today imploding over the issue of homosexuality. To quote Anscombe again:

> If contraceptive intercourse is permissible, then what objection could there be after all to mutual masturbation, or copulation *in vase indebito*, sodomy, buggery (I should perhaps remark that I am using a *legal* term here—not indulging in bad language), when normal copulation is impossible or inadvisable (or in any case, according to taste)? It can't be the mere pattern of bodily behavior in which the stimulation is procured that makes all the difference! But if such things are all right, it becomes perfectly impossible to see anything wrong with homosexual intercourse, for example. I am not saying: if you think contraception all right you will do these other things; not at all. The habit of respectability persists and old prejudices die hard. But I am saying: you will have no solid reason against these things. You will have no answer to someone who proclaims as many do that they are good too. You cannot point to the known fact that Christianity drew people out of the pagan world, always saying no to these things. Because, if you are defending contraception, you will have rejected Christian tradition.

By giving benediction in 1930 to its married heterosexual members purposely seeking sterile sex, the Anglican Church lost, bit by bit, any authority to tell her other members—married or unmarried, homosexual or heterosexual—not to do the same. To put the point another way, once heterosexuals start claiming the right to act as homosexuals, it would not be long before homosexuals start claiming the rights of heterosexuals.

Thus in a bizarre but real sense did Lambeth's attempt to show compassion to married heterosexuals inadvertently give rise to the modern gay-rights movement—and consequently, to the issues that have divided their church ever since. It is hard to believe that anyone seeking a similar change in Catholic teaching on the subject would want the Catholic Church to follow suit into the moral and theological confusion at the center of today's Anglican Church—yet such is the purposeful ignorance of so many who oppose Rome on birth control that they refuse to connect these cautionary historical dots.

The years since *Humanae Vitae* have seen something else that neither traditionalist nor dissenting Catholics could have seen coming, one other development shedding retrospective credit on the Church: a serious reappraisal of Christian sexuality from Protestants outside the liberal orbit.

Thus, for instance, Albert Mohler, president of the Southern Baptist Theological Seminary, observed in *First Things* in 1998 that "in an ironic turn, American evangelicals are rethinking birth control even as a majority of the nation's Roman Catholics indicate a rejection of their Church's teaching." Later, when interviewed in a 2006 article in the *New York Times* Sunday magazine about current religious thinking on artificial contraception, Mohler elaborated: "I cannot imagine any development in human history, after the Fall, that has had a greater impact on human beings than the Pill. . . . The entire horizon of the sexual act changes. I think there can be no question that the Pill gave incredible license to everything from adultery and affairs to premarital sex and within marriage to a separation of the sex act and procreation."

Mohler also observed that this legacy of damage was affecting the younger generation of evangelicals. "I detect a huge shift. Students on our campus are intensely concerned. Not a week goes by that I do not get contacted by pastors about the issue. There are active debates going on. It's one of the things that may serve to divide evangelicalism." Part of that division includes Quiverfull, the anti-contraception Protestant movement now thought to number in the tens of thousands that further prohibits (as the Catholic Church does not) natural family planning or any other conscious interference with conception. Such second thoughts among evangelicals are the premise of a 2002 book titled *Open Embrace: A Protestant Couple Re-Thinks Contraception.*

As a corollary to this rethinking by Protestants, experience seems to have taught a similar lesson to at least some young Catholics—the generation to grow up under divorce, widespread contraception, fatherless households, and all the other emancipatory fallout. As Naomi Schaefer Riley noted in the *Wall Street Journal* about events this year at Notre Dame: "About thirty students walked out of *The Vagina Monologues* in protest after the first scene. And people familiar with the university are not surprised that it was the kids, not the grownups, who registered the strongest objections. The students are probably the most religious part of the Notre Dame. . . . Younger Catholics tend to be among the more conservative ones." It is hard to imagine that something like the traditionalist Anscombe Society at Princeton University, started in 2004, could have been founded in 1968.

One thing making traditionalists of these young Americans, at least according to some of them, is the fact of their having grown up in a world characterized by abortion on demand. And that brings us to yet another irony worth contemplating on this fortieth anniversary: what widespread rejection of *Humanae Vitae* has done to the character of American Catholicism.

As with the other ironies, it helps here to have a soft spot for absurdity. In their simultaneous desire to jettison the distasteful parts of Catholicism and keep the more palatable ones, American Catholics have done something novel and truly amusing: They have created a specific catalogue of complaints that resembles nothing so much as a Catholic version of the orphan with chutzpah.

Thus many Catholics complain about the dearth of priests, all the while ignoring their own responsibility for that outcome—the fact that few have children in numbers large enough to send one son to the priesthood while the others marry and carry on the family name. They mourn the closing of Catholic churches and schools—never mind that whole parishes, claiming the rights of individual conscience, have contracepted themselves out of existence. They point to the priest sex scandals as proof positive that chastity is too much to ask of people—completely ignoring that it was the randy absence of chastity that created the scandals in the first place.

In fact, the disgrace of contemporary American Catholicism—the many recent scandals involving priests and underage boys—is traceable to the collusion between a large Catholic laity that wanted a different birth-control doctrine, on the one hand, and a new generation of priests cutting themselves a different kind of slack, on the other. "I won't tattle on my gay priest if you'll give me absolution for contraception" seems to have been the unspoken deal in many parishes since *Humanae Vitae.*

A more obedient laity might have wondered aloud about the fact that a significant number of priests post-Vatican II seemed more or less openly gay. A more obedient clergy might have noticed that plenty of Catholics using artificial contraception were also taking Communion. It is hard to believe that either new development—the widespread open rebellion against church sexual teachings by the laity, or the concomitant quiet rebellion against church sexual teachings by a significant number of priests—could have existed without the other.

During Benedict's recent visit to the United States, one heard a thousand times the insistence that *Humanae Vitae* somehow sparked a rebellion or was something new under the sun. As Peter Steinfels once put the over-familiar party line, "The pope's 1968 encyclical and the furor it created continue to polarize the American church." On this account, everything was somehow fine until Paul VI refused to bend with the times—at which point all hell broke loose.

Of course, all that Paul VI did, as Anscombe among many other unapologetic Catholics then and since have pointed out, was reiterate what just about everyone in the history of Christendom had ever said on the subject. In asking Catholics to be more like contraceptive-accepting Protestants, critics have been forgetting what Christian theologians across centuries had to say about contraception until practically the day before yesterday.

It was, in a word, *No.* Exactly one hundred years ago, for example, the Lambeth Conference of 1908 affirmed its opposition to artificial contraception in words harsher than anything appearing in *Humanae Vitae*: "demoralizing to character and hostile to national welfare." In another historical twist that must have someone laughing somewhere, pronouncements of the founding fathers of Protestantism make the Catholic traditionalists of 1968 look positively diffident. Martin Luther in a commentary on Genesis declared contraception to be worse than incest or adultery. John Calvin called it an "unforgivable crime." This unanimity was not abandoned until the year 1930, when the Anglicans voted to allow married couples to use birth control in extreme cases, and one denomination after another over the years came to follow suit.

Seen in the light of actual Christian tradition, the question is not after all why the Catholic Church refused to collapse on the point. It is rather why just about everyone else in the Judeo-Christian tradition did. Whatever the answer, the Catholic Church took, and continues to take, the public fall for causing a collapse—when actually it was the only one *not* collapsing.

VI

From time to time since 1968, some of the Catholics who accepted "the only doctrine that had ever appeared as the teaching of the Church on these things," in Anscombe's words, have puzzled over why, exactly, *Humanae Vitae* has been so poorly received by the rest of the world. Surely part of it is timing, as George Weigel observed. Others have cited an implacably secular media and the absence of a national pulpit for Catholics as contributing factors. Still others have floated the idea that John Paul II's theology of the body, an elaborate and highly positive explication of Christian moral teaching, might have taken some of the sting out of *Humanae Vitae* and better won the obedience of the flock.

At the end of the day, though, it is hard to believe that the fundamental force behind the execration by the world amounts to a phrase here and there in *Humanae Vitae*—or in Augustine, or in Thomas Aquinas, or in anywhere else in the long history of Christian teaching on the subject. More likely, the fundamental issue is rather what Archbishop Chaput explained ten years ago: "If Paul VI was right about so many of the consequences deriving from contraception, it is because he was right about contraception itself."

This is exactly the connection few people in 2008 want to make, because contraceptive sex—as commentators from all over, religious or not, agree—is the fundamental social fact of our time. And the fierce and widespread desire to keep it so is responsible for a great many perverse outcomes. Despite an empirical record that is unmistakably on Paul VI's side by now, there is extraordinary resistance to crediting Catholic moral teaching with having been right about anything, no matter how detailed the record.

Considering the human spectacle today, forty years after the document whose widespread rejection reportedly broke Paul VI's heart, one can't help but wonder how he might have felt if he had glimpsed only a fraction of the evidence now available—whether any of it might have provoked just the smallest wry smile.

After all, it would take a heart of stone not to find at least some of what's now out there funny as hell. There is the ongoing empirical vindication in one arena after another of the most unwanted, ignored, and ubiquitously mocked global teaching of the past fifty years. There is the fact that the Pill, which was supposed to erase all consequences of sex once and for all, turned out to have huge consequences of its own. There is the way that so many Catholics, embarrassed by accusations of archaism and driven by their own desires to be as free for sex as everyone around them, went racing for the theological exit signs after *Humanae Vitae*—all this just as the world with its wicked old ways began stockpiling more evidence for the Church's doctrine than anyone living in previous centuries could have imagined, and while still other people were actually being brought closer to the Church because she stood exactly as that "sign of contradiction" when so many in the world wanted otherwise.

Yet instead of vindication for the Church, there is demoralization; instead of clarity, mass confusion; instead of more obedience, ever less. Really, the perversity is, well, perverse. In what other area does humanity operate at this level of extreme, daily, constant contradiction? Where is the Boccaccio for this post-Pill *Decameron*? It really is all very funny, when you stop to think about it. So why isn't everybody down here laughing?

Source: Mary Eberstadt. 2008. "The Vindication of *Humanae Vitae*." *First Things* (185) 35-42 (August/September). Reprinted with permission from *First Things*.

Mary Eberstadt is a research fellow at the Hoover Institution and consulting editor to *Policy Review*, the Hoover Institution's bimonthly journal of essays and reviews on American politics and society. She focuses on issues on American society, culture, and philosophy. Her newest book is *The Loser Letters: A Comic Tale of Life, Death, and Atheism* (Ignatius Press, 2010). She is also author of *Home-Alone America: The Hidden Toll of Day Care, Behavioral Drugs and Other Parent Substitutes* (Penguin/Sentinel, 2004) and editor of *Why I Turned Right: Leading Baby Boom Conservatives Chronicle Their Political Journeys* (Simon and Schuster/Threshold, 2007).

Chapter 22

Abortion

Abortion is the willful termination of the life of an unborn child, the weakest and most vulnerable member of our society. The Catholic Church has unequivocally condemned the practice of abortion under any circumstances.[1]

This condemnation of the Church is nothing new. Since the first century, it has forbidden abortion, a common practice among the pagans of that time.

> You shall not kill the embryo by abortion and shall not cause the newborn to perish.[2]

For a time, so-called "abortion rights" defenders argued that we do not know when human life begins and that holding that human life begins at conception was a religious belief that should not influence the abortion debate in the public square. In fact, as recently as during the 2008 U.S. presidential election, Catholic politicians said as much in support of their position on "abortion rights." However, determining when human life begins is not a religious or doctrinal matter, but a scientific matter. Modern science tells us that human life begins at conception. In the summary of **"When Does Human Life Begin?: A Scientific Perspective,"** Maureen Condic, Associate Professor of Neurobiology and Anatomy at the University of Utah School of Medicine, states:

---

[1] *Catechism of the Catholic Church*. 1997. no. 2270. Vatican City: Libreria Editrice Vaticana.

[2] *Didache* (or *The Lord's Teaching Through the Twelve Apostles*), 90-100.

Resolving the question of when human life begins is critical for advancing a reasoned public policy debate over abortion and human embryo research. This article considers the current scientific evidence in human embryology and addresses two central questions concerning the beginning of life: 1) in the course of sperm-egg interaction, when is a new cell formed that is distinct from either sperm or egg? and 2) is this new cell a new human organism—i.e., a new human being? Based on universally accepted scientific criteria, a new cell, the human zygote, comes into existence at the moment of sperm-egg fusion, an event that occurs in less than a second. Upon formation, the zygote immediately initiates a complex sequence of events that establish the molecular conditions required for continued embryonic development. The behavior of the zygote is radically unlike that of either sperm or egg separately and is characteristic of a human organism. Thus, the scientific evidence supports the conclusion that a zygote is a human organism and that the life of a new human being commences at a scientifically well defined "moment of conception." This conclusion is objective, consistent with the factual evidence, and independent of any specific ethical, moral, political, or religious view of human life or of human embryos.[3]

Now that science has settled the question of when human life begins, the next question is whether the desires of the mother should trump the right to life of her unborn child. How we answer this question has profound implications for our society and for whom deserves to live and to die.

In **"Why Conception?,"** Michael Baruzzini presents the issue of when human life begins in a clear and concise manner. He refers to the Condic paper to support his position.

➤ The Catholic Church teaches that human life begins at conception as a matter of objective fact, not as a matter of faith.

➤ Life differs from other matter in that it grows and develops based on its innate plan and potency. It grows and changes without altering its identity.

---

[3] Maureen L. Condic. 2008. "When Does Human Life Begin?: A Scientific Perspective." White Paper, The Westchester Institute for Ethics & The Human Person (October).

➤ Life possesses an internal unity and capacity, not merely accidental features.

➤ Before conception, neither the sperm nor the egg has the capacity to become anything on its own. The fertilized ovum, however, is a single organism that can develop into a member of its species.

➤ After conception, there is no point where one can say there is a new organism. One must distinguish between developmental change and ontological change.

➤ The human identity comes from a person's own nature rather than its environment or circumstances. All human beings at any stage of development need these things.

➤ We cannot rely on arbitrary criteria to determine when life begins. Reasonable, objective criteria direct us to "the point where an independent being exists that is innately structured and ordered toward development as a member of the species." This point occurs at conception.

Further Reading

Maureen L. Condic. 2008. "When Does Human Life Begin?: A Scientific Perspective." White Paper, The Westchester Institute for Ethics & The Human Person (October).

Dianne N. Irving. 1999. "When Do Human Beings Begin? Scientific Myths and Scientific Facts." *International Journal of Sociology and Social Policy* (19) 3/4: 22-47 (February).

Why Conception?

By Michael Baruzzini

In response to Vice-President elect Joe Biden's erroneous public comments on the Catholic Church's teachings on abortion, USCCB Chairman Justin Cardinal Rigali released a statement asking:

> When does a new human life begin? When is there a new living organism of the human species, distinct from mother and father and ready to develop and mature if given a nurturing environment?

The answer, the cardinal concludes, is conception—and he goes on to make it clear that this answer is clearly derived from science and reason, not from religious doctrine:

> The Catholic Church does not teach this as a matter of faith; it acknowledges it as a matter of objective fact.

In order to preserve their defense of legal abortion, many Catholic abortion advocates have recently made the argument that the Church's position that human life begins at conception is merely a religious doctrine, held purely by revelation, which cannot be binding on others in a pluralistic society. Cardinal Rigali's statement points out that this position is false. The sacredness of human life is the Church's teaching; the beginning of life is a matter of objective observation. The last sentence in the cardinal's quote above is crucial: The Church does not teach that conception is the beginning of life, he pointedly states, it simply acknowledges it as fact.

It can be difficult to see why that's so. The events of conception and early embryonic development are microscopic and buried deep within the human body. They are certainly not easily observable, and even if they were, the structures and events that we observe during conception and development are not familiar to the untrained eye. The level of detail involved can be a bit bewildering. Despite the complexity, though, the events of conception and development are understandable with a little study.

To that end, the Westchester Institute for Ethics and the Human Person has recently released a paper, authored by University of Utah School of Medicine physiologist Maureen Condic, which examines the steps of conception and development and asks the title question, "When Does Human Life Begin?"

Now, life has a peculiar property that separates it from other matter in the universe: It grows and develops, according to an innate plan and potency. Living things change—specifically, they change themselves—over time. Life is, in fact, organic rather than mechanical. It grows and changes without losing its identity; it is not constructed from the outside, like a car on an assembly line.

This fact is crucial to answering the question of when an individual human life begins. When identifying life, we must look for an internal unity and capacity, rather than the simple possession of accidental features. Archbishop Rigali recognizes this when he asks for two criteria: distinction from the parents, and the ability to grow and develop under the right conditions. In her paper, Dr. Condic puts it more technically:

> In considering the question of when the life of a new human being commences, we must first address the more fundamental question of when a new cell, distinct from sperm and egg, comes into existence: when during the interactions of sperm and egg do we observe the formation of a new cell with both a material composition and a developmental pathway (i.e., a pattern of cell behavior) that are distinct from the cells giving rise to it? These two criteria (unique composition and behavior) are used throughout the scientific enterprise to distinguish one cell type from another. . . .

These criteria—distinction from the parents and the intrinsic ability to develop along human lines—are based in reason, not the tenets of any religious faith. To reject them for any other criteria—such as the possession of some specific human faculty or feature—is, as Condic puts it, "logically akin to linking the beginning of 'personhood' to the eruption of teeth in an infant or to the onset of menses in an adolescent—they are arbitrary, variable, and not indicative of any fundamental change in the entity under consideration."

So, taking this internal orderedness as our criterion, why do we say that conception is clearly the beginning of human life? How can a scientific layman understand and make the arguments necessary to defend this position? Conception is the point at which the male gamete, the sperm, fuses with the female gamete, the ovum or egg, and introduces its half of the genetic information to the half already present in the ovum. Adult humans have two complete sets of the genome: 23 pairs of chromosomes, for a total of 46. Each gamete has only one set, so it is genetically only half of what is necessary for a human to live. Of course, an organism is no more reducible to its genetics than a computer is to its programming, so it is also important to note that, in addition to this genetic completeness, the zygote at this point also has all of the additional structures and compounds necessary to proceed along the human developmental pathway.

Conception is the point when the new organism begins to exist because it is the first moment at which a single organism capable of developing as a member of its species—in this case, the human species—comes into being. Before conception, neither a sperm nor an ovum can develop into anything at all on their own. After conception, there is no point that could be identified as the beginning of a new organism, because every significant stage after conception is only the transition from one physiological stage to another. None of those steps could be considered the "beginning" of development, anymore than we consider puberty—a major developmental stage—to be a stage that defines human life (however much we may joke about it). It's crucial to distinguish mere developmental changes from ontological changes. If development had not already begun—that is, if the organism which is developing didn't already exist—we wouldn't see the subsequent stages.

The fact that the potential for human growth is intrinsic to the organism is also crucial: The human identity derives from the person's own nature, not from the environmental conditions in which it is placed. The developing embryo's need for nutrients and a protective environment within its mother are sometimes raised as an objection to the embryo's personhood. But the need for a favorable environment and the need for food are conditions that no organism can evade, no matter what its stage of development. We need food and shelter appropriate for our age when we are in the womb, as newborns, as adolescents, and as octogenarians. This mere need for food and shelter cannot be a condition for humanity, because it is a need we never escape. Nor does the method of obtaining nutrition—the placental and umbilical complex—have a bearing on this issue. Feeding tubes in hospital patients don't negate their humanity; why should a natural feeding tube in the womb?

The point where a life begins is the point where we can say, by reasonable and not arbitrary criteria, that a new organism has begun to exist. We identify it not by looking for the point where the organism can survive on its own, or the point where it no longer needs protection and nutrients. We don't even look for the point where we find unique genetic codes, although that may be a clue. Rather, we identify it by looking for the point where an independent being exists that is innately structured and ordered toward development as a member of the species. We find that point precisely at the fertilization of the ovum by the sperm—not before, because the gametes are incomplete on their own; and not after, because by those points development of the organism has already begun and the organism must already exist. Conception is the only point.

The Church, in her deference to science and philosophy's proper spheres, does not define but rather recognizes this truth. Dr. Condic's paper is a powerful tool in educating ourselves and our society about these objective, observable facts.

Source: Michael Baruzzini. 2008. "Why Conception?" *Crisis Magazine* (December 18).

Reprinted with permission from InsideCatholic (www.insidecatholic.com).

Michael Baruzzini writes from Colorado Springs, Colorado, where he lives with his wife and daughter. His blog on the Catholic faith and science can be found at www.deepsoftime.wordpress.com.

Chapter 23

Stem Cell Research

The Catholic Church supports all forms of stem cell research that respect the dignity of human life in all its stages. This clearly excludes human embryonic stem cell research, since such research involves the experimentation and ultimate destruction of the life of the human embryo. Certainly, the Church has encouraged adult or somatic stem cell research.[1]

Referring to unjust accusations leveled at the Church for being insensitive and unsupportive of research devoted to curing diseases for the good of humanity, Pope Benedict states:

> If there has been resistance—and if there still is—it was and is to those forms of research that provide for the planned suppression of human beings who already exist, even if they have not yet been born. Research, in such cases, irrespective of efficacious therapeutic results is not truly at the service of humanity.[2]

Indeed, all of the therapeutic successes in stem cell research have been associated with adult stem cell research.

> When it comes to stem cells, the public—and the media—tend to focus on embryos. But researchers and analysts say marketable therapies already are emerging from less controversial work with adult stem cells.

---

[1] Pope Benedict XVI. 2006. Address of His Holiness Benedict XVI to the participants in the symposium: "Stem Cells: What Future For Therapy?" (September 16).

[2] Pope Benedict XVI. 2006. Address of His Holiness Benedict XVI to the participants in the symposium: "Stem Cells: What Future For Therapy?" (September 16).

Adult cells make up the lion's share of the stem cell space, mainly because they are easier to come by than embryonic cells, and less expensive to run in clinical trials. They are also derived from mature tissue, like bone marrow or umbilical cord blood, so they avoid the ethical debate that surrounds embryonic stem cells.[3]

In **"What We Know about Embryonic Stem Cells,"** neurobiology and anatomy professor Maureen Condic outlines the many practical problems associated with embryonic stem cell research.

> ➤ Embryonic stem cells and the tissue derived from them tend to be rejected by the patient's immune system.
> ➤ Embryonic stem cells tend to form tumors when transplanted into adult tissue.
> ➤ There is no convincing scientific evidence that embryonic stem cells can be reliably differentiated into normal adult cell types.
> ➤ To overcome the problem of immune rejection, scientists have focused almost exclusively on somatic-cell nuclear transfer, or cloning. No successes have been documented in cloning human embryos, and the medical risks associated with the human egg donation required for cloning human embryos raise serious ethical issues.
> ➤ Despite frequent claims, no scientific evidence suggests that embryonic stem cells can be induced to form all the cells of the mature human body.
> ➤ "In June 2004, Ron McKay at the National Institutes of Health acknowledged in a *Washington Post* interview that scientists have not been quick to correct exaggerated claims of the medical potential of embryonic stem cells . . ."

Tadeusz Pacholczyk, in **"Rethinking Embryonic Stem Cells: The Reprogramming Breakthrough,"** discusses the research published in November 2007 in the journals *Cell* and *Science* that shows that skin cells can be converted into highly flexible or pluripotent stem cells.

---

[3] Anna Kattan. 2009. "Adult Stem Cells Are a Promising Market." CNNMoney.com (June 16).

- ➤ Two research papers by Japanese scientists and American scientists have demonstrated that there is no need to use, much less kill, human embryos to produce the most promising type of stem cells.
- ➤ The technique utilizes "cellular reprogramming" and is a significant scientific breakthrough. The method enables researchers to obtain patient-specific stem cells without using human eggs or destroying embryos.
- ➤ Nevertheless, many are calling for continued research with human embryos for several reasons. First, huge investment has been made in this kind of work. Second, some scientists and politicians do not recognize the immoral nature of human embryonic stem cell research. Third, embryos continue to be destroyed in infertility treatments. Fourth, it provides "moral" cover for the abortion industry.

Further Reading

Amin Abboud. 2005. "Stem Cell Research." mercatornet.com (May 12). http://www.mercatornet.com/backgrounders/view/stem_cell_research.

Juan de Dios Vial Correa and Elio Sgreccia. 2000. "Declaration on the Production and the Scientific and Therapeutic Use of Human Embryonic Stem Cells." Pontifical Academy for Life, Vatican City (August 25).

What We Know about Embryonic Stem Cells

By Maureen L. Condic

Back at the beginning of 2002, there was considerable optimism regarding the promise that embryonic stem cells were said to hold for millions of people suffering from fatal or debilitating medical conditions. Stem cells derived from human embryos, it was claimed, provided the best hope for relief of human suffering. Despite the profound ethical concerns regarding the use of human embryos for medical and scientific research, many Americans embraced this promise and the seemingly miraculous hope it offered.

The challenges facing embryonic stem cells were formidable. First, there was the concern that the cells and their derived tissue would be rejected by the patient's immune system, requiring the patient to undergo lifelong immune suppression. The three proposed solutions to this incompatibility problem (generating large banks of stem cell lines, cloning human embryos to provide a source of cells that perfectly match the patient, or genetically engineering stem cells to reduce immune rejection) were either socially, scientifically, or morally problematic (or all three). Second, there was the serious problem that embryonic stem cells form tumors when transplanted to adult tissues, and the tumorogenic capability of these cells is difficult, if not impossible, to control. Finally, there was the disturbing fact that science had thus far provided essentially no convincing evidence that embryonic stem cells could be reliably differentiated into normal adult cell types, as well as the disturbing possibility that overcoming this barrier would prove a difficult scientific endeavor.

Despite these concerns, many continued to regard embryonic stem cells with hope, believing that further research would overcome these difficulties and harness the power of embryonic stem cells for the benefit of mankind. Such optimists asserted that it was simply a matter of investing sufficient time, money, and research.

Since 2002, considerable resources have been devoted to just such research. A recent query of the grant database maintained by the National Institutes of Health (NIH) indicates that more than eighty research projects investigating human embryonic stem cells have been funded over the past five years. A research effort of this size represents millions of dollars in public money invested in the medical promise of embryonic stem cells. Indeed, the NIH reported to Congress in September of last year that anticipated spending on human embryonic stem cell research in 2006 was "just $24,300,000." Since 2002, approximately nine hundred research papers have been published on investigations of human embryonic stem cells, with more than a thousand additional papers investigating the properties of embryonic stem cells derived from animals. Clearly, research on embryonic stem cells has advanced considerably over the past five years, and it is therefore important to revisit the promise in light of current findings.

Stem cell-based therapies propose to treat human medical conditions by replacing cells that have been lost through disease or injury. Unlike an organ transplant, where a damaged or diseased tissue is removed and then replaced with a comparable organ from a donor, stem cell therapies would involve integration of replacement cells into the existing tissues of the patient. The dispersed integration of the transplanted cells throughout the targeted organ (indeed, throughout the entire body of the patient) would make it impossible to remove the stem cell derivatives surgically should any problems arise. Thus, the problem of immune rejection is of particular concern—if transplanted cells are attacked by the immune system, the entire tissue in which the foreign cells reside becomes the target of a potentially disastrous immune attack.

Over the past five years, the scientific community has focused almost exclusively on somatic-cell nuclear transfer, or cloning, as the best resolution to the problem of immune rejection. During somatic-cell nuclear transfer, the genetic information of an unfertilized human egg would be removed and replaced with the unique genetic information of a patient. This would produce a cloned, one-cell embryo that would mature for several days in the laboratory and then be destroyed to obtain stem cells genetically matched to the patient. Based on the success of animal cloning, human cloning was optimistically predicted to be a simple matter. Once we were able to clone human embryos, those embryos would provide patient-specific stem cell repair kits for anyone requiring cell-replacement therapies.

Human cloning has proved to be more challenging than antici-pated. Human eggs, as it turns out, are considerably more fragile than eggs of other mammalian species, and they do not survive the proce-dures that were successfully used to clone animals. Multiple attempts by several research groups worldwide have been unsuccessful in generating human clones. The few reports of the successful cloning of human embryos were either unverifiable press releases or clear chican-ery promoted by a quasi-religious group for its own publicity.

The elusive prize to generate the first human clone appeared to be won in March 2004, when a South Korean group led by Hwang Woo-Suk reported in the prestigious professional journal *Science* that they had generated a human stem cell line from a cloned human embryo. A year later, in June 2005, this same group sensationally reported that they had successfully generated eleven patient-specific stem cell lines from cloned human embryos and had dramatically improved their success rate to better than one in twenty attempts, bringing cloning into the realm of the possible for routine treatment of human medical conditions. Hwang was hailed as a hero and a pioneer, and his reported success evoked an almost immediate clamor to remove the funding restrictions imposed by the Bush administration on human embryonic stem cell research, lest America fall hopelessly behind South Korea in developing therapies.

By fall 2005, however, the cloning miracle had begun to unravel. Colleagues of Hwang raised serious concerns about his published studies, launching an investigation into possible scientific fraud. By December, it was conclusively shown that all the claimed cloned stem cell lines were fakes. To date, no one has successfully demonstrated that it is indeed possible to clone human embryos, and, based on the failed attempts of Hwang and others, human cloning is not likely to be a simple task, should it prove possible at all.

The scandal surrounding Hwang's audacious fraud raised multiple concerns about the ethics of embryonic stem cell research. Investiga-tions revealed that Hwang had used thousands of human oocytes for his unsuccessful attempts, not the hundreds as he had originally claimed. The medical risks associated with egg donation (the potential complications include both sterility and death) raise serious questions about the morality of conducting basic research on human cloning. Given that Hwang pressured junior female colleagues into donating eggs for his research, how can the interests of female scientists be protected from such professional exploitation? Given that thousands of human eggs from more than a hundred women were used by Hwang and not even a single viable cloned human embryo resulted from this research, how can the medical risks to women entailed by this research possibly be justified?

The technical challenges encountered by Hwang are not particularly surprising. Experience from multiple laboratories over the past decade confirms that it is extremely difficult to clone any animal. Cloned embryos are generally quite abnormal, with those that are sufficiently normal to survive to live birth typically representing between 0.1 and 2 percent. The problems do not end with the technical difficulty of somatic-cell nuclear transfer itself. Extensive evidence indicates that even the cloned animals that make it to birth are not untarnished success stories. Following Ian Wilmut's production of Dolly the sheep, the world's first cloned mammal, it was almost immediately evident that Dolly was not normal; she experienced a number of medical problems that resulted in her being euthanized, due to poor health, at the age of six years, about half the lifespan of a healthy sheep. Dolly was the only clone to survive to live birth out of the 277 cloned embryos Wilmut's group generated, yet this success did not prove that cloning can produce a normal sheep. Dolly was merely normal enough to survive to birth.

In the past five years, a number of studies have carefully examined patterns of gene expression in mice and other cloned animals that survived to birth. Not one of these animals is genetically normal, and multiple genes are aberrantly expressed in multiple tissues. Both the severity and the extent of these genetic abnormalities came as a surprise to the cloning field, and yet, in retrospect, they are not surprising at all. The fact that most cloned embryos die at early stages of development is entirely consistent with the conclusion that somatic-cell nuclear transfer does not generate normal embryos, even in the rare cases where clones survive to birth. Thus, the optimistic contention that "therapeutic cloning" would fix the immune problem facing potential embryonic stem cell-based therapies for humans seems thus far entirely unsupported by the scientific evidence.

The dwindling numbers of therapeutic-cloning supporters defend this procedure by asserting that the genetic abnormalities are only a problem if you are attempting to produce a live birth. Thus, in a 2004

New York Times article, George Daley, a stem cell researcher at Children's Hospital in Boston, acknowledged that cloned animals show multiple genetic abnormalities, yet optimistically asserted, "Cloned tissues are not likely to have the same problems." In light of the mounting evidence that cloned animals experience severe genetic disregulation, such tentative reassurance is wearing thin, with even Daley admitting that his optimistic prediction that cloned tissues will prove normal enough for medical purposes has "yet to be proven."

The question of how normal cloned tissue needs to be is not merely a detail that needs to be worked out. It is, in practice, a fundamentally unanswerable question. If cloned human embryos are to be used as a source of stem cells, we will be faced with this simple question for every single patient: How normal is this particular cloned embryo, the one we are going to use to generate stem cells to treat this particular patient? Without allowing that embryo to develop and observing precisely how abnormal it proves to be, it is simply impossible to know whether it is normal enough for medical use. Every patient will be an experiment with no quality control. Perhaps the particular cells will be normal enough to cure this particular patient, but then again perhaps they will be so grotesquely abnormal that they will create a condition worse than the one they were intended to treat.

The limitation in our ability to determine which cloned embryos are of sufficient normalcy to generate medically useful replacement tissue is one that no research can address unless scientists develop some kind of test to determine in advance which cloned embryos are normal enough. Developing such a test would almost certainly require the horrific scenario of growing human embryos to a sufficient state of maturity that the normalcy of their developing tissues could be empirically determined. This would mean implanting cloned embryos into surrogate wombs and then aborting them at specific times to examine the embryo's development. Based on this information, it might be possible (although difficult) to identify features of very early embryos that predict whether they are capable of generating therapeutically useful tissue. Whether Americans are willing to accept the unknown (yet potentially large) risk of being treated with stem cells of undetermined (and essentially undeterminable) quality or whether we would prefer to accept the kind of experimentation on human embryos and fetuses that would be required to ensure embryonic stem cell safety are questions of profound social and moral importance.

It was unambiguously clear five years ago that embryonic stem cells robustly form tumors (teratomas) when transplanted into adult tissues, and this remains the case today. Teratomas are benign tumors that contain a variety of differentiated cell types (hair, teeth, muscle, etc.). These tumors can often prove fatal because of their rapid growth, but they are not malignant or cancerous tumors, which metastasize into multiple locations within the body. Embryonic stem cell advocates were well aware of the tumor-forming potential of these cells. (Indeed, teratoma formation following injection of embryonic stem cells into adult mice is still today the test of whether a researcher has successfully generated a bona fide embryonic stem cell line.) Embryonic stem cell advocates dismiss the threat of these tumors, however, claiming this would prove a problem only for undifferentiated embryonic stem cells.

These optimistic predictions have not held up to scientific experimentation. The tumor-forming potential of embryonic stem cells has proved a significant problem that does not show signs of being resolved any time soon. More than a dozen papers over the past five years (five papers within the past year alone) have shown tumor formation in animals treated with differentiated embryonic stem cell derivatives. In several of these studies, a shocking 70 to 100 percent of the experimental animals succumbed to fatal tumors. In all cases, tumors were believed to be derived from embryonic stem cells that either failed to differentiate or from cells that somehow de-differentiated once transplanted. Although experimental approaches designed to reduce tumor formation from differentiated embryonic stem cell derivatives are under investigation, it is not clear whether these approaches will ever prove successful, especially if the tumors are due to uncontrolled de-differentiation of the embryonic stem cell–derived tissues back to a more primitive state once they are transplanted to an adult environment.

Even more alarming than formation of benign (albeit, fatal) tumors, several studies over the past five years have raised concerns that the longer embryonic stem cells are maintained in the laboratory (or, presumably, in the tissues of adult human patients), the more likely they are to convert to malignant cancer cells. Embryonic stem cells spontaneously accumulate the genetic abnormalities associated with embryonal carcinoma (a form of testicular cancer). Embryonal carcinomas are believed to be the cancerous equivalent of embryonic stem cells and are a highly metastatic form of cancer. Although the finding that embryonic stem cells spontaneously convert to cancer cells over time remains contested, it is clear that some, if not all, embryonic stem cells undergo this conversion, and the factors controlling the transition are not well understood.

The assertion that embryonic stem cells in the laboratory can be induced to form all the cells comprising the mature human body has been repeated so often that it seems incontrovertibly true. What is missing from this assertion remains the simple fact that there is essentially no scientific evidence supporting it. Experiments have shown that embryonic stem cells are able to participate in normal embryonic development, an observation that is also true of cancerous embryonal carcinoma cells. When injected into early mouse embryos, both embryonic stem cells and embryonal carcinoma cells randomly contribute to every tissue of the developing body.

Even more dramatically, when embryonic stem cells are injected into mouse embryos under specific experimental circumstances (a procedure known as tetraploid complementation), they can be induced to form all the cells of the postnatal body. These experiments prove that embryonic stem cells (and embryonal carcinoma cells) remain capable of responding appropriately to the developmental signals that regulate tissue formation in the embryo, and from these results we can conclude that if embryonic stem cells were intended to provide cell replacement therapies for embryos, they would represent a very promising therapeutic approach. The problem, of course, is that embryos are not the intended targets of stem cell therapies, and there is little reason to believe that the capabilities of embryonic stem cells in an embryonic environment are relevant to their therapeutic potential for non-embryonic patients.

Five years ago, most scientists working in the field of embryonic stem cell research confidently predicted that we would soon determine the precise recipe of molecular factors required to replicate in the laboratory the mysterious inner life of the embryo. David Anderson, a stem cell researcher at Caltech, boldly asserted in a *New York Times* opinion piece that once science had figured out the factors required to replicate embryonic development, specific molecules could simply be "thrown into the bubbling cauldron of our petri dishes," where they would transform embryonic stem cells into an unlimited source of replacement cells for any tissue we chose to produce.

Skepticism regarding this claim was well warranted. While there have been hundreds of papers published over the past five years that stridently claim "cell type X produced from embryonic stem cells," under closer inspection these successes have all been less miraculous than they appeared. It is relatively easy to generate stem cell derivatives in the laboratory that have at least some of the properties of normal, mature cell types. But the test of whether an embryonic stem cell–derived brain cell, for example, is indeed a normal adult brain cell is to put it into the brain of an adult animal and determine whether it survives and contributes to normal brain function. In addition, if laboratory-generated cells are to be therapeutically useful for the treatment of human disease and injury, they must be shown to have therapeutic value in adult animals: It is not sufficient that embryonic stem cell–derived cells merely survive in adults; they must also be able to repair the underlying disease or injury. It is precisely this kind of test that embryonic stem cell–derived tissues have proved unable to pass.

When cells derived from embryonic stem cells are transplanted into adult animals, their most common fate is to die. Indeed, most such transplanted tissue does not survive beyond a few weeks in an adult environment (the only exception is blood cells, where small numbers of cells survive long term in mature animals). The rapid death of transplanted embryonic stem cell–derived cells stands in striking contrast to the robust survival of bona fide adult cells when transplanted to adult tissue. Typically, even the most promising experiments involving the transplant of embryonic stem cell derivatives have reported modest positive effects that persist for only a few weeks. In the few cases where tiny fractions of the transplanted cells survive for months (rather than weeks), this straggling band of survivors typically provides no therapeutic benefit.

The failure of embryonic stem cell–derived tissues to survive when transplanted to adult tissues strongly suggests that science has not yet determined how to generate normal adult tissue from embryonic stem cells. Why then do some studies show modest, short-term benefits from transplantation of such tissues? In many cases, the authors of these studies speculate that embryonic stem cell–derived transplants are not providing benefit because of replacement of lost or damaged cells but rather because the transplanted cells are supporting the survival or function of damaged adult tissues by secreting generic survival factors. Thus, the modest and transient benefits reported for embryonic stem cell–derived cell transplants over the past five years do not appear to require stem cells at all and are likely to be replicated by simply identifying the beneficial factors produced by the transplanted cells and supplying these factors directly.

In light of the serious problems associated with embryonic stem cells," I noted in 2002, "there is no compelling scientific argument for the public support of research on human embryos." Serious scientific challenges are, by definition, problems that have stubbornly resisted the best attempts of science to resolve them. Over the past thirty years, hundreds of billions of dollars and countless hours of research by dedicated professionals worldwide have been devoted to solving the problems of immune rejection and tumor formation, yet these issues remain serious scientific and medical challenges. The mysteries of embryonic development have been plumbed for more than a hundred years by some of the most brilliant biologists of history, and yet, despite the clear progress we have made, we are nowhere near the point of having a "recipe book" for cooking up cellular repair kits to treat human disease and injury. Immune rejection, tumor formation, and embryonic development have proved themselves to be profoundly serious scientific challenges, and they are likely to remain so for decades into the future.

The hubris of scientists in the field of embryonic stem cell research who confidently asserted "Give us a few years of unrestricted funding and we will solve these serious scientific problems and deliver miraculous stem cell cures" was evident in 2002, and it is even more evident today. For the past five years, researchers have had completely unrestricted funding to conduct research on animal embryonic stem cells, and yet the serious scientific problems remain. They have had every conceivable tool of modern molecular research available to them for use in animal models, and yet the serious scientific problems remain. Millions of dollars have been consumed, and hundreds of scientific papers published, and yet the problems still remain. The promised miraculous cures have not materialized even for mice, much less for men.

In June 2004, Ron McKay at the National Institutes of Health acknowledged in a *Washington Post* interview that scientists have not been quick to correct exaggerated claims of the medical potential of embryonic stem cells, yet McKay justified this dishonesty by stating:

"To start with, people need a fairy tale. Maybe that's unfair, but they need a story line that's relatively simple to understand." Isn't it time Americans recognize the promise of obtaining medical miracles from embryonic stem cells for the fairy tale it really is?

Source: Maureen L. Condic 2007. "What We Know About Embryonic Stem Cells." *First Things* (169): 25-29 (January). Reprinted with permission from *First Things*.

Maureen L. Condic is an associate professor of neurobiology and anatomy at the University of Utah School of Medicine and conducts research on the development and regeneration of the nervous system.

Rethinking Embryonic Stem Cells: The Reprogramming Breakthrough

By Rev. Tadeusz Pacholczyk

The recent discovery that regular old garden-variety skin cells can be converted into highly flexible (pluripotent) stem cells has rocked the scientific world. Two papers, one by a Japanese group and another by an American, have announced a genetic technique that produces stem cells without destroying (or using) any human embryos. This technique involves the transfer of four genes into the skin cells, triggering them to convert into pluripotent stem cells. It has been called "biological alchemy," something like turning lead into gold. Many are hailing "cellular reprogramming" as a breakthrough of epic proportions, the stuff that Nobel Prizes are made of, a kind of Holy Grail in biomedical research.

As important as this advance may prove to be scientifically, it may be even more important to the ethical discussion. It offers a possible solution to a long-standing ethical impasse and a unique opportunity to declare a pause, maybe even a truce, in the stem cell wars, given that the source of these cells is ethically pristine and uncomplicated. As one stem cell researcher put it recently, if the new method really produces equally potent cells, as it has been touted to do, "the whole field is going to completely change. People working on ethics will have to find something new to worry about."[1] Thus, science itself may have devised a clever way to heal the wound it opened back in 1998, when human embryos began to be sought out and destroyed for their stem cells. Dr. James Thomson (whose 1998 work originally ignited the controversy, and who also published one of the new breakthrough papers) acknowledged just such a possibility in comments to reporters: "Ten years of turmoil and now this nice ending."[2] Whether this nice ending will actually play out remains to be seen, but a discovery of this magnitude, coupled with a strong ethical vision, certainly has the potential to move us beyond the contentious moral quagmire of destroying human embryos.

---

[1] Gretchen Vogel. 2007. "Researchers Turn Skin Cells Into Stem Cells." *Science Now Daily News* 1 (November 20).

[2] Rick Weiss. 2007. "Advance May End Stem Cell Debate." *The Washington Post*, November 21.

Respecting Ethical Boundaries in Research

Reprogramming addresses significant ethical concerns even as it offers a highly practical technique for obtaining pluripotent stem cells. As Dr. Thomson himself put it, "Any basic microbiology lab can now do it, and it's cheap and quick."[3] Reprogramming also offers a way to avoid getting entangled in "therapeutic cloning," a complex and unethical procedure which uses women's eggs to clone embryos and get patient-specific stem cells. Reprogramming allows researchers to get patient-specific stem cells without using women's eggs, without killing embryos, and without crossing moral lines.

The sheer practicality of the new reprogramming approach, coupled with its ethical advantages, makes it appealing enough that some researchers are in fact changing their research plans. Dr. Ian Wilmut, the researcher responsible for cloning Dolly the sheep, went so far as to announce that he will no longer pursue human therapeutic cloning, but will instead turn to reprogramming techniques. Yet when pressed by reporters, he still insists that all avenues need to be investigated: "Certainly using skin cells is much easier to accept socially than the use of embryos, but this was very much a personal decision and I still think we need to continue to work in both areas."[4] There are a number of reasons that scientists and politicians continue to argue that the bio-industrial-complex emerging around destructive human embryo research must be safeguarded and every avenue of research, even unethical ones, must be pursued.

First, the financial investment that has already been made in this area is significant. Certain state initiatives, like Proposition 71 in California, have earmarked enormous sums of state taxpayer money (about $3 billion) to promote research that fosters human embryo destruction. When such astronomical sums are involved, and researchers, universities, and pharmaceutical companies sense a gold rush in the offing, ethics often become the first casualty of the scramble.

---

[3] Marilynn Marchione. 2007. "Wis. Stem Cell Pioneer Shuns Limelight." *Associated Press*, November 20.

[4] Sarah Freeman. 2007. "Science Is a Wonderful Thing." *Yorkshire Post*, December 5.

Second, some of the scientists who advocate the destruction of human embryos have never really taken the moral concerns too seriously, because the creed they subscribe to is that of the so-called "scientific imperative," namely, that science must go forward, no matter what, as if it were the highest and most incontrovertible good known to mankind. This kind of modern dogmatism results in the view that science must be able to do essentially whatever it wants, and ethical viewpoints should not be allowed to interfere with experiments that researchers might want to do. That, of course, is a completely untenable position, because we regulate scientific research all the time. The very mechanism by which we dispense federal research money and grants imposes all kinds of checks and balances on what researchers can and cannot do. Certain types of research, like germ warfare studies or nuclear bomb development, are strictly regulated by the government today, and have been for decades. Other kinds of research are outright criminal, such as performing medical experiments on patients who do not give their consent. The idea that we ought to allow science to do whatever it wants is ultimately little more than "pie-in-the-sky" wishful thinking.

The Connections to IVF and Abortion

Another reason that embryocidal research in our laboratories can be expected to continue in the foreseeable future is that we have become largely acclimatized to human embryo destruction as part of what happens during infertility treatments. Many thousands of embryos are frozen or die each year at fertility clinics, and hardly a word is mentioned in respectable society. One of the most successful rallying cries in the stem cell debate has been, "Just give us the frozen embryos. They're all going to be thrown away anyway." Because of our unflinching pragmatism as a society, the proposal to get some good out of something that will be thrown into the dumpster seems like a no-brainer. We recycle our aluminum cans religiously, and try to maximize returns on every investment we make, so if young human embryos could be mined for their parts, we conclude that they would "not be wasted" either.

The first lapse in reasoning here, of course, occurs when we grant the assumption that it is somehow okay to discard very young humans. We wring our hands and tell ourselves that this is "inevitable"—we really can't be expected to stop scientists from discarding young human beings as medical waste, because that could have the practical effect of generating suspicion around the sacred cow of *in vitro* fertilization. Hence, it must follow that it is okay for researchers to directly cause the death of young humans who have been thawed out and are now growing in the Petri dish on the laboratory bench, as long as somebody else was going to do the dastardly deed "anyway." So long as clinics were planning to do evil anyway, that makes it okay for me to jump ahead of them in line and do the evil myself as a researcher. The flawed logic here is glaring, yet it sadly passes for respectable thinking and illuminated discourse in our universities and legislative bodies every day.

Yet another reason that embryo-destructive research will still likely be promoted in the future has to do with abortion. Several astute commentators have observed how the whole field of embryonic stem cell research has come to serve as a kind of "hedge" for abortion. In the same way that a hedge is placed around a garden in order to protect it, embryonic stem cells are becoming a place holder for abortion. As long as a kind of medical neo-cannibalism of embryos can be declared necessary for the maintenance of our personal health and well-being, then abortion on demand will more likely curry favor in our culture as well.

We Were Embryos

The argumentative continuity behind this position springs from the fact that each of us, remarkably, is an embryo who has grown up. This biological fact stares researchers in the face every time they choose to "disaggregate" a human embryo with their own hands. It makes many researchers edgy, touching them on some deeper level of their being. It makes many Americans queasy and eager to find alternatives. Dr. Thomson, who has overseen the destruction of numerous embryonic humans himself, had the honesty to acknowledge this fact in comments he made to *The New York Times*: "If human embryonic stem cell research does not make you at least a little bit uncomfortable, you have not thought about it enough."[5] Dr. Shinya Yamanaka, the Japanese

---

[5] Gina Kolata. 2007. "Man Who Helped Start Stem Cell War May End It." *New York Times*, November 22.

researcher who developed the reprogramming approach and published one of the two recent breakthrough papers, memorably described the problem after visiting a friend who worked at a fertility clinic. After looking down the microscope at one of the human embryos stored at the clinic, he later reflected back on the moment: "'When I saw the embryo, I suddenly realized there was such a small difference between it and my daughters,' said Dr. Yamanaka, forty-five, a father of two and now a professor at the Institute for Integrated Cell-Material Sciences at Kyoto University. 'I thought, we can't keep destroying embryos for our research. There must be another way.'"[6]

Drs. Yamanaka and Thomson have managed to pioneer another way, a powerful and practical way, but it is clear that several complex factors will influence how this major new stem cell discovery plays out in medicine and society. One thing is certain, however: those renegade researchers, lawmakers, and Hollywood personalities who have long dismissed ethical concerns and advocated human embryo destruction now find themselves at an important juncture because of this breakthrough. We can only hope that in the wake of this discovery, the siren call of harvesting human embryos will cease ringing in their ears and allow for a new era of ethical science to begin.

Source: Rev. Tadeusz Pacholczyk, Ph.D. 2008. "Rethinking Embryonic Stem Cells: The Reprogramming Breakthrough." *Ethics & Medics* (33) 4 (April). Originally published in *Ethics & Medics* 33.4 (April 2008): 1-4 © 2008 by The National Catholic Bioethics Center. All rights reserved. Reprinted by permission.

Rev. Tadeusz Pacholczyk, Ph.D., earned his doctorate in neuroscience from Yale University and did post-doctoral work at Harvard. He is a priest of the diocese of Fall River, Massachusetts, and serves as the Director of Education at The National Catholic Bioethics Center in Philadelphia.

---

[6] Martin Fackler. 2007. "Risk Taking Is in His Genes." *New York Times*, December 11.

Chapter 24

In Vitro Fertilization

One might ask what could possibly be wrong with a married couple with fertility problems seeking to conceive a child using modern technology such as *in vitro* fertilization. Indeed, such a couple's plight should elicit great empathy on the part of any parent who has been given the gift of children. Nevertheless, our feelings, however well intentioned, should not rule the day in judging the morality of any action.

The Church's clear and consistent condemnation of *in vitro* fertilization stems from a thoughtful consideration of the morality of every aspect of the process. The Church supports and encourages research and procedures that strive to enable couples to conceive a child in ways that are morally licit. However, the Church is a loving shepherd of its flock and strives to teach us what is morally right, while sympathizing with those who suffer from infertility issues. Addressing the broad issue of infertility treatments, the Church specifies the conditions that must be met to ensure that infertility treatments are ethical:

1. Treatments should respect "the right to life and to physical integrity of every human being from conception to natural death."
2. Treatments should maintain respect for the unity of marriage, which refers to "respect for the right within marriage to become a father or mother only together with the other spouse."
3. Treatments should honor the human values associated with our sexuality and ensure that new human life be "the fruit of the conjugal act specific to the love between spouses."

The Church supports methods that assist procreation and indicates that they should not be rejected simply on the basis that they are artificial.[1]

Indeed, the Church is sympathetic to those married couples struggling with problems of infertility and sees their desires as legitimate and proper. However, because of the dignity of every human being, it is wrong to create a child as if he or she were a "product," the output of a biological production process. This would be true even if *in vitro* fertilization could be conducted without the destruction or freezing of unused embryos.

In **"Do Married Couples Have a "Right" to a Child?,"** William May makes the case that married couples have no "right" to children. A child made in the image and likeness of God has such dignity that it can only be a gift, not a product manufactured in a laboratory.

> ➤ Married people do have rights. For example, they have the right to engage in the marital act, an act of interpersonal communion.
> ➤ Married couples do not have a right to a child as if it were a product inferior to its producers.
> ➤ A child conceived through the marital act is not a product but a gift. The spouses conceiving a child in this way do not "make" anything. Rather, they are participating in the act of creation. "The life they receive is "begotten, not made."
> ➤ Artificial fertilization involves the actions of "technicians" who take the sperm and eggs of the spouses and generate a product on behalf of the couple. This life is "made and not begotten," as if it were beneath the dignity of the parents.
> ➤ Human beings, the image and likeness of God, ought to be "begotten, not made," as the Second Person of the Trinity was "begotten, not made."

Father John Doerfler, in **"In Vitro Fertilization and the Person,"** discusses the relationship among marriage, the conjugal act, and the Trinity in providing a perspective on the immorality of *in vitro* fertilization.

---

[1] William Cardinal Levada. 2008. *Dignitas Personae: On Certain Bioethical Questions.* Congregation for the Doctrine of the Faith, September 8.

- ➤ The call to fruitfulness that spouses receive is a symbol and manifestation of the Trinitarian Love. The Holy Spirit proceeds from the "mutual self-gift of the Father and the Son."
- ➤ The spouses' fruitfulness is intimately connected with who they are—"being-in-the-image-of-God." The child conceived through the marital act is a mutual self-gift of the spouses, while a child conceived outside of the marital act fails to reflect the Trinitarian nature of procreation.
- ➤ When a child is conceived through *in vitro* fertilization, he or she comes to be in a manner that fails to reflect his or her dignity as a person created in the image and likeness of God. Rather, he or she becomes the product of a technical procedure.
- ➤ Although a couple unable to conceive a child through licit means may suffer deep sadness, they have not been forgotten by God. It may be that God has given them a different calling, a calling that will bring them great joy as they enter the lives of others in need.

Further Reading

William Cardinal Levada. 2008. *Instruction Dignitas Personae: On Certain Bioethical Questions*. Congregation for the Doctrine of the Faith (September 8).

Tim Drake. 2004. "Couples Ask: What's Wrong with In-Vitro Fertilization?" *National Catholic Register* (August 14).

Christopher West. "In-Vitro Fertilization and the Hermeneutic of the Gift." http://www.christopherwest.com/page.asp?ContentID=77.

Do Married Couples Have a "Right" to a Child?

By William E. May

Frequently, in discussions about fertility and the use of such techniques as artificial insemination and *in vitro* fertilization, the claim is made that a married couple has a moral "right" to a child. After all, one of the goods of marriage is the procreation and education of children. Therefore, if a married couple is not able to have a child through normal genital activity, why should they be prevented from using contemporary biological techniques in order to have a child of their own?

The Church, as is well known, teaches that it is morally wrong to generate human life outside the marital act (cf. Congregation for the Doctrine of the Faith, *Instruction on Respect for Human Life in Its Origin and on the Dignity of Human Procreation*, 1987). Many people, both Catholic and non-Catholic, can readily understand why the Church teaches that it is morally bad for a couple to generate human life by inseminating the wife with sperm provided by a man who is not her husband or by inseminating a woman other than the wife with sperm from the husband (i.e., a "surrogate" mother, who would, after the bearing the child, turn it over to the married couple). They recognize that the choice to generate human life in these ways does violence to marriage and to human parenthood and does a serious injustice to the child.

The Problem of the "Simple Case"

But many of these same people, Catholic and non-Catholic alike, find the teaching of the Church on the immorality of artificial insemination by a husband and the "simple case" of *in vitro* fertilization a different matter. In both artificial insemination by the husband and the "simple case" of *in vitro* fertilization, there is no use of gametic materials from third parties; the child conceived is genetically the child of husband and wife, who are and will remain its parents. In both these cases there need be no deliberate creation of "excess" human life which will be discarded, frozen, or made the subject of medical research of no benefit to them. In these cases, there need be no intention of intrauterine monitoring (although there could be) with a view of abortion should the child conceived suffer from any abnormality. Nor need there be, in these cases, the use of immoral means (masturbation) to obtain the husband's sperm, since it can be retrieved in morally acceptable ways. In these cases there is, apparently, only the intent to help a couple, despite their physical incapacity (either by reason of the husband's low sperm production or the wife's blocked Fallopian tubes) to have a child with whom they ardently desire to share life and to whom they are willing to give a home. Do not such couples have a "right" to have a child of their own? Why, many people reasonably ask, is it morally bad—indeed a sin, an offense against God Himself—to make use of artificial insemination by the husband and homologous *in vitro* fertilization in such cases? Is not the Church's position here too rigid, too insensitive to the agonizing plight of involuntarily childless couples who are seeking, by making good use of modern technologies, to realize one of the goods of marriage? Do not married couples in this situation have a right to make use of these methods so that they can have a child of their own?

It is definitely true that married men and women have rights (and responsibilities) that nonmarried men and women do not have. They have the right, first of all, to engage in the marital act, that is not simply a genital act between two persons who happen to be married but is an act of interpersonal communion in which they give themselves to one another as husband and wife. In direct contrast to genital sex between an unmarried man and woman merely joins two individuals who are in principle replaceable, substitutable, disposable, the marital act unites two persons who have made one another absolutely irreplaceable and nonsubstitutable by giving themselves to one another in marriage.

In addition, husbands and wives, by giving themselves to one another in marriage, have capacitated themselves, as St. Augustine put it, "to receive life lovingly, to nourish it humanely, and to educate it religiously," i.e., in the love and service of God (cf. *De genesi ad literam*, 9.7 PL 34:397). Unmarried men and women to the contrary have not so capacitated themselves. God, in short, wills that human life be given in the marital embrace of husbands and wives, not through the random copulation of fornicators and adulterers.

Is There a "Right" to a Child?

Husbands and wives, thus, have a "right" to the marital act and to care for life conceived through this act, but they do not have a "right" to a child. A child is not a thing to which husbands and wives have a right. It is not a product that, by its nature, is necessarily inferior to its producers, rather a child, like its parents. And this is the moral problem with the laboratory generation of human life, including artificial insemination by the husband and the "simple case" of *in vitro* fertilization.

When a child comes to be in and through the marital act, it is not a *product* of their act but is "a gift supervening on and giving permanent embodiment to" the marital act itself (cf. Catholic Bishops [of England and Wales] Committee on Bioethical Issues, *In Vitro* Fertilization: Morality and Public Policy [London: Catholic Information Services, 1983], n. 23). When human life comes to be through the marital act, we say quite properly that the spouses are "begetting" or "procreating," they are not "making" anything. The life they receive is "begotten, not made."

But when human life comes to be as a result of various types of homologous fertilization, it is the end product of a series of actions undertaken by different persons. The spouses "product" the gametic cells that others use in order to make the end product, in this case, a child.

In such a procedure, the child comes to be, not as a gift crowning the marital act (cf. *Gaudium et Spes*, n. 51), "but rather in the manner of a product of a making and, typically, as the end product of a process managed and carried out by persons other than his parents" (Catholic Bishops of England and Wales Committee on Bioethical Issues, n. 24). the life generated is "made," not "begotten."

But, as noted already, a human child is a person equal in dignity to its parents, not a product or a thing. A child, therefore, ought not to be treated as if it were a product.

In the Nicene-Constantinople Creed that we say at Mass every Sunday, we profess that God's Eternal Word was "begotten, not made." Human beings, as beings made in God's image and likeness, are, as it were, the "created words," brothers and sisters of God's Eternal and Uncreated Word, that manifest the depths of God's personal love for every human person. Thus human beings, the "created words" of God, like his Eternal and Uncreated Word, ought to be "begotten, not made." Husbands and wives have no "right" to make a child. They have the right to give themselves to one another in the marital act and, in and through this act, to *receive the gift of life.*

Source: William E. May. 1991. "Do Married Couples Have a 'Right' to a Child?" *Ethics & Medics* (16) 2 (February). Originally published in *Ethics & Medics* 16.2 (February 1991): 1-3 © 1991 by The National Catholic Bioethics Center. All rights reserved. Reprinted by permission.

Professor William May taught at Catholic University for twenty years and is now Emeritus Michael J. McGivney Professor of Moral Theology at the John Paul II Institute for Studies on Marriage and the Family. He is the author of more than 200 essays and a dozen books, among them *An Introduction to Moral Theology* (Our Sunday Visitor, 2003), *Catholic Sexual Ethics* (Our Sunday Visitor, 1998), *Catholic Bioethics and the Gift of Human Life* (Our Sunday Visitor, 2000), and *Standing with Peter: A Lay Theologian's Reflections on God's Loving Providence* (Requiem Press, 2006). He was appointed by Pope John Paul II to serve on the International Theological Commission from 1986-1997 and to serve as *peritus* for the 1987 Synod of Bishops.

In Vitro Fertilization and the Person

By Rev. John F. Doerfler, STL, JCL

Her rival, to upset her, turned it into a constant reproach to her that the Lord had left her barren. This went on year after year; each time they made their pilgrimage to the sanctuary of the Lord, Peninnah would reproach her, and Hannah would weep and refuse to eat. Her husband Elkanah used to ask her: "Hannah, why do you weep, and why do you refuse to eat? Why do you grieve? Am I not more to you than ten sons?" [1 Sam. 6–8]

The age-old problem of infertility is no less painful today for married couples who long for a child yet have difficulty conceiving. To overcome this problem, some couples seek recourse to various technical means of reproduction such as *in vitro* fertilization (IVF).

The Sacred Vocation of Procreation

Yet before deciding whether to employ a technical means to conceive a child, a married couple's actions to address infertility need to be seen within the context of the sacred vocation of procreation. The Second Vatican Council describes the spouses' call in this way:

> [W]ishing to associate them in a special way with his own creative work, God blessed man and woman with the words: "Be fruitful and multiply (Gen. 1:28). Without intending to underestimate the other ends of marriage, it must be said that true married love and the whole structure of family life which results from it is directed to disposing the spouses to cooperate valiantly with the love of the Creator and Savior, who through them will increase and enrich his family from day to day.

> Married couples should regard it as their proper mission to transmit human life and to educate their children; they should realize that they are thereby cooperating with the love of God the Creator and are, in a certain sense, its interpreters. This involves the fulfillment of their role with a sense of human and Christian responsibility and the formation of correct judgments through docile respect for God

and common reflection and effort; it also involves a consideration of their own good and the good of their children already born or yet to come. . . . Whenever Christian spouses in a spirit of sacrifice and trust in divine providence carry out their duties of procreation with generous human and Christian responsibility, they glorify the Creator and perfect themselves in Christ [*Gaudium et spes*, 50].

Note that in this sacred vocation of procreation, the spouses cooperate with God. They share in his love and creative work.

God's Love and Creative Work

Throughout eternity the Father, Son and Holy Spirit are joined in a communion of love. The Father gives Himself to the Son and the Son gives Himself back to the Father. So sublime is this mutual self-gift of the Father and the Son that the love given and received proceeds from them as another Divine Person, the Holy Spirit. Throughout eternity, a third Person proceeds from the mutual self-gift of the Father and the Son.

When we listen to the language of the body, we learn that by its very nature marital intercourse is meant to symbolize and make present this love of God in a communion of persons. God created man and woman in his own image and likeness and concomitantly gave them the mission to be fruitful and multiply [cf. Gen. 1:27–28]. Their fruitfulness is connected to their very "being-in-the-image-of-God."

The unitive meaning of marital intercourse bespeaks a mutual self-gift and acceptance of persons in love. Through their bodies a husband and wife give and accept each other in love. The procreative meaning flows from this mutual self-gift, disclosing its participation in the life and creative work of the Trinity. Just as the Holy Spirit proceeds in love from the mutual self-gift of the Father and Son, so a child can be the fruit of the spouses' mutual self-gift through their bodies. The unitive and procreative meanings of the conjugal act are inseparable since both flow from the Trinitarian life in which the spouses are called to participate in the sacred vocation of procreation.

In so fulfilling their vocation by the acts proper to marriage, spouses can participate in the very life and love of God as a communion of persons in love from which another person can proceed. Thus, the spouses can glorify God and perfect themselves in Christ, as mentioned above in the quote from *Gaudium et spes*. However, if the coming-to-be of a child occurs apart from marital intercourse, the manner in which the child comes to be no longer discloses the Trinitarian meaning of procreation.

Therefore, the Church teaches that a child's coming-to-be can be sought only as the fruit of the spouses' personal union in marital intercourse:

> Thus, fertilization is licitly sought when it is the result of a "conjugal act which is per se suitable for the generation of children and to which marriage is ordered by its nature and by which the spouses become one flesh." But from the moral point of view procreation is deprived of its proper perfection when it is not desired as the fruit of the conjugal act, that is to say, of the specific act of the spouses' union. [*Donum vitae*, II, B, 4. The internal citation is from the *Code of Canon Law*, c. 1061.]

When a child is conceived through IVF, he or she comes to be apart from the conjugal act. Herein lies the essential moral problem. With IVF, the child comes to be in a manner that violates his own dignity as a person created in the image and likeness of God. Rather the child comes to be as a product of a technical procedure. A technical procedure of its very nature cannot bespeak the Trinitarian meaning of procreation. It cannot bespeak the mutual gift and acceptance of persons in love. It cannot bespeak the procession of a person from a communion of persons in love.

In contrast the "logic" of a technical procedure points to something made or manufactured, something manipulated or dominated by its makers. [Cf. *Donum vitae*, II, B, 4-5. For more on this point see Bartholomew Kiely, "Contraception, *In Vitro* Fertilization and the Principle of Inseparability." In "*Humanae Vitae*": 20 *Anni Dopo* (Milan: Edizioni Ares, 1989), 329–336; and William E. May, "The Simple Case of *In Vitro* Fertilization and Embryo Transfer," *The Linacre Quarterly* 56 (1988) 29–36.]

Only procreation as the fruit of marital intercourse can disclose the Trinitarian meaning of procreation. Only procreation as a fruit of marital intercourse can bespeak the child's "being-in-the-image-of-God," a person proceeding from a communion of persons in love. Thus, the generation of a human person through IVF is deprived of its proper perfection, since it is divorced from the marital act, as *Donum vitae* says:

> Conception *in vitro* is the result of the technical action which presides over fertilization. Such fertilization is neither in fact achieved nor positively willed as the expression and fruit of a specific act of the conjugal union. . . . [T]herefore, even if it is considered in the context of *de facto* existing sexual relations, the generation of the human person is objectively deprived of its proper perfection: namely, that of being the result and fruit of a conjugal act in which the spouses can become "cooperators with God for giving life to a new person." [*Donum vitae*, II, B, 5. Emphasis as in the original. The internal citation is from John Paul II, *Familiaris consortio*, 14.]

Infertility and Love's Vocation

Those couples who have difficulty conceiving may certainly seek technical means that assist the marital act to achieve conception [cf. *Donum vitae*, II, B, 6]. Nonetheless, some couples may still be unable to conceive. Their marital union can participate just as much in the life and love of God, yet He has a unique vocation for them in which their love becomes fruitful.

I know such a couple who very much longed for children of their own. After years of trying to conceive and unsuccessful attempts at corrective surgeries, they adopted two boys with severe disabilities. It seems that the Lord has endowed them with the special gifts that they need to care for these boys. Few people could care for them as they do. Because they were unable to conceive, they discovered their unique vocation to share God's life and love in a manner that few could. Those unable to conceive have not been forgotten by God, rather they have a unique vocation that only they can fulfill. May they listen to God's voice as He calls them to share his life and love.

Source: John F. Doerfler, STL, JCL. 2000. "*In Vitro* Fertilization and the Person." *Ethics & Medics* (25) 5 (May). Originally published in *Ethics & Medics* 25.5 (May 2000): 1-5 © 2000 by The National Catholic Bioethics Center. All rights reserved. Reprinted by permission.

Father John Doerfler has served as a parish priest and in various positions at the Diocese of Green Bay, Wisconsin. He is a diocesan vicar general and chancellor and holds a doctorate in moral theology and a licentiate degree in canon law.

Chapter 25

Human Cloning

In February 1997, scientists in Scotland announced that they had successfully cloned a sheep that was subsequently named Dolly. The world was fascinated, and many were horrified, by this feat. What could science not accomplish? Many ethicists pointed out that Pandora's box had been opened. Would cloned humans be next? Indeed, several years later, researchers in the United States announced the production of the first human clone for therapeutic purposes.

The Church has been very clear in its teaching that human cloning is immoral. The Church has not set itself against science in this matter; rather, it is defending the dignity of the human person.[1]

The Church has been a champion of science and scientific research for the purpose of advancing the well-being of humanity over the centuries. But, scientific endeavors cannot be justified by what *can* be done, but rather by what *ought to* be done in light of the ethical standards that protect the dignity of all human persons.

In **"Reproductive and Therapeutic Cloning,"** Alfred Cioffi, a priest with doctorates in Sacred Theology and Genetics, provides a necessarily technical explanation of some of the biological, philosophical, and theological considerations associated with human cloning.

- ➤ In therapeutic cloning, the human embryo is destroyed. However, in reproductive cloning the intention is for the embryo to survive to become a normal child.

---

[1] William Cardinal Levada. 2008. *Dignitas Personae: On Certain Bioethical Questions,* Congregation for the Doctrine of the Faith, September 8 (nos. 28 and 29).

- Sexual reproduction occurs when fertilization takes place, while cloning is an asexual form of reproduction.
- A zygote generated from human cloning is no less human than one coming from human fertilization.
- Cloning is immoral for at least two reasons. First, both the sperm and the egg have as their ultimate end the purpose of creating a human being, and their integrity must be maintained. Cloning violates their integrity. Second, the process of cloning yields a human life outside of the context of matrimony, making it illicit.
- Cioffi argues that it is reasonable to assume that the human zygote has a soul.
- Therapeutic human cloning is unethical because of the intention to destroy the human clone, which is tantamount to killing an innocent human being.

Further Reading

Juan de Dios Vial Correa and Elio Sgreccia. 1997. *Reflections on Cloning.* Vatican City: Pontificia Academia Pro Vita.

Kass, Leon R.1997. "The Wisdom of Repugnance." *New Republic* (16): 22 (June 2).

Tadeusz Pacholczyk. 2007. "Soulless Clones and Spineless Men." *Making Sense Out of Bioethics* (October).

Reproductive and Therapeutic Cloning

By Rev. Alfred Cioffi

On November 26, 2001, major news media throughout the United States reported the production of the first human clone by a biotechnology company in Worcester, Massachusetts. Officers of the biotech company claimed that the human clone was produced strictly for therapeutic purposes, and that they oppose reproductive cloning.

This is an essay on why one should oppose both forms of human cloning. It examines the issue from the perspective of biology, philosophy, and theology. The biological setting is based on the observation of natural systems; the philosophical setting on the possibility of arriving at objective truth by the use of logical reasoning; and the theological on a Christian mono-theistic system that affirms the existence of One Absolute Creator who endows every individual human being with a rational soul.

I note beforehand that, in any natural system, exceptions inevitably arise. Here I am only concerned with the norm, that is, with the standard pattern arising from the vast majority of observations. Likewise, by the possibility of arriving at objective truth I do not mean that we have absolute access to all truth by mere reasoning; rather, that objective truth is reasonable. Finally, the belief that God freely gives every individual human being a rational soul is itself based upon the belief that all human beings are an integrated union of body and soul. I accept this last point as essential to the Christian faith and thus make no attempt to prove it.

Biological Considerations

All observed living organisms are composed of cells. This is known as the cell theory: the basic unit of organic life as known on Earth is the cell. In general terms, a cell is composed of cytoplasm and nucleus. The nucleus codifies for the function and structure of the cell by means of chromosomes. Genetically, somatic (body) cells are diploid (containing a double set of chromosomes), whereas gametes (sexual cells) are haploid (containing a single set of chromosomes). At fertilization, each of the two gametes contributes its own set of chromosomes, contained in the pronucleus. Upon fusion of the two pronuclei, a new cell with a duplicate set of chromosomes is formed, called a zygote. The zygote is the first diploid cell of an organism.

Zygotes and blastomeres (diploid cells resulting from the first few mitoses of the zygote) are totipotential, that is, any one of them is capable of developing into an entire individual organism of the species defined by the nuclear genome. Stem cells, derived from blastomeres, among other sources, normally are not totipotential but pluripotential. They are progenitor cells that give rise to organs and tissues in a living organism, or to cell lines under laboratory conditions. Multipotential cells are the precursors of fully differentiated somatic cells. Examples of this last category are hematopoietic cells that become the different types of mature blood cells found in the circulatory system. Thus, one observes a progressively narrower scope among living cells from totipotentiality, to pluripotentiality, to multipotentiality, to full differentiation.

In principle, cloning involves the removal of an ovum pronucleus and its replacement with a nucleus from a somatic cell, either of the same biological species or of another species. Because of the complex chemistry of a cell and the possibility of rejection as a foreign object, the greatest success in cloning would be obtained by the transplantation of a nucleus, not only of the same species, but actually of the same female donating the ovum. In humans, therapeutic cloning would involve the creation of a human embryo for the harvesting of stem cells, whereas reproductive cloning would involve implanting the created human clone into a uterus and taking him or her to full gestation. Thus, in therapeutic cloning the embryo is destroyed after a few cell divisions, whereas in reproductive cloning it is hoped that the embryo will be born a normal infant.

Cloning replaces fertilization. When a diploid nucleus is injected into an enucleated ovum, in effect, one no longer has a gamete (haploid), but a new zygote (diploid). Some may claim that, because the injected nucleus comes from either a multipotent or from a fully differentiated cell, the cloned cell cannot be regarded as a zygote. However, the successful cloning of sheep and cows by using the same basic technique proves that the somatic nucleus, once within the ovum cytoplasm, is perfectly capable of reverting to toti-potentiality. Otherwise, the cloned embryo would not give rise to blastomeres capable of producing stem cells.

Hence, fertilization is an example of sexual reproduction, whereas cloning is an example of asexual reproduction.

Philosophical Considerations

A cloned ovum is a zygote. What is the teleology (ultimate end or goal) of a zygote? To become a mature individual organism of its own biological species. The teleology of a human zygote is to become a mature human being. Here it is important to note that organic life, as we know it, is never generic—no observed organic life is unspecific. Rather, one always observes organic life as pertaining to a specific living biological species. We might be the only biological species conscious of belonging to one species and not another, but all observed organic life is seen to occur in organisms of particular species, regardless of what taxonomic system is followed. The same is true at the tissue and organ level. One never observes just a brain or a heart or a liver. Instead, one speaks of the brain of an elephant, the heart of a lion, or the liver of a goose. Even at the level of cell lines, there are no true "generic" cell lines. All have been developed from some organic system, either human, canine, or murine, etc.

Thus, every living zygote is a species-specific zygote. Because there are no generic biological cells, there are no generic zygotes. A human zygote, whether originating from a fertilized ovum or a cloned one, remains a human zygote. The origin of the diploid nucleus may vary, but once integrated with the corresponding cytoplasm, the organic whole remains a totipotential zygote. The most that one could say, in searching for a difference, is that, genetically, the chromosomes of a zygote resulting from gametic fusion have a gametic origin, whereas the chromosomes of a zygote resulting from cloning have a somatic origin; as far as the genetic code is concerned, however, these two sets of chromosomes are equivalent within the same species. A zygote obtained from human cloning, therefore, is no less human than a zygote derived from human fertilization.

Similarly, there is no real half life, quarter life, or any fraction of life. Even though colloquially one may say that a particular organism is only "half alive," strictly speaking, any organism is either alive or dead.

Also, since all observed biological species develop, the same may be said of the various developmental stages of human life. An adolescent is not half an adult, a child is not half an adolescent, an infant is not half a child, a fetus is not half an infant, an embryo is not half a fetus, and a zygote is not half an embryo. Rather, each one of these represents an integral stage of development of the full human individual. The fact that the first stage of development of the human species is unicellular is not inconsistent with the first stage of development of any other observed multicellular organisms, all of which are unicellular. Nor should this surprise us, considering that there are millions of other organic species that spend their entire lifespan in a unicellular mode.

One unique characteristic, though, of each individual human being is precisely his or her integral individuality, that is, that I am myself and no one else—at any stage of development. Given the capacity of the human zygote to give rise to two or more identical twins, can one truly consider the human zygote an integral individual? Yes, if one is willing to acknowledge the scientific fact that there are two fundamental means of reproduction in nature: sexual and asexual.

As stated earlier, human fertilization is an example of sexual reproduction. Cloning is an example of asexual reproduction, because it does not involve the union of gametes. Twinning is another example of asexual reproduction. In fact, twinning, or vegetative propagation, or cellular fission, or budding, are not uncommon in many other organisms. All of these are examples of asexual reproduction. It is entirely plausible, then, that the human species also has retained a vestigial form of asexual reproduction as expressed in identical twinning. This means, quite simply, that under some rare conditions, a human zygote (an integral individual) may give rise to another human zygote (another integral individual) when she radically separates from her twin. Teleologically, a twinning zygote was meant to become twins, whereas a nontwinning zygote was meant to become a single individual. If zygotic cloning is possible biologically, then zygotic twinning is also possible biologically. Both are forms of asexual reproduction, the former artificially and the latter naturally.

Thus it is entirely reasonable to state that a human zygote derived from cloning is as human as a human zygote derived from fertilization.

Theological Considerations

From a Catholic moral perspective, opposition to both therapeutic and reproductive human cloning is fairly straightforward. It is based mostly on the special dignity conferred on human reproductive cells (sperm and ova) on two counts: First, on the fact that the teleology of these two germ cells is to create a new human being, and in order to do so, they must maintain their full integrity. Hence, enucleating a human ovum for the purpose of replacing it with a somatic nucleus is tanta-mount to destroying its integrity. Second, on the teaching that the only valid fusion of a human sperm with a human ovum is within the context of a valid matrimony. Since cloning obviates the figure of the father, human cloning may also be rejected on this second count.

Some might wonder whether a human clone has a soul? In order to answer this question, first one has to understand that, just as there is no generic organic life, likewise at the human level there is no generic soul or generic spiritual life. That is, every human being has a specific and individual soul. It is specific because the human soul pertains to the human species (in contrast with the animal or vegetative soul of which St. Thomas Aquinas speaks), and it is individual because the soul that we each have belongs to each one of us and to no one else. More-over, such is the intimate and intricate union between human body and human soul that the Catholic Church does not even speak of the human body as having a human soul, but rather that each one of us is body and soul. That is also why death is that mysterious temporal separation of the soul from the body. And that is also why the Christian faith proclaims in reciting the Creed: " . . . we believe in the resurrec-tion of the dead. . . ." In other words, the original plan of God is that each human being be body and soul for all eternity.

When does the human body acquire a soul? Consistent with the aforesaid argument concerning the integral and intimate unity of body and soul, this would occur simultaneously with the moment of acquir-ing a body. That is, that we are integral body and soul from the moment of our individual origin. What is our individual origin? Again, the first moment of corporeal existence of any living being which reproduces sexually is the zygote, namely, the moment when the fertilized (or cloned) ovum ceases to be a sexual (haploid) cell and becomes a somatic (diploid) cell. As noted earlier, the zygote—whether arising from fertilization or from cloning—contains in his or her nucleus the entire genetic code necessary to form a new individual of a particular species.

True Therapeutic Cloning

One may conclude, then, that a human clone has at least the potential of becoming a new human being and, therefore, also has the potential for having a human soul. Now, any true interdisciplinary dialogue is going to run into the problem of nonunivocal words. One such word is "potentiality." Within the context of this essay, the potential for becoming a new human being is not meant in the philosophical sense of being potentially a human person. In fact, in the philosophical sense we should equate human being and human person; hence, from the beginning of the zygotic stage, a new human clone is an actual person (with potential for further development). Rather, the reference to the "potential" to become a human being is made here in view of the plausibility of the argument that a fully differentiated somatic nucleus, when implanted into an enucleated human ovum, may not necessarily give rise to a new human being; that is, that the clone might not revert to totipotentiality. In other words, as long as the possibility exists for the cloned human ovum to begin embryonic development, the risk of destroying this cloned ovum is equivalent morally to the risk of killing an innocent human being.

In the case of human life, killing the innocent is an absolute moral prohibition. By the very act of cloning one is risking the death of the clone, not to mention the real possibility of death during subsequent stages of attempted implantation, and dubious successful gestation to birth. While the possibility exists that a cloned human ovum may develop teleologically into a human adult, reproductive human cloning risks the death of an innocent human being and, therefore, may not be attempted morally. Under this perspective, it becomes obvious that therapeutic human cloning also remains strictly unethical, since here the intentional death of the human clone is not merely a possibility but a certainty.

Nor is it sufficient to presume that a human diploid (somatic) nucleus will remain differentiated once transplanted into an enucleated human ovum, for this bypasses the teleology of the ovum itself, which is to give rise to a new human being (thus offending her dignity and purpose). If and when science can guarantee reasonably that a differentiated somatic human nucleus which has been transplanted into another enucleated somatic human cell will not revert to totipotentiality, then and only then will science have achieved a true, ethical therapeutic human tissue clone (not a new human being), capable of developing into an ethical human cell line. Until then, the only provisional moral position that fully avoids the risk of deliberately killing innocent human life is to oppose both therapeutic and reproductive cloning.

Source: Alfred Cioffi. 2002. "Reproductive and Therapeutic Cloning." *Ethics & Medics* (27): 3 (March). Originally published in *Ethics & Medics* 27:3 (March 2002): 1-5 © 2002 by The National Catholic Bioethics Center. All rights reserved. Reprinted by permission.

Rev. Alfred Cioffi is a visiting assistant professor of Biomedical Ethics at St. Thomas University in Miami and a Senior Fellow at the National Catholic Bioethics Center. He is an ethics advisor to the Archdiocese of Miami and the bishops of Florida. After receiving his undergraduate degree in biology in Florida, he entered St. Vincent de Paul Regional Seminary and was ordained a priest in 1985. After five years of parish ministry service, Fr. Cioffi was sent to Rome, where he earned his Doctorate in Sacred Theology, magna cum laude, from the Pontifical Gregorian University. He later received his Ph.D. in Genetics from Purdue University. Fr. Cioffi is a frequent speaker on bioethics and life issues and is fluent in English, Spanish, and Italian.

Chapter 26

Homosexuality

Homosexuality is not a modern phenomenon; reports of homosexuality date back millennia. St. Paul condemns homosexual activity at the beginning of the Christian age (Rom. 1:26–28, 32). It seems there is little agreement as to its cause and the ability of one with same-sex attraction to reverse this inclination. Nevertheless, the Church is clear in its teaching that while same-sex attraction is not inherently sinful, engaging in homosexual acts is gravely sinful.[1]

The Church also makes it clear that while the homosexual condition is disordered, those with this condition deserve our respect and should be treated with charity and not discriminated against. Rather, they should be treated with compassion; for many with this condition, their suffering is a cross that can be united to the cross of Christ.[2]

All Christians are called to live chastely within their state in life. Homosexuals too, despite their particular burden, are called to a life of chastity, supported by a life of prayer and sacramental grace.

Finally, the Church teaches clearly that the legal recognition of homosexual unions is contrary to the natural law and is opposed to the common good.[3] A misguided effort to be "kind" to those with same-sex attraction by legitimizing same-sex unions would be a grave error and undermine the institution of marriage by introducing profound confusion regarding its meaning and purpose.

---

[1] *Catechism of the Catholic Church.* 1997. no. 2357. Vatican City: Libreria Editrice Vaticana.

[2] *Catechism of the Catholic Church.* 1997. no. 2358. Vatican City: Libreria Editrice Vaticana.

[3] Joseph Cardinal Ratzinger. 2003. "Considerations Regarding Proposals to Give Legal Recognition to Unions Between Homosexual Persons," Congregation for the Doctrine of the Faith (June 3).

In **"Homosexuality,"** Janet Smith provides a comprehensive overview of the Church's teaching.

> In the tradition of Judeo-Christian thought, homosexual activity has always been considered contrary to God's plan for the use of our sexual faculties.

> Based on natural law, Scripture, and tradition, the Church has taught that sexuality is meant to be between a man and woman, committed to each other in marriage and open to the transmission of new life.

> The Church's teaching that homosexuality is unnatural and disordered is meant to express the understanding that any act that does not lead to what is good for human beings is unnatural.

> The effect of original sin is the fallen nature of humanity, leading to many disordered passions and desires, including homosexuality.

> We are all challenged to overcome our disordered inclinations, whatever they might be.

> Although the Church teaches that the homosexual condition is disordered and unnatural, it does not teach that the homosexual condition is itself sinful.

> Homosexuals deserve to be treated with justice and charity, recognizing their inherent dignity as human beings.

> Homosexuals are not required to seek the reversal of their homosexual condition. However, they, as all persons, are required to live a chaste life according to their state in life. Living chastely as a single person can be demanding. But, the example of many priests, religious and single lay people demonstrate that it can be done with the support of prayer and an intimate relationship with Christ.

> Special ministries help homosexual persons in their pursuit of chaste lives.

In **"Why Marriage is Inherently Heterosexual,"** Patrick Lee explains the nature of the marriage act and why true marital union can only occur when the act is open to procreation.

> Both faith and reason demonstrate that genuine marriage must be heterosexual.

> In every society, men and women are attracted to each other and engage in sexual acts that lead to offspring. Their communities generally encourage an environment in which families thrive.

- ➢ Philosophical reflection reveals that authentic marriage is sexual in nature and includes bodily union.
- ➢ In marriage, the sexual relationship (which consummates the marriage) is "intrinsically linked, indeed fulfilled by the procreation, bearing, and raising of children."
- ➢ Cohabiting same-sex couples, in contrast, have a relationship with each other. However, if they were to adopt a child, that would form a new relationship since it would have no intrinsic link to their sexual relationship.
- ➢ Some same-sex couples raise children, leading some to conclude that committed same-sex relationships should be considered marriages. However, other communities, such as orphanages, are committed to raise children and no one suggests that they are marriages.
- ➢ The marriage act is not simply a symbol of the love of the heterosexual couple. It is a "unitary action" in which the husband and wife complete one another biologically since the act is procreative in nature. They truly become one, which is clearly not true of same-sex intercourse.
- ➢ Genuine marriage requires two conditions: the couple must form a "union that would be fulfilled by bearing and raising children together" and must perform the conduct that would lead to procreation if all the conditions existing to enable procreation occur.
- ➢ The state's declaration that same-sex unions are equivalent to marriage would seriously confuse the nature of marriage. It would send the "message that marriage is essentially about romantic attachment and sexual relationship of adults to each other rather than about a relationship which by its nature is oriented to and suited for becoming family."

Further Reading

Dwight Duncan. 2005. "Same-Sex Unions." mercatornet.com (May 12). http://www.mercatornet.com/backgrounders/view/same_sex_unions.

Robert A. Gahl, Jr. 1999. "Homosexuality and Gospel Truth: Towards Effective Pastoral Care." *L'Osservatore Romano* (July 14).

The Catholic Medical Association. 2000."Homosexuality and Hope." Statement. http://www.narth.com/docs/hope.html.

Homosexuality

By Janet E. Smith

Few topics require greater sensitivity than homosexuality does. The phenomenon remains very little understood, either by professional psychologists or the general public. There is, for instance, no agreement about how common the condition is nor exactly what constitutes the "condition" of homosexuality. There are those who claim to experience sexual attraction only for members of their own sex, and such individuals may properly be designated homosexual in respect to sexual orientation; but even individuals with a strong heterosexual orientation may at some point in their lives experience sexual attraction for a member of the same sex. Moreover, there is no consensus about what might be the cause or causes of homosexuality and what might be the reversibility of the homosexual condition.

Morality of Homosexual Acts

Many in modern society would like to proclaim sexual acts between homosexuals as moral and would like homosexual unions to be recognized as legitimate alternative "life arrangements" or modes of partnership. Homosexual sexual activity, however, throughout the long tradition of Judeo-Christian thought has been considered incompatible with God's plan for human sexuality. On the basis of natural law principles, Scripture, and Tradition, the Church has taught that the proper use of sexuality is between a male and female who are married and are open to having children; sexual intercourse is meant to be an expression of love by those who are married to each other. Sexual intercourse between members of the same sex is understood to be a misuse of the gift of sexuality: It does not serve to create a bond between male and female; it cannot serve the purpose of bringing forth new life; it creates an inappropriate bond between members of the same sex.

Yet some individuals find themselves with a sexual attraction to members of their own sex. The attraction can be experienced as permanent and seemingly irreversible or as a response to a particular individual in a very particular situation. The cause of such attractions is unknown. Many claim that the homosexual condition is not chosen—that it seems to be innate or the result of certain experiences in early childhood, though all such explanations seem largely speculative and without hard scientific data to support them. The American Psychiatric Association has held varying positions, and these seem to be as much influenced by cultural and political factors as reliable scientific studies.

The argument is made that if some individuals are born with a propensity to a homosexual orientation, then we must proclaim homosexuality to be natural and normal—just one of the many variants of the human identity. Some human beings have blue eyes, some have brown, some have green: We have what we are born with and are not subject to moral evaluation on what is given to us at birth. On this analogy, some individuals are born heterosexual, others are born homosexual, and there is no ground for moral approval or disapproval of these innate conditions.

Nonetheless, were it to be proven that some individuals have a genetic determination to homosexuality, in itself this evidence would not serve to invalidate the Church's claim that homosexuality is an unnatural or disordered condition. Indeed, those who think showing that homosexuality is innate would serve to prove that homosexuality is natural misunderstand what the Church means by "natural."

The word "natural" has a fairly complicated meaning within the Church's moral tradition. "Natural" does not, as some think, refer simply to what is in accord with the biological processes of man. Nor does it refer to what is innate, nor even to what is "normal." Rather, the word "natural" in the context of the Church's moral doctrine has a metaphysical meaning. The Church relies largely on the principles of Thomism to explain its moral teachings. Thomism understands all things to have essences or natures; these essences or natures are good (in fact, designed by God), and everything prospers insofar as it acts and is treated in accord with its essence, or nature. That is said to be natural which accords with what is good for human beings; that is called unnatural which is not good for human beings. Integral human nature, or human nature before it suffered the effects of original sin, was an "ordered" nature. This means that the psychic processes of the human person were ordered: There were no disordered desires, no desires to eat or drink or do anything not in accord with what is good for human nature. Before the Fall, the human person reasoned correctly about reality, and his passions quite automatically and spontaneously followed the deliberations of reason. With original sin came "fallen nature."

The condition of original sin, or fallen nature, brought with it disordered passions and desires. After the Fall, humans began to act against their nature, quite constantly and predictably. As a result of original sin, all human beings, because they are imperfect, are in an unnatural and disordered condition. It is common to the human condition, for instance, for human beings to want to eat, drink, and sleep more than is good for them. It is common to the human condition for humans to want to have sexual intercourse with those with whom they should not or when they should not or in ways that they should not. In the "natural" state (that is, the prelapsarian state, or the state of humans before the Fall), humans would only desire what was good for them. After the Fall, human beings became susceptible to innumerable unnatural and disordered desires.

The Homosexual Condition

The claim by the Church that homosexuality is "unnatural" or "disordered" has been found offensive by some, since these terms seem to suggest that homosexuals are in some special category deserving of particular censure by the Church. Yet, as the above explanation of the term "natural" establishes, any human desire for what is not good is unnatural and disordered. Thus, in this context, homosexuality is simply one more of the "unnatural" or "disordered" conditions to which humans are susceptible.

It should not be surprising if some individuals are born with a propensity to homosexual sexual attractions, for it certainly seems that individuals are born with many propensities, both good and bad: for instance, a propensity to generosity, patience, anger, irritability, or alcoholism. Part of the challenge of the moral life is to learn how to order what we find disordered in our being so that, for instance, if one has a bad temper, one needs to learn how to govern it. Some of us may acquire the orderedness or disorderedness in our psyches through childhood experiences, either good or bad, rather than through heredity. Having good and generous parents who work to impart generosity to their children, for instance, will likely assist the children in being relatively free from greed and selfishness; conversely, having lazy parents may facilitate our being lazy. Such experiences as sexual abuse may deeply scar our psyches and fill us with fears and tendencies that we in no way chose to acquire. It seems plausible that a homosexual orientation is the result of any number of factors or causes. But the fact that it may be inborn—or not the product of our own choosing—does not thereby make it a "natural" condition not subject to moral evaluation.

It is very important to note that, although the Church teaches that the homosexual condition is unnatural or disordered, she does not teach that the homosexual condition itself is sinful. This is true of any disordered propensity that may be in the human soul: Those who are irritable or hot-tempered by nature are not sinful by virtue of these temperamental traits. Sin is a result of the voluntary choices we make in response to what our passions may be driving us to do. For many, there is no moral culpability in feeling irritable or hot-tempered; rather, it is in choosing and acting irritably or out of hot temper that most sins occur. (We can, though, be morally culpable if we do nothing to overcome our temperamental propensities.) So, while individuals may have little or no responsibility for having a homosexual orientation, they can exercise moral agency in respect to their actions.

Some find fault with the analogy between innate or unchosen homosexuality and a propensity to alcoholism or any moral failing. They argue that, since our sexual orientation so deeply influences how we respond to the world (how we fulfill, for instance, our needs for intimacy), to categorize homosexuality with all other human disorders mischaracterizes the plight of the individual with a homosexual orientation. It seems right to acknowledge that the plight of the homosexual is a particularly burdensome one, that the condition of homosexuality presents challenges to the moral agent many times greater than the usual challenge of dealing with disordered passions, for human beings do have a profound need for intimacy, and most individuals will satisfy that need (insofar as possible) through marriage and family.

Moreover, there is disagreement about whether it is possible for those with exclusively homosexual attractions to change their sexual orientation. Some psychologists maintain that no permanent change is possible; others maintain that, with the help of therapy and grace, many homosexuals have been successful in entering and sustaining heterosexual marriages. The Church does not require that homosexuals seek such reorientation; rather, homosexuals are called to a life of chastity, as all Christians are.

Those with a homosexual condition have often suffered unjust censure and discrimination by members of their own families, by society at large, and by some of those who represent the Church. The prejudicial rejection of homosexuals is called homophobia. Those who are guilty of homophobia refuse to recognize the full human dignity of persons with a homosexual condition. Such prejudicial rejection is in manifest conflict with the dictates of justice and Christian charity. Indeed, much love and acceptance should be extended to those with a homosexual condition, since often they find themselves lonely and rejected.

The Celibate Homosexual

The celibate lifestyle to which persons with a permanent or irreversible condition of homosexuality (if there is such) are called need not be lonely and isolating. There are, for instance, many celibate priests, nuns, and laypeople who forgo the intimacy of marriage, sexual relations, and family. Moreover, not only those called to the consecrated life are called to celibacy. Celibacy is lived by some heterosexuals who are unsuccessful in finding a spouse or who have been abandoned by their spouses. They fulfill their needs for intimacy through a deep relationship with Christ, though friendship, and by extending their love more broadly. They often have very rich human relationships in which the lack of a sexual dimension allows other dimensions of the human person and human relations to emerge.

Some object to the claim that, since many heterosexuals successfully lead celibate lives, it should be possible for homosexuals to do the same. Some think false analogies are being drawn here between the celibacy of the consecrated life, the celibacy of unwed heterosexuals, and the celibacy of homosexuals. They note that the celibacy of those in the consecrated life is a voluntary celibacy and often wins them great respect and esteem. Also, they point out, it is possible for heterosexuals who live lives of involuntary celibacy to have some hope that their situations may change. But the celibate homosexual enjoys neither the esteem given to the consecrated individual nor the hope of the unwed heterosexual. Furthermore, as mentioned, there is a stigma attached to homosexuality that makes it very difficult for homosexuals to be open about their condition, often even with family and friends. Given the amount of both overt and subtle unjust discrimination against homosexuals, open acknowledgment of one's homosexuality is often unwise, and thus one is denied even the comfort of self-disclosure. The isolation and alienation that can accompany the homosexual condition can therefore be extreme, and the Catholic demand that homosexuals lead celibate lives can seem unrealistic and cruel.

The cost of Christian discipleship, however, is often very high. While it must be acknowledged that, for many reasons, homosexuals are in a particularly difficult situation, others face challenges that equal or surpass theirs. For example, people with severe physical or psychological anomalies may also face lives burdened with various stigmas, be subject to much discrimination, and find establishing intimate relations extremely difficult; they, too, must learn to rely upon the Lord to meet their needs. Indeed, the Lord promises us that if we pick up our cross and carry it, we will find our burdens light.

Many Christian denominations have ministries designed to help homosexual persons live lives of chastity. Father John Harvey, O.S.F.S., a moral theologian, has founded Courage, an organization committed to helping those with a homosexual orientation draw upon prayer and the sacraments to lead chaste lives. They find that once they submit to the discipline of a committed prayerful and sacramental life, they are able to meet the demands of chastity; their testimony indicates that they find the rewards of remaining faithful to Christ's teaching and to the moral law to be great. (For more information on Father Harvey's organization, contact Courage, c/o St. Michael's Rectory, 424 W. 34th St., New York, NY 10001.)

Source: Janet E. Smith. 1997. "Homosexuality." In Russell Shaw, ed., *Our Sunday Visitor's Encyclopedia of Catholic Doctrine*, pp. 296–300. Our Sunday Visitor Publishing Division, Our Sunday Visitor, Inc., Huntington, Indiana. The permission to reproduce copyrighted materials for use was extended by Our Sunday Visitor, 200 Noll Plaza, Huntington, Indiana, 46750; 1-800-348-2440. website: www.osv.com. No other use of this material is authorized.

Janet E. Smith holds the Father Michael J. McGivney Chair of Life Ethics at Sacred Heart Major Seminary in Detroit. She is the author of *Humanae Vitae: A Generation Later* (Catholic University of America Press, 1991) and *Right to Privacy* (Ignatius Press, 2008) and editor of *Why* Humanae Vitae *Was Right: A*

Reader (Ignatius Press, 1993). She has coauthored *Life Issues, Medical Choices, Questions and Answers for Catholics* (Servant Books, 2007), with Chris Kaczor.

Why Marriage Is Inherently Heterosexual

By Patrick Lee

A recent story in *Newsweek* claimed that the only reasons for opposing same-sex "marriage" are religious. But there are powerful arguments for marriage rooted not in faith but in reason.

In the December 15, 2008 edition of *Newsweek*, both Jon Meacham in his editor's note and religion editor Lisa Miller in her front-page article mock arguments from scripture. At the same time, they invoke that same Bible's authority for a "more general" message of "inclusivity," in order to lobby for making gay marriage a sacrament. Meacham and Miller paint all opposition to the radical re-definition of marriage as hateful bigotry, comparing it to racism, and labeling appeals to the authority of the Bible against homosexual "marriage" and homosexual acts as fundamentalism. Indeed Meacham goes further: it is "the worst kind of fundamentalism." How much worse than suicide-bombings and beheadings he does not make clear.

Others can dissect the theological and factual howlers in these essays. Here I want to correct the assumption made by Meacham and Miller that the case against same-sex "marriage" must be a Biblical one. Instead, both by faith *and* by reason one can see that genuine marriage must be heterosexual, that sexual acts outside of marriage are immoral, and that the state, therefore, should not declare any same-sex unions "marriages," nor actively encourage sexual acts outside of marriage.

Consider Some Facts

In every society we find the following type of community: men and women committed to sharing their lives together, in the sort of community that would be naturally fulfilled by their conceiving, bearing, and raising children together. This is marriage. That such a community does exist in every society is indisputable.

In every culture men and women are attracted to each other, wish to commit to each other in a stable relationship, and perform sexual acts that might result in children. Hence every society encourages men and women—ideally, before they perform such sexual acts—to form the sort of community that will be a suitable environment both for the flourishing of their romantic love and for the flourishing of whatever children they may produce: marriage.

Sound philosophical reflection helps us identify what is going on here. The marital communion of the spouses is both good in itself (and so not a mere means to bearing and raising children) and at the same time *intrinsically fulfilled* by bearing and raising children together. Genuine marriage is sexual in nature and includes a bodily union: without sexual intercourse the marriage has not been consummated, that is, completed. But this sexual relationship is intrinsically linked, indeed, fulfilled, by the procreation, bearing, and raising of children. By contrast, co-habiting same-sex couples form one relationship. If later they decide to collaborate in raising an adopted child, they form a new and distinct relationship, since there is no intrinsic link between their sexual relationship, on the one hand, and their cooperation to raise a child, on the other. Unique to marriage is the fact that the bodily, emotional, and volitional relationship between the man and the woman is intrinsically oriented to being prolonged and fulfilled by their becoming a family. It is the same community that begins between the spouses on their wedding day, and may be prolonged and enlarged by becoming a family later on.

Advocates of same-sex "marriage" often argue that since marriage is a community oriented to raising children, and same-sex couples sometimes do raise children, such couples should qualify as marriages. But if having the purpose of raising children were sufficient to qualify as marriage, then orphanages, and some groups of religious women or men, could also be labeled as "marriages," which is absurd. Likewise, other arrangements are sometimes called "marriage," but in reality these are different types of relationship. For example, men and women often cohabit and view children as an optional extra or as burdens to be avoided. Or two or more individuals sometimes form alliances for the sake of raising children (for example two sisters, or several celibate religious men or women). But neither of these relationships are marriages: they have distinct purposes or goals.

Other advocates of same-sex "marriage" view marriage as only an emotional relationship, and the sexual acts as extrinsic symbols of that emotional connection. Since same-sex couples can intend their sexual acts to symbolize their love or affection, these unions (they contend) qualify as marriages. But, as just noted, genuine marriage is in fact a multi-leveled relationship that encompasses the bodily, emotional, volitional, and intellectual aspects of the spouses. In genuine marriage the bodily sexual acts are *part of* the marital union, not just extrinsic symbols. In sexual intercourse between a man and a woman (whether married or not), a *real* bodily union is established. Human beings are organisms, albeit of a particular type. In most actions—digesting, sensing, walking, and so on—individual male or female organisms are complete units. However, with respect to reproduction, the male and the female are incomplete. In reproductive activity the bodily parts of the male and the bodily parts of the female participate in a single action, coitus, which is oriented to procreation (though not every act of coitus actually reproduces), so that the subject of the action is the male and the female as a unit. Sexual intercourse is a unitary action in which the male and the female complete one another, and become really biologically one, a single organism. In marital intercourse, this bodily unity is an aspect of, a constitutive part of, the couple's more comprehensive, marital communion.

When a couple have mutually consented to marriage—the kind of union that would be fulfilled by bearing and raising children together—then the biological unity realized in their sexual intercourse embodies that community. In sexual intercourse they unite (become one) precisely in that respect in which marriage is defined and naturally fulfilled. They have consented to a *communion* procreative in kind, so their *acts* that are procreative in kind embody their communion. In that way the loving sexual intercourse of a husband and wife realizes a basic aspect of human flourishing: the good of marital union.

Given the above considerations, it is clear that the charge that the denial of same-sex "marriage" is unjust discrimination, or hateful bigotry, is a canard. In order to be genuinely married, a couple—*any* couple—must: (a.) commit themselves to the type of personal union that would be fulfilled by bearing and raising children together; and (b.) perform the conduct by which they become biologically one, conduct that, with the addition of conditions extrinsic to that conduct, might result in procreation (and even if those extrinsic conditions do not obtain, as in infertile couples, their act has still biologically united them). (a.) and (b.) together constitute the beginning of a marriage and are necessary for consummated marriage. *Any* couple who is unable to fulfill those conditions is unable to marry. Not only same-sex couples, but opposite-sex couples who are too young to form a commitment and opposite-sex couples who (because of impotence) cannot consummate their union are unable to marry.

Along these same lines, we can also understand by reason that sexual acts outside marriage—including therefore homosexual acts—are immoral. Within marriage, sexual acts embody (consummate or renew) the marriage. By contrast, in non-marital sexual acts, either the participants do not become biologically one, or they have not committed to sharing their lives in a way that can be embodied by a sexual act. People build up friendships or personal communions by pursuing together a common good. In marital intercourse the common good is their marriage, embodied (consummated or renewed) in that sexual act. But if a sexual act does not embody marriage, it does not embody any other community (sexual acts do not embody sports communities, scholarly communities, or generic friendships), and no genuine good is realized in the sexual act. (Pleasure alone cannot be the common good of their act, since pleasure is a genuine good only if it is attached to a condition or activity that is already genuinely fulfilling. Their *experience* of embodying union when they are not actually doing so is not a genuine good but is illusory.) Thus, in nonmarital sexual acts, the couple (or, in cases of polyamory, the group) instrumentalize their sexuality (their bodies-as-sexual) for the sake of a mere experience—either the experience of pleasure or the illusory experience of the bodily-personal union without its reality.

What does all of this mean for public policy? In a well-ordered society, the state should give legal recognition to real marriage, promote it, protect it, and privilege it over other sexual arrangements—as a good for the spouses and the children their union may form. The state has an essential interest in the health of marriage. Generally speaking, children will receive the best and most loving care if they are raised by their biological parents, who have formed a community aimed at providing the most suitable environment for any children they may help bring into being. Almost always, children can count on their mothers to care for them when they are young; the institution of marriage is dedicated to ensuring, as much as possible, that fathers also will fulfill their responsibilities to the children they help procreate, and to the mothers of their children. Furthermore, where the institution of marriage is strong, people's sexual passions and energies—frequently difficult to control, often leading to self-centeredness and exploitation—are channeled toward intelligible goods, namely, marriage and family.

If the state declares same-sex unions to be equivalent to marriage, it will profoundly obscure the nature of marriage. In effect, it will send the message that marriage is centrally about the romantic attachment and sexual relationship of adults to each other rather than about a relationship which by its nature is oriented to and suited for becoming family. Doing that would almost certainly further weaken the institution of marriage.

These points are open for all to see, whatever faith one has, or if one has no faith at all. To pretend that only religious "fundamentalists" oppose the radical re-definition of marriage advanced by same-sex "marriage" advocates is doubly distorting: first, the biblical and theological cases are not fundamentalist; second, there are reasoned arguments that do not presuppose faith against that proposal as well.

Source: Patrick Lee. 2008. "Why Marriage Is Inherently Heterosexual." *Public Discourse* (December 19). Reprinted with permission from *Public Discourse*. Copyright 2008 the Witherspoon Institute. All rights reserved.

Patrick Lee is the John N. and Jamie D. McAleer Professor of Bioethics and the director of the Institute of Bioethics at Franciscan University of Steubenville. He is known nationally as a keynote speaker and author on contemporary ethics, especially on marriage and the value of human life. He attended University of Dallas, receiving a B.A. in 1974. He received an M.A. in philosophy from Niagara University in 1977 and a Ph.D. in philosophy from Marquette University in 1980. His books include *Body-Self Dualism in Contemporary Ethics and Politics* (Cambridge University Press, 2008) with Dr. Robert P. George of Princeton University, and *Abortion and Unborn Human Life* (Catholic University of America Press, 1996).

About the Editor

Stephen Gabriel was born in Quincy, Massachusetts. The son of a merchant sea captain and a homemaker, he moved with his parents and five siblings to Fort Lauderdale, Florida, and then to the Panama Canal Zone, where he attended high school. He graduated from Loyola University of Chicago with a B.A. in economics. He received an M.S. in finance and a Ph.D. in agricultural economics from the University of Illinois.

He is currently a senior financial analyst with the federal government. In 1986, he coauthored an award-winning book entitled *Financing the Agricultural Sector: Future Challenges and Policy Alternatives* (Westview Press).

Over the years, he has written for *New Covenant*, a magazine of Catholic Spirituality, and *Our Sunday Visitor*. Gabriel has written two books on fatherhood: *To Be a Father: 200 Promises That Will Transform You, Your Marriage, and Your Family* (Moorings Press, 2010) and *Speaking to the Heart: A Father's Guide to Growth in Virtue* (Our Sunday Visitor Books, 1999).

Gabriel lives in Falls Church, Virginia, with his wife, Peggy. They have eight adult children and 14 grandchildren (at this writing!).

———✸✸✸———

Moorings Press Welcomes Your Comments

Moorings Press welcomes your comments and suggestions for future editions of *Catholic Controversies*. Please send your thoughts to us at publisher@mooringspress.com.

23776422R40323

Made in the USA
San Bernardino, CA
30 August 2015